Mark Andrews is from Warwickshire and has lived and worked in the UK, Egypt and now Belgium. He is the author of a series of long articles for *The Quietus* on the early years of the Sisters of Mercy. He has also written for the *Middle East Times*, *Bangkok Metro*, *Flanders Today* and *Louder*.

Paint My Name
in Black and Gold

The Rise of the Sisters of Mercy

Mark Andrews

unbound

First published in 2021
This paperback edition first published in 2022

Unbound
Level 1, Devonshire House, One Mayfair Place, London W1J 8AJ
www.unbound.com
All rights reserved

While every effort has been made to trace the owners of copyright material reproduced
herein, the publisher would like to apologise for any omissions and will be pleased to
incorporate missing acknowledgements in any further editions.

Earlier versions of some parts of this book first appeared in *The Quietus*.

This book is a wholly unauthorised work written independently by the author.
It is neither endorsed nor approved by the Sisters of Mercy, who make no warranties
as to the accuracy of the information contained in this book, which is
exclusively the opinion of the author and the interviewees.

Text design by Ellipsis, Glasgow

A CIP record for this book is available from the British Library

ISBN 978-1-80018-197-7 (paperback)
ISBN 978-1-80018-038-3 (hardback)
ISBN 978-1-80018-039-0 (ebook)

Printed in Great Britain by Clays Ltd, Elcograf S.p.A

1 3 5 7 9 8 6 4 2

For Richard M. Holtom

(1968–2019)

Superfans

Rohan Edward Baboolal

Alex Bark

Keith Barton

Mark Bartrum

Paul Bates-Shuker

Bruno Bossier

David Brownlee

Steve Burnett

Moric Butstraen

Helen Campbell

Ian Campbell (Version)

Eugene Carey

George Carless

Neil Cross

Paul Cuska

Clive Davies

Lothar Dittmann

Oliver Fahl

Jason Feinberg

Aldo Framingo

Jochen Friedrichs

Sarah (Chaotican) Schneider Gold

Charles Greth

Ian Hartley

Paul Hurd

Gabriel Husek

Matt Jutras

Jonathan Kewell Michaelsson

Andrew J Khoury

Stuart Kingston

Rob Koning

Johnny Lancaster

Antonio Luberto

Hrvoje Matovinović

Alessandro Meteori

Christian Misje

Chip Mosher

Sean Pledger

Aaron Quinton & Noah Quinton

Karl Reinsch

Jon Rimmer

Mark Robertson

David Brent Roundsley

James Ryan

Dirk S

René Schraven

Andrew William Small

Chris Smith

Juha Sorva

Stadium Anthems (Feature Film)

Nicholas P. Stathoulopoulos

Alexandra Superbonita Tolksdorf

Ariock Van de Voorde

Stan Verbeken

Phil Verne

Ingo Wennemaring

Chris York

'And I want to remember it. I never want to forget it. I never want to forget. And then I realised, like I was shot, like I was shot with a diamond, a diamond bullet right through my forehead. And I thought: My God, the genius of that. The genius. The will to do that. Perfect, genuine, complete, crystalline, pure.'

Apocalypse Now, 1979

'With Swann, you forgive a lot, you know.'

My Favourite Year, 1982

Contents

FOREWORD

Indelible – adjective describing marks (typically of ink)
that cannot be removed

I received my copy of the book in the post, took it out of the pack-aging, admired the dust jacket and then put it down on my desk. It stayed there for some time, untouched – those four shady, almost imaginary, boys staring back at me accusingly every time I tiptoed past. I don't know why, but I was reluctant to wake them from their slumber and actually read the book. My trepidation didn't make any sense; I already knew the story it would detail far better than most.

Finally, one Saturday morning we had a power cut that lasted around ten hours. A world without electricity: not one that the Sisters could inhabit. I read it straight through, from the first jack being eagerly plugged in, to the final unsettling feedback loop. As soon as I put the book down the lights came back on. No sorcery involved, just a connection to the National Grid re-established. I'm not sure what connection was re-established for me.

I lost count of the number of times I howled with laughter. I cried somewhere near the middle… By the latter stages I just wanted the power to come back on so that I could play my old Ramones albums at full volume. I knew the Sisters' story intimately, but I'd forgotten what a fantastic story it is – how all the individual stories dovetail and provide counterpoint to create this monumental *orchestral* piece.

I only have one lasting scar from my time in the Sisters: the one on my left arm picked up in Newcastle circa 1983. When I got up after finishing the book, I took my shirt off to inspect it – I wouldn't have been at all surprised if it had disappeared. It's still there. Everything joined to the scar looks different now, but it's still as it was. The Sisters are a permanent thing – indelible, some kind of damage done.

Way, way before I ever heard from Mark Andrews, I'd toyed with the idea of writing a full-length account of my time in the Sisters of Mercy. It had the working title *Romance and Assassination*. His title is much better and his book is much, much better. I thank him and all the people who play their parts, big or small. The next time the lights go out I will do my best Ketty Lester impersonation and read the book 'again right from the start'. Hey, love letters, vendettas, it's all the same to me.

For the moment, we have power! My earlier need to hear 'Blitzkrieg Bop' has been usurped by a new craving. I pull a large, round slice of shiny black vinyl out of a large, shiny, black cardboard sleeve and place it on the turntable. Solid gold: 'Heartland' has rarely sounded better.

Gary Marx, March 2022
Co-founder and former member of the Sisters of Mercy

PREFACE

There Have Been
Better Plans

On a Sunday afternoon in the late summer of 1980, Craig Adams arrived for an audition at 12 St John's Terrace in the Hyde Park area of Leeds. Adams was eighteen and already a veteran of numerous Leeds bands. His most recent had been a short-lived electro-pop duo called Exchange. Adams and Jim Bates, the flamboyant bar manager of the Faversham Hotel, played synths. Bates was the singer. They had played a student sit-in at the university and done little else. By Adams' own admission, Exchange had been awful.

Adams had been playing some form of keyboard since he was seven; Exchange was the last straw. He arrived at 12 St John's Terrace carrying a bass guitar and a fuzzbox. The fuzzbox was his, the bass guitar wasn't; Adams did not own a bass. This one had been borrowed from Ken Brown who was in a Leeds band called

YOU.* Brown was left-handed so Adams had had to restring it before heading over to St John's Terrace.

The street consisted of a row of three and four-storey houses. Number 12 had been converted into bedsits. Waiting for Adams in the cramped top-floor flat were Mark Pearman and Andy Taylor. The duo had a band they were calling the Sisters of Mercy. Pearman played guitar, Taylor played the drums. They shared the singing.

The Sisters of Mercy had neither gigged nor recorded. Taylor and Pearman had four songs between them: 'The Damage Done', 'Home of the Hitmen', 'Miser Rate' and 'Watch'. None of the songs sounded any good when they played them.

Taylor had been playing his instrument – a second-hand drum kit, which he had painted black – for less than a year. His style was primitive, tribal and eschewed most of the kit; a result of both his technical limitations and a Glitter Band obsession. He was twenty-one.

Pearman was the same age. He had tried – and failed – to get a band going in Hull before moving to Leeds in early 1979. Pickings there were slim too. He'd been the singer in Naked Voices but the band had barely gigged and couldn't settle on a line-up or a style, ending up as an unappetising mishmash of Wire, the Jam and Elvis Costello. So dispiriting was this experience that Pearman had decided to teach himself guitar. This venture was still on-going when Adams arrived for his audition: Pearman knew only a

---

* Adams recalls another member of YOU, Pete Master, working in the mortuary of Leeds General Infirmary, which might explain why one of the tracks on the band's *The Night and Music* EP is called 'Autopsy'. 'How goth is that!' Adams adds. (In fact, Master worked in the haematology department, next to the mortuary.)

handful of chords and his lead playing was as erratic as it was undeveloped.

Nevertheless, the Sisters of Mercy did have a great logo – a five-pointed star overlaid with a diagram of a flayed head adapted from the *Gray's Anatomy* medical textbook; Taylor and Pearman suspected it would look great on T-shirts, or as the label of a 7-inch single spinning on the turntable of a record player.

Adams, Taylor and Pearman all knew each other from the F Club, the city's itinerant punk club, at that time in Brannigans, a cellar dive on Call Lane. Taylor's girlfriend, Claire Shearsby, with whom he lived on St John's Terrace, had been the resident DJ at the F Club since its inception in the summer of 1977. She was therefore a well known and central figure in the Leeds music scene. Taylor could usually be found sitting next to her in the DJ booth, from where the best view of the bands could be had.

Objectively, Adams was slumming it by auditioning for Taylor and Pearman. Before Exchange, he had been in another, better known Leeds band, the Expelaires, also as the keyboard player. They had been signed to Zoo Records, early home of the Teardrop Explodes and Echo & the Bunnymen. The Expelaires had recorded a Peel Session, released a couple of singles and gigged outside of Leeds. Of all the local bands that formed in, or orbited, the F Club, the Expelaires were the leaders of the pack. Adams had walked out on them when they turned down a major label deal. (They had also told him a riff he had written for them was 'heavy metal shit'.)

Adams was better friends with Shearsby than with Taylor. He knew their flat well: a bed and Taylor's drum-kit took up most of the available space; a pair of shabby armchairs pointed towards a small black-and-white TV; a coffee table glued together from spent Marlboro packets sat between them. Posters lined the walls: Devo's *Are We Not Men?*, Bowie's *Low* and a homemade one, completely blank apart from a dot near the middle with 'There Have Been Better Plans' written next to it. Also on display were Taylor's fencing mask and sword – a sabre – and an Airfix model, the Angel Interceptor jet fighter from *Captain Scarlet and the Mysterons*, which he had assembled.

Scattered about the room was the Sisters of Mercy's meagre collection of musical equipment, most of it junk. Adams was not spoiled for choice for amplification. Pearman played through a cheap portable record player, which he'd wired through to serve as an amp. It functioned as long as the turntable was revolving. That was positioned on the bed. The only other amp available was Taylor's, a battered Woolworth's 3-watt practice amp, which he used with his bargain-basement guitar.

There was a tray of cat litter in the bedsit: the third witness to Adams' audition would be Spiggy, Taylor and Shearsby's black cat. Shearsby was not there that afternoon.

In this room, and in such inauspicious circumstances, can the precise moment of birth of the Sisters of Mercy – the Sisters of Mercy proper – be identified: Craig Adams plugged his borrowed, restrung bass guitar – and, crucially, his fuzzbox – into Andy Taylor's puny Woolworth's practice amp and played his shit heavy metal riff.

The riff itself was a low-budget punk interpretation of Motörhead. It was aggressive, distorted, devoid of any subtlety or sense of fashion. It sounded exactly as if it was being played by an unruly teenager whose overriding musical fantasy was to play bass like Lemmy.

Taylor and Pearman were shocked by the volume and the ferocity of the sound Adams was able to generate.

Their immediate reaction: 'You're in.'

Unlike the Expelaires, Taylor and Pearman loved Motörhead and Hawkwind, in Taylor's case to the nth degree. Fortunately for them, Adams was prepared to join any band that would let him play super-heavy fuzz bass – even the Sisters of Mercy.

The core trio of the Sisters was now in place.

What Adams had played would soon become the central riff to 'Floorshow'. At the time, it was the only riff he had. It was the first brilliant piece of Sisters music that would debut in that top floor bedsit; yet more would enter into the world in cramped spaces across the Burley and Hyde Park areas of Leeds. Mark Pearman would adopt the name 'Gary Marx' while Andy Taylor would become 'Andrew Eldritch'; Craig Adams, although he had been nicknamed 'Lerch' at school, would do without a rock 'n' roll *nom de guerre*.

The three present at that bedsit audition were soon to become four. Waiting for them at Kitchens, Leeds' large and venerable music shop in the Victoria Arcade – or being assembled in the Roland factory in Hamamatsu, Japan – was the first of their drum machines, a BOSS DR-55 Dr Rhythm. It, like all its successors, would be given the name 'Doktor Avalanche'.

The Sisters would later add human fourth members. At the time Adams was auditioning in the St John's Terrace bedsit, Ben

Matthews was a fifteen-year-old schoolboy living at home in Otley, a market town ten miles to the north-west of Leeds. From late 1981 until late summer 1983, he would play guitar in the Sisters under the name 'Ben Gunn'. As Adams was joining the Sisters of Mercy, Wayne Hussey was twenty-two, living in Liverpool and in the process of leaving Hambi & the Dance, another in a sequence of failed bands. He would replace Gunn and play in the Sisters for two years until September 1985.

In their first five years the Sisters would rise from the no-hopers in that St John's Terrace bedsit to local heroes, then one of the premier alternative bands in the UK and Europe, before blowing apart on the verge of major rock stardom. Their path would be strewn with brilliant singles, astonishing EPs, exceptional album tracks and legendary live shows. When they peaked, the Sisters of Mercy would be all bang and no whimper.

The Sisters achieved greatness by force of will and their own peculiar talents but they did not do so alone; they also needed the support of friends and the kindness of strangers. Key allies would be found in Bridlington, Brussels, New York, London, York, Los Angeles, Rome, Wakefield – and, primarily, in Leeds itself; the band and its inner circle of crew and uberfans would often closely resemble a tight-knit Yorkshire family. Throughout their ascent the Sisters remained steadfastly a Leeds band. Amid its violence and decay, Leeds had one of the most extraordinarily vibrant post-punk scenes in Britain. This was their spawning ground: Sisters songs are Leeds songs.

As the Sisters grew in stature, multitudes of fans began a relationship of unusual and enduring intensity with the band. The Sisters dug their claws in and, for many, they never let go. The story of the Sisters of Mercy is therefore one of the shared joy of performance between a band and its followers, one that has spanned time and distance. The band themselves also had tremendous fun, embracing the glorious stupidity of being in a Leeds rock group: smoke machines, leather trousers, blood, vomit, speed, reckless driving and reckless sex.

Yet, being in the Sisters of Mercy was no doubt an ordeal for long periods of time. Rage, sickness, misery and bitterness are integral to their story. The version of the band that was initiated on St John's Terrace would survive for no more than five years. Nor would Taylor, Pearman and Adams' friendship. Taylor and Shearsby's relationship was also doomed. As was Spiggy the cat. In different ways, all would leave indelible marks on Sisters records.

Eldritch ends this narrative as the last man standing: wounded, almost consumed by his own myth, but on the verge of taking the Sisters on to new heights. He was the most peculiar and compelling member of the band, a singular and mesmerising amalgam of T. S. Eliot, David Bowie and the countless fragments of data he squirreled away, processed and launched back at the world. As Andrew Eldritch, Andy Taylor staked a powerful claim to be the greatest rock star of his generation. Against the odds and all reasonable expectation, he and the other Sisters of Mercy would make transcendent and life-changing music.

1

The Swamp

If 12 St John's Terrace was the birthplace of the Sisters, the F Club was the womb. For five years, from 1977 to 1982, these club nights were held across Leeds and hosted virtually every major punk and post-punk act.

The F Club was the brainchild of John Keenan. While Keenan was not single-handedly responsible for the Leeds music scene, he was undoubtedly its central figure. What he created was extraordinary, and the Sisters of Mercy could not have existed without him.

'I created the swamp they could crawl out of,' Keenan says proudly. 'And what a fine, fetid swamp it was too,' Eldritch has observed: 'We couldn't have got anywhere without the support he gave us.'[*]

---

[*] Most quoted material is derived from interviews carried out for this book between May 2016 and March 2021. Where a quotation has a different source, it is given in the Notes on Sources.

9

When Keenan began promoting in Leeds in early 1977, punk rock was well under way. Although a colossal figure in the history of the Leeds music scene, Keenan was not involved at punk's outset. By the time of his first gig as a promoter in the city, the utterly un-punk Alan Price at the Grand Theatre and Opera House, the Sex Pistols had already played in Leeds twice – once at the Fforde Grene on 12 September 1976, and then at Leeds Polytechnic in December of the same year (as part of the Anarchy Tour). Before Keenan promoted his next Leeds gigs three months later, a Leeds punk scene had begun in the Cellar Bars underneath the Corn Exchange. Gang of Four – supported by the Mekons – debuted there in April 1977. SOS, Leeds' first indigenous punk band, had also formed. In the wake of the Pistols, Leeds Polytechnic hosted a series of punk gigs in the first half of 1977, including the Jam, the Stranglers, the Ramones and the Clash.

With the mindset of an entrepreneur as much as of a fan, Keenan began putting bands on at the height of punk in the summer of 1977 in the common room of the polytechnic. These nights were billed as Stars of Today. The music was 'basically punk – the Slits, Slaughter & the Dogs, XTC,' he says.

Keenan promoted Stars of Today with Graham Cardy. Cardy, like Keenan, was a generation older than the punks in the audience. Cardy was essentially a hippy. He had reformed the Mirror Boys – once a Beefheart and Zappa-inspired band at art college in Harrogate – as a 'compact new wave group' in Leeds. Cardy was also playing drums in SOS, whom he thought were 'terrible'. Throughout his time promoting the F Club, Keenan was working at Yorkshire Television (YTV) on the Kirkstall Road in Leeds.[*]

The Keenan–Cardy partnership did not last long. Keenan's time at the poly was also short-lived. 'When the students came back after the holiday, the new Common Room Committee wouldn't let me have the regular weekly club. So basically I said, "Fuck the poly."' This was the original 'F' in F Club. Keenan later re-branded the F Club, as 'the FAN Club'.[†]

'It was such a good group,' remembers Keenan. 'All the intelligent kids – not necessarily university kids; there were kids from the estates, who realised change was in the air and had attached themselves to the club . . . When I moved from the poly I thought, "How am I going to keep them together?"'

Keenan's answer was to 'form a club and give them a club card that cost a quid and would get them reductions at some of the punk shops in Leeds, like X Clothes . . . They had arty ideas – it wasn't safety pins and plastic bags – there were some very inventive people around. One girl used to come in with jewellery made out of cake decorations. Another guy came in once and he had all these very colourful laminate passes. When I looked closer they were all fannies cut out of porn magazines. It wasn't just a

---

[*] Keenan trained as a film editor but worked as a unit assistant and in the costume department at YTV. He 'got to meet and converse with a lot of great stars in that job: Ringo Starr, Spike Milligan, Les Dawson', and 'even worked with Harold Wilson and David Frost on a series about prime ministers.'

[†] For its regulars, 'the F Club' was usually used as a catch-all term covering Stars of Today, the F Club (which only ran to July 1978) and the FAN Club. 'The F Club' remains the common parlance for John Keenan's series of punk and new wave club nights, 1977–82.

musical movement, it was a total youth movement – artistic and creative.'

Craig Adams was one of Keenan's regular patrons from the outset. He was known as 'Hippy Craig'. 'There was "Gay Craig" and another Craig. I was "Hippy Craig" because I still had long hair,' he explains. Adams was most definitely not one of Keenan's 'kids from the estates'. He was born in Otley and had a middle-class upbringing in Horsforth and Rawdon, just outside the city to the north-west. His family had even had an interlude in Haworth – home of the Brontës – where his mother had an antiques shop on the main street called the Eye. Adams' father was Head of Publishing for Grattan's catalogues.

'A lot of the early punks were from the north and east side of the city,' Adams explains. 'There wasn't many of us from my end. It was more Seacroft, Crossgates, that side of the city. The people I came into Leeds with, definitely we were the posh kids.'

Although the Sisters of Mercy would become one of the quint-essential Leeds bands, Craig Adams was the only one of the St John's trio who had roots in Leeds and its West Yorkshire hinter-land.

The F Club's first home was the Ace of Clubs – a decaying cab-aret joint – where it only ran from September to December 1977. 'I put a fair selection on – Wilko [Johnson], Siouxsie,' remembers Keenan. 'The classic one at the Ace of Clubs was X-Ray Spex and the stage collapsed,' according to Adams.*

---

* Keenan: 'The stage didn't collapse. It was Poly [Styrene, the singer] who collapsed after a couple of songs. We had to carry her into the dressing room.'

Keenan's residency at the Ace of Clubs ended because 'there was a fire and the insurance wouldn't pay out.' After the Ace of Clubs, Keenan moved the F Club to the Roots Club, a primarily West Indian venue in the Chapeltown area of Leeds and a former synagogue that had gone under various names: the International Club, the Cosmopolitan Club, the Glass Bucket. As the venue for the F Club, it hosted, among others, Suicide, Magazine, Wayne County & the Electric Chairs, Wire and Joy Division.

In October 1978, the F Club moved to Brannigans down the bottom end of town near the Dark Arches, a complex of vaults under Leeds railway station. 'I used to do at least two nights a week down there,' Keenan recalls. 'The manager of Brannigans was very forward-thinking: two discos on top, punk club below.'

Brannigans was the F Club's longest-lasting location. The roll call of bands that played there is astonishing: Ultravox (with John Foxx); Wire; the Damned; the Only Ones; Penetration; Generation X; Cabaret Voltaire and Joy Division (on the same bill); Pere Ubu and the Human League (ditto). These were just some of the F Club's offerings in its first three months at Brannigans. Early 1979 saw, among others: Adam and the Ants; the Cure and the Teardrop Explodes (on the same bill); the Cramps, the Psychedelic Furs, the Raincoats and Joy Division again (this time with OMD).

Danny Horigan, who would roadie for the Sisters (and would later sing in Salvation under the name Daniel Mass) remembers the F Club in Brannigans: 'At the bottom of the stairs, there was a pool room and then you went round the corner to where the bands were on – stage at one end, DJ at the side of the room. Really low ceiling, proper dirty, sweaty punk club.'

There was nowhere to hang coats, which added to the clamminess; the low ceiling meant there was a low stage. The bands – whether great or abysmal, legends in the making or the instantly forgotten – went virtually toe-to-toe and nose-to-nose with the crowd. The sweat cannot be understated. One of Horigan's abiding memories of the venue is – besides a close-up view of Bryan Gregory of the Cramps' tattoos – the perspiration dripping off John Foxx's prominent chin.

'It was an intense and gruelling experience to go to concerts at Brannigans,' says Stephen Barber, an F Club regular from Crossgates. Another regular, John Lee, who put out the fanzine *Damaged Goods*, remembers the F Club as 'a real dive, brick walls . . . terrible, terrible beer. Pretty ropey sound – but it was our place. There used to be a lot of glue sniffers down there; it used to stink in certain corners.'

The F Club should not be overly romanticised, but it was certainly a haven for outsiders, misfits and music fans. It was 'occasionally a bit dangerous, that predictable nihilism,' says Lee, 'but you never saw much trouble there, the odd punch-up and that was about it. There were people who *were* complete fuckwits but [they were outnumbered by] those who were curious about the music.'

Compared to the violence above ground in Leeds, the F Club was remarkably peaceful. Much of Leeds was inhospitable in the late 1970s. 'It's a cosmopolitan place now but it was dark satanic mills back then,' says Paul Gregory, the singer in the Expelaires. 'It was a dodgy place to be a punk rocker.' Adams concurs: 'It was an awful time. Dangerous. You always felt: Be careful. Be careful where you go.'

Teddy Boys radiated violence from their favourite pub, the Whip, targeting punks with special malice. An even graver threat – because they were more numerous – were the Flickheads, football hooligans, then at the apex of their malevolence; Leeds United, famed for its on-field brutality as much as its success, had the ultras to match.

Yet, the greatest danger was not subcultural antagonism, but the common-or-garden, alcohol-fuelled near-psychotic hostility that was endemic in British towns and cities. Leeds was lousy with Tetley Bittermen looking to complete their evening with a punch-up. 'It was a shithole, pretty horrible really but it was ours,' is how Adams remembers his hometown.

As well as a large minority of women among its patrons, the F Club also had a female DJ, something almost unheard of in Britain in the late 1970s. Claire Shearsby DJ'd at all the locations of the F Club, even at Keenan's Stars of Today night in the poly common room, but her roots in Leeds music went back even further. She had been one of the few at the Sex Pistols' debut in Leeds at the Fforde Grene: 'It was 35p to get in and Johnny Rotten was just staring out at people and eating honey out of a little jar; he said his voice was going,' Shearsby recalls. She left with an autographed poster off the pub's door (which is how she knows how much the gig cost) and a safety pin, given grudgingly off Rotten's lapel.

Shearsby's tastes straddled glam and punk but in her early days of DJing there was a scarcity of actual punk records. The MC5, the Stooges, the Velvet Underground and the New York Dolls all bridged that gap; nevertheless, her guaranteed floor-fillers at Brannigans were 'Another Girl, Another Planet' by the Only Ones and OMD's 'Electricity'.

Shearsby was an extraordinary presence in the F Club: more than good-looking enough to earn the inevitable Debbie Harry comparisons after she dyed her hair blonde, she was tall ('Five feet, eight inches in stocking feet', 5ft 11 inches in her cowboy boots) fit and strong. The whole time she DJ'ed at Brannigans she was training to be a PE teacher and had been an accomplished school-girl sprinter and long-jumper. 'She could have smacked any of us out easily,' is Craig Adams' recollection. 'I was not an aggressive person, but people might have been wary nonetheless,' Shearsby explains. 'I used to stop fights, if I could get in between people.'

The F Club at Brannigans would provide Shearsby with a long-term boyfriend: Andy Taylor, a closet Deep Purple fan reading Chinese Studies at the university. 'Andrew just impressed me when he turned up in his leather jacket and Ramones T-shirt and stood next to the DJ booth. He just asked for Stooges all the time. I thought he was quite handsome and we started going out.'

'Andrew made quite an entrance into Leeds,' says Stuart Green, who was the bassist in Problemz at the time. 'He wasn't there and suddenly he was going out with Claire. Everybody knew Claire and suddenly this new guy in town's going out with the DJ.'

Mark Johnson (who would go on to start the fanzine *Whippings & Apologies*) used to think: '"Who's that fella in silver lurex kecks like Iggy's?" I never saw him more than two yards away from the DJ booth.' Yet there were sightings elsewhere in the F Club. Dave Wolfenden, the guitarist in the Expelaires 'can remember Andrew standing by the pool table. I thought, "Who's that fucking bloke looks like Lenny Kaye, who never speaks to anybody?"'

By rights, Andy Taylor should never have been in the F Club – or Leeds – in 1978. He should have been at Oxford University beginning the second year of his Modern Languages degree. He wasn't because he had been sent down from St John's College for failing his Prelims, his first-year examinations. Boyd Steemson, a PPE student at St John's, and a friend at the time, describes Taylor's time at Oxford as: 'Bowie, cigarettes, Bowie, cigarettes, Iggy, cigarettes, Bowie.' His sending down was 'the result of an impressively determined refusal to do any non-Bowie or cigarette-related work at all. He did nothing. He did no work at all.' Taylor's request to change course to Chinese was therefore emphatically denied by his college.

Being sent down from Oxford in the late 1970s was a rare accomplishment: a young man would really have to put his mind to it. Taylor disliked the French language and loathed the German literature course, claiming later – with no small amount of embroidery – that it consisted mainly of studying plays in Viennese dialect.

In many ways Oxford was Taylor's natural environment. Most of his secondary education had been at Merchant Taylors', a private school in Northwood, Middlesex, from which pupils regularly went to Oxford and Cambridge. Taylor was gifted at languages, highly intelligent, with an idiosyncratic mind and sardonic world-view that impressed those who knew him. This included his tutors. They were reluctant to let him go, but Taylor gave them no choice. They, like his fellow students, saw little of him while he was at St John's.

Steemson was one of the exceptions. His room was on

the North Quad 'in the hideous Beehive thing' (one of the post-Second World War additions to the college); Taylor's was over on the seventeenth-century Canterbury Quad. Steemson 'was a terrible student as well: I would get up in the middle of the night and write an essay . . . about half an hour later there'd be a knock on the door and it'd be bloody Andrew, prowling about college looking to see where a light was on.'

Although Taylor 'was a complete Bowie nut,' it was the Velvet Underground and Pere Ubu where his and Steemson's musical tastes intersected. As stuffy as the 1977 matriculation photograph made the St John's students look in their formal dress of dark suit, white bow tie, mortarboard and short commoner's gown, Steemson and Taylor were far from alone in their interest in, for want of a better word, punk. Furthermore, Friars in Aylesbury, one of England's great music venues, was a bus ride away. Oxford was not infertile ground in musical terms, but, despite this, Taylor made no attempt to form a band there, and played no instrument. As well as being a basic requirement for the Sisters of Mercy to exist, Taylor's exit from St John's College was a blessed relief: he absolutely hated his time there.

Taylor arrived in Leeds to begin his Chinese Studies degree at the university in October 1978. He had parted company with St John's so late in the previous academic year that there was little in the way of student accommodation left. Taylor was lodged way out of town near Leeds United's Elland Road ground in what he later described as 'a housing estate of utter grimness, which has since been declared uninhabitable and knocked down'. This was Hunslet Grange, also known as the Leek Street Flats, one of the UK's great architectural disasters: the buildings were under-heated and wringing wet with condensation on the inside, streaked black and crime-ridden on the outside. Although only built in 1968, they were near the end of their lives when Taylor moved in in 1978. Steemson, who visited him in Leeds several times, remembers his Hunslet Grange flat as an 'absolute hole, a horrible place . . . low ceilings, dark, fucking freezing, and a real trek to get into the centre of town . . . It seemed to be in the middle of nowhere . . . It was a big jolt to go from Canterbury Quad to Hunslet Grange.'

If Taylor needed any reminders that Leeds was a new beginning, Hunslet Grange provided it in spades. Taylor was in an alien city. His knowledge of the North of England had been limited to episodes of *Coronation Street* ('I discovered it was a documentary,' he once recalled). Despite his lodgings, he loved Leeds, its people and its music scene, almost instantly. The Ramones were playing the university the week he arrived and 'I must have gathered from that, from flyers or talking to people that there was this F Club.' Brannigans reminded Taylor of an 'oversized toilet' but it felt like home. There was also the lure of 'the glamorous DJ'.

Coming to Leeds was surely a shock to the system, stressful but also liberating and pleasurable. Steemson speculates that 'there was a sense in which Andrew could start again. He was in a different place; nobody knew him. I think the construction of the personality was a way of coping with that.' Leeds shook loose something hitherto supressed: Taylor was born in Ely; Eldritch was born in Leeds.

Steemson 'made the godawful coach trip' to Leeds several times. He found Leeds 'a dark and grimy and mysterious place, cold and wet. Coal mines all the way up [the M1 motorway].' His first trip there involved going to a gig at the F Club: Pere Ubu with the Human League supporting. Both Steemson and Taylor thought it was the best gig they'd ever seen. 'I'm still haunted by the dual genius of it,' Eldritch has stated. 'I just can't think of that happening anywhere else, at least not with the same intensity.' Steemson was 'quite struck by how they created a really exciting rock and roll atmosphere with minimal reliance – and in the case of the Human League, no reliance – on the standard pieces of kit: two really interesting bands on blistering form in a small provincial club.'

At the time of the Pere Ubu/Human League concert, the UK was on the verge of its Winter of Discontent: a wave of mass strikes at the fag-end of a Labour government. Margaret Thatcher's election was a certainty. The winter of 1978/9 was particularly bad in Leeds: the whole centre of the city was already a disintegrating environment; right-wing political violence was peaking; the Yorkshire Ripper was at large. 'That winter,' Stephen Barber notes, 'was also one of the intensive phases of punk rock club culture in Leeds.' As objectively awful as it no doubt was, 'it was quite exhilarating to experience an urban environment like that.' The pyroclastic cloud of Thatcherism would later sweep through the city, laying further economic waste and dealing debilitating blows to the musical culture there, but Taylor had arrived at an optimum moment: Leeds was decaying but intensely alive.

The beating heart of that was the clammy, noxious and very loud cellar club on Call Lane. 'I practically lived in the F Club,' Eldritch has said, and there was one band he would have seen more than any other. 'The Expelaires were like the house band of the F Club . . . They had their tendrils in pretty much everything,' he concluded. According to Adams, 'Leeds and the Expelaires went hand in hand.'

2

Cat People

Fittingly for the ur-Townie band, the Expelaires started right in the city centre, in the bar of the Guildford Hotel on the Headrow. 'We all used to drink in the Guildford,' says Craig Adams, 'and when I say "drink in the Guildford", I mean I sat in the pool room and asked people to buy me drinks, because I looked about ten.' The best-known Expelaires line-up was Adams on keyboards, Dave Wolfenden on guitar, Carl 'Tich' Harper on drums, Mark Copson (known as Johnny, despite the surfeit of Johns in the Leeds post-punk scene) and Paul Gregory (nicknamed 'Grape') as the singer.

Adams was no three-chords-and-form-a-band punk autodidact. 'I started playing piano when I was about seven,' he says. 'My teacher was a very old lady who looked a bit like Barbara Cartland. She used to beat us with a knitting needle. Then most Saturdays I'd have to spend at the Heaton School of Music in Bradford. Mornings were Theory and after lunch it was Piano.' He soon got sick of playing Classical music. 'My dad would drop me off at the music school and I'd do the old pretend walk in and then go off somewhere in Bradford until he came to pick me up.' This rebellion, which would eventually lead Adams into the Sisters of Mercy, began with ragtime. 'Instead of playing Bach and Mozart every night . . . I started looking at Scott Joplin.' Adams soon bought the *200 Rock Hits* book of sheet music from Virgin Records. 'It was a slippery slope from there.'

Adams was in various bands at school, including the Village Green Preservation Society, in which he sang and played keyboards. 'We used to play at the school Youth Club a lot; Faces covers like "Stay With Me",' Adams recalls. Wolfenden was in Anorak Faction, who also 'used to play at the Rawdon shit Youth Club. Craig's band used to support us. They used to do this really fucked-up version of "Paranoid". We used to just play Clash and New York Dolls songs. Craig liked that we could play Dolls songs.' Adams was also in Anorak Faction – for one rehearsal. 'We rehearsed in my bedroom when my parents were on holiday. The local people got up a petition to make sure it never happened again.'

Adams was too young to experience the stirrings of punk in Leeds first-hand: he was fourteen and had never even been to a gig when the Sex Pistols played the Fforde Grene in September 1976. His mother banned him from the polytechnic gig on the Anarchy Tour; the infamous Bill Grundy interview on the *Today* show, during which Steve Jones called Grundy a 'dirty fucker', had immediately become national news. Adams also had his paper round the day after the poly gig and had to be up early. Nevertheless, he went to virtually every punk gig at Leeds poly in 1977 and 1978.

When he left school at sixteen in 1978, it was the end of 'Hippy Craig'. With a mother-mandated haircut, he got a job in a clothing warehouse. 'I'd bump into Craig to or from work,' remembers Stuart Green (who was working at Kay's Catalogues), 'both of us really pissed off with doing these really shit jobs that we knew we were not going to do for the rest of our lives.' Adams was in a short-lived band called the Paris Riots with Green and Reg Forbes, otherwise known as 'Reggie Riot' or 'Riot Reggie'. 'We never did a gig but we rehearsed a few times at Stuart's house,' Adams says. 'Fantastic name; a great idea, in search of a band,' is Green's view. 'I remember Craig trying to teach me how to play bass and me not really getting it. He tried to tune us up using the old stand-up piano my mum had in the back room.'

Adams' next band was the Expelaires. By early 1979, they had become one of the leading local Leeds bands. Keenan put them on at a showpiece event at Brannigans on 20 February 1979, which he called the Sheepdog Trials. It featured Leeds' other most-likelies: the Butterflies, Abrasive Wheels and the Faction.

That month, the soon-to-be Gary Marx arrived in Leeds from Hull. Mark Pearman had spent his teenage years in Withernsea, a depressed and isolated resort town on the East Yorkshire coast, before moving to Hull in the summer of 1977. 'While others might have become jaded in the Leeds music scene,' Pearman arrived full of vim. 'In truth I was just kicking against my background. I'd felt so starved of excitement living in the back of beyond, it just gave me a certain energy and openness when I got to Leeds. If others in the splintering punk scene there were guilty of complacency, it was all still thrilling to me and I was prepared to throw myself into situations while others were busy checking themselves in the mirror.'

Pearman came to Leeds with his best friend, Graeme Haddlesey. They had failed for two years to get a band together in Hull but thought Leeds and the F Club scene would be the solution. 'I'd keep asking Keenan to make an announcement over the PA to find other members,' Marx explains. 'Through that we got Martin Taylor to drum and he just brought in a succession of bass players he knew. We rehearsed over at Martin's mum and dad's in Beeston [South Leeds].' This band was Naked Voices. 'The band barely played a gig and never really developed much of an identity. I had no say in the music because I couldn't play an instrument and my singing was pretty tuneless.'

Pearman got to know the Expelaires through his Beeston/Naked Voices connections and because the Guildford 'was one of the best places to hang out, drink, play snooker, pool or pinball . . . Craig seemed the junior member of that band. He was significantly younger than Dave [Wolfenden] and his appearance was still that of a schoolboy really. The fact he was playing keyboards also meant he was a bit in the background whenever you went to see the band. He always had a sense of humour though; that was his way of holding his own. I liked him, although exchanges were limited.'

Fewer and fewer of these interactions took place in the Guildford. Leeds was a regional centre for the far right in the late 1970s and many of the patrons of the Guildford, like other Leeds pubs, reflected that political ugliness. It 'got hairy with the NF – *a lot* of NF,' recalls Wolfenden. 'Right-wing types were always warning us,' adds Gregory. The Expelaires therefore graduated to the Faversham ('the Fav' to its regulars), a hotel with a bar and a late licence, right on the western fringe of the university, well away from the city centre. It was known for its great jukebox, pool tables, the strength of its lager (Holsten Export, especially) and the acid tongue of the bar manager, Jim Bates. The nightclubs of choice for the Faversham crowd soon became the Warehouse and Le Phonographique, depending on the day of the week. The Warehouse began as a New York-style disco, but its main clientele rapidly became New Romantics, post-punks and devotees of electronic music.* Le Phonographique (often called simply 'the Phono') was a basement club inside the Merrion Centre, Leeds' 1960s beast of a shopping centre. Like the Warehouse, it catered to those of an alternative persuasion, but in a far less slick, spacious and salubrious environment.

At the time of the migration from the Guildford to the Fav, Pearman was sharing a house on Hares Avenue with Haddlesey and had a job in a carpet shop on the nearby Harehills Road. 'I had the keys, so I did sleep there sometimes, if I was out late or whatever. I'd just lay down on the big rolls of carpet.' This is the origin of Craig Adams' misunderstanding – to this day – that when he joined the Sisters, 'Mark lived in a carpet shop.' Pearman's job would go on to fund the Sisters of Mercy on at least one occasion: 'There was no accurate stock-taking and money could easily go walkabout,' he explains. In 1979, Pearman was 'just someone else

---

* If the Expelaires were the house band of the F Club, the nearest equivalent at the Warehouse was Soft Cell.

holding down a crap job while trying to get something off the ground.' Adams was in the same boat, but he and the Expelaires were far more advanced in their endeavours than Pearman and Naked Voices.

Andy Taylor was still, nominally, a student at the University of Leeds and had yet to make any move to form a band. He and Pearman met through mutual friends of friends at the university, encountering each other in the union bars or in the Faversham. Their friendship was cemented in the F Club. 'It was clear Andrew was pretty sharp,' Marx recalls. 'Conversations could be involved, often political. He could be very pedantic. I remember him pulling John Keenan up on his use of the word "metaphysical". He liked to argue, liked to test his intellect . . . Although these are the traits people would sort of expect given the public persona that developed, there was another side to him: he was very friendly and approachable.'

Stephen Barber met them both in the F Club at the last concert of his band, the Wanking Cunts*. 'Mark especially had this expansive friendliness in this era, and I got to be good friends with him,' says Barber, known to Pearman as 'Laughing Boy' because of the effect cheap Polish spirits had upon him. Barber 'always found Andy really chatty. He liked his soap operas: he liked *Coronation Street* and *Emmerdale Farm*. He liked to talk about writing, to talk about the Stooges especially. So if you got into common ground

---

* Keenan refused to put the name of Barber's band on his flyers, posters or any other promotional material, instead billing them as the Konky Wonks or the Wonky Konks.

with him, he was very friendly. Andy was always interested in Leonard Cohen and he liked T. S. Eliot and Kerouac. I was very interested in French writing, but we didn't find much common ground with that.' John Lee's reaction to Taylor in the F Club was typical: 'Andrew had a really wry sense of humour, dry, a dark view of the world. He'd come out with critical lines about whatever we were talking about that would make me laugh. He wasn't big for social interaction, but a nice enough lad.' Keenan puts it like this: 'Andy had something about him. He was never one of the lads; he was always in his own little space. He was not a follower.'

To his F Club friends, Pearman was 'Peach'. Despite his best efforts, his primary school nickname had followed him to Leeds and stuck. A third fruit-related name in the F Club seemed excessive to him: there was already a Grape and a Johnny Plumb in his immediate circle. Sometimes his crowd would go to the Warehouse. 'Peach used to dance around to "20th Century Boy" in his own inimitable way,' recalls Lee. 'Very enthusiastic dancer he was.' The same could not be said for Taylor.

Nor did he and Pearman have much in common in their upbringing; 'It was clear his name wasn't on the list for free school meals with mine,' says Pearman. But their taste in music overlapped: the Fall, Pere Ubu, the Stooges – their first album in particular – the Human League, Patti Smith and Suicide. They also looked very different. Not only was Pearman a head taller than Taylor but he was powerfully built, whereas Taylor had the slight and skinny physique of a long distance runner. Furthermore, Pearman 'was always wearing this stuff he got from jumble sales,' says Barber, 'or he got from people in his family.' Dr. Martens shoes and thick socks pulled up so far they looked like puttees were his signature look. Taylor – leather jacket, winkle-pickers, tight jeans (and, occasionally, 'silver lurex kecks'), long soon-to-be-dyed black hair – stood in marked contrast.

As a couple Shearsby and Taylor were also a striking pair, looking more New York than Leeds: if Shearsby was successfully channelling Debbie Harry, Taylor was 'essentially Joey Ramone, crossed with Lenny Kaye,' as Marx puts it. 'I knew Andrew just from the look for a while before I knew anything more. He was out of step with your standard punk appearance.'

Although not long out of school, Shearsby was already one of the most iconic and recognisable figures of the whole Leeds music scene. 'She was there at the birth of it,' Eldritch has noted. 'Absolutely. People don't give her enough credit. A lot of DJs would have baulked at playing the stuff she did. She was like the John Peel of Leeds.'

Taylor and Shearsby were later sketched by the Mekons:

> In the flat above the chemist's
> Andy and Claire are dressing to kill
> But they don't come out till after dark
> Down in Charlie Cake Park*

When Taylor and Shearsby moved in together, Shearsby brought

---

* Taylor and Shearsby's bedsit on St John's Terrace was, of course, not above a real chemist's – Leeds was the amphetamine capital of England.

Spiggy with her. 'When I first met Andrew, I was living at home and this cat from down the road had kittens in our hall. One of them we decided to adopt. He was a little boy, Spiggy, a lovely little black long-haired cat.' Taylor named him after Spiggy Topes, the *Private Eye* character that satirised John Lennon and the Beatles. Taylor was a fan of neither, but he adored the cat.

At university, as in the F Club, Taylor was neither gregarious, nor anonymous, and well liked by those with whom he did mix. 'Andy's a smart fellow obviously. I found him funny,' says Tim Strafford-Taylor, then an Engineering student and bassist in the New Fauves. It was he who had originally introduced Pearman to Taylor.

Strafford-Taylor and Taylor bonded over *The Times* crossword ('He was much better than me and I'm not bad'), the Ramones (they had both loved the concert in Freshers' Week) and the Stooges. 'The first place I ever heard *Funhouse* was at Andy's flat, when he played me it on a battered old cassette recorder, for which I've been eternally grateful,' says Strafford-Taylor. 'Andy came to a few New Fauves gigs. I borrowed his leather jacket a couple of times. We used to swap clothes back then.'

Strafford-Taylor was part of the sprawling group of Leeds university students that were in bands and who drank in the Fenton. The Guildford and the Fenton were focal points of two separate worlds, not least because the Fenton was packed with left-ists. 'Everybody thought fondly of the Fenton,' Eldritch has observed. 'In the days when there was street-fighting, the Fenton was very unwelcoming of Nazis and welcoming of the likes of us.

The whole atmosphere was very politically charged and we were very clear which side we were on.'

Gang of Four, Delta 5 and the Mekons were the best known of its bands. Many of their members were – or had been – Fine Art students. The Sisters of Mercy would intersect with all of these 'art school bands', but the Mekons, especially their drummer, Jon Langford and their guitar player, Kevin Lycett, were the most significant.

Taylor could be seen in the Fenton but 'he did prefer to be at home than in the pub, so you'd go round,' says Lycett. 'Many evenings would just be me, Andy and Claire, sitting and listening to music through his stereo. The speakers were called Dan and Doris, from *The Archers*. To be an *Archers* fan at that age!' Langford met Taylor through Lycett. 'Andy and I didn't go out on the razz together, but we did see a couple of movies and I did go round his flat to watch *Doctor Who*. He wasn't one of the guys down the pub like the rest of us.'

Lycett also detected something of the dandy in Taylor, something 'Wildean: he'd wait for a long time before he said anything, and then you'd realise he'd been polishing it for quite a while before he said it.' Taylor's studied manner was the means by which an essentially shy person interacted with the world. Before he had the Sisters as a vehicle within which to develop his own aesthetic, Taylor was already constructing ways of presenting himself. 'He was fairly arch,' recalls Tim Strafford-Taylor. 'There was an element of acting up.'

All interactions are performative, but Taylor seems to have been especially aware of that. Boyd Steemson is inclined to believe that in Leeds, wrenched out of his usual milieu, Andy Taylor began 'initiating a programme of constructing a personality . . . and Bowie is implicated heavily . . . I think one of the reasons he quite liked seeing me up in Leeds was because there wasn't any need for that. Our relationship was built on the fact that I was a vestigial bit of his previous life. I think he liked that he could maintain contact with that.'

The Sisters of Mercy are an extension – the apotheosis – of these acts of self-creation: highly artificial and at the same time completely authentic. Hence, of those from the F Club who formed bands, Eldritch has been able to describe himself as 'the representative of camp' i.e. 'expressing what's basically serious to you in terms of fun and artifice,' as Christopher Isherwood once wrote: 'You can't camp about something you don't take seriously. You're not making fun of it; you're making fun *out* of it.'

F Club regulars also had the sense that Taylor was an expert observer. 'He would kind of lean against walls at the back of places and watch what was going on, taking it all in,' says John Lee. 'Andy was definitely introverted,' Dave Wolfenden asserts, 'but he would have been logging everything.' Paul Gregory has a sense that drafts of the Sisters of Mercy might have been assembled in Shearsby's DJ booth, in Taylor's mind as he watched the bands: 'He must have been sat there [adopting the dastardly voice of a moustache-twirling villain], "Mmm, I'll have *that*. I do *not* like that. *That* will do."'

Taylor not only loitered in the DJ booth in Brannigans: he sometimes functioned as substitute DJ. 'He'd be down at every gig with Claire,' recalls Keenan. 'When Claire was DJing and wanted to go to the bar or the toilet or whatever, Andy would take over for a bit and all he ever played was Iggy Pop, David Bowie and Gary Glitter.' 'You could always tell when I'd taken over,' Eldritch has confirmed, 'because on came the Glitter.'

Even though Taylor was significantly happier in Leeds than he had been in Oxford, completing a university education remained a low priority. If he had been expecting to coast through and get a 'groovy' year in Taiwan, then he was sorely disappointed. There was no year abroad and the early stages of learning modern Chinese made huge demands on the time and brain power of its students. The F Club was of far more interest to Taylor than his degree – so he dropped out.

Packing in his studies left Taylor in something of a hinterland. The division between the city and the university was stark: young people born and raised in Leeds and those who came there to study were two separate tribes; on leaving the one group, Taylor did not become a local by default. His accent, and to some extent his class, marked him out as different from other habitués of the F Club. 'By virtue of being displaced, both Andrew and I didn't really fit fully in either camp,' says Pearman, who had crossed from the East Riding into West Yorkshire when he relocated from Hull.

Yet Taylor was a rarity: he had his connections to the world of the art school bands, but as someone 'who virtually lived in the F Club' and formed a couple with Shearsby, he was definitely at ease on the other side of the divide. 'To a much lesser extent I also straddled these two camps and that was partly what pulled us together,' Pearman says. Their band would be instrumental in closing the schism between town and gown. When they took their place at the head of the next great wave of Leeds bands, the Sisters of Mercy would redefine what being a 'townie' band meant.

3

Under the Jungle Sky

Since Taylor considered being unemployed a 'perfectly reasonable way to live,' the only job he had after university was brief: he sold merchandise on a couple of Undertones tours. Shearsby and Taylor, in her red VW Beetle with its fur-lined interior, used to drive over to York and hang out at Priestley's, a T-shirt shop just outside the medieval city walls. Paul Ireson, a Priestley's employee, recalls that 'if you hung out in the shop for long enough, you ended up doing some work somewhere along the line.'

Ireson was another who found Taylor visually distinctive. 'He'd be sitting in the shop with his leather jacket, winkle-picker shoes, scarf tied around his wrist, sunglasses on. It wasn't punk. The kids who were the punks were a bit younger and they were still wearing bondage trousers, tartan stuff. Andrew was something a little bit different. It was a little more refined.' Taylor was also no longer a teenager and, as Kevin Lycett witnessed, old for his age, to the point of being something of a fogey. Ireson noted that 'he probably related more to us – I was twenty-five at the time – than the younger kids.'

He knew Taylor as 'Spiggy', a Mekons-appointed nickname that had followed him to York from Leeds university. Taylor obviously understood the *Private Eye* reference but seems not to have seen any humour when it was directed at him. 'He got a bit annoyed when people called him that,' Ireson says, so the Priestley's crowd stopped using it to his face. The nickname is an example of the cleavage between the worlds of the university and the city of Leeds. 'It would never have occurred to me to call him Spiggy,' says Marx, 'either to his face or when referring to him. In no sense was he Spiggy to me . . . I don't remember anyone in the F Club scene using it.'

Literally around the corner from Priestley's was Red Rhino, a record shop, which provided the sleeves Priestley's was using as the inspiration for many of its T-shirt designs. Rhino was also distributing records out of the tiny backroom of its Gillygate premises. From his frequent trips with Shearsby, Taylor was well aware that it was York, not Leeds, that had the two most important hubs for merchandise and record distribution in the region.

Post-university, then, Taylor was not unpleasantly adrift in Leeds. 'We were taking a lot of medication,' he has commented. 'We were doing what we'd always done: going down the F Club, moshing and mincing around . . . Gigs weren't going to watch themselves.' On many an afternoon he and Shearsby would play snooker at the university, this in turn sharpening their pool-playing skills in the Fav. Shearsby was especially adept. Adams would often join them for a game. He too was adrift and, although the junior member of the Expelaires, was the most focused and ambitious, the least tempted to idle. 'I was essentially the manager of the Expelaires,' he says. Adams used the upstairs office of Virgin Records (where he worked after the clothing warehouse) to phone around on his lunch break getting gigs.

The Expelaires got a Peel Session at their first attempt: they had handed their demo directly to John Peel at a roadshow at the university. 'His producer, John Walters, called my mum,' says Adams. If Adams was the manager of the Expelaires, his mother 'was like the secretary.' They got their first record deal off the back of the same demo tape. The deal with Zoo was for one single: 'To See You'/'Frequency' came out in September 1979.

Although he played the instrument – a Vox Jaguar combo organ – that made the Expelaires a good fit as a Zoo band, Adams' core taste lay elsewhere. 'I was into the harder end of things,' he says. The epitome of this was a Destroy All Monsters gig at Brannigans on 2 October 1979. As Adams puts it: 'Ron Asheton and Michael Davis onstage – yes! I couldn't wait, I was just like: "This is *it*!" Ron had his Iron Cross on and his glasses. He was amazing. Michael Davis broke a string: Holy Crap! Niagara – she was gorgeous! I've got all their records – everything.'

Although Dave Wolfenden also loved the MC5 (and Sabbath and Zeppelin), Adams' heavier, hard rock musical tastes were near impossible to indulge in the Expelaires. Before he'd even been to a punk gig, Adams was already in thrall to Hawkwind, especially the way Lemmy played the bass guitar. He also had a considerable soft spot for Thin Lizzy and had seen them in Bradford at St George's Hall in November 1976, one of his first gigs.

At the Destroy All Monsters gig musical differences in the Expelaires were clear. 'I was dancing at the front, pretty much on my own,' says Adams, 'and Grape came up with a pint in his hand and just started laughing at me.'

Soon after this gig, in November 1979, a protozoic version of the Sisters of Mercy came into being in the Hyde Park area of Leeds. After being sacked as the guitarist of Dance Chapter (as the Faction renamed themselves) 'for incompetence and not being a good enough musician,' Stuart Green found himself playing with three habitués of the F Club he thought 'looked fucking amazing': Keith Fuller, Johnny Plumb and Andy Taylor.

In this nameless band, Plumb played bass. 'He wore a nice line in charity shop suits,' remembers Green. 'He had an interesting background: raised in a Catholic family, he had rebelled and run away to join the Navy.' Fuller was the singer. He was an F Club regular who had immediately become one of the faces at the Warehouse. 'Keith was a handsome bastard,' observes Green. 'Great physique and he would slick back his hair and wear a tuxedo . . . We used to call him the Prince of Darkness.' Taylor was the drummer. He had bought his drums – dubbed the 'fish-kit' – from Jon Langford earlier in the year. 'It was a second-hand Olympic kit,' Langford explains. 'Me and Andy Corrigan [of the Mekons] went to Woolworth's and bought fish-tank bathroom lino. We carefully took all the pieces off the drums and stuck the lino down and put all the fittings back, so it looked like a beautiful fish tank. Andy painted it black. He painted it black, maaaan!'

Fuller knew Taylor well from the F Club: 'Andy stood out from the crowd mainly because of his long hair.' Fuller liked him a lot: 'He made me laugh like a drain. He was very droll, which was lost on a lot of people. I think people found him aloof because of his posh accent and him going to university to study Japanese.' As well as dry humour, Fuller and Taylor shared a taste for leather. Fuller would often sport a complete leather jacket/leather trouser outfit; it was a look Taylor would later adopt. 'I was channelling Elvis Comeback Special, whereas Andy was more Alvin Stardust with a little bit of the Lizard King thrown in' is how Fuller distinguishes them.

For a couple of months in the winter of 1979, this fucking-amazing-looking four-piece very occasionally rehearsed together, on one occasion in the cellar of Priestley's in York. All Fuller can remember of any of these rehearsals is 'going through one of John's songs, which included the line: "My enemies stalk each other under the jungle sky."'

The band, however, was a shambles. Green was the first to quit. The F Club would almost immediately offer up a replacement: Mark Pearman was over by the arcade machines when one of the regulars (either 'Johnny Copson or his mate Andy Padgin') asked him if he 'knew any guitar players because well-known Leeds face, Stuart Green, had just left this band,' Pearman recalls. 'I remember saying: "I've got a guitar." I remember clearly that I didn't actually go as far as saying I could play it.'

By this point, Pearman had had enough of Naked Voices. He had become convinced the group needed a lead guitar player. 'I even went so far as to buy an instrument and quickly try to learn it myself to show how much better we could be. Of course the rest of the band just laughed when they heard my attempts to play with absolutely no technical ability . . . That's the point when I started looking for somewhere else to branch out to as a guitar player.'

Shearsby also joined the unnamed band playing a borrowed electronic keyboard. The Fuller/Pearman/Plumb/Shearsby/Taylor line-up was extremely short-lived. 'It was an hysterically dysfunctional set-up,' Marx recalls. 'I can even remember a lengthy argument between Andrew and Johnny Plumb about Claire having a copy of *Cosmopolitan* magazine – as if that somehow made her unsuitable as our keyboard player in Johnny's eyes.' At that same rehearsal, Shearsby remembers, 'down the road from St John's Terrace . . . downstairs in a dilapidated building . . . That's where my amp caught fire.'

Plumb and Shearsby both quit. She was much happier as a DJ than a keyboard player. 'I was always really scared there was going to be a gig at some point,' she says. 'I don't think I could have got onstage. I'd rather be in the dark . . . playing records.' Fuller also concluded 'pretty quickly that I couldn't sing for toffee, so I decided to leave forthwith and save any dignity I had left. We were still friends and there wasn't a hint of malice.'

Taylor, however, hadn't given up on the band and was prepared to scrape the very bottom of the barrel to find a bassist. Boyd Steemson was back in Leeds for New Year's Eve at Taylor and Shearsby's bedsit, 'drinking in the 1980s, probably with Special Brew . . . Andrew had this idea that I might become a bass player in this band. I soon proved otherwise. I had never played before and was utterly inept.'

Pearman also remained committed. During his brief stint in the band 'it hadn't really emerged that I couldn't play, because when we weren't arguing, we only went over one song ad infinitum in the rehearsal: all I had to do was play an A minor chord, luckily one of the handful of chords I knew.'

In fact, only Plumb and Taylor had displayed any talent so far. It is a myth that Taylor was such an awful drummer that he would eventually replace himself with a machine. His band members liked the way he played his fish-kit. 'He was a very limited drummer,' says Green, 'but made an amazingly brilliant use of limited resources . . . Andy not only played the drums like Kenny Morris [of the Banshees], he looked like him too. It was a time for tribal drumming.' Pearman also 'really liked Andrew and his drumming', noting a similarity to 'bits of PiL and Joy Division': 'He would ignore the more standard kick, snare and hi-hats approach to playing and he definitely did not include any fills.'

With Taylor and Pearman resembling 'the last two kids to be picked for the team in the playground' (as Eldritch once put it), the Expelaires seemed to be transitioning from local heroes to a national act. 'To See You' hadn't made it into the Independent Charts, but it had been played by John Peel. The Expelaires also played in London for the first time. This was at the Electric Ballroom, on 19 January 1980. They were fourth on the bill beneath the Teardrop Explodes, Echo & the Bunnymen and Scritti Politti. A Flock of Seagulls went on before them. Less than two weeks later they supported the Clash at Leeds university.

Had they continued their ascent, Craig Adams would never have found his way into the Sisters of Mercy. However, the Expelaires were soon foundering. Mark Copson severed an artery and tendons in one arm in an accident, which meant he could no longer play bass and had to leave the band. He was replaced by Tich Harper's brother, David ('Tubby' to Adams). Zoo were not interested in a second single, but Rockburgh – a short-lived label founded by an expat American, Sandy Robertson – were. The A-side, 'Sympathy (Don't Be Taken In)', emerged as weak reggae, the B-side, 'Kicks', as weak funk. 'The single was supposed to sound like PiL or Chic,' says Dave Wolfenden, 'but then Robertson got his hands on it and, as far I was concerned, fucked it up. We weren't strong enough to say no.' Adams had recorded an extended piano intro to 'Kicks' – several minutes long – that Gregory and Wolfenden still rave about. Mirroring the ill fortunes of the band, this was cut to a few seconds on the single and the tapes lost.

The fissures in the ranks of the Expelaires started to widen. Wolfenden remembers that 'Craig had this bass-line for a song. He played it for us. "Sounds like fucking Motörhead. We're not doing that." We told him it was shit.' Gregory wryly admits: 'It became one of the very best Sisters songs and we gave it away. Hindsight is a wonderful thing.'

Adams' time in the Expelaires was hurtling to a close. 'We got offered a deal from CBS,' he says. 'It came via my house and I put it to them. CBS wanted three singles and an album for £25,000. Tich and his brother Tubby, they wanted to stay independent; I think Wolfie might have been in that clan. I was like: "Screw that!" and that's when I left. "You just turned that down? OK, that's the end. See you later." Grape, to this day, cannot remember the offer even being there. That's why I left, Grape! I was beyond livid. How stupid do you want to be?'

Taylor and Pearman had become a duo by accident. Marx jokes that 'Andrew had such a Bowie fetish that he couldn't resist having his very own guitarist/sidekick straight off the bus from Hull.' In reality, 'I don't imagine for one minute that he looked at me and muttered anything similar to Bowie's immortal: "I've found my Jeff Beck."'

Taylor and Pearman were not an entirely unnatural pairing: both were academically able, rather quiet and self-contained young men. Yet, there was an imbalance, which both of them enjoyed. Although only a month apart in age, by dint of 'his personality and his education Andrew sometimes assumed the role of elder to a greater degree than that gap would warrant,' says Marx, who had dropped out of school two weeks into his A Levels and 'was picking up my education piecemeal mostly prompted by my love of music.' Although his formal education had been abbreviated, he wasn't devoid of cultural knowledge: 'When I met Andrew I had a loose grasp on certain things: I didn't just stand there slack-jawed, if he inadvertently mentioned Dadaism in the same sentence as the new Pere Ubu album.' Nevertheless, the first time Taylor invited him to the cinema, Pearman 'imagined popcorn and a blockbuster; what I got instead was an all-night showing of the films of Luis Buñuel in the university.' Taylor went 'into a long post-match analysis on that occasion,' Marx recalls, 'possibly because he'd chosen to view them with chemical supplements.'*

Pearman and Taylor tried again – and failed again – to find a bass player. Taylor asked Tim Strafford-Taylor: 'Andy was too po-faced about it,' Strafford-Taylor recalls. 'He was quite intense; he had a plan even then. I just wanted to get up on a stage, drink some beer and make a row and have a laugh. So I turned down the Sisters.' Kevin Lycett went to just one rehearsal: 'I didn't have any skill as a bass player and they clearly wanted musicians not nihil-istic art school post-punk arses, who couldn't even play two chords properly. Like me. Also, they didn't really do the left-wing shtick back then and I would've felt a bit awkward in a band that was more interested in black leather and pointy boots than politics, fine though black leather and pointy boots indeed are.'

They also tried to replace Shearsby on keyboards. Like Lycett, Jon Langford managed one rehearsal. 'One day we sat around and I made explosion noises on the Mekons' Korg synthesiser,' he says. 'It was never a proper rehearsal with tunes.' Langford could have joined the Sisters, but never turned up to rehearsals: 'I was just too busy with other things.'

Stephen Barber was exasperated by Pearman and Taylor's slow progress. 'I had this sense even then, that if you hadn't got going with a band by sixteen or seventeen you were finished. You were over it. So for them to get into their twenties and have not really got going with these plans for a band, I guess I thought nothing

---

* Marx can also recall watching *Tron* in a big cinema in the city centre of Leeds with Taylor, Shearsby and a big group of their friends, many of them lysergically adjusted and artificially stimulated.

was going to happen and they were wasting everyone's time – completely feckless. They used to talk about it and time went on and on and on . . .'

At this unformed stage of the band's development Pearman had the extraordinary idea of making a record. 'I approached Andy to go into the studio with me, despite the fact the only thing I had was the money I'd pilfered from work to pay for the time. I could barely play at all and had no material.' Taylor consented. 'I suspect he viewed it as having very little to lose at that point.' Pearman was literally prepared to give blood to make a record. He 'played a variety of cheap and/or borrowed guitars . . . The one which sticks in my mind from that initial period was an Arbiter Les Paul belonging to a mate, which I used for a while. He had modified the bridge and tail-piece for some reason, and it meant I continually sliced my hand open on its jagged metal.'

Pearman booked Ric Rac Sound Studio in Wortley, the same studio where Naked Voices had made their one demo. For the recording session, Taylor offered a song he had written called 'The Damage Done'. Pearman was delighted because the band now had one proper song. 'I quickly threw three ideas down, which became 'Watch', 'Home of the Hitmen' and 'Miser Rate'.

'Miser Rate' is the first of the Sisters' lost songs; perhaps just as well. 'It really was the most cobbled-together piece of the lot, which is some boast,' Marx concedes. 'I'd been desperately trying to come up with some material for a couple of days to show Andrew, fearing he'd back out if I didn't deliver. I'd seen the 'Economy' setting on the control for my gas fire was named 'Miser Rate'. It amused me and so I fired off some stream of consciousness

47

lyrics and invented some music triggered by a tune from Pere Ubu I really liked. I had a sort of speeded up variation of the same pattern halfway through, which Andrew pointed out was of course almost note-for-note 'I Wanna Be Your Dog'. Because I was so unmusical I really didn't know. He thought I was being kind of arch and knowing, post-modern even.'

The Captains of Industry was a serious contender for the name of the duo's band. Taylor was going to be Captain Black ('No shit, Shylock!' Pearman quips), while Pearman was to be Captain Orange, 'an in-joke about my limited singing – zero range.' Instead they chose the Sisters of Mercy. This was taken from the song 'Sisters of Mercy' on Leonard Cohen's first album, with a definite article added. Cohen, according to his biographer Sylvie Simmons, 'wrote the song during a blizzard in Edmonton, Canada, after encountering two young girl backpackers in a doorway. He offered them his hotel bed and, when they fell straight to sleep, watched them from an armchair, writing, and played them the song the next morning when they awoke.' Referring to them as nuns indicated the chastity of the encounter.

Pearman and Taylor were also well aware of the ironic use of the song in Robert Altman's 1971 revisionist Western *McCabe & Mrs Miller* – 'Sisters of Mercy' plays over the introduction of the prostitutes in the make-shift brothel that McCabe (Warren Beatty) has set up in a frontier mining town. 'The name's nice and ironic,' Eldritch once noted, 'very corporate. A nice 50-50 balance between nuns and prostitution, which seems like a very suitable metaphor for a rock band. All this pseudo-faith business and high ritual, and yet – prostitution.'

'Nurses were always part of that mix as well' in Marx's opinion. They too were capable of corporal and spiritual acts of mercy. 'We'd both spent a fair bit of time in our late teens in the company of nurses,' he continues. Both young men had concluded that proximity to illness and death often gave nurses an inner steeliness and a greater zest for life. And 'we were both aware of the power of uniforms.'

With the name of the band decided, the name of their record label soon followed: Merciful Release. This was already the front-runner when Pearman and Taylor were watching *The Oblong Box*, a 1969 adaptation of an Edgar Allan Poe short story on late-night TV, when Vincent Price noted, after the death of his badly disfigured brother: 'There's no need for sorrow. In his case, oblivion was a merciful release.'

Taylor produced various drafts of a logo for Merciful Release, soon arriving at combinations of a five-pointed star and a tracing of a diagram labelled 'Dissection of the head, face and neck' from *Gray's Anatomy*. With the star blacked-in, the design resembled the emblem of a macabre radical leftist cell: part Red Army Faction, part Alice Cooper.

On the verge of going into Ric Rac, the Sisters of Mercy finally found a bass player. Craig Adams had ignominiously followed up the Expelaires with Exchange, his synthesiser duo with Jim Bates from the Faversham. They gigged twice and made an 'appalling' demo at RAM in Leeds. Adams 'was still going to the F Club and I would sit with Claire when she was DJing. Her boyfriend Andy was going on about doing a band, and not having a bass player anymore. Blah blah blah. "I can play bass," I said. Which was not necessarily true. That's how I fell into the Sisters.'

At the time, Adams was sharing a house with university students on Burchett Place. This was a twenty-minute walk from Taylor and Shearsby's bedsit. Adams' walk to his life-changing audition – between two non-descript Victorian houses, with his restrung guitar and a fuzzbox – took him right across Woodhouse Moor, known locally as Hyde Park; it is fitting that the creation of the Sisters of Mercy – the Sisters of Mercy proper – one of the most iconic Leeds bands, was initiated by a stroll across one of the city's great landmarks.

4

Slow, Slow, Quick, Quick, Slow

The Sisters of Mercy were now a trio, but they had already committed to making a record as a duo. Things went badly wrong at Ric Rac Studios. The Sisters were under-rehearsed, inexperienced and muddle-headed. They needed a sympathetic producer. Mick Robson, the owner of Ric Rac, was not that man. Ric Rac's core business was showbands and advertising jingles, but recording options in Leeds were limited. Mark Pearman also suspected that Robson was a Supertramp fan: Pere Ubu, the Fall – or any band the Sisters might want to sound like – were not remotely within Robson's frame of reference.

An account of this shambolic non-meeting of minds was written by Eldritch (if we assume it was he, despite the third person) for the Sisters' official website:

So it came to pass that our intrepid sonic explorers booked themselves . . . studio time at Ric Rac Studios, which was (and possibly still is) a shed in Wortley. Wortley is a run-down indus-trial area south of Leeds . . . The studio owner was, naturally, the only one who knew how to operate the studio, so he did the engineering. With a beard. Our heroes found it difficult to convey to him what a non-cabaret act might sound like. As a result, *nobody* knew what they were supposed to be doing. The engineer lost himself in a place where no engineer had gone before (or since), somewhere near the worst of both worlds.

Marx is equally even-handed in apportioning blame. 'Mick Robson had an understandably one-size-fits-all approach to producing local bands. We didn't really conform to anything he was used to and we didn't have the know-how to wrestle it away from him and create something better. All we really managed to achieve by badgering him was make it sound worse than if we'd left him to it.'

An additional problem was that it was often quite apparent when Robson did not like the music he was recording.* Nick Toczek, who published the Bradford fanzine *Wool City Rocker*, remembers that 'Mick was not someone who suffered what he thought were fools.' He clearly thought Taylor and Pearman were prize idiots. When Toczek was dropping off copies of *Wool City Rocker* at Ric Rac, Robson said: '"Jesus, Nick have a listen to the band practising downstairs. I'm recording them. Just listen to this

---

* While there are other examples of Robson's disdain (such as his telling the Mekons to their faces that they sounded like a cow farting in a bath), other acts including the Keighley band Skeletal Family happily recorded many times at Ric Rac.

shit." He opened the door,' remembers Toczek, 'and it was the Sisters. "This is the worst band I've ever had in this studio. I don't know what they are trying to do."'

Kevin Lycett visited the Sisters in Ric Rac and his reaction was exactly the same: 'I don't get these sounds at all. I don't know what's going on here.' Pearman and Taylor would have agreed with him. In fact it took two visits to Wortley to complete 'Watch'. 'We decided to go back a second time with a clearer idea of what we were doing – that meant dropping "Miser Rate" completely,' Marx says. Even in its finished version, 'Andrew's attempt at playing a sort of disco beat on "Watch" wasn't great.' 'The Damage Done', Andy Taylor's first ever song, was similarly bungled. 'The combination of electronic pulses from the Wasp synth with overlaid live drums didn't really gel either,' Marx thinks.*

A fragment of 'Home of the Hitmen', Pearman's other song, did make it onto the B-side after 'Watch'. Its opening lyric – 'the sun shines on the aluminium' – was an in-joke about window frames. Taylor and Pearman 'used to howl with laughter watching Everest double glazing adverts' featuring the farmer-turned-celebrity Ted Moult. 'There were these ever more bizarre variations on the ads, which usually involved the turning on of a wind machine at some point to prove how airtight the glazed units were.'

Although 'The Damage Done' single was a false start and not a product of the authentic band, it clearly exhibits fragmentary proto-Sisters elements. Taylor's voice is already recognisable, as is the

---

* The dinky yellow and black synthesiser was most likely borrowed from Adams, who had played one in the Expelaires.

intention to combine simplistic riffs with overdriven trebly barre chords and to use echo on voice and drums. Even the desire to synthesise percussion is apparent. In his lyrics, Taylor – not for the last time – references the work of T. S. Eliot ('The Hollow Men' in this case). However, the results that came out of Ric Rac were genuinely bad. 'I wasn't exactly concerned about sounding amateurish. I loved the Fall after all,' Marx concedes, 'but I did know the attitude had been lost somewhere in the process. Attitude was pretty much all we had going for us, so it's no shock the first single doesn't stand up to repeat listening.' Yet the single was a form of praxis, of self-constitution through music, the very act of making it far more important than what it sounded like. 'The Damage Done' is therefore an important record, those two days in Ric Rac vital: the Sisters had launched their pebble in the water and the consequences were numerous, enormous and immediate.

After Ric Rac, the Sisters of Mercy 'started using a drum machine because a decision was made Andrew should be the singer,' says Marx. 'It may be the case that he had the biggest ego and desperately wanted to be a frontman from the outset . . . It was a simple decision based on the fact he was self-evidently a much better singer than I was. Although we both had similar registers he could sing in tune and there was a richness to the timbre of his voice that was markedly absent in mine . . . As soon as we had started thinking about possibly playing live, there was no way we would have a singing drummer. Genesis, 10cc, the Eagles: no fucking way.'

There was a technological solution at hand. 'None of us saw the drum machine as a poor man's option, far from it. We loved bands like Suicide and the Human League . . . It seemed to make sense because in Andrew we had a drummer to program it and, although it was never said, that unshakeable bedrock meant it really didn't matter how wayward my playing was; it almost made a virtue of it.' Although he didn't play a note there, the session at Ric Rac solidified Adams as part of the trio. 'Craig came into Ric Rac with us that second time,' says Marx. 'I really remember him making me laugh uproariously for most of the time. He told jokes . . . an endless repertoire of stupid jokes but told with such gusto; he was great fun and very easy to be around. He instantly brought something extra to the party, both in terms of his musical outlook and his personality. Neither contribution should be undervalued.'

Adams' arrival in the band created a kind of ground zero. Each member of the band had roles they had no or little experience in. Marx puts it like this: 'I didn't play guitar, Andrew didn't sing and Craig didn't play bass . . . That seemed a pretty healthy, even-handed starting point to me.' Joining the Sisters, after the Expelaires 'was a sizeable step down in profile for Craig but he seemed to relish the new freedom he found with us.'

'The Damage Done' single also deployed a much-improved version of Taylor's 'Head and Star' as the Merciful Release logo. Still using the flayed head from *Gray's Anatomy* in combination with a five-pointed star, this iteration was excellent: stark white on black, it was surely inspired by Joe Petagno's design for the cover of Motörhead's first album and Arturo Vega's Ramones logo. The new 'Head and Star' was graphically striking and so excessively macabre as to be more than a little funny: the head is divided into segments, each with its own flap of skin ready to be peeled back. Eldritch would later insist that the star was an indicator of the band's leftist credentials, but it was just as redolent of a pentagram and heavy rock's flirtation with the occult. Taylor himself appeared to have absolutely no interest whatsoever in esoterica and black magic, but he was most definitely interested in exploring the stupidity of rock 'n' roll. The image neatly sums up Taylor's approach to rock 'n' roll: a desire to embrace, and then archly re-contextualise, its more ludicrous aspects. The Merciful Release logo hovered somewhere between satire, post-modern bricolage and the sincere desire to exude power and violence. First and foremost: it looked great. Taylor strongly believed that aesthetics could be divorced entirely from morality. He loathed Nazis, past and present, but was quite capable of recognising the design choices of the SS: the Merciful Release logo is a kind of Death's Head.

At this point, Taylor was perhaps more interested in graphic design than he was in being in a band. It was therefore apt that the Merciful Release logo appeared on clothing before it did on a record. Taylor had a batch of T-shirts printed up at Priestley's, so called because the premises had previously been a butcher's and the name was still clearly visible in the tiles on the frontage. Somewhat fittingly, given the macabre subject of the logo design, the first ever Sisters T-shirts came into the world in what had once been meat freezers, repurposed as drying rooms, where freshly screen-printed T-shirts were hung up in rows in front of electric heaters before being made available for sale in the shop above, or via mail order from the Priestley's catalogue. The first buyers, however, were down at the F Club, the Warehouse and in the Faversham. John Lee remembers, 'Peach came along one night with a bag of them.' Claire Shearsby would also wear one during her DJ set.

The process of making 'The Damage Done' single also provided Pearman with a better stage name than Peach: 'One of the early Ric Rac Studio invoices was made out to "Gary Marks" – their spelling. That came about because Claire used to mistakenly call me Gary when we first met and I never corrected her . . . Mick who ran the studio was a bit puzzled by Andrew calling me Mark and then Claire would pop in and call me Gary. When it came to paying, he asked me what he was supposed to put on the bill. I just gave him the two names . . . It was a little later that I refined the spelling based on my credentials as a working-class hero.' Another inspiration was an incident at school when one of Pearman's teachers had asked the whole class if anyone knew who Lenin was. 'My mate just replied, "Didn't he play guitar with the Beatles, sir?"'

According to Eldritch on the Sisters' website (still assuming he is the author): 'Andrew went off to York with the master tape and a proposition for Red Rhino . . . "You put up the money to press a thousand singles, and we'll pay for any that don't get sold".' Red Rhino 'had nothing to lose but cashflow,' Eldritch believed. 'The record was mastered with George Peckham (of "Porky Prime Cut" fame) in Portland Place, near the BBC building in London. News had not yet reached Leeds that Porky did his best work before lunchtime . . . The artwork was swiftly put together and it also went down to London, but news had not yet reached Leeds that printers have to be reminded to put the labels on the correct side of a piece of vinyl. Thus a collector's item was born.'

The cover of the first Sisters of Mercy record, like many of those that would follow it, was a found image. This one was lifted from a photography book in Leeds Central Library: an Edwardian-era photograph of a group of worshippers attending service at St Andrew's church in West Tarring, Sussex. Caslon Antique font for the writing was selected by the band from a Letraset catalogue.

'The Damage Done' was played on the radio by John Peel in late October 1980, in between Scientist and John Lee Hooker. A week later Peel played 'Watch' between the Damned and Adam and the Ants, although he was confused by the labelling error and wasn't sure what exactly he was broadcasting. After hearing Marx's singing, Peel concluded, 'the nation seems to be packed to bursting point with tormented young men who want us to stare deeply into their souls.' Marx has no strong memory of either epochal moment, but does vividly remember 'when we first played the acetate . . . It was only good for a few plays because the thin surface coating is degraded every time the needle passes over. That meant we had to go to the person's house with the best record player we knew, and that was Claire's mum's . . . It was a strange ritualistic event, to listen so intently to it. In a way it would have been more fitting if we'd only ever made the acetate and not pressed up any actual records. We could have just played it over and over until we got down to the metal and then Andrew and I could have gone our separate ways . . . It might actually have started to sound better the more we cut through the lacquer and corrupted the sonic information.'

Any further progress by the Sisters of Mercy was extremely slow. Equipment remained an issue for a long time. 'We had to borrow amplifiers at some point,' remembers Adams. 'I borrowed Kevin

Lycett's, until he found out I was playing bass through it and then he went bloody mental. We were all borrowing things.'

'I think it's important to remember just how time-consuming the most basic things could be when you had little or no money,' Marx adds. 'Those endless bus rides or walks across town to borrow an amp or whatever, only to find no one at home; countless broken arrangements. Neither Andrew nor Craig were on the phone, none of us drove a car, I was still working full-time . . . Andrew lived up on the second floor, so even if you walked all the way over to his you couldn't necessarily get hold of him – you wouldn't know if he was in or not or just sleeping through the day. With that and his desire to live a nocturnal existence for some of that period, it's no surprise things didn't happen quickly.'

Nevertheless, the Sisters of Mercy did manage to rehearse. Taylor and Marx could be relied on to trot out a line from Ted Moult, the double-glazing hawker: 'Sound-proofing, that might be important to you,' before starting the drum machine in the bedsit. 'All kinds of people and things became referred to as 'Ted Moult' or 'son of Ted Moult' during that period,' Marx explains. 'Andrew may have had *The Glass Bead Game* [by Hermann Hesse] on his bookshelves but he always had a great flair for inanity as well.'

'We'd take regular breaks,' says Marx. 'I'm not sure how many cigarettes a day Andrew was smoking then but he seemed to be continually going to the corner shop to buy more. He was well known and well liked in the shop – I always found it one of his more endearing qualities that things like that seemed to matter to him. In . . . his normal day-to-day exchanges with people, he really was friendliness and charm personified.'

Once on a visit to St John's Terrace, Adams, upon being buzzed in and climbing the stairs to the top floor, discovered Taylor 'sat there in a deckchair in a corner with an air rifle. "We've got a fucking mouse, man." He'd made this makeshift wall into a little trap and was waiting for this mouse to stick its head out, so he could shoot it.' Taylor's determination to get rid of the rodent stemmed from his intense loathing of insects and vermin: 'Hell is probably run by cockroaches,' he once observed.

In the middle of this period of semi-activity, Adams bought his first bass. 'I was working the night shift at Morrisons with Simon Denbigh (soon-to-be the singer in the March Violets). On my first paycheque I got some sort of tax refund.'

Something more extraordinary also happened: by the time 'The Damage Done' was in the shops, the Sisters of Mercy had three new songs and they were very good indeed. They got the chance to record them thanks to Adrian Collins at Red Rhino, with whom they had made the arrangement to fund 'The Damage Done'. Collins and Tony Kostrzewa – Rhino's owner – ran the distribution out of the cramped backroom of Rhino's Gillygate shop. Collins had been hired by Red Rhino to help transform it from being simply a seller of records into a regional distributor, but he had ambitions of his own: he wanted to form his own label and was on the lookout for bands. He was perfectly aware that, objectively, 'The Damage Done' wasn't any good, but he could see potential there. 'Spiggy, for all his bombasticness and his obnoxiousness at times, I could see he had some talent,' Collins says. 'He had something about him. He was the focal point of the band. The band had something there, that quality, which you can't always put your finger on.'

Acting on this instinct, Collins funded the Sisters' return to the shed in Wortley for a day's recording. There they made demos of new songs: 'Floorshow', 'Lights', 'Teachers' and 'Adrenochrome'. The runt of the litter was 'Teachers', a cover of the Leonard Cohen song, which kept his lyrics and dispensed with his music entirely. The other three were nothing short of a revelation. 'Floorshow' supplemented Adams' metal bass riff with the Doktor, live drums and lead guitar, which largely doubled Adams' part. Taylor's lyrics seemed to be a haughty and stinging attack on the clubs and discos of Leeds, pitched as an eyewitness account of the death of Western culture; several brazen lifts from *The Waste Land* slotted right in. 'The lyric shows Andrew's fluency, as well as a sense of humour,' says Marx. 'It's a barbed attack in the great snarling tradition of Dylan and the Stones, but it would sit equally well with a punk or post-punk figure like Howard Devoto or Richard Butler.' The irony was that a song equating dance-floor hedonism with systemic cultural decay would eventually become a floor-filler at alternative clubs.

'Lights' is slow and sparse, in sharp contrast to the speedy torrent of noise of 'Floorshow'. It's strong on atmosphere and is one of Taylor's first 'tingle, tingle, tingle "was that a minute or was that an hour?"' amphetamine songs. With the Doktor and the guitar saturated in delay, the dabs of Wasp synthesiser and the booming bass, it's a kind of dub. The Doktor also does a more than passable imitation of the drums on Iggy's 'Nightclubbing', themselves performed by one of the Doktor's older Roland relatives. The lyrics of 'Lights' seem to be about finding one's place – finally, and surprisingly – in the damp and dark north of England.

Taylor plays the drums in his usual restricted style on 'Teachers' before it segues into 'Adrenochrome', at which point the Doktor takes over. The shift between the two songs is symbolic of a great leap forward by the primitive iteration of the band. 'Adrenochrome', like 'Floorshow', has excellent lyrics and seems – and we can never be definitive with Sisters lyrics – to be Taylor revelling in his unplanned migration from the dreaming spires of Oxford to Leeds, the land of strong speed and personal liberation.

Yet the demo tape was only a transitional artefact. Taylor had clearly not worked out how to make best use of his voice or his drum machine; but the way ahead was clear. 'If we take Craig's arrival to mark the real start,' says Marx, 'all kinds of aspects of what we did excited me from day one and, by and large, they were the things that I still found compelling two or three years on. Andrew as a lyricist was already commanding although perhaps not so multi-layered. Something in the way Craig played and the sound he used took us up several notches even from the first rehearsals – he just seemed to soak up all the missing frequencies.'

In their efforts to become a properly functioning band, the Sisters of Mercy had their first photos taken together. These were done by Jon Langford near Belle Vue House where he lived, over-looking the valley of the River Aire. The photographs offer no evidence that within a few short years these three men would become iconic and define a whole cultural and musical trend. There's little-to-no sense of a visual identity. Taylor is at least in all black – shirt, jacket with upturned collar, well-worn trousers – and in shades. Marx is in a Harrington jacket, slacks and his trade-mark big socks. Adams looks like a Dickensian urchin, in a scarf, cardigan and extremely baggy trousers. In fact, Adams was so lacking in presentation he now wonders if he had come straight from the night-shift at Morrisons, or an early morning potato delivery for a local entrepreneur, Dave Hall.

'You'd get back from the Warehouse and you'd all be cranked up,' Adams explains, 'so you'd go to Leeds City Station and meet Dave and the trains, pick up the newspapers and deliver them to newsagents with Dave in his van. And then we'd go to a warehouse to pick up vegetables to deliver to schools. We'd get back into Leeds to Hessle Terrace [where Hall lived] around nine in the morning and Dave would pay us and buy us breakfast.' Hall would later become a significant figure in the Leeds music scene as a manager, promoter and merchandiser, but in the early 1980s he was a small-time go-getter – 'a man with a van' – who was working at least three jobs and rarely slept.

As a further part of the strategy to generate some interest, Taylor made cassettes containing the Ric Rac demos and the 'The Damage Done' single. He blacked out the inlays of every one with meticulously applied, thick Rotring ink. One of the recipients of these cassettes was the founder of Rough Trade, a key independent label and distributor. 'Geoff Travis gave it one listen,' recalled Eldritch. 'It was eighteen minutes long, lots of tracks, tapped his feet all the way through and turned round and said, "It's like Bauhaus."' Taylor thought this was even less of a compliment than Travis did. 'Nobody likes being compared to Bauhaus. Not even Bauhaus,' Eldritch once quipped. 'Andrew did as he often did, and all but burned that particular bridge within a matter of minutes of speaking with him [Travis],' says Marx. If he usually played 'the good cop in our particular odd couple', then Taylor was perfectly content to be the bad cop. 'They disagreed over the importance of the Sisters to Rough Trade,' Marx continues. 'Andrew always believed the band should command the highest respect. Travis wouldn't have had much to base a similar sense of belief on at that stage, just an awkward bastard cluttering up his office.'

'I am indeed pretty fucking good at alienating everybody. To be honest, I'd be pretty good at it even if I wasn't fronting a rock 'n' roll band,' Eldritch once admitted.

With songs, a demo and publicity shots, the Sisters of Mercy were almost a fully functioning band. They now intended to play live.

5

White Witch Ceremonies

The trio's first gig was a CND (Campaign for Nuclear Disarmament) benefit on Monday 16 February 1981 at Alcuin College at the University of York. The Sisters were support for the Thompson Twins, well before the Thompson Twins trimmed down to a trio and had pop hits. Eldritch – in presumed website third person and vivid present – remembers the show: 'Marx has connected his guitar to a record-player pre-amp which feeds back uncontrollably and Eldritch has shifted the vocal echo into overdrive. It's metal dub without any spaces, on a shuddering mechanoid backdrop.' This is likely more fun to read than it was to listen to.

The first song the Sisters of Mercy ever played live was their fucked-up version of 'Teachers'; the first thing an audience ever heard was their intro tape. Adams refers to it as 'the White Witch Ceremony'. Taylor had bought a cassette of a magickal ritual from an occult shop in Burley called the Sorcerer's Apprentice. The

Sisters had so few songs that the ceremony played for ages before the cue to begin 'Teachers' arrived. Adams (in portentous voice) recalls that it was: '"And those who blah, blah, blah must now depart . . . depart . . . *depart*" and then we used to start the drums.' Therefore the first voice heard at a concert by the Sisters of Mercy was not Andy Taylor's but that of Chris Bray (aka 'Frater Marabas') the adept who owned the Sorcerer's Apprentice and recorded the spells and incantations he had for sale. Like the logo, the Sisters' intro tape seemed another wry dig at rock 'n' roll's dance with the devil.

A month after the gig in York, the Sisters made their Leeds debut: Thursday 19 March 1981. They were support for Altered Images. Fittingly, it was in the F Club in Brannigans. Stephen Barber was there. 'They were totally shambolic, completely a mess. However, for me and a lot of people in the audience, to do something totally chaotic, cacophonic and inept was really okay.' Mark Johnson was there too and thought the Sisters were 'noisy but poor; poor to the point where you couldn't really decipher what the songs were like or what they were singing. It was just some locals from the F Club . . . just Andy, Craig and Peach who just got onstage and made a racket.' John Keenan's first impressions were that 'they didn't have the drum beat right . . . and Andy was trying to sound like Bowie doing "Heroes".' Taylor was immediately making excuses to Mark Johnson in *Whippings & Apologies*: 'That was a real balls-up because of the bad sound . . . A lot of the stuff we do depends on us having a good PA. Without a decent PA, we sound really crap.'

'It was basically kids learning to play onstage,' comments Keenan. The Sisters of Mercy did get better, but progress was slow, not least because they played live so rarely. Taylor told *Whippings & Apologies* that this was tactical. 'We don't see the need to play in every toilet every week because there's no percentage in it. We could play the Pack Horse or the Royal Park every week but it wouldn't be worth it. It's not that we think we're better than those places, it's just that we know we'd sound shit in them.' Nor had the Sisters honed their chops in the Sheepdog Trials, John Keenan's showcase evenings at the F Club for local bands. 'Because I knew Andy, they went straight to supporting,' Keenan explains.

There was considerably less largesse forthcoming at the university. Andy Kershaw, the future BBC radio DJ, was the powerful Ents Sec (Entertainment Secretary) at the time. Part of his remit was to book bands into the Refectory, one of the UK's most prized venues, not least because the Who had recorded *Live at Leeds* there. Kershaw was astonished when Taylor asked him for the support slot at an upcoming Motörhead show, and dismissively informed him that he should pay his dues on the pub circuit or play a small room somewhere on the campus at a local band night.

'Motörhead in the Refectory is what I asked for,' was Taylor's reply. 'I'm not interested in any of those other toilets.'*

Kershaw, perhaps used to far more deference from local bands, was so infuriated by Taylor's gall that he informed him that the Sisters of Mercy would never play in his beloved Refectory while he was the Ents Sec. Marx, who was also at this meeting recalls:

---

* When Motörhead played in Leeds on 28 March 1981 it was at the Queen's Hall, the largest venue in the city. Whether the gig was moved there from the Refectory due to the success of *Ace of Spades*, or whether Marx has mis-remembered the venue that Taylor was demanding, Kershaw certainly had the power to broker a Motörhead support slot in Leeds for the Sisters of Mercy.

'Andrew didn't bother searching through his extensive vocabulary for his parting retort: "Fuck you!" worked just fine.' Eldritch would later summarise his relationship with Kershaw: 'He fucking hated us. And it was mutual.' Taylor and Marx went straight from the Ents Sec's office to the snooker tables of the Union. Taylor's ire, not untypically for him, gave him additional focus and resolve. He thrashed Marx, who remembers 'Andrew pacing round the table in an approximation of a long-haired Alex Higgins.'

The second time Keenan put the Sisters on in Leeds was on Sunday 22 March 1981, three days after their Brannigans show. This was an all-day fundraiser for the International Year of the Disabled Person that featured twelve bands and five poets. The Sisters were third from bottom of the bill. This took place in Tiffany's, a huge, mainstream, city-centre nightclub. This was 'the only show we ever played where Danny [Horigan] joined us onstage to play synth,' says Marx. 'I kept pushing to get him in but he only made it up that one time, playing white noise as a mad, surrogate Eno through a ramshackle version of "Silver Machine".' The excess of Space Echo that the Sisters deployed was the outcome of dual Suicide and Hawkwind fetishes. Ben Matthews was apparently in the audience and thought the Sisters were hilarious.

At their next gig at York University, the Sisters met Pete Turner for the first time. Turner, a sound engineer, would have a major impact on the band for more than a decade. He was a partner in KG Hire, a Bridlington enterprise that rented out PAs in the north and north-east of England. 'KG' stood for Ken Giles, Turner's business partner. That night in York, 'I generally looked after the Sisters. We were all northern people,' Turner says. 'You get some support bands: so arrogant. They were nothing like that. They were trying to keep their cool, but I did like them.' Turner was being assisted by John Spence, a regular monitor engineer for KG Hire and the engineer at Fairview Studios in Hull. 'When we'd sound-checked the main band, we asked the support to get their gear onstage,' Spence recalls. 'One of them – probably Andy – pointed at a small guitar combo amp and said: "That's our gear." So one amp with four inputs into which were plugged a drum machine, a bass guitar, a rhythm guitar and a vocal mic . . . all overloaded and distorted.' Taking pity on them, Turner 'sorted things out so they could be more independent,' he says, 'so Craig could plug straight into the sound system. I put whatever drum machine they were using straight into the PA too. It sounded a lot better than it would have done through one amp.'

The Sisters obviously agreed that Turner had made significant improvements. Two tracks from the show ('1969' and 'Sister Ray') were added to the B-side of the Sisters' demo tape. On these tracks – unlike at the F Club gig – you *could* hear what they were trying to do: a primitive brutal groove – thick bass and brittle tick-tock drums – slathered with head-slicing fuzz, feedback and screams. It was a bewildering amalgam of the Stooges, Suicide and the Human League. At a push, you could imagine people dancing to it, albeit while bleeding from the eyes and ears.

'1969' had been added to the set, not just because of a love of the Stooges, but because 'Now, I'm going to be twenty-two' was true in Taylor's case. His birthday was coming up on 15 May. Marx 'was going to sing it when we got a gig near to mine [18 June] but that didn't materialise.' Both were included because of 'that punk thing of needing to do a Velvets song or a Stooges one,' Marx says. The band even 'talked about doing a whole bunch of songs with Sister in the title, so "Sister Anne" by the MC5, "Sister Morphine", "Sister Midnight", "Sister Europe". It was one of the ideas that amused us for a little while but never made it to any form of rehearsing.'

The month Taylor turned twenty-two, their demo cassette – now with a rehearsal at St John's Terrace added in addition to the Ric Rac recordings and 'The Damage Done' – initiated a connection with the Psychedelic Furs that, over the next two years, enabled the Sisters' first great record, earned them their most high-profile gigs and brought them significantly closer to the centres of industry power in New York and London.

At Tiffany's in Leeds on 26 May, 'while lurking at a Furs soundcheck', Andy Taylor 'foisted' the cassette on Duncan Kilburn, their saxophone player. If not quite an origin myth, the handing over of the cassette in 1981 has acquired legendary status in the Sisters' narrative.

Shearsby was the DJ that night, so access to Tiffany's would have been easy for her and her boyfriend. The tape handover took place during the Furs' tour to promote their second album, *Talk Talk Talk*. Taylor had seen the Furs' 'first gig in Leeds at the F Club, all twenty-five of them lined up across the front of the stage, a six-inch-high stage, nose-to-nose with the crowd. They just blew the place away, all of them in black, all of them wearing shades and just bringing the house down.' Marx had also seen the Furs live 'and liked them, but Andrew really saw some strong parallels with what he was trying to do.' This included the 'density' of Richard Butler's lyrics and his way with cigarettes as stage props.

Although meeting a member of one of his favourite bands for the first time, Taylor maintained total sang-froid in Tiffany's. Perhaps this was a function of the insouciance of the Leeds' music scene or the democratisation of punk; perhaps it was the clarity and confidence that a dab of whizz brings. Despite having been 'not that well, if you catch my drift' in this era, Kilburn does remember a lot about this encounter with Taylor. 'In that early exchange, he came across as interesting, cool and extremely intelligent. He managed to let me know that he finished *The Times* crossword typically in under ten minutes, he'd been sent down from Oxford and dropped out of Leeds; all impressive and eye-catching factors for me.'

Eldritch's gratitude to Kilburn has remained deep over the forty years since they first met. 'I have to credit Duncan Kilburn for listening to the cassette, which was handed to him by a kid. Famous and halfway famous bands got cassettes handed to them all day long, as subsequently did I. I never listened to any of them. Life's too short. But Duncan, bless him, did listen to it. He passed it on and was encouraging and that gave us a massive boost . . . I can't thank him enough. None of this would have happened without him.'

Kilburn doesn't have any memory of what was on the tape, but John Ashton (then one of the Furs' guitarists) remembers that 'Duncan and I both listened to it a lot' in the transit van they were touring in. 'This tape stuck out,' Ashton continues. 'It was rock with drum machines. At the time there were bands that were electronic-y sounding but this was much more aggressive and metal. The closest thing to it was the Human League and their drum sound but the Human League was all synths and this had guitars and it was pumping. It was Suicide-meets-Iggy-meets-Motörhead.' Both Kilburn and Ashton became proto-Sisters fans; Taylor gave them both 'Head and Star' T-shirts.*

Independently of one another the pair each told Howard Thompson how impressed they were by this almost unknown act. Thompson – only twenty-seven at the time – was already an A&R legend who had signed Motörhead and Suicide to Bronze and the Furs to CBS. Thompson met Taylor in his office at CBS on London's Soho Square. 'He was smart, and I liked him immediately,' Thompson says. As well as 'the infamous cassette,' Eldritch gave Thompson a print of one of Jon Langford's photographs. On the back in neatly Letrasetted Caslon Antique was the line-up, in which Taylor billed himself as 'A'. He was: 'vox, rhythm.' In his own distinctive handwriting he had added: 'This is the nucleus; onstage we use an extra guitarist, and a drummer for synthesised percussion, as well as the drum machine.'

The live drummer never materialised but the extra guitarist, the first of several, did. This was Dave Humphrey. He was short, had close-cropped blond hair and was from Wakefield. His brother and sister, Claire and Andy, played in a band called the Screaming Abdabs. Humphrey played with the Sisters at their next Leeds gig in the Riley Smith Hall at the university at the end of the summer term of 1981.

Also on the bill were the Expelaires (now with Johnny Plumb on

---

* Ashton was photographed wearing his T-shirt for a Furs photo shoot in Canada in July 1981. Kilburn still has his, unlike many of his belongings: 'I lived on a boat for ten years, so really had to pare it down.'

bass) and Pink Peg Slax (with Tim Strafford-Taylor on bass). The Slax singer, Mark Wilson, was no fan of the Sisters. 'They seemed to be very inexperienced and they had this drum machine on a stool and it fell off,' Wilson recalls. 'It all went wrong; they were just a bunch of amateurs . . . We used to call Andy Taylor "The Poodle" because of his hair, like a black poodle . . . We were having a bit of a laugh at them.' Even some of the Sisters' friends were unimpressed. 'Langford and I were in the audience and were laughing our socks off,' admits Kevin Lycett. 'It was like: "Andy, this is a bit clunky." We were all mates, so we didn't say anything cruel.'

Howard Thompson was also in the audience. In stark contrast to most of the audience in the Riley Smith Hall, he thought the Sisters had huge potential. 'Bands at this stage of their careers are usually pretty undeveloped, figuring it out. I don't judge them by how unformed their act is, the shitty sound or the crummy environment. I thought Eldritch was a commanding frontman from day one. Reminded me a little bit of Dave Berry. Both wore black and leather well, and could "slink" better than everyone else . . . I like singers who don't sound like anyone else. Andrew fits right in there. Also, he had infinite appeal to both boys and girls.' (Eldritch has ascribed his 'general demeanour onstage at the time' to the fact that he 'just clung onto the microphone stand – in what must have been a fairly attractive way obviously – out of sheer terror.') Thompson, however, had no intention of signing the Sisters. 'At that point, it would have been too early in the band's development for a label like CBS to jump in.'

Taylor's cassette fell on stony ground when the Birthday Party played Tiffany's on 23 June 1981. 'He just appeared backstage,' says

Mick Harvey, one of the Birthday Party's guitarists. 'He collared Nick [Cave] because he thought the Birthday Party was the best thing he'd seen in a long time. He talked to Nick for ages and gave him a cassette . . . When we got back in the car, Nick put it in the cassette player, played it for a little bit, fast-forwarded it a little bit, played it for a little bit more, onto the next song, Then he just wound down the window, pressed the eject and threw the cassette out the window.'

John Keenan put the Sisters on at the Warehouse on 2 July 1981. This show gave the Sisters a massive boost in the Leeds scene; Iggy Pop played the university and Music for Pleasure played Amnesia, a club near the main railway station, that evening.* Parts of these crowds converged on the Warehouse for the Sisters, looking to prolong their night out. 'All this heat and energy was in this one small club,' remembers Paul Gregory. The Sisters impressed him and many others. They were 'kind of chaotic but there was a noise there.'

By this point the Sisters had another new song, the ironic 'Good Things'. Marx's lead playing remained so unpolished that he 'can distinctly remember us playing "Good Things" at an early Warehouse gig and it was as if I was playing the TV theme tune to a Japanese melodrama over the top of it.' The song's themes of post-imperial decay, economic collapse and political violence – and turning a blind eye to them – Taylor would revisit more obliquely later.

---

* After his time playing bass in the Expelaires abruptly ended, Mark Copson became the singer in Music for Pleasure.

Taylor eventually cooled towards 'Good Things' because its irony
– he sang it from a disengaged, 'I'm all right, Jack' standpoint – was
too much of a blunt instrument. Another reason it eventually got
dropped and never made it onto a record was because, 'when
Eldritch sang "The lines are dead and the cars explode," we used to
shout, "The lambs are dead and the cows explode,"' admits Adams.
'He used to get really pissed off. "We" probably equals "me,"'
he clarifies.*

The gig at the Warehouse was a late finish and required the
Sisters to seek impromptu early morning haulage. 'The only transport we could get back to Belle Vue Road† was an electric milk
float,' Adams remembers. 'Three amps, three guitars and the four
of us and a guy driving us back through town. I mean, how cool
were we!'

The Sisters' only gig outside Yorkshire in 1981 was low down the
running order on the Saturday of Keenan's Futurama III festival in
the Bingley Hall in Stafford. They were added so late that they did
not appear in the line-up in most of the advertising. The Sisters
went on at three-thirty on the Saturday afternoon, Taylor suggest-
ing, 'Bring out your dead' to the sparse crowd milling around
what resembled a very large cattle shed. The Bingley Hall was the
main pavilion of the Staffordshire County Showground; during

---

* Taylor was sure to have found Adams' Yorkshire take on Bauhaus's 'Bela Lugosi's Dead'
(called 'Ben Lugosi's Dad') much more amusing. Adams would adopt a Peter Mur-
phy-like stance and with the requisite po-face intone: 'Flat-cap on the hat-stand, the
pigeons have been fed: Ben Lugosi's dad.' Also in Adams' repertoire was the ability to
deliver a very convincing Louis Armstrong impression.

† St John's Terrace, the location of Shearsby and Taylor's bedsit, forms the northernmost
stretch of Belle Vue Road.

Futurama III it still smelled of livestock. Nine hours after the Sisters, Gang of Four headlined.

Rather than use a milk float, this time the Sisters had hired a semi-professional driver with a transit van to get to Futurama III. This was Graham Cardy, erstwhile drummer of SOS and briefly co-promoter of punk nights with Keenan. Marx remembers that 'Graham almost wrote the van off pulling out at a junction before we'd even got out of Leeds that day: "I've got a bit of a blind-spot, man, sorry."' Cardy's (cannabis-hazy) memory is that 'the Sisters had very little equipment . . . they had sunglasses and were sniffing amyl nitrate.' This was broadly correct. Neither Marx nor Humphrey took drugs, but Adams' poppers would make their presence felt en route from Leeds to Stafford.

'Andrew was always paranoid that the van was going to get pulled by the police,' Marx explains. Having 'crazed punk/hippy looking Graham at the wheel in his battered old van made Andrew even more worried . . . so he made Craig unscrew his fuzz pedal and hide the poppers inside near the battery. The bottle broke in transit (literally) with the result that, depending on where you were seated in the vehicle, you either got the benefits of the poppers or in true Monopoly-style you did not pass Go and went straight to a splitting headache. Dave got the latter and for one reason or another had an awful day all round – he came to say he was leaving the band soon after.'

'He felt so ill at ease with so many aspects of what we did,' Marx continues. 'My connection with him was that we liked the Fall. After a while it did seem he was only interested in being in a band like the Fall. He was anti-rock and whereas I cherry-picked, he had a zero-tolerance attitude.' Humphrey's anti-rock guitar sound – the thinner the better as far as he was concerned – was particularly loathed by Adams, who would refer to Humphrey as 'Cheese Grater', when he was out of earshot. Humphrey was only ever an auxiliary, rather than an actual member of the Sisters of Mercy.

After Futurama III, Cardy was amazed that Taylor paid him the agreed fee for the van hire – and on time. Working with musicians – and being one himself – he expected neither: 'This was very professional from my point of view'. So he drove the Sisters to other early gigs. Taylor once 'got me round to his gaff . . . He didn't want to do whatever silly little gig you could in a pub locally, he was aiming higher than that. He wanted to get onstage where there was a 10 k rig. That was all like new to me. I hadn't seen anybody who worked like that before.' Cardy had been in bands on and off for over ten years by this point.

Without Dave Humphrey, the Sisters of Mercy played at Brannigans on 2 October. For their next Leeds gig at the university on 7 November, they recruited an art student from the Jacob Kramer College. Tom Ashton had come to Leeds from Alva in Scotland to join the March Violets, a band that his school friend Laurence Elliot (also known as Loz) had started at the university with Simon Denbigh and Rosie Garland.

'I guess Von [a later nickname of Eldritch's] must have asked me in the pub,' recalls Ashton, 'and I said, "Fuck it. Why not?"' Ashton already 'knew Craig pretty well because he'd shared a flat with Simon. It was Craig who got me into the Stooges and Hendrix. All the Sisters were just mates, nice guys really, even Von. I always thought he was a lovely guy.'

'I got my copy of that cassette that he'd painstakingly written out by hand . . . I went round to the flat on St John's Terrace and we just worked through all the guitar lines – just me and Von. He taught me what he'd written. I think Craig came in and we had a bit of a jam with it on the drum machine and then we did the gig. It was only two or three run-throughs, tops.'

The gig was in the Tartan Bar, the third and least of the Student Union's venues. 'I had a lot of fun with it,' Ashton says. 'Craig is a fantastic bass player. It wasn't a long set . . . just songs from that cassette. It was a headline show for the Sisters. About a hundred people turned up,' many of them from 'the scene around the Faversham.'

Ashton was clearly a better technical guitarist than Marx. 'I don't think we gave a fuck back at that point,' Ashton says. 'Mark was playing the lead stuff and I was doing more of the rhythm.' Marx puts it like this: 'I really didn't play chords that much – I'd bypassed that part of the usual process guitar players tend to go through. It was typical for lead guitar to be seen as the next step up from being proficient as a rhythm guitar player. That struck me as utter non-sense – far easier to play on one or two strings at a time than master all six. I'd removed the lowest string anyway, so I only had five and I struggled to keep all those in tune.'

Ashton was aware that 'Mark was definitely doing a visual show, which might have detracted slightly from what he was playing.' Marx usually occupied stage right. The key dynamic was between him and Taylor. Taylor, slightly built, languid, half-clutching, half-caressing his microphone and its stand; Marx, tall and athletic, charging hither and thither, working up a sweat, his size elevens clattering. If any coffee had been consumed in the hours before a gig, Marx's already high energy levels shot off the chart. Both he and Taylor would develop their stage personas further, but their dichotomy remained at the core of the band for the four-and-a-bit years they played together.

The Tartan Bar was Ashton's only gig in the Sisters. 'I was under pressure not to join them from the rest of the Violets,' says Ashton. 'As well as that, I already had a plan with the Violets myself.' Marx was not too fussed about losing another second guitarist. 'I think Andrew might have made a bigger play to nick Tom from the Violets but, as much as I liked him as a person, I never thought it worked that well.'

By the time Tom Ashton played in the Sisters of Mercy, the band had already recorded a new double A-side single. Not only was 'Adrenochrome' about to get its time in the sun, so was a new, as yet untitled song. It had lyrics that referenced Walt Whitman, the Tower of Babel and a 1970s cinema gimmick that used ultra-low frequencies to vibrate audiences in their seats.

6

Electric Warriors

On 4 November 1981, the trio of Adams, Taylor and Marx went into an eight-track studio in Bridlington, a seaside resort town on the East Yorkshire coast. Ken Giles Music, also known as KGM, or simply KG, was one of the key locations in the history of the Sisters of Mercy. All the Sisters of Mercy's singles and EPs over the next year and a half would be recorded there. Andy Taylor would put in long hours at KG, transforming himself from studio ignoramus into skilled record producer.

KG was in the courtyard of a large, three-storey house, one block from the seafront. Giles, his wife and their young children lived on the ground floor. The rest of the building comprised holiday flats they rented out. In the mid-1970s, Giles had demolished a greenhouse and a brick outhouse in the courtyard and built a recording studio on the footprint. Although KG was small – not more than ten metres by six metres – with a very narrow control room that bands squeezed into to listen to takes and hear mixes, it was well equipped. Giles was a connoisseur of professional audio gear.

Next to the studio was a former coach-house, which had been converted into a double garage with a flat above. On the lower level, Giles stored the sound systems he rented out. The Sisters had already played live through one of these at York University when they first met Pete Turner.

Yet Turner was not the band's connection to KG; instead 'Leeds face' Stuart Green had provided the link, having made a demo at KG with Chris Oldroyd [drummer in Girls at Our Best! and later Music For Pleasure]: 'The demo came out really well – best thing I was involved in,' says Green. 'I went round and played it at Andrew's. Craig and Andrew really liked it. So I gave them Ken's number.'

In 1981, Giles was the lone engineer at KG. 'The daily rate was around fifty pounds plus tape. I never clock-watched and typically the days would start at between ten a.m. and ten-thirty a.m. and continue through until around two a.m., typically with a break for a bite to eat around six p.m. It was very good value for clients . . . consequently the studio was regularly booked up for two and three months in advance.'

Despite Giles' best intentions, the recording of 'Adrenochrome' and the untitled song that would become 'Body Electric' was fraught. The single was recorded for CNT, the record label co-founded by Adrian Collins, who had funded the Ric Rac demos. CNT (named after Confederación Nacional del Trabajo, a Spanish anarchist trade union), although usually described as a York label, was in fact a Leeds entity. Collins' two partners in CNT

– Jon Langford and Rob Worby – both lived there; if CNT had headquarters, they were the attic of Worby's house in Harehills. Collins had formed CNT after leaving Red Rhino to work for Jumbo Records in the Merrion Centre in Leeds. His split with Tony Kostrzewa was so bitter and enduring that it would hamstring CNT for the five years of its existence and have a debilitating impact on Collins' relationship with the Sisters of Mercy. This was not immediately apparent in KG, but a whole host of other issues were.

'Adrian was pretty straightforward, a music fan and very keen to be involved,' Marx says. 'I don't remember him being particularly forthright or wanting to direct us in any way. That was the job Rob Worby took on with less than glorious results, either in terms of the finished recordings or in fostering any working relationship going forward.'

Worby could have been a good fit for the Sisters. He was no novice in the studio, extremely knowledgeable about music and his band, the Distributors, had used a drum machine taken out of a Hammond organ. The problem was that, to the Sisters, he seemed to be more interested in his own ideas than theirs. Worby, who had 'played tapes, like a *musique concrète* band', in the Distributors seemed overly inclined towards the avant-garde and the experimental. With Worby at the controls, the Sisters felt they were being experimented *on* rather than embellished. Worby recognises that the Sisters 'had everything worked out, all the arrangements', but he felt his role was to 'encourage them to do things they hadn't thought of.'

'I don't think it's a secret that Craig came close to physically assaulting Rob during those sessions,' Marx remembers. 'It was not a winning partnership. There were lots of flashpoints during the time in the studio, but I think it came to a head when Worby insisted on spending an eternity getting this one note of feedback to sustain for a particular section on "Adrenochrome". It was very indulgent of him, added precious little to the track and killed the atmosphere and momentum of the session.'

Worby has no memory of nearly being hit by Adams, although he does recall the band being appalled by his highly polished Oxford shoes and his socks. 'What the fuck are those red socks, you prat?' Adams apparently enquired at one point. Yet, it is Taylor – or Spiggy, as Worby still refers to him – who has lodged most firmly in Worby's mind.

'Very thin; loads of speed' is his pithy summary.

Taylor knew how good his songs were and what he wanted them to sound like, but he had no idea how to operate any of the equipment in the studio. This was not quite 'somewhere between the worst of both worlds' of the first visits to Ric Rac, but Worby had him at a disadvantage, something for which he had a bone-deep loathing. Worby remembers Taylor repeatedly hanging over his shoulder as he sat at the desk in the control room.

Taylor had come to Bridlington with very precise ideas. 'Spiggy had the drum patterns written out on graph paper,' says Worby. 'He had a score, like a proper piece of music. Sixteen semi-quavers in a bar, sixteen spaces on the graph paper.' Taylor was musically untrained and Worby doubted he knew what a semi-quaver was, but was fully aware that Taylor had an 'obsessive-compulsive detail thing . . . Anyone who's sitting night after night with graph paper, drawing out drum patterns: nobody does that! But I can see Spiggy with his Rotring pen and his graph paper [doing] something mind-numbingly repetitive.'

In a primitive way, Taylor did actually play the drum part he had programmed into the Doktor. 'The DR-55 had sixteen different patterns but could only play one pattern at a time,' Worby explains. 'You couldn't chain them together. Spiggy had the brilliant idea of just turning the knob to the next pattern. Do it manually: pattern one, pattern one, pattern three, pattern one, pattern one, pattern two . . . he sat in the studio turning the knob. That's how we could have fills. He was the drummer: he had that rhythm mentality.'

Even working with a machine, Ken Giles was intent on getting 'a good drum sound early on in the session at the backing track stage,' just as he would have with a live drummer. The Doktor allowed for techniques that were impossible with a human. 'I would bring in the gig amplifiers and, where we would have normally set up a drum-kit, the live room was full of big amp racks. It looked like the side of the stage at a big concert . . . We would put mics directly in front of the bass speakers, directly in front of the horns, even facing a wall with the sound coming off it. It was not just DI'd into a console, it was in the air, like a live gig.'

Nevertheless, the DR-55's end product was feeble. Jon Langford (who had been 'called upon to keep the peace', according to Marx) had come over to Bridlington and remembers 'EQing a bass drum all day which we pumped at maximum volume through a huge PA that was crammed in Ken's tiny studio. . . It was hilarious. Hours of thump thump thump rocking the whole seafront but when we listened back to what we had on tape it always sounded like a mouse tap dancing.' The DR-55 was so puny that Taylor had to augment it with a live snare drum.

Taylor was also very specific about his vocals. Worby recalls that 'he wanted the mic to be in a particular place, and we'd dim the lights – standard stuff when you're recording – but there was an issue about the microphone: he didn't like the *look* of the one we were about to use. It was actually a better microphone.'

Worby was convinced that, although Taylor had no musical training, he had studied records in detail. These included a particular kind of sixties pop record: 'Spiggy would have liked that big Wall of Sound . . . he would have liked a sixteen- or twenty-four-track studio, where we could add layers.' Even on 'The Damage Done', Collins and Worby thought they could detect it. 'It's that sixties/Righteous Brothers/kind of operatic [voice] . . . with that vibrato, that basso profundo.' Worby was sure Taylor was a connoisseur of epic and atmospheric pop arrangements and productions, including those by Norrie Paramor (who produced the Shadows and Helen Shapiro) and Ivor Raymonde (who wrote arrangements for Dusty Springfield and the Walker Brothers). 'Spiggy would have known about those . . . everything is smothered in reverb and echo.'

Worby found plenty to admire about Taylor. 'Spiggy and I shared characteristics: clear vision, attention to detail and the notion that if something is to be done it might as well be done right,' he says. 'And he was desperate to learn a few studio techniques.' Therefore Worby felt he did develop a kind of creative relationship with Taylor in KG, if not with Marx and Adams. Taylor and Worby agreed that not only the vocals, but also the drums should be slathered in reverb and delay. Taylor was thinking of Hawkwind, Worby was thinking of dub reggae and the Human League, especially 'Being Boiled'.

The single was supposed to be finished in one day. 'As far as we were concerned, it was done and dusted,' says Worby, 'but Spiggy wasn't entirely sure . . . He had a notebook and he did a kind of focus group exercise. He went to see people like Kevin [Lycett] and he had a list of questions: "Is there enough reverb on the snare drum?" Tick. Then he came back to us and said: "We don't like this production." He twisted Adrian's arm. A fortnight later – 18 November – we went back and remixed it. He redid the vocals.'

Typically for KG, that day's session had run on into the early hours of the next morning. Driving back to Leeds, Worby and the Sisters were stopped by the police. Worby noticed that Taylor did not need reminding to hide his whizz and loathed the idea of being in trouble with the law. 'I think with Spiggy there was this strange kind of moral thing. He had this sense of right and wrong, in a slightly corrupted way . . . principled, in a certain sort of way. There were things that you did and things that you didn't do.' Worby was reminded of the *Belle Époque* in Paris 'with a kind of degeneracy with absinthe and opium, but at the same time a kind of respectability . . . I think he liked the idea of degeneracy, but it was refined. It wasn't like Keith Richards, a total collapse . . . [it was] coupled with complete self-assurance. Complete self-assurance with a bit of paranoia. Dear old Spiggy . . .' Worby trails off. Like the Priestley's crowd, neither Worby nor Collins ever called him that that to his face. 'You always called him Andy,' Worby notes.

'There were points within the actual recording of the second single where we sounded great,' says Marx. 'There's a point near the end of "Adrenochrome" where it drops down to the bass and drums . . . before I come in with a variation on the main riff and Andrew plays the power chords that crash in. Something about those thirty seconds was so perfect at the time – a thumbnail of all the best bits of the band. Sadly that didn't translate into the final mixes of "Adrenochrome" and "Body Electric". We were still a long way short on studio know-how.'

Despite the problems in KG, the Sisters liked Giles immensely. 'He was a lively, engaging, funny and talented man who actually made being in the studio enjoyable,' says Marx. 'Something it had never been for any of us prior to going to KG.' That it was in Bridlington especially appealed to Marx, 'not just because it was a far from fashionable location in music business terms and added to our feeling of being outsiders and underdogs, but it's a town I knew really well having spent countless summer holidays there as a child. It was easy to feel at home at KG.' The next time the Sisters wanted to make a record, there was no question that they would return to Ken Giles' studio.

Nevertheless, one member of the band had doubts about the Sisters' direction of travel. At the end of the session in KG, Adams announced that he was going to the Canary Islands and would miss a gig the Sisters had booked at Vanbrugh College in the University of York for early February 1982.* Adams' father had offered him a job as a gofer on a Grattan's Catalogue photo shoot in Tenerife. Since the Sisters 'were not really happening', Adams recalls that his father suggested he do some proper work. 'You've

---

* Adams insists that the gig was booked *after* he had agreed to the job in the Canaries.

got to do *something*,' was his logic. Adams needed little persuading. 'I'm nineteen and you want me to go to the Canary Islands? And I'll get paid? I'm not turning that down.' All he had to do was 'deal with all the camera crap and bring the film back to London.'

Taylor and Marx 'did get a bit grumpy about it,' Adams concedes. They did indeed. Adams was fired from the Sisters of Mercy. The Sisters did not look far – or long – for their new bass player. He was sitting at the mixing desk in KG. 'I'd never played bass,' says Jon Langford. 'They seemed quite amused by that idea.'

The Sisters by this point had also recruited a second guitarist. Rob Worby remembers that, as well as 'Langy' coming over for the second session at KG, 'so did a really young guy.' This was Ben Matthews.

When Marx had rung him up and asked him to join, he had refused before he even heard the name of the band. 'I was in the middle of my A Levels,' was Matthews' explanation, 'so they spent ages convincing me that they were going to be the biggest thing Britain had seen since the Stones or the Beatles.' When Marx finally gave the name of the band, Matthews said he'd join immediately. Not that he believed any of the wild claims of future success, but because the Sisters had been so funny at their Tiffany's gig in March 1981.

'Ben was still at school . . . around five years younger than Andrew and me,' says Marx. 'He lived at home in Otley. I used to go over to teach him the tunes. It was all very nice, very suburban. You went up into his room and he'd got the walls covered in black plastic and Crass posters, but it was like *Blue Peter* punk. He was so clean-cut and at odds with the perception of what the band was about. That never made us think twice about inviting him in.'

Matthews 'was the first of those fourth members to stick it out,' Marx observes. One of the previous occupants of that role was among the first to hear the results of the KG sessions. Dave Humphrey was sitting in Claire Shearsby's car when Marx played him a cassette of the finished mix of 'Adrenochrome'. 'He was horrified. He thought we'd sold out. I might as well have been playing him Foreigner.'

The car was parked up outside 7 Village Place in Leeds. This was Taylor and Shearsby's new home. They had moved westwards from St John's Terrace into Burley, less than a ten-minute drive away. Instead of a bedsit, this was an archetypal British semi-detached with three bedrooms. Like many of the houses in Burley and Hyde Park, 7 Village Place had a cellar. The potential of an on-site rehearsal space made it attractive, as did the presence of a telephone.

Marx joined them as the third occupant when Graeme Haddlesey moved out of Hares Avenue because he 'was freaked out by the Chapeltown Riots [of July 1981]. He woke up to find our backyard ablaze . . . Once I couldn't afford the rent on my own I pitched in with Andy and Claire pretty quickly.' Marx's first floor room was better appointed than his Hares Avenue one: it had a chair as well as bed. He has a memory of decorating 7 Village Place listening to *No Sleep 'til Hammersmith*. Eldritch has recalled that the first Imagination album was also played.

Langford played the Vanbrugh College gig on 5 February 1982 and loved it. 'It was always very theatrical . . . very particular, stripped down . . . no amps onstage . . . The biggest piece of equipment onstage was the smoke machine.' Marx confirms that 'we travelled over on the train with our guitars, leads, and a fuzz-box each and plugged everything directly into the PA.' His fuzzbox was 'a home-made one a friend of Craig's put together . . . His hand-built device had an old Bakelite light switch to turn it on/off. I took that part out of the wiring because, obviously I couldn't see any circumstance where I'd want it switched off!'

Langford 'was impressed by the minimalism and professionalism . . . I was a Mekon though, so it's all relative. I was amazed how packed it was . . . kids went mad mad mad mad!'

Taylor had even told Langford what to wear:

'You'll have to wear black.'

'I can do that.'

Langford wore a dark suit and supplemented his look: 'I even had some glasses with no lenses in. I looked like Clark Kent.'

Langford was one of those who found the Sisters – and Taylor – extremely funny. 'I thought it was all hilarious. Andy wasn't humourless at all. He was a very funny guy. He was severe though.' That oscillation between humour and severity, which defined Taylor, also defined his band.

In the crowd at Vanbrugh College was Adam Sweeting of *Melody Maker*. He was there completely by chance. 'We had this idea at the *Melody Maker* to get out of London and write pieces about the music happening in places around the country. We called it "Awaydays". I'd been at university in York so I thought I'd go back there and see what was going on.'

And so it was that the Sisters got their first press in one of the national music weeklies. They were doubly fortunate that it was Sweeting. Not only did he like the band, he was one of the more perceptive and talented music journalists of his era. He wrote:

Attached to the mic like it was a failing life-support system is Spiggy, alias Andy, a skinny black-clad thing from the corners of the night, kept alive by ginger beer . . . Spiggy oozes a sickly sort of charisma, which is surprising considering his lank black hair and specs. As Dr Avalanche pumps through the PA like a battery of AK-47s, the bespectacled Ben Gunn cowers behind his guitar at the back of the stage. Gary Marx has no such scruples. A burly figure in boots and thick socks, he storms and rages through the songs, flaying chords with his hands and crushing the stage with his feet.

Not only did Sweeting enjoy the gig, he enjoyed interviewing Taylor. His piece in *Melody Maker* was the first of many he wrote on the band. Indeed, Sweeting and Taylor formed a friendship that was, according to Marx, 'very useful and very genuine'.

Taylor had clearly thought long and hard about what he wanted to articulate about the Sisters of Mercy and fully recognised how crucial the music weeklies were. In his first major interview Taylor deployed a battery of Eldritchisms, the likes of which would beguile, entertain and infuriate journalists over the coming years.

Taylor raved about his legs ('These are the finest legs in rock 'n' roll . . . These legs are the thinnest in Leeds'), the Stooges (the 'one great heavy metal group'), as well as Motörhead and the Birthday

Party: 'We're not as good as Motörhead but we're better than the Birthday Party. That makes us pretty damn good.' Taylor's self-confidence was there in blatant abundance. 'We're not a provincial band, we're a MAJOR ENTITY . . . There's no reason we shouldn't be able to carry on playing more or less like we do at the moment and be IMMENSE.'

After Vanbrugh College and with Adams persona non grata, Langford continued rehearsing with the Sisters in the cellar of 7 Village Place. 'I remember walking over there and some local kid shouting: "Oi, Shakin Stevens!" at me, which was quite disconcerting,' he recalls. However, he felt that 'I was never really in the Sisters of Mercy, except for that one gig. I was just a mate helping them out. I was waiting around wondering when Craig was going to come back. He was gone quite a while.'

When Craig Adams did rejoin the band he was, for Marx at least, in the doghouse. 'After inviting him back into the band, I told him that that we wanted him back because it suited our purposes but I would never trust him . . . I suspect we never truly got past that barrier . . .. [but] we got along well and my happiest memories are when Craig was on top form and he'd go into that mad Jack Nicholson mode.'

7

Metallic K.O.

The Sisters of Mercy entered 1982 with several significant new relationships: Ben Gunn, 7 Village Place, Ken Giles and CNT. Another was burgeoning with Les Mills, the manager of the Psychedelic Furs.

Mills had become the Furs' manager around the time they were making their first album in 1979. As John Ashton drolly recalls, 'Les had expertise: he'd roadied for the Banshees. What more do you need?' Mills had been responsible for the infamous 'Sign The Banshees Do It Now' graffiti campaign. 'That was in my amphetamine-fuelled days,' he says. 'I made a list of all the record companies in London, got a pack of fat magic markers and went round every record company. The West End was easy, but I even went out to Island in Hammersmith. I walked all night long.'

'We used to joke that Les wiped the gob off Sioux's mic stand,' says Duncan Kilburn. 'He was a hustler, spiv and hyperactive. All the things you need in a manager,' he adds sarcastically.

By the end of 1981 it had become clear that Howard Thompson would be moving to New York to become an A&R executive at Columbia. He persuaded Mills to guide the Sisters in his absence.

Mills worked out of an office complex in London near Southwark Cathedral. One day, as he was arriving, he noticed someone sitting outside. 'There was this skinny guy with long hair and aviator shades sitting on the stairs outside my office,' Mills recalls. 'I just assumed he was a typical Furs fanboy. A few hours later my assistant came back from lunch and told me: "That weird little guy is still sitting there. Why don't you go and see what he wants?" I went out and spoke to him. That was my first meeting with Andrew.' Mills concluded immediately that 'he definitely marches to a different drummer. He could have got my number off Howard and phoned and set up a formal meeting, but that set the tone. This made sense the more I got to know him. He was a very peculiar character. Initially, he seemed almost introverted. He wasn't difficult to start with because he wanted something and he felt I could help him. As long as it was to his advantage, I felt he was willing to play along.'

Mills had obvious appeal to the Sisters. The Furs were in the ascendant and were preparing for another assault on the USA. When Mills met Eldritch for the first time, they were recording *Forever Now*, with Todd Rundgren at his studio in Bearsville in upstate New York. Although he was prepared to help the Sisters, the Furs were the only band Mills managed at that point and he intended to keep it that way.

The Sisters of Mercy and the March Violets were also edging closer together. The first time the Violets played live was as support to the Sisters. This was on 29 March 1982 at the Funhouse, a first-floor club in the centre of Keighley in West Yorkshire. This was also the debut of the first classic line-up of the Sisters of Mercy: Taylor, Marx, Adams and Gunn. They were now using a Roland TR-606 drum machine, which had noticeably more heft than the DR-55. The Sisters were billed by the promoter, Nick Toczek, as a 'Leeds cult band.' That Keighley is less than twenty miles from Leeds indicates how small a shadow the Sisters cast at this point.

The Sisters and the Violets already knew each other well. Simon Denbigh had lived with Adams on Burchett Place, worked the Morrisons nightshift with him and socialised with Marx and Taylor. Denbigh and Taylor were even interviewed together in late 1981 (with Denbigh using the astonishing pseudonym of Clit Gothic) for a Leeds fanzine named *Box of Rain*.

Rosie Garland (the lead vocalist along with Denbigh) thought Taylor was 'a quiet guy, who thinks a lot before he answers questions . . . reserved and difficult to get a word out of but there's quite a lot going on behind the quietness.' She felt she 'saw the tail end before he became Andrew Eldritch. He'll always be Andy Taylor to me.'

'The one time I ever made him think I might be more than just a bore, was when he was chatting to me sometime in 1981 when I first met him and he said: "What have you done musically?" in that kind of way that he did.

'"Yeah, I was in a band in Devon with the bassist from Hawkwind."

'At which point, he almost lost his breakfast. He thought I meant Lemmy. I actually meant Harvey Bainbridge – not anywhere near as cool. That was my life's experience of almost impressing Andy.'

Adams had also made an impact on Garland. 'I seem to remember Craig's room was entirely wallpapered with porn, including the ceiling,' she recalls. Adams clarifies this: 'I took someone's room over when he moved out. The room was indeed a collage of ladies, in underwear from catalogues that he had decorated it with.'

Les Mills came up from London for the Funhouse gig. Marx recalls that Mills 'had a digital tuner sent by express courier the next day. By his reckoning we spent almost as long tuning up between songs as playing. That involved me wandering over to Craig and him turning my machine heads for me – we still did that at full volume. Usually Andrew would be baiting the crowd at the same time. A rough recording did exist but sadly I don't possess it: it was our *Metallic K.O.*'

'He'd just stand there smoking and insulting people,' is how Adams puts it. Eldritch's taunting of the crowd, throwing out non-sequiturs and rhetorical questions, and engaging in an internal dialogue with himself – out loud – all became an integral part of Sisters' shows.*

Keighley – and other gigs of this era – illustrated some of the more slapstick elements of Marx's stagecraft. Anyone who thought

---

* A later iteration of the Doktor actually increased the delays between songs. For a time, instead using an actual drum machine onstage, 'we ran it from four-track cassettes, so I had to change the cassette every song,' says Adams. 'I had to check the master book and mix the four channels before we could start a song.' Marx had a few short instrumentals he could deploy to fill time: 'Ghost Riders In The Sky', the main theme from *Lawrence of Arabia*, 'Hava Nagila' and, 'if the mood took me, "Yankee Doodle Dandy", one of the first things I learned to play.'

the Sisters were a straight-faced extrapolation of Joy Division or Bauhaus needed only look stage right. Marx was the drum machine operator at this point. 'At its simplest,' he explains, 'it might be one pattern all the way through a song with no end point programmed in. I would stop the machine with a footswitch. All good in theory but if you're rolling around on the floor it's not always easy to deliver that Vegas moment . . . I would manage to stop the thing a beat or two late only to restart it by mistake. Sometimes Andrew and Craig would manfully try and make something of the cock-up yelping wildly over some borrowed Hawkwind riff.'

Stephen Barber, who enjoyed the cacophony, thinks 'the Funhouse is the one where they really stepped up. I remember Andrew was standing on this dais away from the band. They were really focused and pummelling away, really letting rip. There was hardly anyone there, so it had this gratuitous energy, this aberrance and extravagance which was not dependent on having an audience.'

The previous time Nick Toczek had heard the Sisters play was in Ric Rac. He also thought they were fantastic in Keighley. 'They actually did a proper rock show, the whole taking-the-stage-and-making-a-drama-of-it, which was such a change from the original punk idea of "anyone can get up there and do this" when you got people with no stage charisma, nothing. The Sisters also were incredibly loud, one of the loudest bands I've ever heard.'

Claire Shearsby was key to this early Sisters live sound. 'It's always a good idea to have someone who knows what sound you want by the mixing desk; we've had gigs ruined by "mixers",' Taylor had explained in *Box of Rain*. 'At first she would mostly concentrate on dealing with Andrew's voice and timing delays for the Space Echo on different numbers,' says Marx. 'She then grew in confidence and muscled in on the desk because more often than not the in-house engineer would be killing us.' Shearsby puts it like this: 'I used to stand next to the people who did the mixing to begin with. I turned up at one gig the Sisters were doing and said, "I'm the engineer" and they stood next to me for a change.'

'There were occasional clashes over Andrew's special treatment . . . but Claire helped a lot through those early gigs,' says Marx.

Part of the Sisters' 'proper rock show' was utter artifice. They used two large speaker cabinets adorned with hand-painted 'Head and Star' logos onstage. The speakers were still inside but had been disconnected. Before there were any roadies to move the gear, these heavy props were a cause for annoyance, at least as far as Adams was concerned. The Funhouse was a particular flare-up because the club was up a flight of stairs: 'I can't believe I'm breaking my back carrying these fucking things . . . speaker cabinets with no fucking speakers,' is Marx's recollection of the bassist's grievances.*

The month after the Funhouse, 'Body Electric'/'Adenochrome' came out on CNT. For all the ill-humour of its making, it remains a fantastic record. *Melody Maker* made it Single of the Week. *Sounds* was also complimentary, noting that 'Motörhead compared to SOM are Mickey Mouse. These two songs drill into your skull with the sort of electric persistence the Human League tried early on.'

It also has a great sleeve for which Taylor had repurposed a Francis Bacon 'Screaming Pope'. The run-off groove saluted the

---

* They were Adams' own speaker cabinets. He had used them as part of a miniature PA system when he was in the Expelaires.

now-deceased Spiggy the cat. 'He didn't live very long,' laments Shearsby. 'Maybe three or four years. Andrew found him dead. It was awful. Very sad. We had him in St John's Terrace. He didn't make it to Village Place.'

Although intended as a CNT record, Taylor delivered the artwork with 'Merciful Release' emblazoned on the reverse of the sleeve, much to Rob Worby's chagrin: 'It's *got* to say CNT! It *cannot* be a Merciful Release,' was his view at the time. His view did not prevail. Having already spent 'a lot of money', Adrian Collins could not face going into battle with Taylor again because 'Andy wasn't the easiest person to deal with.'

The single was key to making converts in Leeds. Two of them were Danny Horigan and Jez Webb. Horigan had been at a Gary Glitter gig at Unity Hall in Wakefield with Taylor and Marx when 'Mark said, "Come back to ours." They played "Body Electric"/ "Adrenochrome". It was the Ramones, Stooges, Suicide . . . I thought: "This is the future!" No one sounded like that.'

Webb's introduction to the single was down at the Warehouse. 'It was like nothing I'd ever heard,' he says. Webb was used to drum machines in electro music but 'this was rock!' When he saw the Sisters live for the first time he thought: 'Doktor Avalanche was as fuelled-up as the band, it seemed. Loved it. A wall of sound, great frontman, good songs and they were ours, from Leeds.'

Webb was actually from Derby but had relocated to the city with his family in 1980. Horigan was Leeds-born and bred. Together they would become the Sisters' first two roadies and key parts of an inner circle that was developing around the band.

Horigan was already friendly with the band through the F Club;

Webb's route in was different. 'One night at the Phono, somebody pointed out Craig. I don't know why but I wandered over to tell him I loved the single. From this one moment my life changed forever. We got chatting and as the Phono closed, we wandered back to his flat. [We] drank and smoked until the early hours and as I was leaving Craig said: "We're doing a gig next week, if you'd like to come along. Be at Village Place around lunchtime."'

Webb's first gig working for the Sisters was the band's London debut. 'There's nothing to be said for playing in toilets in your hometown, but we're perfectly prepared to play in toilets out of town,' Taylor had conceded in *Box of Rain*. The Embassy Club on Old Bond Street in Mayfair was most definitely not 'a toilet'. It was then – just about – clinging to its reputation as London's equivalent of Studio 54: bisexually hedonistic and the haunt of coked-up celebrities, Eurotrash aristocrats in exile, petrodollar Arabs, New Romantics and Lemmy on the slot machines. However, London discos – even ones that looked like they were owned by Joan Collins in *The Stud* – needed to fill their off-nights.

Taylor hired an ageing coach to transport anyone from West Yorkshire that wanted to go to the Embassy. Rosie Garland puts it like this: 'All the gear . . . and all the girlfriends and some poor sod drove us [to the] schmaltzy end of London.' Stephen Barber thought it 'was a really strange environment. I remember Mark or Andrew saying to me that the exiled King of Greece or Romania would be there.' Marx, for his part, 'did feel a bit like we were hicks from the sticks.'

'This was another great gig,' Barber recalls, 'where you got a sense they were gelling very well, even playing to this strange audience: half exiled monarchs of Eastern Europe, half idiots from Leeds and Wakefield.' That combination, unfortunately, left the Embassy Club largely empty. Regardless, Jez Webb was hooked: 'I lifted the gear onto the stage, but the band set up their own stuff. So basically I ended up watching the show, having a dance, loading stuff back in the van . . . and getting free booze backstage. What's not to like?'

At least one celebrity did turn up: Tony James, in an electric blue leather jacket. James was then without a band. Generation X had split up and Billy Idol had relocated to New York. James had heard the as-yet-unreleased 'White Wedding' and was 'completely thrown . . . [and] completely jealous'. It was clear Idol was about to eclipse him, so James was looking to put a new 'big idea band' together. This would eventually be Sigue Sigue Sputnik.

James had been tipped off by a *ZigZag* journalist called Marts and was at the Embassy on the hunt for a lead singer. 'We watched the band go through their set for us and the other two people in the room and they were really great,' James says. 'The singer was especially great – a kind of Jim Morrison meets Suicide and the Velvets.'

'"Damn", I thought, feeling that euphoric rush of excitement when you see something special, "that guy would be so great to work with."' James was exhilarated by what he had seen, so Marts introduced him to Eldritch and they talked excitedly. 'There was an instant connection,' James recalls.

James asked Taylor 'if he would leave this unheard-of group . . . to join me in my new vision' but he 'couldn't entice him away from the Sisters . . . They were his dream, just as Sputnik was mine . . .

I wished him luck, knowing he was destined for greatness. . . and my search for a singer went on.'

Had Taylor taken James up on his offer, he would have been a subordinate in someone else's project – an intolerable state of affairs. Also, despite the poor turnout at the Embassy Club, it would have been clear to him by this point that the Sisters of Mercy were now a properly functioning band. 'It wasn't simply a glorified hobby,' as Marx puts it. 'It wasn't just what the members did when they'd finished work or at the weekend. Although we weren't exactly blazing a trail in those first years, we were doing all the things a proper band does, just on a smaller scale.' He adds that 'the Sisters family was evolving as well, so there was great camaraderie among that core of people. You definitely felt something was building, something important on a personal level as much as anything.'

Although Taylor was unchallenged in his role as main songwriter in the band, Adams and Marx believe they shaped the Sisters sound and what he was writing. 'My lack of musicianship and Craig's bloody-mindedness forced us down particular roads in those first two years,' says Marx. 'Very quickly our limitations became the sound and Andrew in effect was writing with me and Craig in mind as the people who would have to get out in front of an audience and make it look as if it meant something. I suspect my playing dictated the kind of things he wrote – the guitar-line came to be one of the key Sisters signatures on many tracks.'

After the Embassy, the Sisters did wonder why a band that had a Single of the Week couldn't get a bigger crowd and why 'Body Electric'/'Adrenochrome' was selling little more than 'The Damage Done'.

The reason was the ongoing feud between Tony Kostrzewa and Adrian Collins. In Leeds, Collins was able to circumvent Rhino but elsewhere Rhino stymied the distribution of CNT product. 'Tony did everything he could to prevent CNT succeeding: refused distribution, bad-mouthed Adrian,' Jon Langford explains. Collins understands why the Sisters left CNT. 'We may have re-pressed it but one thousand or two thousand is all that record ever sold. When they got Single of the Week, the Sisters thought they were going to be very famous overnight. I think they realised then that they were on a record label that was never going to make them famous. I don't think I was the right person to take it forward.'

The Sisters were also political misfits on an openly socialist label like CNT, alongside the Redskins, the Mekons, the Three Johns and the Newtown Neurotics. 'Eldritch was not overtly as political as the other stuff,' says Collins. 'I don't think I ever had a political discussion with him . . . There was a lot of ambiguity about him and what the Sisters did.' During 1982, Taylor, a young man who loathed fascists, would take to wearing an SS *Totenkopf* badge on the lapel of his leather jacket.

The Sisters of Mercy reverted to using Merciful Release as their record label and working directly with Rhino for distribution. However, the next record to come out on Merciful Release was not by the Sisters. It was 'Religious As Hell' by the March Violets.

The Violets had followed the Sisters' lead and gone to KG to make demos. 'Andy being a star, came out and helped us with the mixing,' Garland says. Adam Sweeting reviewed the demos positively in *Melody Maker*. 'I think Von saw an opportunity there,' says Tom Ashton. 'He saw this band getting some national coverage and got involved. He was an astute businessman.'

Taylor offered to put four of the songs from the demos out on Merciful Release. Ashton thought it was a no-brainer: 'The graphic looked great and we knew Andy.' Denbigh and Laurence Elliot, the bass player, the pair who wielded the greatest power in the band, agreed. Although the Sisters had only put out two low-selling singles, Taylor and Merciful Release were growing in stature in Leeds.

Taylor was also influencing some of the older generation of bands. 'The Mekons owe him a debt,' says Jon Langford. 'Days of EQing a fucking drum machine through a PA in a garage in Bridlington' had made an impact on him. 'When Andy got a 606, I got one and that's when we did a whole Mekons record [*The English Dancing Master*] based on that machine. It was our attempt at weird dub reggae, drum machine, electronic English folk music – a big switch for us. That was basically down to Eldritch showing us that technology . . . God, I'm blowing so much smoke up his arse . . . I must love the man!'

The Mekons and the Sisters were both trying to find new routes out of the dead-end of punk. Taylor certainly had little time for the Mekons' diversion into what he termed 'country-folk'. He preferred their 1980 dalliance with synths on songs like 'Teeth'.

Most of all, the Sisters influenced the Three Johns, the band Langford started on the day of the Royal Wedding in 1981 and had on the go in parallel with the Mekons. 'We sort of fell into the Sisters' wake,' says Langford. 'It was all kind of informed by what Andy was doing. He did push it in a new direction, technically . . .

He realised there were volume knobs for each of the instruments, so he got someone to put separate mini-jacks in each volume knob. He showed me that: "Ah, now you can completely control the sound and make it more apocalyptic and less like a drum machine." Andy became my drum machine guru!'

With the March Violets' single recorded and set for release, the Sisters went back to London for another important gig: the ZigZag Club on 10 July 1982. They were support for the Birthday Party who, allegedly, thought the Sisters of Mercy were the worst band ever to support them and told them as much. In fact, it seems no one in the Birthday Party even saw the Sisters' set.

At Taylor's urging Chris Carr (the Birthday Party's manager) went into their dressing room to get feedback from the Australians. 'I used to get very tense,' says Mick Harvey, the guitarist, 'because I was quite sober before a show and the others – anything could happen. So I really did not like talking to anybody. And Chris just kept asking this question. He went out and came back again: "They really, really want to know what you thought of them."' Nick Cave, Tracey Pew and Roland S. Howard were unable to offer an opinion, so it was up to Harvey. 'I said: "Just tell them they were shit! Fuck off and leave us alone!"'

Craig Adams can confirm that the Birthday Party did indeed seem stressed that evening. 'The dressing rooms at the ZigZag Club were up one staircase. On the first level were the Birthday Party. We were on the second level, the last door. The Birthday Party came off and they started having a proper punch-up, a proper fight. We were like: "Holy shit, it's going off downstairs!"

They were punching the shit out of each other. I remember us closing our door and going: "Let's stay out of this."'

Les Mills met up with the Sisters at the ZigZag Club. He still had reservations about taking the band on. 'The Sisters didn't really present themselves as a band. Mark looked most of the time like a builder in a string vest and a leather jacket. Craig looked like Craig and Ben looked like a schoolboy. Andy made a bit of an effort but it was still a bit gauche.' Mills' sartorial doubts about Marx went both ways: Marx notes with mild disdain that Mills 'did have a habit of turning up wearing Mickey Mouse sweatshirts and pastel slacks.'

Ben Gunn alone prevented the Sisters resembling an archetypal rock band. Sometimes the incongruity could be extreme. When the Sisters supported Nico at the Venue in London that June, 'we had to promise his mum we'd get him on the last train home because he had an English exam the next day,' says Adams. He also remembers that 'Ben's mum drove the Sisters in her Volvo estate to support the Clash at Newcastle City Hall.'

If anything eventually convinced Mills to become more involved with the Sisters, it was Taylor's self-belief and focus. 'It was his bloody-mindedness. He was very single-minded and was very much a detail-oriented person. When I first stayed round 7 Village Place, I remember looking at his cassette collection. He'd taken cigarette boxes and glued them together and made little shelves. Who else would do that? Every cassette tape was handwritten in this meticulous writing. People who have that kind of attention to detail . . . can really go somewhere.'

At the ZigZag Club, the Sisters of Mercy played a new song live for the first time. All John Ashton's dreams of making pumping Suicide-meets-Iggy-meets-Motörhead music were about to come true.

8

The Hyacinth Girl

In the late spring of 1982, John Ashton was in the living room of his top-floor flat on Kingwood Road in Fulham. Andy Taylor was with him. They were there to begin the process of making a new Sisters record. Taylor showed no sign of nerves despite having to play guitar in front of the guitarist of one of his favourite bands.

'He said, "I've got this riff,"' Ashton recalls. 'I had a little amp and we mic'd it up.' Taylor played his riff on the B string. Then he stepped down to the E string and played a slight variant. 'What's it called?' Ashton asked. 'Alice' was the reply.

'Alice' had – atypically – been written very quickly by Taylor. His recollection is that it was on a sofa. Most probably it was the one in the front room of Village Place, but Marx doesn't 'remember ever hearing him messing about with the guitar lines. It just arrived as a fait accompli. My memory is of him coming back from a stay with John Ashton in London with the song complete . . . Andrew brought the demo in, pressed play on the cassette machine and it was like he'd found the turbo charge on the Sisters-mobile.'

The lyrics are almost as direct as the riff: 'Alice' is a 'mentally wayward' (according to Eldritch) young woman with a taste for downers and the occult. Like many of his songs, 'Alice' is probably rooted both in the very specific and the highly personal, but has been sufficiently abstracted and coded to allow him to sing it.

Taylor also played the rough demo for Les Mills, who had set up the Kingwood Road meeting. Mills liked it and arranged for Ashton to go up to 7 Village Place to make a full set of demos. Ashton set his gear up in the kitchen while the Sisters played as a band in the sitting room at close to full volume. The next morning, Claire Shearsby remembers, 'The neighbours going: "What was all that carry on round yours last night?"'

Ashton stayed at 7 Village Place. The time he spent making the demos allowed him to get to know the Sisters better, especially Taylor. 'He had very specific views. He ran the show . . . Andrew made no bones about being very smart but he didn't boast about it. I'd say he was a bit of a nerd.' Ashton was impressed by Taylor's obvious aptitude for programming drum machines. Like Rob Worby, he was struck by Taylor's book of drum patterns. 'Obsessive, written out like the old Football Pools, with Xs,' Ashton remembers.

Ashton recalls one aspect of Village Place very clearly. 'There were a million videos. This was just when VCRs with the big clunky buttons hadn't been commercially available for that many years. Andrew had a stack of tapes and they were all Motörhead or AC/DC; more Motörhead than AC/DC. I began to put this together: this guy is a metalhead! This is really what it's all about and he just put a twist on it. Definitely a rock guy who dressed it up a little bit differently.'

Ashton was also impressed by Taylor's focus on work, not recreation. 'He would use speed like a technician would: just the right amount. He wasn't a big drinker. I never saw him drunk. One time I asked him, if he was going to have a drink. "No, I'm pure of heart," he replied.' However, they did go to what Ashton remembers as 'a huge Victorian-style pub' where 'Andrew had a gin and tonic.'

'Normally he was dressed in tight blue jeans and a pair of trainers. This time he got a bit dressed up: black shirt, black pants and super-long pointy boots. I think Andy Taylor was the guy in the blue jeans, in the sneakers, who was the metalhead.' The other person(a) was shortly to be named 'Andrew Eldritch'.

By the time of Ashton's arrival, the Sisters had very nearly got 'Floorshow' into peak condition. '"Floorshow" was a track we demoed several times and never quite got it right,' says Marx. 'I think Andrew wanted to accentuate what he saw as the rap/dance-floor aspects of the track; something akin to Talking Heads was even mentioned at one point. He wanted Craig to play what we mockingly called a "honda-honda bass-line,"' which was one that hopped back and forth between octaves the way many Theatre of Hate/Spear of Destiny tunes did. 'Craig, as was often his way, told him to fuck right off.' It was Lemmy or nothing. 'Just play the fucking chord' was Adams' attitude at the time.

Marx made an eleventh-hour addition to the track by deciding to 'play anything but the actual riff' on guitar. Ashton was impressed. 'I remember the first time I heard "Floorshow" I was blown away by the riff Mark played . . . He was definitely a good foil for Andrew, the right guy for Andrew at the time' is his conclusion.

This new riff was Marx's first significant writing combination. As well as being the 'good cop' and the frenetic hunk onstage, he now began to compose some of the Sisters' best music, nearly all of it written as economical but potent guitar lines. The contrast between the physicality of his stage persona and the delicacy of his best music would be one of the most compelling aspects of the whole Sisters project.

The Sisters all loved Ashton's demos, so it was natural that he was asked back for the studio sessions that followed at KG. 'Andrew had everything planned out, everyone had their parts, everybody knew what they were doing,' says Ashton. 'In a lot of ways they already had everything together.' Ashton provided a vital missing element: the ability to properly capture the Sisters' sound (or 'noise' as Taylor called it) onto tape. This included Taylor's voice, which he was progressively using more as a baritone amalgam of Bowie and Iggy at their deepest (on 'Sweet Thing' and 'Tonight', for example). It was this that would become his signature, much imitated, although Taylor also often sang an octave higher, much closer to his speaking voice, and there were also the echo-soaked Alan Vega screams and yelps. This assemblage, as derivative as its individual parts might be, was distinctive and had great power and dynamic.

Four songs were chosen for the sessions: 'Alice', 'Floorshow', 'Good Things' and '1969'. The recording of these tracks took place over consecutive weekends. 'I remember riding to Bridlington with the Sisters singing "Bohemian Rhapsody" word-for-word in the back of the car,' recalls Ashton. For those seeking added incongruity, the car was a Renault estate.

The Renault also contained a new, temporary, member of the Sisters: Ashton's freshly purchased 808 drum machine. For these recordings, the Sisters benched their 606. The new drum machine was again recorded live through a mic'd-up sound system 'which immediately gave everything a fattened sound,' says Ashton. The 808 included highly artificial handclaps as part of its repertoire. These ended up all over '1969' in a pastiche of Mike Leander and Gary Glitter.

Ken Giles' most vivid memories of his time working with the Sisters are these 'Alice' sessions. He remembers Adams as 'quite a lively youth . . . with the smile of an angel . . . who liked to have this slightly distorted bass sound' and that the band had 'to go to Otley or somewhere and pick up this schoolboy called Ben and ask his mother if he could come out.' Unsurprisingly, it was Taylor who stood out, not just in the Sisters, but among the hundreds of clients Giles had at KG.

'This guy was very dogmatic. Many, many young musicians come in and they're full of it. They want this and they want that, but it's an over-compensation because they don't know what they want. He didn't necessarily understand how to get there but he knew *exactly* what he wanted.'

'He would put the headphones on, and he would just want the red lights we had in the studio on. Then he wanted very precise echo and reverb, which were only going in his headphones, not to tape, only for his performance. He was *so* pedantic about this stuff. Clearly, all he was seeking was atmosphere and an environment that made him feel how he wanted to feel."

Sometimes the Sisters' roots in DIY punk clashed with Giles' more refined musical background. 'I'd spent what seemed like days getting this drum sound. We had this pulsating sound of all these different microphones being mixed, even with some DI stuff that was completely dry. And then Andy and Mark would get out these home-made fuzz-boxes and get their guitars and just plug them into this thing which sounded like a chainsaw. In a way, I quietly resented it . . . I'd come from a progressive rock background, where we had self-indulgent music, very hi-fi, so I had to relearn everything.'

The next weekend the Sisters, Ashton and now Mills, who had been impressed by rough mixes, were back in Bridlington for final mixing and overdubs. 'John and I went down the pub with Craig,' Mills recalls. 'In fact, he was the only one who was really interested in going down the pub. You could talk to him about football: he was a real Leeds fan . . . if you got him one-to-one, he really opened up. I said: "Look, what do you really want to get out of this?" He said, "I had a chance once before. I was in the Expelaires and I really thought we'd make it. There was major record company interest, A&R sniffing around but we blew it. If I get into that position again, I won't blow it."'

On one occasion at KG, Mills 'was sitting in the control room

---

* Giles even wonders if there was dry ice in the studio 'or is that a false memory from nearly half a century ago? There was certainly a misty atmosphere and red light and all this stuff in his headphones.'

and Andrew handed me a piece of paper and written on it were various permutations of "Andrew" and "Taylor" and "Christian" and "Eldritch", so it was like, "Christian Eldritch", "Eldritch Christian", "Andrew Christian". He asked me which one sounded the best. Maybe he was looking for someone to confirm his own bias, but I told him, "Andrew Eldritch."'

Perhaps Taylor was drawing on his knowledge of H. P. Lovecraft and the Eldritch Abominations, the fearsome, strange and unnatural creatures in his cosmic horror stories. More likely is that the pseudonym is a reference to fellow speed freak Philip K. Dick's 1965 novel *The Three Stigmata of Palmer Eldritch*.

'From my point of view, that's the earliest I can define the use of "Andrew Eldritch". That was a sea change. To me it was always "Andy", but when he became "Andrew Eldritch", there was a change in his attitude too. It was almost like he put on this persona and decided he had to be a bigger arsehole.'

Ashton however speaks overwhelmingly positively about the 'Alice' sessions and about Andrew Eldritch. He regards Eldritch as 'an artist, a creative person, a fan of music, studious. He wasn't there to get high, to get wasted, he was there to make art and make music.'

About a week later Ashton and Eldritch went into central London for mastering and to cut a lacquer. This was again done at Porky's cutting room. 'Kenny Giles walks on water' is cut into the vinyl of the run-off grooves. 'Quite extraordinary,' notes Giles, who still has his copy of the single the band gave him in 1982.

The process of rehearsing and recording those four songs meant the Sisters were in great shape for their first Peel Session, recorded in late August and broadcast in early September. Tony James was in the control room. 'I won't go so far as to say he produced,' Marx says, 'because that wasn't how the radio sessions worked – the BBC engineer "produced" you.'

'Tony's role seemed to be more as a motivator, helping generate a vibe in an otherwise sterile studio environment . . . he'd turned up for the initial recording in full camouflage gear, with this bright red headband looking like the coolest guy never to fight in the Vietnam War.'

'When he came back in the evening he'd changed his outfit completely. He was wearing this beautiful George Raft, gangster-style tailored suit and a shirt and tie – he might even have been sporting a fedora hat as well. I'm not sure any of this helped make the tracks sound better [but] Tony served to reinforce the idea that how things looked was at least as important as how they sounded – just a shame radio was the chosen medium!'

Eldritch and James had remained friends after their meeting at the Embassy Club. 'We hung out together a lot during the following months,' according to James. Eldritch would sometimes stay in the house in Pindock Mews in Little Venice in London, which James and his partner Magenta Devine had bought from Malcolm McLaren. Sid Vicious had been the previous occupant. His redecoration of the main bedroom remained in place when Eldritch visited: black floor, black carpet, black walls, black ceiling and blacked-out windows.

James became a member of Eldritch's 'incredibly funny postcard mailing list. I received cards from all these obscure places detailing the Eldritch exploits, often made-up but always funny, biting and incredibly articulate . . . We used to play Scrabble and to be extra clever, he wouldn't turn the board around, but played upside down just to be. . . well, difficult and intimidating.'

Scrabble-playing, flamboyant friends were optional extras when navigating a route through the lower echelons of the UK music industry. The Sisters of Mercy had already achieved three of the essentials: a manager who could pull strings, John Peel's seal of approval, and being written about in the music weeklies. All were much easier than making a great record, but they had now managed that as well.

John Ashton is fully aware that he produced a wonderful record that broke new ground. 'The crossover between machine and guitars hadn't really been explored. These guys got a drum machine and squashed it and distorted it. They created a genre that had hitherto not existed. They expanded on bands like Can, Neu!, Kraftwerk and brought in "metal" elements.'

Ashton's work as a first-time producer had been extraordinary. Mills finds it hard to believe it was done in an eight-track studio. 'That shows what a genius John is, to get those sessions out. I'm not even trying to boost John up. He was not the most professional musician ever. I mean, he was usually stoned and a bit of a flake. But he knew what he was doing and he took it seriously. Astonishing.'

The TR-808 that is on 'Alice' would become synonymous with hip-hop and house music. Ashton and the Sisters had also made a dance record, albeit one of a different kind, one virtually contemporaneous with Afrika Bambaataa's 'Planet Rock'. 'It wasn't a conscious thing,' Ashton notes, adding (in a Londoner's approximation of a northern English accent), '"Oh they're going to love this in the clubs." But they did love it in the clubs. Still do.' Ashton laconically notes that 'Alice' 'was a good one to sway to; the Goths love to sway.' 'Alice' has endured, like a transpennine 'Blue Monday': both tracks instantly recognisable from their ultra-simple opening drum patterns, both floor-fillers for nearly forty years.

'Floorshow' is even better: an outrageous melange of 'In Zaire' by Johnny Wakelin, Lemmy-like fuzz bass, T. S. Eliot and possibly even 'Stormbringer' by Deep Purple. 'The finished result seems to exemplify everyone doing what they did best and that includes the drums,' Marx says.

Before 'Alice'/'Floorshow' came out as a 7-inch single, the Sisters of Mercy would complete another piece of the puzzle thanks to Les Mills: going on tour with a bigger band.

In October 1982, the Psychedelic Furs toured the UK promoting the freshly released *Forever Now*. For five of those dates, the Sisters were the support band. John Ashton thinks of these dates as being as important for the Sisters as the Furs getting on Talking Heads' *Remain in Light* tour in autumn 1980, almost exactly two years earlier.

John Ashton took care of some of the out-front sound. 'I ran the mixing of Andrew's vocals and the addition of a Space Echo,' he recalls. Despite this extra assistance, the Sisters of Mercy remained wildly unpredictable onstage. Their Leicester gig was unrelentingly bad, a procession of bum and missed guitar notes, false starts from the Doktor, squeals of unwanted feedback from Marx's guitar (which had also clearly been nowhere near Mills' digital tuner) and pitchy Eldritch vocals. This farrago was topped off by the singer's unusually witless scolding of a heckler. Eldritch's 'fuck you, whoever you are' would not have been an unreasonable response from the crowd that evening.

However, the shows in Leeds and York were vital in cementing the band's reputation in its Yorkshire heartland. Numerous fresh converts were made on those nights. Their hometown show was a particular triumph. The Sisters – with the connivance of the stage manager, and to Mills' displeasure – played their first ever encore. Eldritch was sufficiently elated to request a copy of the mixing desk tape. However, such was the paucity of the band's repertoire at the time, they needed to play '1969' for a second time.

For some, the Sisters were shockingly good in the Riley Smith Hall. Rodney Campbell, one of Eldritch's Faversham acquaintances, hadn't seen the Sisters play until that point. 'Craig and Ben and Mark started – they had a crappy TR-606 that went tick-a-tick – and I thought, "This is not bad". And then Andrew walked on. He was a star from the moment he walked onstage. He had a cigarette and he went up to the microphone and when he opened his mouth: "Holy shit, the angels have spoken. Holy fuck, what is this? This is astonishing." It's engraved on my memory.'

Campbell – as Rodney Orpheus – was then in the early stages of putting together his own Leeds drum machine band, one that also sought to fuse electronic, synthesised music and aggressive guitar-based rock. The Cassandra Complex sprang very much from the same Suicide/Stooges roots as the Sisters. 'I very much wanted there to be that conflict between machine-progammed and very live rock 'n' roll attitude,' Orpheus says.

'Alice' was the first Sisters record to get a release in the USA. This was due to Steve Pross, one of the Psychedelic Furs and

Howard Thompson's East Coast connections. Pross worked at Dutch East India, a distributor based on Long Island, and the primary conduit for UK independent records into the USA. Pross had also set up a small label called Brain Eater Records, which put out a 12-inch EP of 'Alice'. When the EP was also released in the UK and European markets, it became a massive success on the Independent Charts.

The quality and popularity of the 'Alice'/'Floorshow' single had a huge impact on Eldritch. 'I thought: this band's going to go the distance, one way or another, however long it takes. Up until then I was still wondering what a proper job was and when I was going to have to get one.'

Originally Eldritch 'didn't foresee a career as musician. One of the great things about punk was that it allowed people to express themselves without the pressure of careerism.' In their earliest incarnations, the Sisters shared this outlook with other Leeds bands like the Mekons, Delta 5 and the Three Johns, 'who had no careerism in them whatsoever' in Eldritch's opinion.

After 'Alice', the possibility of a sustained future within music, whether as rock star, label boss, producer, svengali – or all four – opened up.

9

Heartland

7 Village Place was at the epicentre of the rise of the Sisters of Mercy during 1982 and 1983. 'The popular myth appears to be of Hunter S. Thompson taking over Bruce Wayne's Batcave,' Marx states, 'with hi-tech excess being the order of the day. The curtains downstairs stayed closed at the front of the house all the time, which no doubt gave it the air of a drug den. It had its moments but nothing to ring Ross and Norris McWhirter [co-founders of *The Guinness Book of World Records*] about.'

'The reality is that it was in a quiet street of about twenty houses and our neighbours – Jack and Nora – were people we got on well with, amazingly given the racket they had to tolerate.' Also, injecting some reality into the myth, Adams says that, 'we played football in the park nearby which was hysterical, seeing Andrew Eldritch, Gary Marx and me all with stupid haircuts trying to play soccer in winkle-pickers.'

'Our landlord/lady couple, Mr and Mrs Kavinde, were lovely

people who put up with a lot,' Shearsby observes. Eldritch was called into action should one of them visit 7 Village Place. 'Andrew would absolutely charm the landlady whenever she called round,' Marx recalls. 'Clearly he would need to because we could hardly be considered the ideal tenants. He had ear-marked that as his area of expertise – dealing with people in positions of power, especially if he thought they were well educated.'

'It was a really dirty house,' Danny Horigan remembers. 'There'd be dust everywhere. The magnolia colour of the walls wasn't paint – Andy and Claire used to smoke constantly.' The ashtrays were usually full, Eldritch's cigarettes put out vertically, clumped together like soldiers in formation. The kitchen was often strewn with unwashed crockery and cutlery, Marlboro packets, bin-bags and flotsam from various Burley takeaways. The bath upstairs was regularly filled to the brim with Shearsby's and Eldritch's clothing soaking in detergent. 'It always seemed to be overflowing with dirty black socks,' Marx remembers.

'The main living area was dominated by Andrew's collections of books, VHS tapes and cassettes,' says Marx. 'He had all these Penguin Classics arranged in order . . . Some visitors found it a little forced and pompous, as if he was thrusting his intellect as a challenge to others entering his space.' For Marx, who was working his 'way through just a tiny sliver of [the] collection,' it was a chance to catch up on the education he had missed. Not that Village Place should be seen as a kind of miniature Burley salon or book club. 'It wasn't remotely high-brow, as if we sat around dunking our biscuits, presenting a thesis and discussing the relative merits of the works,' Marx says. 'We were as likely to be sat watching *Hi-De-Hi!* and *Last of the Summer Wine* as we were *The Magnificent Ambersons* or Fritz Lang's *Metropolis*.' On occasion Eldritch and Marx could even be found 'singing along together in falsetto to the Supremes' *Greatest Hits* or Sylvester and Donna Summer on Andrew's disco compilation tape.'*

Living together in Village Place strengthened Marx and Eldritch's friendship. 'Ours was not an intense or outwardly obvious friendship,' Marx says, 'but it was a meaningful friendship all the same. I gave him items of clothing I'd grown out of – a cherished pair of straight-leg Levi's, an old Alice Cooper T-shirt that I valued beyond most of my limited possessions.'

A lot of Eldritch's stage-wear also originated in Village Place: Claire Shearsby was an excellent seamstress. 'I had a Needlework O Level and I learned from my mum,' she says. 'I used to make clothes and Andrew would wear them. We were the same size. I made this lovely long velvet jacket – he nicked it. He wore my boots as well. I liked black suede ankle cowboy boots – so did he.' Shearsby was also the source of many of the leather trousers that spread like wildfire through the Leeds music scene, including Eldritch's pair. No wonder Shearsby 'always thought Andrew was much better looking than anybody else.'

'Andrew lived a nocturnal existence,' Marx recalls, 'which required much more focus and planning back then. TV closed down around midnight, so there was continual recording of TV shows and hiring of videos to watch through the early hours.'

'The TV was never not on', says Adams. Episodes of *Blake's 7*,

---

* Taylor and Marx had a particular fondness for Fruit Shortcake biscuits.

Hogan's Heroes and *On the Buses* were viewed over and over. As well as the soap operas Eldritch also loved, *The Gong Show* and *Countdown* were also particular favourites. One of John Keenan's abiding memories of Village Place was of 'Andy sat in the dark, curtains closed, drinking a cup of tea and watching ABBA videos. He was a big ABBA fan.' Eldritch had recorded Futurama 2 when it was broadcast by the BBC in October and November 1981 and had filled up any spare tape at the end with ABBA. Keenan borrowed the tape to try to rustle up financial backing for a commercial release of the Futurama footage.

Eldritch's tape went missing while Keenan was attempting to broker a deal with the owner of a Bradford nightclub. "His son switched the tape for a copy of a Michael Caine film,' Keenan explains. 'I had to say sorry to Andy. He sent me a few terse postcards. I think he wanted the Futurama tape back more for the ABBA.'

'That is mischievous but not exactly untrue,' Eldritch has commented. 'What's not to like about ABBA? If it was *The Ipcress File* or *Get Carter*, then he might have come out ahead.'

'It was *Ashanti*,' Keenan admits.

On another visit to Village Place, Keenan realised just how intent Eldritch was on crafting a public image. Keenan had booked Mark Wilson (as his crooner alter ego Vince Berkeley) for Futurama 4 on Deeside in September 1982. Wilson had jokingly told an interviewer that he had to go back to Leeds to pick up his washing from the laundrette. When Keenan relayed this to Eldritch he was informed with more than a little disdain that Wilson 'should have said something like he had to catch a plane to New York. That's an insight into how Andy was thinking . . . Andy was into myths.'

For friends and the inner circle around the band, 7 Village Place was an open house. Jez Webb and Horigan would regularly come back from the Fav or the Warehouse and watch the results of Eldritch and Shearsby's meticulous recording habits: the tapes were numbered and catalogued in a file of papers indicating the contents of each tape. 7 Village Place had a fine collection of comedown film and music clips. For anyone wanting to watch the New York Dolls on *The Old Grey Whistle Test, Apocalypse Now, Blade Runner, The Blues Brothers* or *My Favourite Year* with Peter O'Toole for the umpteenth time, 7 Village Place was the destination of choice. Although by nature private and introverted, when on home ground Eldritch seemed undisturbed by the traffic through his house. He always had the option of retreating to his bedroom in the windowless attic, or not being awake.

Once American football began showing on British TV, it could also be watched at Village Place. Tim Strafford-Taylor remembers 'ending up down there with pizza from the take-away around corner.' For him Village Place 'equals pepperoni, Super Bowl, amphetamine and beer.'

David Owen (a Fav regular who would later sing in the Hollow Men) remembers Eldritch making bacon sandwiches for those who had come back to Village Place for a late-night session after the pubs had shut. Eldritch occasionally provided other entertainment. 'For a time Andrew got obsessed with a long distance phone number in New York that he'd call up,' Owen notes. 'It was a recorded sex message tape. He'd dial it, then let you listen, then complain that it was costing about ten pounds per call! But he'd do it again and again for everyone who was there . . . it amused him greatly!'

Danny London, another hungry late-night visitor, also experienced Eldritch's catering. '"There's some toast in the kitchen," Andy said. He had already toasted the bread. All you had to do was warm up the toast. He had pre-toasted his toast! He was such a weird, strange guy, but he was absolutely cool.'

There were, however, limits to the hospitality afforded. 'As the band became more successful there were more people wanting to get in on the act and would turn up after the Fav,' Marx explains. 'Andrew could be pretty nasty if he took a dislike to someone. God bless him, he did like an argument.' In his role of paterfamilias, it was clear that Eldritch held dominion over this portion of Burley. One anonymous visitor recalled: 'Even in the dark room Andrew never took off his leather jacket or his dark glasses, and never said a word. He was like a god to the collected masses! Someone would say: "I think Andrew wants to hear *Junkyard*," and someone would dutifully put it on. Later, someone would say, "Andrew wants everyone to go away." So everyone did.'

Sometimes, those between accommodation used 7 Village Place as a place to sleep. This had its hazards. Paul Gregory recalls that, 'You'd end up playing Scrabble with Andrew all night.' Eldritch on speed was impossible to beat. 'I'd have Double Word Score – four points. He'd have "discombobulate".' An option was to feign exhaustion and retreat to the 'one bed in Claire's dressing room.'

As well as being a social space, it was also a private one. 'Most of the plotting and planning happened when there was just me, Andrew and Claire around,' says Marx. And there were drugs, of course. Amphetamine was everywhere in Leeds. 'The speed wasn't cheap but it was very good,' Horigan states. 'Very professional. Not much of that shit speed that makes your teeth itch.' Amphetamine was not good for the immune system, but should you be so inclined, as Eldritch was, it was perfect for staying up night after night reading, watching videos, drafting and redrafting lyrics, tinkering with the Doktor or playing one's trusty Woolworth's guitar.

Village Place was also a kind of design studio. Kevin Lycett remembers, almost with a gasp: 'The Rotring pens!' One time when he called round, 'Andy was sat in the half-light the whole time we were there. He was blacking out centimetre squares. To do that, absolutely meticulously!'

Eldritch certainly did not remind Lycett or Jon Langford of the art students they knew. 'We were all over the map,' Langford says. 'He had a very tight, organised idea of how he was going to approach the band, not at first, but as he went on. He was more like a scientist, actually. His drive and his focus were unlike most of the art students that I know. Actually, maybe he was more like an engineer. He knew exactly how it was going to work. It was a very controlled project. All the art school bands I knew were a load of people thrashing around, trying to get out of bed in the morning and arguing.'

Lycett had the identical impression: 'Andrew was more driven than most people and was able to be clearer in his vision. He was a planner. He thought things through. He worked from ideas, which is certainly one type of artistic practice, one way of being an artist. He could be an arrogant little shit and rub people up the wrong way, but basically he was finding his way like everybody else was.'

Lycett didn't especially like the end results of Eldritch's designs: 'because art was my medium and I swam easily in it, the early sleeves . . . seemed to me to be really clumsy. He wasn't fluent in art history or in visual iconography, but he later became incredibly fluent. It was almost like he willed himself to learn it. It wasn't a natural thing for him. In fact, the whole music project was a bit like that. It was a decision: "Music: That's what I'll do. I don't know anything about it, but now I will, and I will *become* that . . . My will will take me through. And my intelligence."'

Indeed, rock 'n' roll could be learned. Taylor, ever the linguist, once called it a dialect, and therefore one that was possible to become fluent in. Or, put another way: he understood rock 'n' roll (and being a rock star) as language systems of audio-visual signs and symbols.

7 Village Place was just one of many Sisters addresses scattered across Leeds 4 and Leeds 6. Adams seems to have lived in many of them. After Burchett Place (and then Hyde Park Corner) with Simon Denbigh, he lived in Dave Hall's house on Hessle Terrace with Chris Reed and Mick Brown from Red Lorry Yellow Lorry. Then he was on Elizabeth Street with Jez Webb, Steve 'Winker' Watson (aka 'Stevie Sex Pistol') and a pet snake. 'Ben Gunn and a mate of his were on the other side to us,' says Webb. 'His was a nice tidy place, and quiet – a pleasure to visit; ours seemed to be the hub of late-night visitors.'

After that, Adams lived on Beechwood Mount, again with Webb, plus Paul Gregory this time. 'Me and Craig even shared a bedroom,' Webb continues. 'Separate beds though: it wasn't totally Morecambe and Wise. We were up in the loft: bloody freezing, no heating up there. Craig's bed was near the window, which was faulty. One night it snowed in on him: "Sisters of Mercy bassist gets hypothermia – in his bedroom!"' At one point, Adams reckons there was only one bed: 'One of us had to sleep on the bed base, one slept on the mattress, one on the floor.'

As well as two members of Red Lorry Yellow Lorry in Hessle Terrace, members of other bands were in walking distance, or 'staggering distance' as Tom Ashton puts it: the March Violets, the Mekons, the Cassandra Complex, the Three Johns, Salvation and later the Dead Vaynes and 3,000 Revs.

This proximity created a scene. It contained a mutual support network but also intense rivalries, which Eldritch in particular thrived on. This was miniaturised in the Faversham, in which each band had marked out its territory. The Sisters' area was by the pool table, where Shearsby thrashed allcomers with the skills she had honed on the snooker tables of the university. The records the bands had made were regularly played from the jukebox, which further added to the sense of the Fav being a field of combat or a cockfighting arena.

Yet, the Faversham also showed how the divisions between city and university had broken down. It was a stone's throw from the university and was used by staff and students, as well as by the subculture that had brewed in Burley and Hyde Park. The Sisters of Mercy built on – and benefitted from – the healing of that fracture. By 1983, the division had definitively disappeared. No one thought of Red Lorry Yellow Lorry as a townie band or the March Violets as a uni band (though they clearly fell either side of that divide). They were *Leeds* bands. The first, the best and the most enduring of this new phenomenon were the Sisters of Mercy: Eldritch, Marx, Adams (and Gunn) were in the vanguard of that change. After them, came only 'Leeds bands'.

Dave Hall, the 'man with a van' for whom Adams (and Horigan) delivered potatoes, was firmly established as the Sisters' regular driver in this period. His red Ford Transit was in an appalling state. On the outside, it was 'battered because I used to drive like a numpty, if people got in my way,' Hall admits. On the inside, 'the whole of the front was full of empty Marlboro packets.' Hall himself was often wired on caffeine. 'I used to go through a catering tin of coffee a week on my own,' he recalls. 'I overdosed a couple of times.'

As an ex-Bradford City hooligan, Hall could also summon up an air of genuine menace, when required. Eldritch once instructed him to glower at a journalist accompanying the band for the whole journey from Leeds to London, in order to soften him up for the ensuing interview.

In November 1982, Hall drove the Sisters to one of the odder entries in their gigography. Not only were they on the under-card at the Lyceum for Aswad, one of the UK's premium reggae bands, but Hall's van 'couldn't turn left. I had to find some convoluted route to get to the gig on the Strand,' he recalls. The ensuing Sisters' set featured the usual songs but the atypical sight of Webb and Horigan 'surrounded by a whole bunch of Rastas as we chicken-danced,' Webb says.

The original headliners, the Birthday Party, had cancelled but the Sisters had no intention of backing out of a gig in the capital, not least because they were being interviewed for a *Sounds* cover story and were having their photos taken backstage. The best one had Webb's leather jacket – emblazoned with the Sisters' 'Head and Star' insignia – hanging in the foreground, the band reflected in the dressing-room mirrors in the background. Webb had recently removed 'Killing Joke' from the back of his leather to make way for the Sisters. 'Andrew duly obliged in one of his all-night sessions. The Sisters of Mercy had become my life,' Webb says. The jacket is still in his attic.

Eldritch 'didn't have any trouble understanding Aswad' and had seen them when they had played with the Clash, but he doubted the Sisters' crossover appeal to reggae fans. 'I can't imagine they'd find us remotely interesting: we're far too exciting and we don't smoke dope.' Eldritch did not speak for the entire band on this. 'The Aswad brass section offered us a spliff,' recalls Webb. 'Me and Craig took them up on their offer. We were stoned all the way back to Leeds. It was the real deal.'

They were therefore oblivious to yet another malfunction in Hall's van: the alternator had broken. Not only could the van not turn left, Hall could not use the headlights. 'At the end of the gig I had to get John Curd [the promoter] to drive the best way out of London without hitting traffic, with me following him with my lights off.'

On other nights, rather than face the drive back from London, the band would park up and sleep in the van. 'St John's Wood was a popular place . . . a nice, quiet posh area,' says Webb. Sleeping in the van was never ideal: 'Oh God, bits of condensation dripping on your head,' is Adams' memory. On this occasion they could not risk it, in case Hall's van expired while they were asleep.

Hall – and his van – added spice to the logistics of playing gigs, but the key elements were Webb and Horigan. 'The importance of Jez and Danny to the band shouldn't be underestimated,' Marx explains. 'People may assume the chemistry is between the members of the group but in actual fact it's that wider team . . . They were a great double act and kept everything buoyant. You needed that on a six-hour drive. It provided something to draw those different personalities in, to make Ben feel part of it, to allow Craig to be himself, for it to be fun. Whatever had been eating Andrew, we always knew Jez could make him laugh, bring him back down to earth.'

As well as roadying, Webb and Horigan were the cheerleaders. 'As soon as everything was set up, they'd both go into the crowd and get everybody dancing,' says Adams. 'You'd see Jez's blond head bobbing about.' Webb confirms that, 'We covered a hell of a lot of miles in that red Transit of Dave Hall's, up and down the motorways of England, Danny's ghetto-blaster entertaining us with people's playlists, until the batteries ran out – which was frequently. Then we'd have to have a sing-along: TV adverts of the era (Toblerone and Morrisons) and I seem to remember 'Ghost Riders in the Sky' being popular as well. I think Andrew liked these moments: "The family" close together. You were either in, or out with him.'

As the Sisters got more gigs, both Webb and Horigan had to quit their jobs. Webb 'was just dead on my feet' and resigned from the Ministry of Defence in Harrogate. Adams helped him write the letter in Swindon before a gig at the Solitaire. Horigan 'had to pack my job in at a kitchen-making factory. I was driving back from gigs and then going to work and not sleeping for days and days . . . I was having to take loads of days off when the band started touring.' The kitchen factory gave him an ultimatum. Horigan naturally chose the Sisters.

In the wake of the Psychedelic Furs tour, a tiny band of hardcore fans had also begun to gather around the Sisters. This tribe dubbed itself the 'God Squad'. The majority were from Wakefield. 'Wakey', although a city in its own right, almost functioned as a suburb of Leeds – in punk terms – the Bromley to Leeds' London; the Outer Boroughs to Leeds' Manhattan.

Dave Beer and his best friend, Ali Cooke, were the first of this Wakefield contingent. They had met at art school there and were obsessed with the same bands, first the Clash and then the Cure, but their love of the Cocteau Twins was the key overlap with the Sisters. 'Same drum machine. It's all about that for me,' says Beer. 'The 606 and the 808 just cut through everything. I also really enjoyed German bands like Kraftwerk and the snappiness of the sound.'

'There was only about half a dozen of us at first,' Beer continues. The Wakefield element grew the quickest – based around Raffles, a club on Cheapside (with Sizzlers, the legendary kebab shop, around the corner) and the Black Swan pub, where Cooke worked behind the bar. Richard 'Reg' (with a hard 'g') Newton was another regular and Sisters acolyte. He was allowed to put whatever he wanted on the jukebox, since he owned a record store in the market. Chris Pugh, Marcus 'Carcass' Furniss, Jason Wild, Neil 'Emmy' Hemingway and Martin 'Paddy' Callaghan were also part of this early Wakefield contingent.

Although, Wakefield was the epicentre of the God Squad, members came from other Yorkshire cities, as well as the East and West Midlands and ultimately from as far south as Wiltshire and Devon. One of the most influential was Scott Ackroyd from Harrogate. His distinctive greeting of 'fella' became part of the lingua franca of the Sisters and their inner circle. 'Whether this was a Harrogate thing or not, I don't know,' Marx explains, 'but . . . it became the way most people would greet and refer to each other in "the family." That developed into "dobber-fella" which could be used as a term of endearment or mockery depending on the context."

Beer thinks the God Squad was 'like this little incestual bubble, this gang . . . They were the most diehard fans I've ever known.' Beer also describes the God Squad as 'a bunch of reprobates . . . dancing at the front of the stage and getting into trouble all the time. *All* the time . . . all blokes, all on the pull.'

'I think it put me in good stead, as did Scouts when I was a little boy' is Beer's more laconic summary of his time in the God Squad.

There was, however, a small but significant minority of women that followed the band from the outset, especially a trio from Leeds: Anne Merrick, Theresa Bickers and Carla Pope. Bickers and Pope were responsible for some of Marx's outlandish fashion choices. 'They would bring shirts for me to wear as a sort of thank you for getting them on the guest-list,' he explains. 'Increasingly they would bring the most garish or ridiculous items to see if I'd dare to wear them.'

As the God Squad grew, it became ever more tribal, displaying

---

* Dobber is slang for penis in several parts of Britain.

its colours – the 'Head and Star' insignia on leather jackets and T-shirts – engaging in territorial fighting at gigs and its signature formation dancing. 'Some were strange and unique to say the least,' Beer explains. The most obvious was the Pyramid 'which was basically a gymnastic acrobatic move' creating a three-storey, or more, human structure, usually with Beer 'the daftest out of the bunch,' balancing at the apex.

The God Squad had particular affection for Marx. Beer thought Marx 'was like Speedy Gonzalez. He was so fast it was almost like he was transporting himself from one place to another. "Where's he gone now? Ariba! Ariba!" So much energy; an insane amount of energy. He wore you out just looking at him. He was just going hell for leather, sweating like a racist at a carnival. He was like a water feature from B&Q when he came off stage. There was floods of it just coming out of him.' That Marx was in a relationship with Kathryn Wood from Wakefield and was often in the city only increased the bond between him and the God Squad.

Eldritch, for his part, fully embraced the role of tribal leader. As a Bowie nut, he completely understood the potency of the *amour fou* between fans and rock 'n' roll performers. He took his responsibilities seriously and was willing to play the parts of idol, shaman and guru to the hilt. The God Squad reciprocated. 'Bless him, Andrew was amazing,' says Beer. 'We all looked up to him. He was smarter than the rest of us: "Wow, that's pretty profound that shit this geezer knows." We were almost not worthy of his intellect. He'd mention authors when he was talking to you. He'd mention directors of movies. We were learning from him.' Beer continues: 'He knew how to turn you on. He knew what to talk about in any company. He could be talking about Shelley to one person and punk rock to another.' For many, being in the God Squad was formative and transformative. For Beer – as for many in the God Squad – his relationship with the band and its music was hugely important. 'They were divine intervention. Basically, I'm straight up Sisters of Mercy. They probably did save my life.'

The intensity of the bond between the band and the God Squad was replicated again and again as the Sisters collected new sets of fans around the UK, then in Europe and then globally.

By nature and by design, Eldritch kept his fans, even the God Squad, at arm's length.

'Andrew was so aloof for a while at the beginning. He'd purposefully isolate himself,' says Beer. 'While the rest of us would have a crack on, he would be with Claire . . . It really worked for him. She could keep people away from him, which made him even more aloof and enigmatic and mysterious than he really was.'

The Eldritch persona was therefore cooler than the person behind it; colder also. 'Andrew: he's a love,' Beer says, 'but not many people saw that side of him, he'd purposefully keep that behind a veil.' Beer is not sure if the 'keeping the sunglasses on, the cloak and dagger, not really talking to anyone' was because 'he didn't want to be exposed or because he started to believe his own myth to a certain extent.' Either way, 'it was very clever because people didn't approach him very easily from very early on. If you got a nod from him, it made you feel like a million dollars.'

As the Sisters were welcoming new intimates in the winter of 1982/83, Eldritch expelled the March Violets from Merciful Release.

Eldritch's version was that 'the Violets turned rancid . . . they sort of turned around and bit my hand. So I threw them off. I just got rid of them.'

'Our time on Merciful Release came to a rather crunching end,' says Rosie Garland. 'I would put it all down to ego problems,' concludes Tom Ashton. 'Loz [Elliot] was quite a difficult character, quite driven. He had quite a spiky personality, him and Von just rubbed each other up the wrong way. To be honest, they were control freaks that repelled each other.' Garland further suggests: 'Let's be more generous to Laurence: even though he was a complete fucking control freak, it was three control freaks.' Simon Denbigh was also part of the dysfunctional triad. 'Sooner or later, that is just going to blow up in your face,' concludes Garland.

The Sisters of Mercy and the March Violets played their last shows together in October 1982. These were back-to-back gigs at Klub Foot in Hammersmith and at Vanbrugh College in the University of York. Vanbrugh College was also Pink Peg Slax's last gig with the Sisters. In the year since their Riley Smith Hall show, Mark Wilson hadn't changed his opinion of Eldritch. 'I remember being in their dressing room and him getting a bit cross. We would have been doing George Formby impressions: being in a band was all about mucking about and having a laugh and having fun. He definitely didn't like it. He was like the opposite of what I thought punk rock was supposed to be; he was more like the prog rock people.'

The God Squad gained another recruit that night: Jez D'Netto. He was working at Red Rhino at the time and 'fell in love with the Sisters. After that, I started going to see them practically everywhere in the North,' he says. Like Beer, he responded to the groove and the sense of communalism. 'It's dance music at the end of the day,' D'Netto says, 'because of the drum machine it was very full on . . . It was tribal.' Although D'Netto does concede that at Vanbrugh College, 'there was only three of us dancing and one of them was Jez Webb.'

The following month, Les Mills went with the Psychedelic Furs on a long tour of the USA, Australia and New Zealand. Aside from the occasional postcard, he was out of touch with the Sisters of Mercy for the best part of three months. 'The way we left it was with things bubbling along nicely,' says Mills. '"Alice" was already out. Everything was in place, the vibe was good; it was a case of light blue touch-paper. They were getting major articles in the music press and great reviews and they had Peel behind them. Let that build: a three-month hiatus, waiting for the reality to catch up with the perception.'

The Sisters of Mercy utterly ignored him. They increased the rate at which they played gigs and they recorded a new single. Mills' days were obviously numbered.

So were Dave Hall's. His return visit to Klub Foot in the Clarendon Hotel just before Christmas 1982 – or 'my escapade in Shepherd's Bush', as he calls it – hastened his end as the Sisters' driver. 'I basically used to use the van like a battering ram. It was steel, so I would just pull out into traffic. If they got in my way, they got in my way. Even in London. Andy started to believe he was a bit more precious than that . . . I was out of control, if I think back on it.' The Sisters replaced him with Steve Watson, who was 'as wired as me, but a bit more mellow about it,' Hall says.

Eldritch replaced the March Violets on Merciful Release with Salvation, the epitome of a town band. They were formed by Horigan, James Elmore, a fellow F Clubber, and Mike Hayes, who worked at Jumbo Records. Eldritch produced three songs for them at KG in the depths of the Bridlington winter of 1982/83; there was snow on the beach and his fee was paid in amphetamine. The first session was aborted when Horigan 'lost a tooth while I was eating a liquorice stick . . . We had to go back and do the vocals after I had a crown.' Eldritch liked the end results of the sessions and put the 'Girlsoul' single out on Merciful Release. Salvation's time on the label would prove to be almost as short-lived as the March Violets', however.

Although the Sisters had transformed themselves in the recording studio, their metamorphosis as a live act took place over the autumn and winter of 1982/83. 'There were some wild gigs . . . two Birmingham shows were riotous,' says Marx. 'The second in particular I remember as being great.' These were at the Bournbrook Hotel in Selly Oak and the Fighting Cocks pub in Moseley.

Jez Webb remembers that the Fighting Cocks gig 'had a few incidents . . . the ["Head and Star"] backdrop which me and Danny were in charge of sticking up, fell down. It had been painted by Andrew onto a kitchen blind and was a bit too heavy to be held up by a few bits of tape. But you live and learn. At that same show, Mark's bullet belt proceeded to fall to bits . . . shells everywhere. Looked like attempts at a stage invasion had been repelled by the tour Gatling gun.'

Outside of Yorkshire, the West Midlands would provide the largest cadre of Sisters fans. Fighting Cocks was the first Sisters gig for Ian Hill, a teenage steel worker from Wolverhampton. 'From the first notes I was hooked,' he says. 'It encapsulated everything I wanted in a song at that time in my life. I can listen back to the songs – which I still do – and straight away I'm transported to the feeling of energy and hope I had back then. Sisters in their original form were simply amazing – and *loud*. The drum machine had a clinical edge and I loved . . . the metallic thrum from Craig's bass, Mark's wonderful guitar . . . topped off by Andrew and his vocal style.'

Hill was at the gig with Rik Benbow, a painter, also from Wolverhampton. Benbow was known for 'his chain trick,' says Hill, 'which was snorting a chain and bringing it out his mouth then flossing his nasal and throat passages. Hilarious when you've had a few beers – a guaranteed ice breaker.' Benbow had seen the Sisters at Futurama 3 and nearly a year later at the ZigZag Club. By the time of the Birmingham shows he was hooked. He loved the music but 'with the Sisters you had, for want of a better word, the depraved side, the drug-induced-wish-you-were-around-in-1969 thing,' he notes. 'The Sisters were for people like me who grew up listening to the Velvet Underground and Iggy and the Stooges and the MC5.' And Slade. Benbow's high regard for his Black Country local heroes was something else he shared with the Sisters.

Both Benbow and Hill became part of the God Squad. Hill would do so as 'Surfin Merb'. His nickname combined a shortening of the extraordinary 'Merbert Bruntwinkle', his nickname from school, and the Cramps' version of 'Surfin' Bird'. The latter was due to his 'liking for going apeshit when dancing, including as if [I was] surfing.' Merb remembers his time following the Sisters of Mercy as: 'Madness. Energy. Togetherness. No fear. Youth. The excitement of the next gig. Optimism. Freedom.'

10

Choose Your Masks

The Birmingham gigs were the early band at one of their live peaks. As later line-ups would prove, Sisters songs could easily be played by one guitarist: that they used two meant that their sound could either feel deconstructed or be in lockstep, a wall of distorted sound. The overall effect was unrelenting. The band played each song with the same guitars, through the same couple of pedals; Eldritch sang in a fewer-than-two octave range and Adams kept as close to the root notes of chords as possible. The cumulative effect could be extraordinary. Although Gunn 'was living on crumbs', as Marx puts it, he was vital.

Also, as Marx admits, 'of course, we were five in total. As dumb as it sounds, the drum machine was a massive part of the band's personality.' The Doktor in its 606 incarnation was both cutting-edge and primitive. The Doktor was still not able to play anything complicated, even if its programmer wanted it to. And the programmer did not. The Doktor was operated in the realm of the genius dum-dum boy and girl drummers like Nick Knox, Tommy Ramone, Moe Tucker, Scott Asheton and whatever Martin Rev had rigged up to make drum noises in Suicide.

The band's visual presentation onstage was also simple, to the point of austerity: usually no smoke, minimal light show, not much backline, just four men virtually in a row. Left to right: Marx, Eldritch, Adams, Gunn. The key dialectic remained stage right. Marx: one winkle-picker held together by gaffer tape, febrile, often smirking, hacking at his guitar; and Eldritch in shades, a riot of black leather, svelte and sinuous, wafting his cigarette around, manipulating his mic stand and twitching his crotch. Neither of them was afraid of the ridiculous in rock.

'In terms of what I brought to the party,' Marx recalls, 'most obviously I wasn't Andrew.' Marx refers to it as him playing 'Dave Hill to his Alvin Stardust in some weird Glam era mash-up.'

There was indeed a huge dose of Alvin Stardust in the early Eldritch stage persona: black leather jacket, trousers *and* gloves. There had once been practical reasons for these. 'I wore them because I used to bite my nails, and stages in those days, particularly at the F Club, were only six-inches high and the audience was literally nose-to-nose with you. I thought "I can't be showing them nails like these."' By the time of the Birmingham dates, the gloves – sometimes, even more ludicrously, Eldritch wore just the one – were an affectation. The signature Eldritch look 'ties together with every kid of [my] generation's Alice Cooper fetish,' he once explained. 'There are no breaks in the spectrum that also includes Motörhead and the Ramones . . . and goes back to Gene Vincent and "That's All Right (Mama)".'

Eldritch therefore took his place in the long line of preening leather boys in British rock. He was both Billy Fury and his own Larry Parnes, openly mining the broad seam of queerness that has always run through rock 'n' roll and been embraced by straight male performers. This attitude had been fostered down at the F Club. 'It was a very tolerant and inclusive place,' Eldritch has stated. 'Everyone liked to have at least one item of gay wear on their person.'

Eldritch did not become a gay icon – to his own disappointment – but his performance was industrial grade catnip for a lot of straight women. He became aware that 'the audience's attitude changed to me . . . particularly the way the girls were reacting changed a great deal.'

Eldritch's routine – a series of rock star *tableaux vivants*, as staged and as stylised as a body builder's routine, with its transitions from one pose to the next – was strongly rooted in the delicate, languorous shtick of Robert Plant, Ian Gillan and Paul Rodgers: straight dudes – obvious alpha males – but also highly feminised. His stage act was strikingly at odds with the jittery, angular shapes and the gurning that most punk acts – and those that came in their wake – deployed. As with so much else, Eldritch's inner Bowie surfaced in ways other than crass copyism.

The rest of the band also had their own sex appeal: Marx played up to his role as high-energy proletarian beefcake; Adams' youth and prettiness were in stark contrast with his short temper and filthy sense of humour, and Gunn had his own fans who fancied 'Baby Ben'. But Eldritch's stage show was the most ridiculously and genuinely erotic. Even straight men were drawn into the *coup de théâtre*. Dave Beer recognised the sexual excess of Eldritch's shtick. 'Andrew used to hold on to the microphone for dear life . . . That's how to hold a microphone, like Jim Morrison. Wrapped around it, almost making love to it. Snogging it.'

Eldritch's crotch-thrusting was also hard to miss. 'He'd always done that,' Beer notes. 'It was very about that with his leather trousers. Summat kinky going on in his head, which he would never share with the rest of us. I'm sure he must have had some socks or something down the front. Definitely. Unless it was the fact he had a constant hard-on when he was onstage. You can't have a penis that big. He had a lump in his leathers no one else had. I think it got bigger the bigger his head got.'

Such validations – whether male or female, straight or gay – reached a critical mass. As 1983 dawned, Eldritch began an intensification of his persona that would become ever more extreme. Over the next two years, Eldritch would refine a visual iconography and mode of performance that would define the Sisters of Mercy and make him a star.

'Eldritch' was of course not just deployed at gigs. The off-stage persona became that of the remote and nocturnal Philosopher King of Leeds 6, the droll Übermensch, a Renaissance man elevating rock 'n' roll to his level. Much of it was merely an extrapolation of Andy Taylor: slightly reclusive, sardonic, ruthlessly logical, intellectual. Eldritch therefore deployed the persona as a mask but also as a device to project; the *persona* – 'mask' in Latin – when worn by a Roman actor would amplify the voice of the actor, as well as offer a disguise.

This dual function was apparent as Eldritch became more of a public figure: the more powerfully the persona articulated Eldritch's view of the world – onstage, on record and in interviews he told you *exactly* who he was – the more it was deployed to distancing effect. This was also true off stage, especially in Leeds. Never gregarious, Eldritch spent more and more time in Village Place with the Sisters' inner circle, but often alone at night. Even those closest to him felt him withdraw – and wield his power. This was especially true within the band.

In January 1983 Eldritch described the Sisters to *Melody Maker* as 'ludicrously democratic'. This simple phrase – and the making of the 'Anaconda' single – give a clear indication of shifts in the power structure taking place within the band.

Eldritch wrote the words to 'Anaconda' – about a heroin addict, and some of his least opaque – and Marx the music. In KG, Eldritch had the whip hand and properly began his project of learning how 'to work a desk . . . and bend some needles', as he has put it. As a novice, Eldritch was out of his depth, even in a small eight-track studio like KG. There was nothing unusual in this. Eldritch spent a huge amount his time in the Sisters deliberately overreaching himself, but the rest of the band were not impressed by the results or his high-handedness. 'As for the actual recording I was disappointed that we weren't able to get the most out of the track,' says Marx. 'There was an element of it being a bit of a stop-gap single.' Adams agrees: 'It was Andy's first attempt as producer, and it sounded weird.'

Ken Giles and Eldritch worked into the early hours. 'I remember one night with Andy, I couldn't take any more,' Giles says. 'I sat down on the bench that was on the left in the long, narrow control room, and just fell asleep. I woke up at three-thirty maybe four in the morning. I remember looking at Andy – he was never a healthy-looking youth – and he was just *white*. He looked like a man that needed to go to bed . . . He was hunched over the mixing console, sitting in my chair. He'd figured out the console, how to rewind and play the 1-inch tape machine. For two hours he's just been rewinding, playback, rewinding, playback, rewinding.'

'He said something like: "I think we're getting there."'

'Anaconda', for its flaws, is much closer to the Sisters' best work than their worst. It still sounds like the Sisters, albeit the Sisters sometimes sliding towards abrasive, mutant funk, like the Stooges' 'Scene of the Crime'. The star of the piece is Marx's staccato, scratchy lead riff played high up the fretboard, his approximation of surf guitar.

The B-side, 'Phantom', is completely sensational, a quasi-dub of 'Floorshow': 'Rock and Roll Part 2' to 'Floorshow's 'Rock and Roll Part 1'. 'Phantom' occupies some rarely explored place between the Glitter Band, Ennio Morricone and the Shadows.

It actually dated back to improvisations during the 'Alice'/ 'Floorshow' sessions. Marx had borrowed a vintage Burns guitar from Stephen Barber. He had never used a tremolo arm before and tested it out at KG with the 'Floorshow' drum pattern. 'Everyone was leaping up and down in the control room saying it sounded great and not to forget what I'd been playing,' Marx recalls.

Back in Village Place after the 'Alice'/'Floorshow' sessions Marx had worked up a full instrumental. 'Once I'd given Andrew some indication of how much I'd got, he modified the drum track.' For the return to KG, Marx 'couldn't get the Burns guitar. Jon Langford came to the rescue, but his guitar had the tremolo arm snapped off. To operate the action you had to wedge a fork in and use that as the lever. Bands of similar status [as us] that we'd run into doubtless all had these pristine Gretsch guitars. I love that jumble sale aspect of what we did.'

Les Mills returned to the UK in the early spring of 1983 to find that the Sisters had ignored all his advice. 'That's why I asked them to sign a management contract: bring it to the boil, force the issue. I said: "Show it to a lawyer." I left them some time to sit on it.' Mills' final meeting with the Sisters took place in the sitting room of 7 Village Place. 'I pretty much knew which way it would go,' he says. 'It was like a Harold Pinter play. I was sat there on the couch. Andrew had taken the strategic position in the living room and the rest of the band were kind of stood off in secondary positions. It came down to a quick verbal joust between me and Andrew.' Eldritch rapidly brought the Sisters of Mercy's relationship with Les Mills to an end, and the Sisters walked away from a manager who had overseen the global rise of the Psychedelic Furs. *Forever Now* and its single 'Love My Way' were both minor hits, but hits nevertheless, even in the USA.

'My interpretation,' concludes Mills, 'is that I stopped working for them when Andy's ego ran out of control. His interpretation would probably be that he had taken as much from me as he needed and could move on. With the Sisters, I always felt it was Andy calling the shots, pulling the strings. More and more, he became the dominant character. It wouldn't have been so bad except for the fact I felt a lot of his decision-making was very irrational.'

Eldritch indeed had his own logic. He was by nature a contrarian, profoundly anti-authoritarian and with a considerable amount of rage, not someone who readily sought, or submitted himself to, the management of others, and certainly not by someone like Les Mills who, by his own admission, 'tended to be hands-on with all the bands I worked with.' Eldritch had a highly developed and hard-earned sense of self and correctly surmised that signing with Mills would have meant surrendering an intolerable amount of power and control.

Although they often bristled against Eldritch's tutelage, the other three Sisters remained loyal to him during the showdown in Village Place. Mills interprets this as weakness or naivety. 'I was quite surprised that the rest of the band didn't have anything else to say. I'm surprised that Craig didn't speak. I said: "Do any of the rest of you have anything to say?" and they all looked sheepishly at their shoes or looked away.

'I often see statements like these, and it puzzles me,' says Marx. 'Why is it assumed that at any given time, everybody in a room has to say something? It wasn't an episode of fucking *Friends*. On a number of levels, I guess some things were taken personally – I've no need to lash out. Les had Ian Hunter in his record collection and in some way facilitated the recording of 'Alice'/'Floorshow', which makes him OK by me. I think there is ample evidence to suggest Les and the Sisters weren't a good fit for each other.' He continues: 'I may have come to view his as a London-centric attitude . . . It may have been a much more practical thing, that we felt he could never give us the time we needed because of the way the Furs were heading.'

The band's confidence and self-belief were sky-high. Les Mills had become surplus to all their requirements. 'At the time we weren't going to sign anything,' says Adams. 'We were on the same page as Eldritch . . . The plan was world domination whatever. I think all of us were: "We're the best and we're going to show off."'

During his final visit to Village Place, Mills had been struck by the contrast with his first meeting with Eldritch in his Southwark office. 'Now he was not introverted at all. And he was even more paranoid. After it became apparent that the Sisters were not going to sign a management contract, Mills submitted an invoice. 'I did a line-by-line itemised account of every expense that I'd had. I never billed them ever for my time or for the pictures I shot for them. I billed them specifically for the cost of the session, John's expenses getting up to Leeds, any equipment rental, the studio time and train fares when I went up there on business. It worked out as a fraction over £1,000 over the course of a year-plus.'

'I felt Andy should acknowledge the debt that he owed me. He quibbled over it, but I did finally get a cheque from "Andy Taylor" for the full amount.' The connection with John Ashton was also severed.

Ashton claims he 'never saw a penny' from his work on 'Alice'. 'Andrew never paid me anything, but I was more miffed he took my name off it,' he admits. The label of the Merciful Release 7-inch – MR015 – did indeed say, 'Produced by John Ashton at KG', whereas the 12-inch – MR021 – simply featured one of the Sisters' enduring bon mots: 'Rise and Reverberate'. Ashton is convinced this is a deliberate act of erasure.[*]

---

[*]   It is possible that Ashton might not have been deliberately omitted at all. There were no writing or production credits, nor were any members of the Sisters of Mercy named, on 'The Damage Done', 'Body Electric'/'Adrenochrome', 'Anaconda' or the 'Alice' 12-inch EP. The 7-inch bearing Ashton's name could simply be an anomaly.

'Actually, I was angry and quite upset,' he adds. 'That was a pretty shitty thing for Andrew to do. That was not cool. I did put my heart and soul into it. I did it because I loved it. I didn't know it at the time, but I was a consummate detail-oriented producer. It would be nice to get a cheque one day.'

Mills is probably correct when he states that the Sisters 'could have been a much, much bigger band in America, if they had signed a management contract and gone the way I wanted to go.' Eldritch would in fact consider that a vindication of turning his back on Mills. 'We chose not to get in bed with their [the Furs'] manager and we were proved right subsequently because it didn't take him long to try and translate that band into "John Mellencamp and Friends". That didn't turn out well.'

The David 'Kid' Jensen BBC radio session they recorded in the first week of March 1983 accurately represented just how good the Sisters were when they showed Mills the door. Two tracks ('Burn' and 'Valentine') would appear on their next release, *The Reptile House* EP, one ('Heartland') would be a B-side, yet the pick of the four tracks is an extraordinary cover version of 'Jolene'.

The Sisters came to praise, not to bury, the original. Their version of the wonderful Dolly Parton number is properly camp, hilarious and profoundly groovy. In part, 'Jolene' was intended to rebut any argument that lumped Eldritch in with (what Simon Reynolds termed in *Rip It Up and Start Again*) 'the hunky Goth singers' like Peter Murphy and Ian Astbury, or indeed the entire phallocentric tradition in rock. Drenched in overdriven guitars, four-on-the-floor drums with a discoid hi-hat, the Sisters' 'Jolene' is radical, delicious and perfectly balanced on that fine line between very clever and very stupid. In this sense, its true antecedents are John Cale's 'Heartbreak Hotel' or Devo's 'Satisfaction'.

As ever with the Sisters, with the humour came severity. Rodney Orpheus was particularly aware of Taylor's metamorphosis into Eldritch. 'It shocked the hell out of me. Pure Nietzschean strength of will . . . We both reinvented ourselves into the people we wanted to be. And I completely respect that and understand it.' He felt that he and Eldritch were 'manifesting an unconscious desire into reality . . . a completely willed, conscious act; to take an inner me and build it into an exterior world I wanted to be and make the world accept that. I think that's very much what I was doing and others, like Andrew, were doing as well. It was the idea of becoming the Total Man.'

The two 'shy intellectuals . . . hit it off early on because we were very similar in a number of ways, but I think Andrew was more single-pointed than I was,' Orpheus says. 'I wanted to do a million different things. Andrew just wanted to be a rock star and that was it: laser-focused on that idea. Sometimes, I used to be jealous of that ability to want nothing else than to be the world's greatest rock star. But when I saw what it did to him in some ways, I was actually quite glad. When you have that single-pointed focus of will it can be extraordinary; you cut out everything else in your life and that can be problematic too.'

The more Eldritch's amplification of self-achieved epic and symbolic proportions, the more Eldritch risked being consumed by a myth of his own making. His hauteur, intelligence and verbal dexterity disguised just how much the ultra-rational Eldritch flirted with chaos and outright disaster: the Apollonian could not forever corral the Dionysian.

The *becoming* of Andrew Eldritch was also a descent.

11

Upon Thy Belly Shalt Thou Go

The gigs either side of the Jensen Session were a typical Sisters mixture of this era: sometimes technically ragged, sometimes virtually empty, always loud, increasingly sexy and with bursts of slapstick. The Liverpool Warehouse was attended mainly by the 'berserk' God Squad and their 'ferocious electrical dancing' (as a local fanzine editor and BBC Radio Merseyside presenter, Roger Hill, recalled). New Order played in Liverpool the same night, so almost no one heard Eldritch mis-sing his own lyrics to 'Kiss the Carpet' as 'I kissed the curtain, I climbed the carpet.' Reappearing for the encore after minimal applause, Adams correctly stated: 'It don't take much to get us back on.'

'Kiss the Carpet' was the very bold beginning to the Sisters' set in this era. It was one of their very slowest and sparsest songs, which mixed the slow-burn and build of something like 'Dirt' by the Stooges and the twitchy, synthetic menace of Suicide. 'It was an edgy way to start,' recalls Marx. 'I often looked across at Ben who seemed a bit unsure how to behave when he was doing so little.' Several minutes into the gig, Eldritch would slink on with a breezy ''ello'.

There were also practical reasons for the slow build-up. 'It certainly made good sense to introduce elements one by one,' Marx continues, 'to leave plenty of time and space to sort out technical problems. It gave me a little time to feel my way in. I can hardly overstate the fact I was often playing stuff that was tricky for me to do sitting down and concentrating, never mind when I was revved up and trying to throw a shape or two.'

The Sisters played in London three times in February and March 1983, twice at the Brixton Ace, but it was the one time at the Venue that drew reviews. Adam Sweeting weighed in yet again: 'The Sisters' macabre fusion of hideous raw power with black and twisted humour may well be unmatched in the annals of rock. Certainly, they tread this wicked razor's edge with malicious deadpan glee, and I find the keen blade of their irony a splendid thing . . . How the entire band managed to keep a straight face while Andy Snakeman negotiated the higher registers of their preposterous cover of 'Jolene' will probably have to go unexplained.' Eldritch's shtick was also not lost on Elissa Van Poznak, a rare female reviewer: 'He unleashes a torrent of prowling malevolence and brooding sexuality like other Lizard Kings we have known and loved (to death). He's posey as hell.'

Also in March, the Sisters played an infamous gig at Franc's in Colne, near Burnley. 'It was tiny and when you got there you had to help assemble a small stage out of plastic beer crates and plywood,' Marx explains. 'The gig was great but as Craig and I got more and more into it we lurched ever nearer with the headstocks of our guitars until finally we both turned too quickly and he hit me right above my eye with the end of his bass splitting the brow Henry Cooper-style. I guess we thought medical facilities round there might be as make-shift as the stage and decided to administer some first aid Sisters-style: I rubbed speed straight into the gaping cut as a sort of act of experimentation and bravado . . . "Tonight Matthew, I am Iggy Pop, in bloody Colne."'

At the Porterhouse in Retford, Adams performed one of his occasional onstage party pieces. He went back on for the encore with his one-string Hondo bass – one string being enough to play 'Sister Ray' or 'Ghost Rider' – and smashed it. Over two years into his time in the Sisters of Mercy, Adams still did not own a decent instrument of his own. The Hondo was such 'a piece of crap' that it came apart easily and could then be reassembled in order to be rent asunder on another night.

In Retford, 'this was all captured, albeit in very poorly lit conditions, on the VHS tape we were given to take away,' Marx explains. 'The Porterhouse had a fixed video camera aimed at the stage which captured basic footage of the gigs – I think its main purpose was actually for security.'

The next day Johnny Plumb called round to Village Place to collect an ornate and rather beautiful violin bass that he had loaned the band for the gig, and which he believed Adams had played at the Porterhouse. 'We invite him in and tell him we are just finishing watching the footage from the gig, if he wants to sit down and see the end,' says Marx. 'This he does in all innocence, just in time to see this murky footage of Craig destroying what he genuinely believes to be his bass, his absolute pride and joy. I just wish we had set up a camera to record his reaction."

As well as 'Jolene' – in case anyone thought Eldritch's tight trousers made him a cock rocker – the Sisters had also added 'Gimme Shelter' – in case anyone thought his long hair meant he was interested in peace and love.

Marx and Adams had first rehearsed it at KG in the flat above the double garage that housed the PAs. Other cover ideas had been floated at the time. 'I always wanted to do "Music" by John Miles,' says Adams, who can do a fair impression of Eldritch melodramatically singing the opening lines.'

'That would have been brilliant,' Adams says, 'but it was really difficult and we couldn't work it out.'[†]

With the addition of 'Gimme Shelter', the Sisters main set was now usually tailed by Eldritch as a camp *primo uomo*, exiting the stage accompanied only by Adams' bass after twisting Mick Jagger's lyrics. 'The original was about how love is just a kiss away and war is just a shot away. We turned it around.' This was part of Eldritch's refinement of his 1969 mythos: 'a way of saying . . . we are the children of Altamont' who had come of age in a post-hippy world after 'the trip turned sour'. It had the additional function of locating the Sisters 'as part of the rock 'n' roll tradition, which is where

[*] In the year of the 'great bass shortage' (as Marx puts it), the violin bass actually belonged to Mark Copson. Plumb 'was only the temporary custodian.' Adams would eventually mime playing Copson's bass in the video for the Mission's 'Serpent's Kiss.'

[†] Adams was the main, perhaps only, advocate for 'Music'. Eldritch suggested 'Bess You Is My Woman Now' from *Porgy and Bess* and Marx 'They Call the Wind Maria' from *Paint Your Wagon*. Neither of those made it to any kind of rehearsal.

we differ from all those people [that] make a big deal about being some brand-new thing,' Eldritch explained. 'We're very aware of the tradition and we're keen to own up to it.'

Adams particularly enjoyed this fetishising of Altamont, but much of Eldritch's high-concept theorising and posturing Adams regarded as utter twaddle: 'I think he was just saying stuff to be controversial, which he specialised in. He said all sorts of crap all the time to any audience that would listen. He might have been mentally bored. We didn't have a lot going on: we had this many songs, the show was what it was . . . He talked all kinds of shit all the time. Maybe he would say things to get a rise.' At worst, Adams suspected Eldritch was an outright fantasist.

In fact, in the unnaturally large amount of time Eldritch spent awake – most of it in his own company – his mind turned easily to the abstract. Rancour also came easily, especially towards bands he considered inferiors. Among those deluding themselves about not being rock bands were 'the new spiritualist, ludicrous, positive punk bands who I've got no time for whatsoever. Mostly because none of them can write a good tune.' Even before it was called goth, Eldritch was against it. Put another way: 'We don't know who the fuck Alien Sex Fiend are, and we don't want to know.'

It was at this stage that the Sisters made *The Reptile House* EP, for many their early masterpiece. It was a record so unusual and singular that it simultaneously remade and transcended gothic rock. 'I would say that's my favourite Sisters' stuff ever,' declares Adams. 'It was just great. That's what we were doing at the time; we weren't playing "Body Electric" in rehearsals. They were definitely a different set of songs, tapping into a bit of Sabbath and bits of

Hawkwind and seventies bands that never got big, just got really stoned and played heavy, slow music for two hours.'

The Reptile House was radio poison: no singles and tracks so slow you couldn't dance to them unless you were utterly fucked up. 'This record is completely unarguable: take it on its own terms, bearing in mind that it doesn't give a damn whether you like it or not,' is how Eldritch put it. 'The mix is obtuse, the pace relentlessly, unyieldingly slow.'

Lyrically, the EP is a vortex of tenderness and horror: 'romance and assassination', 'love' and 'genocide', 'a shiny love song' and 'a quick incision', 'kissing' and 'carnage'. Its high points are on the second side, a mini suite of oblique political songs. In 'Valentine' Eldritch flays a certain kind of recurring English national sickness, describing his fellow countrymen as 'a people fed on famine' who 'eat each other', 'waiting for another war.'

On 'Fix', Eldritch's lead vocals – he also sings the falsetto back-ups – relish each bone-dry pun and juxtaposition: 'corpse and corporation' and 'death and defecation' stand out. On its surface, 'Fix' is poised and witty; beneath, it is packed with rage and disgust – at the pestilence of nationalism, especially.

'Burn' seems to contain the impulse to incinerate the Palace of Westminster and bring the particular 'Reptile Houses' of Lords and Commons crashing down. The EP came out in the month Margaret Thatcher's Conservatives won a second term with an increased majority. Eldritch loathed Thatcher and her policies, which had cruelly targeted working-class towns and cities – in the North especially – and were turning Britain into a spiv nation of conspicuous consumption and compromised morality. His countrymen therefore lived in a Reptile House of their own making.

Yet he was fully aware that his own skull housed a reptilian brain, which contained the primal drives of sex, violence and self-preservation. 'There are no windows in the Reptile House, and there is no handle on the inside of the door. The rules of the game are house rules, and it will take you a long time to understand them,' Eldritch wrote on the test pressing he sent to a journalist.

For such a serious collection of songs, *The Reptile House* was also very playful. 'Valentine' has drums like 'We Will Rock You' on quaaludes, a guitar line that alludes to 'Venus in Furs' and lyrics adapted from Eliot's 'Sweeney Erect'. 'Fix' is also allusive, including a bassline like 'I Want You Right Now' by the MC5, made grindingly slow and fuzzy.

The Reptile House was recorded at KG with John Spence, not Ken Giles, as the main engineer. Giles' generous definition of what constituted a working day in the studio had burned him out and he had decided to concentrate on his other business as a distributor of high-end audio equipment, which he had moved to Wakefield. Nevertheless, Giles was in the studio for some of *The Reptile House* sessions. When Eldritch 'insisted on having the backing track to "Valentine" ever louder in his headphones,' says Marx, 'Kenny told him the sound from the cans was spilling into the vocal mic. Andrew did his vocals wearing a bobble hat to help combat the sound bleeding through – the supposed Prince of Darkness looking like a cross between Mike Nesmith of the Monkees and Benny from [the soap opera] *Crossroads*.'

'Recording the vocal was challenging,' confirms Spence, 'because

Andy sang very, very quietly. I suspect it was the only way he could hold the pitch in the lower register . . . At one point Andy asked me to point a mic directly at his throat and mix it in with the main vocal mic. We pursued that for a while but it didn't really work. He always wanted his voice to sound lower and deeper.'

Eldritch's approach to working in a studio already displayed the tendency to extreme laboriousness that would mark the remainder of his time as a recording artist.

'The mixing process was not difficult but very time consuming,' recalls Spence. 'When he had mixed the drums down onto one of KG's eight tracks, Andy would step in and start tweaking it. He would sit for hours listening to just the bass drum mic and fiddling with the EQ, then the same with the snare channel and the hi-hat channel . . . During this time I would hover around, smoke, drink coffee and read. When he declared himself happy with the drum sound I would then bring up the bass and the process started again followed by the guitars and vocals.' Spence continues: 'At first I assumed that he was trying to achieve a certain sound but I later realised that he didn't actually know what he was doing, he was just finding out what each frequency sounded like.'

Whether Eldritch's approach to making *The Reptile House* was arrogance or bravery – or both – he was learning at a rapid pace. Its creation also contained a contradiction: it was both obsessively laboured over, yet cobbled together and, at times, rushed. One was very likely an Eldritchian corollary of the other.

The EP was an assembly of pre-existing material as much as it was a concept mini album. 'Kiss the Carpet' had first appeared in the live set in autumn 1982. 'Valentine' – under the working title

'Bell' – had also been 'kicking about for a while,' says Marx. 'Lights' was on the Ric Rac demo. 'Burn' had been unfinished when the Sisters went into KG. 'It didn't have a fully formed lyric and so all the backwards vocals were spun in to try and flesh it out – it's only moderately successful and was much better live,' Marx thinks. The lyrics for the backwards vocals on it were repurposed from a track the band had demoed called 'Burn It Down'.

Eldritch however couched the production of 'Burn' as part of the concept: 'The last track especially promises something to hold on to, and then proceeds to recede away before the reprise of track 1 puts you right back where you started - the door of The Reptile House had swung shut behind you again. Welcome.'

Of all the early Sisters records, *The Reptile House* is the one closest to an Eldritch solo record. He wrote it, produced it and was responsible for virtually all the major creative decisions. A decade later, Eldritch would even claim he was the only member of the Sisters of Mercy who played on it. 'They weren't into recording that much, they just wanted to play live. They were sleeping in some corner until I woke them up after I had played and recorded everything on my own. When they asked me how their guitar and bass parts had turned out, I used to say to them they performed very well. Gary didn't even listen to *The Reptile House* until it had been released on vinyl and I handed it to him with the words: "This is our new record, you'll like it!"'

'While it is quite amusing and convenient to say the rest of the band slept through the sessions while Andrew did everything, it simply isn't true,' says Marx. 'To suggest Ben didn't play on the sessions or that I didn't is a nonsense.'

Adams, who on occasion refers to Eldritch as 'the Thin White Duck', puts it like this: 'The description from the Duck saying Mark and I never played on that record: What a load of old choff! I don't know where he comes up with it.'

Whatever actually happened, Eldritch certainly dominated the artistic direction of the EP and continued to obsess over it long after recording. He had it test pressed twice because he was dissatisfied with the first and 'he slaved over the lyric sheet insert night after night laying it out in Letraset,' says Marx. He individually positioned and dry-rubbed each letter from a transfer sheet.

Boyd Steemson sees the Letraset – as Kevin Lycett views the Rotring pens – as emblematic of something deeply embedded in Eldritch. 'Andrew had – probably still does – a preoccupation with absolutely mindless activities,' Steemson says. 'The Letrasets – absolutely insane. Justifying by eye, which takes hours and hours, even then could be taken to a typesetter. Letrasetting a lyric sheet: absolutely ridiculous! But of course he was probably right that it was more accurate – his justification was better than a computer could do at that stage.'

David Owen, who was then a budding graphic designer, agrees with Steemson that this was 'something bordering on madness and obsession. He'd spent God knows how long doing it as a single piece! This one moment is pretty much everything you need to know about Eldritch: obsession, patience, detail. Years later, when I read Mervyn Peake's *Gormenghast* and *Titus Groan* . . . I realised that Eldritch is very much like Steerpike!'

When printed, someone had to put the lyric sheets into sleeves in Red Rhino's Fetter Lane warehouse in York. Eldritch 'duly bowed out,' says Jez Webb. 'Craig, Mark, me and Danny were given that duty.' The cover was a collage made from a photograph in the December 1968 issue of *National Geographic* entitled 'Mekong: River of Terror and Hope'. *The Reptile House* therefore cast Eldritch as a Marlow/Willard figure on a journey upriver into political and personal hearts of darkness.

His days as Kurtz were still ahead of him.

The EP was the last of the Sisters' fully Yorkshire records: demoed and rehearsed in the cellar of Village Place; the artwork designed and the lyric sheet hand-made in the sitting room above; recorded at KG in Bridlington, and distributed by Red Rhino of York. Village Place and Rhino would remain in the Sisters' story, but *The Reptile House* was the last Sisters record made at KG. Forty years later, Giles remains proud of his work with the Sisters and his part in crafting, what he terms, 'their exciting noise.'

'It's impossible not to be positive about Kenny Giles,' says Marx. 'Without him and KG it's perfectly likely that there is no Sisters story beyond CNT. Kenny was crucial to the band's development and success.' He credits Giles as 'the person who encouraged Andrew to take himself seriously as a producer and gave him that platform,' adding, 'the most precious commodity in the studio back then was time . . . Kenny was young enough, energetic enough, and generous enough to adopt an attitude that said: "while it's sounding good and we're enjoying ourselves no one needs to look at the clock". That took a lot of pressure off all of us, but was most valuable to Andrew because he tended to be just getting warmed up once you got into the early hours.'

Not long out of the studio, the Sisters played four-fifths of *The*

Reptile House at their last ever Leeds Warehouse headlining gig in early April 1983. 'Kiss the Carpet', Valentine' and 'Burn' were all live staples, but that night, 'Lights' got a rare airing. It would be over a year before 'Fix' finally made it to the stage. Twice in June 1984 and once at the Albert Hall in June 1985, as if it was on some extraordinarily long fuse, it was finally detonated live.

Eldritch was personally ambivalent about the Warehouse. 'The drinks were more expensive [than the F Club] and the carpet wasn't sticky,' he says. Nevertheless, the DJs at the Warehouse played his records a lot. It was also the venue the Sisters of Mercy played the most in Leeds: five times in total, more than Brannigans, the Riley Smith, Tiffany's or the Tartan Bar.

The Warehouse was also one of the incubators of the new Leeds that merged the city and the university bands. It functioned as a melting pot in ways the F Club had not. Where portions of the F Club had stunk of glue, the dancefloor of the Warehouse reeked of amyl nitrate. Its American owner, Mike Wiand, courted West Yorkshire's devotees of electronic music, its Roxy/Bowie freaks, New Romantics and the punks for whom punk was clearly over and were looking for the next thing.

The other option for the Faversham crowd was Le Phonographique. This dive was loved by many, but not by Eldritch. 'I was not a citizen of the Phono,' he has stated, even taking issue with the pronunciation – 'faux-know': 'I know it shouldn't be, but it is.' If there was one place that typified the demarcation between Eldritch and his audience, it was here. In quasi-Charlie's Angels font, Le Phonographique promised 'Vin. Bière. Cuisine. Discotheque.' All were sort of true. There was food and alcohol for sale and there was dancing – on a tiny dancefloor with a mirrored pillar in the middle of it. There were also famously foul toilets, usually in some state of inundation. One of the DJs was Claire Shearsby – often in a 'Head and Star' T Shirt – proselytising with her playlist.

The Fav, the Warehouse and Le Phono therefore housed the core of the Sisters' audience in Leeds. Here was a coalition of overlapping tastes: punk rock, with the emphasis on 'rock'; those with a penchant for electronic and industrial music; vestigial traces of glam and heavy psych. In this post-F Club intersection of Le Phono, the Fav and the Warehouse, Northern Goth was born.

It did not recognise itself in the London version. When the Batcave Tour (Specimen, Alien Sex Fiend and Flesh for Lulu) arrived at the Warehouse on 19 May 1983, 'We went down in whatever brightly coloured clothing Claire could find for us,' remembers Jez Webb. 'Mark had a fetching orange paisley number, I remember. I wore a shirt with a Noddy print.'

This protest was part of a losing battle. The Batcave style – Halloween, vampires, whey-faces, *The Road Warrior*, bondage, and often something redolent of seventies KISS and LA glam metal – swept north, pulling northern scenes like Leeds' into more theatrical directions. Many went willingly. When Ben Farvak (future Salvation guitarist) arrived in Leeds from Lille in 1984, 'it was Rocky Horror.' Eldritch looked on aghast.

12

Seven Samurai

In late April 1983, the Sisters played their final gig in Leeds for more than a year, as part of a short tour supporting the Gun Club. Apart from festivals, this was one of the very last times the Sisters would ever be a support band. The pairing of the two groups made sense, although they sounded wildly different. Both ran unlikely elements of rock's heritage through the post-punk blender: American roots music in the Gun Club's case, stomping glam and hard rock in the Sisters'. They were both fronted by highly literate young men, who wrote superb lyrics and delivered them in idiosyncratic vocal styles.

The Sisters might not have been note perfect by the spring of 1983, but increasingly regular gigging had sharpened them up no end. The Sisters had indeed come a long way from the cock-ups and debacles that had spattered 1981 and 1982. At the Lyceum Ballroom in London with the Gun Club, 'everything seemed to click,' Eldritch has stated. The Sisters were the equals of the Gun

Club, themselves a ferocious live act. That iteration was: Dee Pop, Jim Duckworth, Patricia Morrison and Jeffrey Lee Pierce.

In most bands, Morrison would have been the most flamboyant: part Suzi Quatro, part Bride of Dracula. However, on this tour Pierce was looking like an amalgam of Debbie Harry and Marlon Brando and dressing like a transvestite deserter from the Vietnam War. The tour was the beginning of a six-year relationship between Eldritch and Morrison that would eventually transform the Sisters of Mercy and need lawyers to draw to a close.

At the Hacienda in Manchester, the Sisters contrived to look even more striking than either Pierce or Morrison. Even with the Hacienda's awful sightlines, 'it was obvious they were dragged up, wearing dresses and make-up,' says Andy Booth (a student at Leeds university, and future guitarist in the Cassandra Complex), who had gone back to his hometown for the gig. 'I'm pretty sure Eldritch was wearing a dress. Someone was wearing a suspender belt with stockings.' Even when they were dressed normally, Booth thought 'there was always something humorous about the Sisters. They were a bit cartoony . . . they had a smirk on their face about what they were doing, rather than being earnest musicians. They weren't the Clash, you know. It was obvious they had a sense of humour. Once you realised that, you were kind of in on the joke, but that didn't mean the music wasn't great and it wasn't a serious artistic endeavour. You got both. It was ironic.'

Nothing encapsulated this duality more than a new cover version the Sisters had brought on tour with them: 'Emma'. Hot Chocolate's version was already a slow-burning, sparse heartbreaker; the Sisters made theirs even slower, even sparer and even more of a tear-jerker. Their 'Emma' is incredibly moving, and yet such fun, even more perfectly camp than 'Jolene'; a masterpiece of artifice and exaggeration, yet deeply and truly emotional. It was often the high point of their sets for the next two years.

The visual identity of the band was also beginning to pull together, although a far cry from the more uniform presentation of 1984 and 1985. Marx recalls that 'on the third date of the Gun Club tour in Norwich, we were all getting ready in the tiny dressing-room and Andrew looked into the mirror and said, "Finally we look like a band."'

Marx explains further: 'When we started, it was still so close to the height of punk that I stubbornly stuck to that idea of avoiding what I saw as the trappings of rock stardom. The *Sounds* cover shot [in December 1982] gave a fair indication, with Andrew up front looking like Johnny Thunders and I'm behind him with a basin-cut and one of my dad's old cardigans. I soon got sick of looking like the village idiot and any principles got the squeeze.'

One of the reasons for Eldritch's approbation in Norwich was that it was one of the few times Marx wore sunglasses onstage. Eldritch was well practised at this, but Marx was not. 'I fell off the side,' he says. 'Thankfully it was only a very low riser.' Eldritch had also mastered the even trickier stage business of smoking in gloves.

The Gun Club tour also resulted in another of Marx's not infrequent, bloody, Sisters-related injuries. While out front watching the headliners in Newcastle, 'I felt this whack, as if someone had hit my arm with a mallet. Next thing I knew I was pouring with blood. The guy – who was nowhere to be seen – had broken a glass and jabbed it into my arm. I was whisked off to the hospital and for a while no one from the band knew what the hell had happened to me.'

Jez Webb recalls that the tour 'was a whole different ball game; the rock 'n' roll levels turned up a bit: me and Danny sleeping on Jeffrey Lee Pierce's hotel room floor and being woken by the great man offering us a breakfast swig from his Wild Turkey bottle.' Steve Watson, the Sisters' cranked-up driver, was also up for a challenge: the bands raced their vans from Norwich to Newcastle. 'They beat us by thirty seconds,' laments Adams.

In the middle of the Gun Club tour, the Sisters had a headlining date booked in the sports hall of Peterborough Technical College. Peterborough is an unremarkable city in the east of England then, as now, rarely visited by travelling rock bands. Hijinks and violence were in evidence in rapid succession during 'Floorshow'. The inner circle was full of fun but, like a street-gang, it also carried with it more than a whiff of aggression. Marx explains: 'Some of it was territorial, as the Yorkshire-based following took over a venue. Equally, there were aspects of the band's personalities that could be the trigger for it. Craig in particular had a very short fuse.'

'There was a throwback punk kid stood in the front of Andrew,' recalls Marx, 'who had some connection with a local band on the bill and had the big spiked hair and "The Exploited" or some such stencilled on his leather jacket.' The punk was staring too intently or mouthed something or spat – his exact infraction has been forgotten – but as Adams began 'Floorshow' the punk attempted to climb up on to the stage. Adams let go of his instrument, rushed forward and kicked him in the face. As the punk scurried off the stage, Adams carried on with 'Floorshow'. Justice had been swift: Adams had only missed one bar.

While Adams was still guarding the front of the stage and eye-balling the locals, Dave Beer and Ali Cooke ran onstage and shoved custard pies – paper plates full of shaving foam – onto the heads of Marx and Gunn. 'I think they were going to do Craig and Andrew as well,' recalls Marx, 'but sensed they weren't exactly in the mood.' Beer insists that, 'the custard pie thing came about because we couldn't find an ostrich.'

The high point of the British comedian Bernie Clifton's act was him cavorting in an orange ostrich costume which gave the impression he was riding the bird. 'We wanted one of them,' says Beer. 'The Sisters in the peak of the moment and we were going to Bernie Clifton across the back of the stage.'

Even without a giant bird costume, 'the gig had a definite mood shift,' Marx recalls. 'Craig played out of his skin for the rest of the show. Something clicked for Andrew as well.' For Marx too: always the boisterous performer, he ended the show sprawled on his back having slipped over in the remnants of the shaving foam.

The show was recorded on VHS video from a balcony at the rear of the sports hall. So too was its aftermath. The camera kept run-ning as the DJ played a King Sunny Adé track. 'The punk throw-back returned with his nose splattered,' remembers Marx. 'He had obviously rallied all these mates of his from the area.' After initially loitering backstage the Sisters and their inner circle soon had enough and decided to bring things to a head. 'The camera recorded us all coming out for the showdown,' says Marx.

'The Peterborough punks huffed and puffed a bit but ultimately turned and ran,' remembers Marx. 'We did look kind of magnificent. I use the word advisedly because it was more like those samurai or Western films. Shot from above with all of us walking through the frame at some point: Steve, Claire, Danny, Andrew, Dave and Ali, and Craig of course – all these special people.'

It was in moments like these – and the less charged ones on long journeys in vans, idling backstage, hanging around the pool table in the Fav or watching videos in Village Place – when being in and around the Sisters of Mercy went beyond music and comradeship. 'It was my first experiences in a band that made me realise what a family is supposed to be like,' Eldritch has said, 'and I thought it was good.'

Dave Beer felt the sense of belonging just as intensely. 'It was a family. We lived for it. I would have died for it without a doubt . . . I came from a one-parent family . . . My mum married a few times . . . I didn't have much of a family. I think I was quite dysfunctional.' Eldritch's own upbringing was more privileged, but he – for whatever reasons – was wont to agree with Sartre that: 'I loathed my childhood and everything to do with it.'

Peterborough was one of the last gigs in which Shearsby, in her role as sound engineer, was part of the inner circle on tour. 'When the Sisters got to a certain size, they were able to pay somebody, so Pete Turner took over from me,' she recalls. 'I did realise that maybe I wasn't, at that point, experienced enough as a sound engineer to do the band's sound justice. When "Wall of Pain" Pete came on the scene I got left behind a bit. I was quite sad about that. They went off touring and I got left. We'd still play pool in the Fav though. I remember vowing to gain the experience necessary, and maybe would be asked to work with them in the future.'*

Turner had been a sound engineer for nearly ten years by this point and had toured with Bad Manners, the Blues Band, Orange Juice and Aztec Camera. He was a seasoned pro and no one in the Sisters, not even Eldritch, encroached on his role. 'Andrew, bless him, the whole band just trusted me to do what I needed to do,' says Turner. 'We had such a good rapport.' Part of the understanding was that Turner should make the gig as loud as possible, hence his nickname. 'I prefer Wall of Sound,' Turner jokes, 'but yeah, it had to be loud. Red sound. That happened quite a lot . . . You don't get that excitement if it's not killing you.'

After touring with the Gun Club, the Sisters plugged more and more into the established touring circuit in Britain, including universities and polytechnics like those in Sheffield, Coventry, Kingston upon Thames and London. Yet there were still oddities: Solitaire in Swindon, which only a few people came to, and the Union Rowing Club in Nottingham, which was packed.

Another oddity was the Boscombe Academy on the south coast of England. 'The only people in the audience when we played there were a jazz funk band, a couple of widows, a retard and a dog,' Eldritch tastelessly recalled the following year. The band and crew had a day off in Bournemouth before the Boscombe gig. 'We all put some money in and bought a load of booze, to while away the hours,' explains Jez Webb. 'By the end we only had gin and Coke

---

* In 1985, Shearsby went on to do the sound for Salvation, then Ghost Dance and later for the Mekons on a tour of Europe. 'That was the best fun!' Shearsby says. 'It sounded really good,' Jon Langford remembers.

left. This became known as "Van Death Cocktail" and subsequently a favourite for Andrew on tour.'

The Sisters have a well-deserved reputation as a hard-living band but that needs qualifying. On 'a sliding scale Craig and Steve Watson were usually vying for top spot,' says Marx. Eldritch's consumption of speed 'was a sort of "little and often" approach,' adds Marx. 'By and large, there was a code of get the job done first – a discipline that came from Andrew and me.'

'Andrew called me "Captain" – it could have been a Sensible reference or it could be from . . . the Captains of Industry . . . I think it was mainly because I was organised and got things done, I could be relied upon to have my act together and take one for the team if need be. In that sense, I was something of an oddity in a rock band, as he was in his own way. Neither of us had much patience with people who got stoned – I would estimate ninety per cent of anyone I ever met in or around bands liked to skin up and get stoned. It was equally true of most of the people traveling anywhere with us.'

'As "Captain" [later to be rechristened "TC", Tour Coordinator] a good deal of the paperwork fell to me. I was the one booking vehicles and accounting, hanging on to the scribbled bits of paper with who'd spent what on fuel or whatever in the UK.'

At the University of London Union (ULU), the Smiths opened for the Sisters. 'Morrissey came into the dressing room and asked us to keep it down,' Dave Beer remembers. 'We were all there eating Kentucky . . . I just didn't get the Smiths then. We were throwing chicken bones at Morrissey as he went onstage with daffodils in his back pocket. "*You* keep it down, you cunt." We just got a bit hyper: Jack Daniel's, speed, chicken and sleep deprivation. He was ducking as me and Ali lobbed chicken bones at the back of his head.'

Another member of the God Squad also made his feelings clear to Morrissey in the backstage that evening. 'It was a shared dressing room – or the Smiths had to go through the Sisters' to get onstage, recalls Rik Benbow. 'Andy was laying down under the table sleeping and Morrissey pushed his feet out of the way. I smacked Morrissey in the mouth for doing it and told him to show a bit more respect.'

An important part of Eldritch's pre-gig routine had been disturbed. 'Before sound-check Andy would be quite friendly,' Benbow explains, 'but after he would go quiet for an hour, two hours before a show. In fact, very often he used to curl up under a table and sleep before a show and then crawl out, probably do some speed and get ready to go onstage . . . Like many frontmen and lead singers, he had to get into character. It was a kind of acting. He'd lie down as Andy Taylor having a kip under the table and emerge as Andrew Eldritch. When he came off stage he'd be very aloof, on his own, and shortly after that, he was back to his normal self.'

Backstage at ULU, Adams was 'running down the corridor with a pair of tights on his head,' recalls Webb, when he also encountered the Smiths' singer. 'Morrissey looked as unimpressed with this act as we had been with his live performance.' Marx's was the minority view: 'Coming on to the stage with all the flowers still scattered around – you definitely felt they'd left a calling-card.'

Johnny Marr, where perhaps his singer didn't, liked the Sisters, as performers and as confrères. 'They had an admirable attitude towards their audience, who they seemed to regard more like guests at a communal gathering than fans,' Marr concluded. 'Their attitude to support acts was admirable too . . . the Sisters and their crew went out of their way to make sure we were looked after, and I would occasionally spend time before we went on with their singer, Andrew Eldritch, who was very cool.'

At Sheffield Dingwalls, God Squad tribalism curtailed the Sisters' performance. Jez D'Netto recalls that a 'stand-off in the mosh-pit started in the middle of the gig between this punk and Chris Pugh. Chris is well over six foot and built like a brick shit-house. Why this punk had decided to have a go at Chris, I don't know. Dave Beer jumped on the back of this punk guy and a massive fight started. Eldritch went: "David Beer, I'm *very* disappointed in you." The Sisters walked off and didn't come back on.'* Beer did feel that with Eldritch, 'There is this element of the Headmaster.'

Of the songs they were already performing, there were no likely candidates for a new single. Something fresh had to be written and recorded. Marx offered two tracks of his that he had demoed: one was an instrumental nicknamed 'The Scottish One' because of its vaguely Celtic lead guitar riff, the other had verses and a chorus and was called 'Temple of Love'.

Eldritch had one guitar riff and no lyrics.

'Andrew was more concerned than I was about the exact nature of that release,' says Marx. 'We all knew it needed to be a more

---

* The early exit may well have been a relief to Marx. He played the gig in a pair of German jackboots he had borrowed from Steve Watson: 'beautiful boots, but the leather was far from supple . . . excruciatingly painful.'

obvious single, I just thought it needed to be catchy and direct, he believed it had to work at a very high tempo.'

Eldritch pulled rank and elected to turn his guitar riff into the single. Marx disagreed and they 'never really saw eye-to-eye again' until the recording was finished. 'We booked the studio with just a skeletal version of how it might be and Andrew's determination to make it work,' Marx continues. 'For the bulk of those sessions Craig and I let him get on with it and play with his gadgets.'

This time the Sisters were at Strawberry Studios in Stockport in Greater Manchester – '10cc's studio, very posh,' as Adams puts it. Neil Sedaka and Joy Division had also recorded there. Other evidence that the Sisters were moving up in the world was that 'we had a boarding house in Stockport and we'd get a cab to the studio,' recalls Adams. At KG, they had slept on the studio floor. This was also a new way of working for Eldritch: rather than piecing a track together as a demo or beating it into shape on the road, he was chasing an idea in the studio; it would become his modus operandi for most of the rest of his recording career.

'We spent longer than envisaged and moved across to the lesser of their two studios,' recalls Marx. 'There were quite long periods of experimentation with Andrew chaining up noise gates and delays to produce sequenced bass or whatever metronomic effect he thought was going to bring his flimsy idea to life.' Adams' abiding memories of his time at Strawberry are watching TV and playing pool downstairs. Every time he went back up to the studio he found 'nothing had happened, since I was last upstairs.' Eldritch seemed to be spending his entire time doing nothing other than EQing a snare drum.

Marx also thought Eldritch was wasting his time and suspected the track – now also called 'Temple of Love', but containing none of Marx's words or music – would be botched.

Eldritch returned to Village Place in the early hours one morning after finishing the mix on his own. He woke Marx up, placed a ghetto-blaster on the landing outside his first-floor room and cranked up the volume. All Marx's 'doubts were obliterated. Hearing the chorus kick in for the first time is one of the landmark moments of my life. Boy, did he gloat!'

'Temple of Love' was constructed as a 12-inch single, designed to run for nearly eight minutes. For many bands, the 12-inch was a padded-out extrapolation of the 7-inch, but this was purpose-built. Its roots were on the dancefloor in the extended plays of disco. Eldritch himself was rarely, if ever, seen dancing, and he loathed most nightclubs, but he understood his constituency: the kids who had emerged energised from punk and with their minds and ears opened by post-punk, still loved to get down. Having a DJ for a girlfriend would have clarified this for him, if there was any doubt.

'Temple of Love' contains an utterly golden riff, a thumping chorus and a cynical torrent of lyrics: it is an anti-love song wrapped inside an enigma inside a gargantuan Eldritch production, his finest work behind the desk to date. Fast, furious, danceable, 'Temple of Love' guaranteed that the Sisters' days as a small-time indie band would soon be over. It was obviously going to be their biggest hit so far.*

---

* Eldritch's guitar riff became the verse of 'Temple of Love'. The origin of the music for the chorus is disputed between Adams and Eldritch. Eldritch is the sole credited writer.

'Heartland' – faster and more cavernous than the Jensen version – and 'Gimme Shelter' completed the 12-inch single. 'Heartland' is also peak Sisters. It plays with minimalism and repetition to the same degree as *The Reptile House*. Rooted in a motorik drum groove, it's Adams at his most economical – his down-stroke bass simply shifting up an octave is absolutely key – and Eldritch intoning the title over and over again, in lieu of a chorus. Yet, for a song that trades in monotony, 'Heartland' has great beauty and drama, especially Marx's interlacing guitar lines, variants of which are played ever higher and with extra vibrato – in lieu of a guitar solo. Eldritch's lyrics seem to salute his West Yorkshire following and his need for speed, two of the key ingredients enabling his will to power.

Marx was initially against recording 'Gimme Shelter'. 'The rest of the band out-voted me,' he says. 'I'm glad I went along with the decision to commit it to tape because that 12-inch . . . is probably as good as Andrew ever got us to sound on record. It is one of the tracks which reminds me most of Andrew's Bowie fetish. The way the multi-tracked vocals sound is very reminiscent of the *Diamond Dogs* album for me – no bad thing.'

'I hear the Stones version of the track now on the radio or TV and love the fact that ours is so removed from it. This is where all that "band-by-default" stuff paid off – Andrew could have hooked up with Tony James, Brian James or Sidney-fucking-James back when they came a-knocking and I know they'd have put together this shitty copy-cat Keef version of it.'

It seems that Tony James was not the only one looking to recruit Eldritch into a band he was forming. The Lords of the New

Church, Brian James' band after the Damned, 'had just surfaced and attracted a bit of attention,' Marx explains. He has a (vague) memory that 'Andrew turned to me and said something like, "I can't believe he's gone for that junkie piece of shit, [referring to their singer Stiv Bators]. I'm glad I wasn't interested. Does he really think I'm like *that*!?"'

When they left Strawberry, the Sisters of Mercy had very little material left over. 'There was never any danger of being labelled prolific,' admits Marx. Left to wither on the vine along with 'Good Things' were 'Burn It Down', which provided lyrics for the backwards section of 'Burn', and 'Driver', some of the lyrics of which got shunted over into 'Heartland'. 'I really liked "Driver" or parts of it at least,' says Marx, 'but Andrew never made any real claim for it to be considered.'

'The track that didn't surface which could have easily had a seat at the top-table was called "Dead and American". I really loved it and nagged the hell out of Andrew to finish it. The problem was that it was the nearest we ever came to doing something that you could say had a groove. Suddenly all these two-bob indie funk bands came through. We must have decided to distance ourselves from that trend. The main chanted chorus line was this staccato, ". . .two wings meet the mountain I'm dead and American twen-ty-one . . ."'

To all intents and purposes, the Sisters of Mercy had no new songs to draw on. The consequences of this lack of material were a year in the future, but in the summer of 1983 the Sisters of Mercy were still super-powered by the white heat of Andrew Eldritch's first great burst of creativity.

13

The Western Allies

Before 'Temple of Love' was released, the Sisters of Mercy played in Europe for the first time. They headlined the final night of Parkingang, a well-funded alternative arts and music festival in Ancona in late July 1983.

'It had the feel of a holiday,' recalls Marx 'because it was just one gig with a few days' stay.' Jez Webb, Danny Horigan and various members of the God Squad certainly approached it in the time-honoured fashion of young British men on a European summer holiday: an excess of sun and booze. En route to Ancona 'we started to get stuck into our duty free: Blue Label Smirnoff, one bottle each,' Webb explains. 'The train journey was my down-fall. Feeling sick, I went to put my head out of the window, but at that same time a train came the other way. I was forced back in and regrettably threw up . . . Everybody was so comatose, they slept through it and awoke to the horrific scene later. I think I nearly got away with it.'

One of those vomited over was Craig Adams. He had not brought a change of clothes with him. While others were out enjoying the beaches and the bars, he was stuck in his room washing his clothes and waiting for them to dry. 'I never went out because I was covered in puke!' is his summary of his first day in Ancona.

'The gig in a central plaza was awful, but the trip was memorable,' in Marx's opinion. 'Ben took his expensive camera, which I managed to drop in the sea. I then trod on several sea urchins and spent the next few days almost crippled, walking around in my brothel creepers with the skin around the spines getting more and more infected.'*

Band and crew were accommodated in decent apartments in Ancona and the festival organisers spent a lot of time 'running around on scooters looking after us,' recalls Horigan, but were nonplussed when asked to procure some speed. 'We might as well have asked them for heroin.'

After Ancona, there was a sleeper train through the Alps and onward to Belgium. 'Me and Andrew ended up sharing a cabin with a young couple, newly-weds,' Webb says. 'Andrew insisted on keeping a light on. His nocturnal ways would keep them up most of the night. I did see their hands reach across to each other a few times: "What have we got ourselves caught up in?"'

A few days after Ancona, the Sisters played outdoors in another square in another European city. The Mallemunt festival in Brussels

---

* The gig was in the most beautiful square in Ancona, the Piazza del Papa (otherwise known as the Piazza del Plebiscito). The eighteenth-century baroque Chiesa di San Domenico and a large statue of Pope Clement VII faced the band as they played.

degenerated into one of the most notorious episodes in early Sisters' history.

On arrival in Brussels, many of the Sisters' following managed 'to locate a bar next to a tattoo parlour which served incredibly strong beer,' says Marx. 'For whatever reason, some locals got involved in a couple of messy scraps with our lot that boiled over into the day of the gig.'

The gig itself had problems. Other than being in broad daylight and in a downtown shopping district, 'We had a power spike just before we started and the drum machine wiped,' remembers Adams. 'So Ben had to get the master book out and program the drums from scratch.' By this point Gunn had taken over 'those drum minder duties but he didn't cope well with the pressure,' Marx believes. 'By then we were using a more sophisticated machine. When he made a mess of things . . . Andrew tore into him and Ben became ever more anxious.'

In Brussels 'Ben kept messing up with starting the drums and got us all wound up,' Marx adds. The Doktor even blurted out repeatedly during the very solemn and lengthy introduction in Flemish the band were being given. There were further technical issues. Eldritch immediately complained about the sound mix and then Adams' only pedal broke. 'The pedal's fucked. That's Belgian for "fucked", by the way,' observed Eldritch. 'I don't think the state of my foot was helping either,' adds Marx. Eldritch, no Francophile, introduced 'Emma' in perfect, English-accented French: 'Il y a quelqu'un ici qui se souvient de Hot Chocolate?' afterwards summing up his own and the band's performance with 'Errol Brown, eat your heart out.'

The gig then descended into a bad parody of Altamont. Several of the travelling contingent climbed into a large water fountain in the square. 'Who in their right mind puts a fountain directly in front of the stage?' Rik Benbow still wonders. 'It was crying out . . . It wasn't until we'd thrown ourselves in half a dozen times and were dancing around, that the police came along.' As the Sisters began 'Gimme Shelter', police vans entered the square.

The police were still looking for troublemakers after the gig. 'We tried to get away but we were a bunch of wet English people in a crowd of dry people,' says Benbow. The police tracked them down in a side-street where the Sisters were in the middle of a photo shoot. 'We all got kind of arrested,' says Benbow, the band along with dripping wet God Squad members.

'The photographs with me, Danny and Jez grinning as we are being herded into the meat-wagon took pride of place in my house for many years,' says Marx. The Sisters were let out of the van without charge. The sodden were driven away. Benbow woke up in a cell, naked, shivering and still wet. 'Our clothes were handed back to us in plastic bags . . . None of us were charged either,' he stresses.

Brussels, unlike Ancona, provided the Sisters with a proper bridgehead into Europe and a vital long-term ally. The band had been booked to play at Mallemunt by Herman Schueremans. Although his surname is not pronounced 'like those tanks in World War Two,' he explains, Schueremans is nevertheless referred to by many Anglophones in the music business as 'Herman Sherman'. Eldritch, who is quite capable of correct Flemish, has affectionately referred to him as 'HermanShermanHe'sNotGerman.'

At the time of Mallemunt, Schueremans was part of a concerted effort to put Belgium on the map for international rock acts, especially those that were part of the great wave that punk unleashed. 'The key was to pick up-and-coming bands when they were small and still had a lot of time to come to Belgium,' Schueremans says. The Sisters became a prime example of a band that 'grew up and stayed loyal. When you do something good for them when they are small, they have a memory like an elephant's.' Indeed, in Eldritch's hierarchy of strangers who have showed him kindness, Schueremans is near the top, along with Duncan Kilburn, Ken Giles and Pete Turner. 'I feel very good about that,' Schueremans comments.

By the fountain on the Muntplein, the Sisters played for the first time in what would become one of their continental European heartlands; if there is an overseas equivalent of West Yorkshire, then it is Brussels and Flanders.* '*De zwarte jassen* – the guys in the black jackets,' as Schueremans calls them, developed a special affinity for the Sisters. The band would return to Belgium for gigs booked or promoted by Schueremans twice in both 1984 and 1985.

The day after Mallemunt, the young couple from the sleeper train found themselves, to their horror, travelling with the Sisters on the coach from Brussels to London. This was stopped at the France-Belgium border and, after one look at the Sisters and their coterie by customs officials, searched for drugs. The couple complained loudly to anyone on the coach who would listen how the Sisters of Mercy had ruined their entire journey from Milan to London.

In the week after Brussels, the Sisters played two gigs the same

---

* In Eldritch's recollection, the Sisters played in Belgium before they played in London. This was not the case, but the Sisters were embraced much more warmly there (and in the Netherlands and West Germany) than they were in many parts of the UK.

night in London. The first was supporting the Virgin Prunes at the Electric Ballroom, the second was a headline show at the Camden Palace. 'It was a brilliant night because we hammered out one set and then went on . . . marching down the road taking our audience with us Pied Piper-style to the next gig,' Marx says. Benbow remembers that 'there was no guest list at the Camden Palace, so the Sisters had twenty or thirty "roadies" that night. Instead of putting the gear into the van, each person was carrying a little bit down the street: an amp between two people; someone had a guitar; someone else had the guitar case.'

Waiting for the band in the Music Machine (as many still referred to the Camden Palace) was Howard Thompson, along with his friend Ruth Polsky.

Polsky channelled alternative UK bands into the US in her role as the booker for Danceteria, a multi-floor club and venue in midtown Manhattan. Polsky was an extremely articulate Anglophile, who would regularly come to the UK to meet bands who were being covered in the UK music press and offer them gigs at Danceteria and sometimes fix up mini tours for them within striking distance from New York. She especially liked what she termed the 'doom glam' bands. She had lined up a series of NYC and East Coast dates for the Sisters.[*]

---

[*] Eldritch had already met Polsky by this point. He had stayed in New York City in July 1983 during the New Music Seminar, a conference and festival held each summer. That trip had further consolidated the Sisters' support network on the East Coast. Eldritch deemed the visit sufficiently important to miss a John Cale concert at the Venue in London. Eldritch's admiration of former members of the Velvet Underground had strict limits though. Just before his departure for the US, Eldritch lamented to an interviewer that he could not find a buyer for his Cale ticket – and referred to Lou Reed as 'a boring old twat.'

Not all bands got on with Polsky – the Smiths famously did not – but the Sisters liked and valued her enormously. Adams became good friends with her and, according to Howard Thompson, 'one of her favourite people was Andrew Eldritch.' Polsky photographed him backstage at the Camden Palace, grinning, barefaced, making the Devil horns, Thompson next to him wearing his sunglasses. This is one of the least iconic photos of Eldritch in circulation. The next year, Polsky would take one of the most indelible.

Before heading to the US, the Sisters began their first proper tour of Europe: Trans-Europe Excess. The pun could be on the title of the Kraftwerk album, but with Eldritch's taste for European art cinema, it could just as easily have been the Alain Robbe-Grillet film. Any tour, especially one out of the country, had to be short, so not too many dole signing-on days were missed. Adams remembers telling the DHSS that he was going 'camping in Wales' in order to allay their suspicions.

The Sisters' first European tour naturally did not pass without incident. Before the show at the Paradiso in Amsterdam, 'Mark unwittingly ate a hash pizza,' says Webb. Marx remembers the 'tight spiral staircase in and out of the dressing-room. I know this because I fell down it at the height of my post-pizza wooziness . . . as I tried to go back for the encore. Prior to that I had just enjoyed all the warm glow and giggles you'd expect.' During the encore a semi-incapacitated Marx 'fell down a gap in the stage,' remembers Webb. 'He was left there for a while because it looked like it was just one of his moves gone a bit wrong.'

'Also at that gig, there was a guy in the RAF stationed out in Germany, who came to quite a few Euro shows,' Webb says. 'Craig asked him to go and buy some hash for us, gave him the money and off he went. He returned later, looking reasonably stoned, with a nice bit of "black." On close inspection it was a piece of rubber, obviously not what he'd sampled. He was soon brought out of his stoned stupor by a shouty Craig.'

Neither crew, nor God Squad and other sundry followers, had accommodation on European tours. They were reliant on the kindness of strangers. Merb remembers 'a top gig in Hamburg followed by a stay in a disused fish factory' arranged by local Sisters fans. Any offer of a floor or a bed was gratefully received. 'Copping off' was therefore multi-functional.

A shortage of cash and hunger were also the mother of invention: 'To get some money to eat, me and Jez did this busking thing in Amsterdam,' Benbow recalls. 'Jez used to be able to turn his feet round. He'd be standing looking one way, but his feet were pointing in the other direction. And I used to do the chain trick . . . and then we'd pass the hat around. We actually made quite a few guilders; fed all of us travelling together.'

Stamina was tested but spirits were high. Before the show at the Odeon in Münster, Merb and other fans locked themselves 'in the cellar dressing room and competed to be dunked into buckets of beer.' Münster also featured one of the first demonstrations of Benbow's signature acrobatics. He was swinging from the ceiling of the Odeon 'when Mark climbed up the PA and handed me his guitar. So I had the guitar in one hand and was hanging by the other.' Benbow then flipped upside-down, hung by his feet and played Marx's guitar, 'just bashing the strings more or less.' The Odeon also featured a rare instance of the Sisters allowing a fan,

Mekons-style, onto the stage to perform. With Eldritch AWOL for the encore, the fan managed a verse of 'Ghost Rider' before the band called it a night.

Horigan and Webb had official duties to perform but only one could fit in the van (so they were informed by Eldritch), so they shared an Interrail pass between them. Getting to and from stations and gigs, waiting for trains, regularly sleeping on platforms – often simply not sleeping – made roadying for the Sisters in Europe tough work.

Benbow and Merb also had Interrail passes, which they got by collecting vouchers from the back of washing powder packets. The rest of the God Squad usually relied on hitchhiking. Since this was forbidden through East Germany, most of the travelling faithful were ruled out of the Sisters' gig at the Loft in West Berlin. Benbow was the only one of the God Squad to get there. On arrival at the venue, he went straight up to the dressing room and was met by Eldritch with an offer he could not refuse: German speed pills. 'We had a couple and we went: "These are shit." So we had another couple. The band went onstage and then they all kicked in. *Really* powerful stuff.' Even in an altered state, it was still obvious to Benbow 'that quite a few in the audience had pet rats on their shoulders.' Adams, suffering from 'horrendous food poisoning' at the time observed that 'the rats were also on the stage just walking about!' In the middle of the Sisters' set a small pre-teen German punk with a Mohican (and also transporting a rodent) took a shortcut across the stage past Eldritch. With a brief pause for effect, Eldritch informed the crowd: 'That's my manager.'

Benbow had to assist with a piece of subterfuge after the gig during the load-out. A woman connected to the Loft – and 'notorious for chasing singers' according to Adams – had taken a shine to Eldritch. 'He was desperately trying to get away,' Benbow recalls. 'In the end, we carried him out in a flight case and put it in the van. She came and stood outside waiting to collar him, so we couldn't let him out [the flight case]. We had to shut the doors of the van and drive off round to the hotel and let him out there.'

Eldritch freed, the group found the staff at the hotel's reception less than welcoming, chuntering about the tour party among themselves. 'They didn't know that Andy spoke fluent German,' Benbow explains. 'He understood every word this bloke was saying about us "dirty English punk scum."' When Eldritch asked for the keys in excellent German, 'that shut them right up.'

Accompanying the band as driver and tour manager on Trans-Europe Excess was Martin Docherty. The Sisters had encountered him several times when he was running gigs for the promoter John Curd at various London venues, including the Lyceum and the Electric Ballroom. Docherty's main appeal was that he was a known entity and liked to drive, which fit well with his minimal interest in drinking. However, Adams observes, 'Martin was not good on his "left/right" skills. If Andy said "take a left", Martin could easily go right . . . or straight on.'

The morning after the gig at the Loft, Docherty had to drive the band out of West Berlin back into East Germany. 'Andrew was in the passenger seat,' Docherty recalls. 'The border guard checking the passports looked at Andrew, trying to work out if it was him.' This was difficult since Eldritch, as usual, was in sunglasses. 'The guard indicated to him to remove his sunglasses.' Eldritch in turn indicated that he didn't wish to do so. The East German border guard, clearly unused to having his authority questioned, immediately shouldered his rifle and aimed it directly at Eldritch's head. 'Andrew took his sunglasses off faster than I've seen anyone take their sunglasses off. Ever,' Docherty remembers.

On arrival at the Kir Club in Hamburg, Docherty and the band discovered the city was strangely quiet. This was not simply because the gig was in Poppenbüttel, a leafy and residential suburb in the far north of Hamburg, but because 'the Germans were thinking World War Three was about to break out,' Docherty says. One of the worst crises of the Cold War since the Cuban Missile Crisis had just begun: a Korean Air Lines flight from New York to Seoul had been shot down by a Soviet fighter, killing all 269 people on board, including an American congressman.

Eldritch was not averse to the idea of imminent nuclear Armageddon. In fact, he found 'the gesture of total atomic oblivion wonderfully fascinating and attractive: I know that when the balloon goes up, it's going to look really good, and it's going to make a noise like you've never heard.' He was evidently upbeat during the gig, engaging the crowd in German and English, including introducing 'Gimme Shelter' with, 'OK hippies, here it comes.' Gunn – in a rare turn at the mic – stuck with English: 'The next person who chucks a fucking bottle gets his head kicked in,' he announced after 'Kiss the Carpet'. Eldritch did not usually welcome projectiles being hurled at the stage, but two days later he told a German interviewer that sometimes 'tension sets the right mood' ('*Spannung macht Stimmung*').

Less than a week after Trans-Europe Excess, the Sisters of Mercy paid their first visit to the USA. Waiting for the band at JFK was John Hanti, whose company, SST, offered a combination of tour management and backline rental, with him as the sound engineer and driver. Hanti's time in rock 'n' roll spanned two decades: a pro musician in Pennsylvania, club owner in Florida (until the mob muscled in) and then a mover and shaker in New York. He had co-founded the cassette-only label, ROIR, which had already put out music by Suicide, Television, Nico, James Chance and the Contortions, and the Dictators by the time the Sisters arrived in the city.

Hanti drove the Sisters to their gigs in Philadelphia, Trenton, Washington DC and Boston. At the East Side Club in Philadelphia, the Sisters pulled in enough of a crowd for the promoter, Bobby Startup, to book them for a second night. Startup thought Eldritch was 'a really good guy . . . he got this diagnosis as a nasty person, but he wasn't. He was just so *serious* about his music.' The East Side Club was also the gig at which Adams first met Lisa Levine, who became his girlfriend. She found Adams as 'adorable' as his Yorkshire accent was impenetrable.

In DC, at the 9:30 Club, the Sisters also played twice: an evening and a late show. Afterwards, Hanti freaked out everyone in the van by careening through a back alley, splattering rats. Adams remembers Gunn crimping his hair in 'this shitty DC hotel room before the show' and resting his crimping irons on the hotel room Bible. 'And when we came back the Bible had all burned.'

Ruth Polsky also put the Sisters on twice at Danceteria. She was clearly not the only one with a thing for doom glam. Yet, reviews of the US shows varied wildly. One observed that the Sisters were 'painfully close to the heavy metal end of things when they dirge out . . . his Morrison meets Moses voice thoroughly cloaks the band's slower stuff as completely as clouds of dry ice hide the rest of the stage. Yep, dry ice – and green lighting and leather trousers and shades and haircuts.' The same reviewer called Eldritch 'a skinny little weasel.' Another reviewer was plainly enraptured by the 'slight, dark figure . . . with finely-chiselled nose and chin, eyes concealed by glowing mirror-frames and a mop of onyx hair. His lithe, snaky, black-gloved hands wrap around the mike stand . . . His shoulders slip from side to side as he pulls the mike stand back and forth around his wiry form, his bony hips pumping seductively like some uncontrollable piston.'

During one of the Danceteria shows the Sisters heard some of their West Yorkshire in-jokes and catchphrases – including 'dobber fella' – being shouted out from the audience in the lulls between songs. 'Of course we found this hilarious and curiosity led us to seek out the person responsible,' says Marx. This was Bryan 'Brain Damage' Christian, 'who let us in on the joke, that his old pal Scott (Ackroyd from Harrogate) had once lived in NYC and had rung him and set it up.' Christian lived up to his nickname: 'Some of his late-night driving though Manhattan was straight out of *Mad Max,*' Marx observes.

Gigs only took up a small portion of the band's time in the US, leaving plenty of opportunity for recreation. Adams remembers 'being sat with Ruth and Andy in Danceteria and she asked, "Do you want a line of coke?" And we were like: "Have you got any speed?" We were cheap, man.'

'Ruth was plugged into the scene; you could go places with her and bypass some of the nonsense,' recalls Marx. 'She was used to dealing with English bands and seemed to like our "Northern thing" . . . I suspect we drove her mad . . . Craig and I weren't overly concerned with the dangers inherent in running wild in a city like that. She was all too aware.'

Eldritch was too: he refused to use the subway and walked anywhere he needed to go. Howard Thompson also gave the band instructions on how to be safely mugged at knifepoint. 'Don't fight back' was the gist of it, recalls Adams. In New York, Adams 'didn't actually go out much anyway.' There were two reasons: 'You could get beer delivered', and Lisa Levine had travelled from DC.

Ben Gunn's time in the Sisters was coming to an end. He hated the American tour. 'Ben's reaction to the US was markedly different from everyone else's,' believes Marx. 'He got worked up about the poverty we saw on our travels. We'd asked to go "sight-seeing" through some of the boroughs and it all got a bit "cheap holidays in other people's misery" for Ben.' Also, being in a band and under twenty-one in the USA could be ignominious. Not only could Gunn not drink in the clubs, he could barely get through the door. Adams recalls that, 'Ben had to sit in the van and be pulled out just before we went on and had to go straight back out again after the show had finished.'

The end point of Gunn's time in the Sisters was triggered when 'Ben delivered an ultimatum demanding more of a role within the band,' according to Marx. 'We didn't really appreciate being presented with ultimatums.' The second of the Danceteria shows was Ben Gunn's last gig in the Sisters of Mercy.

'As to Ben's role and importance, history will show he's there on the best records and all those fantastic gigs,' Marx explains. 'While not exactly being central, he was certainly crucial. In much the same way that my chief contribution was by virtue of not being Andrew, Ben was not any of us.'

'It must have seemed like a meteoric rise for him. A lot happened in a much shorter space of time and the band's stock just kept rising once we had that Indie Chart presence up there with the Smiths and New Order. He was a nerdy school kid suddenly on the front cover of magazines . . . it meant he was understandably very up, a cheery presence . . . Ben brought an innocence to the group.'

A year after his departure, Gunn explained that his exit was due to 'personal differences . . . general band policies, which are obviously derived from one member, began to stink. They were always taking the piss out of the system, which was why I was in the band, until they started taking themselves seriously. Now they're no better than anyone else. Worse, in fact. They're just not funny any more. So I got out . . . I've received no money whatsoever. I'm owed hundreds of pounds and intend suing them shortly.' 'He tried to get all legal with us lot with a local lawyer,' Adams remembers. His reaction at the time was: '"He's trying to get money out of Andrew: *that* ain't gonna work!"'

The Sisters still had a trio of dates booked for October 1983, which they played as a three-piece. With a beard. Eldritch had grown one and dyed it black as he did his hair and eyebrows. In his leather jacket, aviator shades and gloves, he resembled the louche – and probably sexually sadistic – leader of a biker gang in a Roger Corman exploitation film.

'The shows were actually great with the three of us,' remembers Marx. 'I knew I was going to be more exposed as a guitarist but by then it wasn't quite the problem it would have been in '82.' Stockholm was first and after that the Sisters had two dates in California. 'The idea to carry on and do the few shows we'd got booked in the autumn may have been partly to do with whatever relationship was going on between Andrew and Patricia Morrison,' suggests Marx.

The Sisters certainly travelled cheaply to America. 'We didn't even have guitar cases,' says Adams. 'You had a guitar in a plastic bag with your cable, fuzz box and your other cable. That's how we landed in Los Angeles.'

That Eldritch was able to spend time with Morrison 'was a source of some resentment for me and Craig,' states Marx. 'He got to stay with her and hang out with her circle in LA while we were holed up in a crappy single room in the Tropicana Motel, living on next to nothing for a week.'

John Hanti was back on duty with the band on the West Coast. His role enlarged to include that of Eldritch's driving instructor. 'Andrew and I used to go down to an arcade . . . I can't tell you how many quarters him and I put through a cart race game. And that's when I said to him: "Andrew, you love driving so much, let's go." I took them to Disneyland and put Andrew in one of those self-drive little motor cars. He was out there with all those little kids in Disneyland in this go-kart.'

The Los Angeles show was promoted by Gary Tovar whose lucrative marijuana smuggling business was subsidising punk and new wave in Southern California. Tovar put the Sisters on in the mezzanine of the gargantuan but utterly dilapidated Alexandria Hotel, once luxurious then stranded in a part of downtown LA abandoned to the homeless, the drug-addicted and the criminal. 'It was a no-go area,' remembers Adams.

That mixture of ornate grandeur, sleazy decrepitude and hard-edged rock 'n' roll was perfect for the Sisters. As Iggy and MC5 connoisseurs, they were well aware of the Grande Ballroom and the Michigan Palace, the latter where the Stooges met their ignominious and violent end (as recorded on the live album *Metallic K.O.*) fleeing the stage under a barrage of projectiles. At the Alexandria Hotel, the Sisters came closer to an LA re-enactment of that event than they intended.

'The promoter had put out folding seats,' Adams recalls. 'Well, that didn't last long.'

'People in Los Angeles have no legs – too many cars,' Eldritch told the sedentary audience early on. However, what really got them stirred up was the huge delay after Adams broke a string. Marx played a long version of 'Ghost Riders in the Sky' in an attempt to occupy the restless crowd, while Eldritch continued with his variation on a theme: 'You know you can get bed sores if you stay there too long,' he announced.

The chairs met their fate shortly after. 'Anybody got any more furniture? I just stand here like a lemon,' Eldritch observed. Marx, ever the good cop, then began playing 'Yankee Doodle Dandy' in an attempt to keep the peace. 'I'm perfectly happy with the number of teeth I've got, thanks,' Eldritch dryly informed the crowd. 'One less would not be very good for me, so that's the last chair I'm going to accept up here.'

To make matters worse, the band then made such a mess of 'Temple of Love' they couldn't complete it, either because they were unnerved, or because it was so hard to execute. The crowd again made its opinion known. 'We're going to try again when this frank exchange of views has finished,' Eldritch announced. 'Maybe we should tell you some leper jokes, like we did in Boston. Are there any lepers in the house?' Even when the band got their act together, Eldritch still couldn't resist riling the audience further: 'So this is what sunshine does to you, huh?' he told them. 'I think that I can live without it.'

The show at the I-Beam in San Francisco was two days later, at Halloween. 'We had to judge a fancy-dress competition after we finished the set,' Marx recalls. 'There was a woman naked apart from three very small pieces of sticky tape and a great Jackie O, complete with butcher's shop brains, all over her jacket. Andrew had to do his game-show host bit.' Andrea Ross (who performs as Angel Corpus Christi) was in the crowd that night and recalls that, 'The costume that the band voted number one that night was a kid with a cardboard TV on his head. His was the lamest costume.'

After the I-Beam, the band were tipped off to a house party being held for Joe Jackson, then a sizeable star in the US thanks to his Grammy-nominated single, 'Steppin' Out'. On their arrival, in no way did the Sisters of Mercy look like invited guests, more like Charles Manson and his sweaty Droogs. They were met with a mixture of appalled silence and genuine horror. Their excellent manners only made them more unnerving. The cost of getting rid of them was cheap and easily negotiated: cold beer from the fridge.

After San Francisco, and with the money saved on Gunn's

airfare, the Sisters went on holiday. They hired a station wagon and went on a road trip that included Reno, Las Vegas and Death Valley. John Hanti had offered to do all the driving, but because their rental vehicle 'was an automatic and had cruise-control, Andrew insisted on taking the wheel on the long straight roads, despite the fact he didn't drive at the time,' Marx explains.

'He drove almost all the way from San Francisco to Las Vegas,' says Hanti. 'Those three days . . . were gloriously fun days, in which they really came out of being a band and enjoyed being kids again.' Adams recalls the trip less fondly: 'We couldn't afford to do anything. I kept getting carded all the time. We had to get our passports out constantly.' To save money they stayed in Reno [at Circus Circus] not Las Vegas. 'If you filled the car up you got vouchers to spend,' Adams recalls. 'I also bought forged drink tickets in the casino.'

The year 1983 had brought extraordinary changes for the Sisters. If Eldritch had a master plan, it had worked brilliantly, but it also contained a paradox. 'Of course at the heart of this master plan was the decision to invite two people along who had no interest or desire to be governed by anyone's over-arching strategy,' says Marx. 'How's that for planning? How should we interpret that?'

In late 1983, the Sisters of Mercy were in peak condition. They had had a Number 1 single in the UK Indie Charts and major record labels were sniffing around looking to make a deal. The twelve months from 'Alice' to 'Temple of Love' contained one of the great runs of singles by any post-punk band and is the bedrock of the Sisters' reputation and longevity. It was an astonishing time, even for those in the eye of the storm.

'I suppose the clearest memories I have of being aware of how special the band were becoming,' remembers Marx, 'were on the occasions I left the stage early during the last number. I would sometimes run around to the back of the hall to stand and watch, having left my battered guitar feeding back while the other three carried on with "Sister Ray" or whatever number it happened to be . . . There was something about the way it looked, as well as how it sounded. The casual destruction brought to mind the footage you see of kids playing in the bombed-out ruins of a city; a scene of devastation but the children treat it as if it's completely natural, almost like they've been waiting for the buildings to topple all along.'

It would be another five months before they played live again, and another eight before they released a record. The band that re-emerged scaled new heights; it also rapidly initiated its own death march.

14

New Skin for the Old Ceremony

'Ben's leaving was really just another in a line of similar departures, so nothing we felt threatened by,' Marx explains. The Sisters were in no rush to find a replacement, but Gunn's spot in the band remained vacant for less than a month. Unlike all the other previous fourth members – Tom Ashton, Dave Humphrey, Jon Langford – Ben Gunn's replacement was not found in the Leeds post-punk scene. This time, Liverpool filled the gap.

Wayne Hussey was a seasoned musician, who had toiled away behind charismatic frontmen in the Ded Byrds (aka. the Walkie Talkies), Hambi & the Dance and Dead or Alive. None of them had taken him to the land of milk and honey. Hussey had scented, but never experienced, success.

The matchmaker between him and the Sisters was Annie Roseberry, A&R at CBS. She had been courting the Sisters and knew Hussey didn't have a band. The Sisters were not really on

Hussey's radar. '"Alice" and "Floorshow", I recognised from club nights at Planet X in Liverpool,' he says, but the rest of the Sisters' material was unknown to him. 'I was more of a pop boy.' His dream job would have been the guitarist in the Teardrop Explodes 'but that offer wasn't forthcoming,' so his response to Roseberry was: 'I don't really know that much about them, but give the guy my number.'

'Have I got a guitar player for you!' was the gist of her pitch to Eldritch, according to him. Marx remembers 'getting this Dead or Alive single sent to us. I suspect it was just to show us roughly what he looked like on the cover.' Marx's overall impression was 'Robert Smith lite' which was neither ideal, nor off-putting.

As ambitious as Hussey was, he was also an opportunist and a pragmatist: he took the bait and went to Leeds to meet the Sisters. Hussey was driven to Village Place by his friend Kenny Dawick, who was a DJ at Planet X. Hussey's immediate reaction was that he was at the wrong address because Number 7 'was completely blacked out.'

Hussey's induction began in the sitting room. Tea was drunk. Cigarettes were smoked. Amphetamine was taken. Adams, unlike Marx, 'didn't know what Wayne looked like' so when he arrived – while Hussey was upstairs having a pee because of all the tea – he spent several minutes in the murky living room quizzing Dawick about his experience as a guitar player and his suitability for the Sisters. He was shocked to find it was virtually nil. When Hussey returned to the living room and was correctly identified to Adams, 'We got on instantly,' Adams recalls. 'We left Andrew and Mark and went to the pub. Apparently, I asked Wayne to lend me a fiver.' A long-lasting friendship and musical partnership was born.

Before leaving Village Place, Hussey had been given 'a pile of Sisters' records', including 'Temple Of Love'. Hussey liked that song, but it was 'Gimme Shelter', that piqued his interest the most. As for the rest of the Sisters' catalogue, 'I wasn't blown away to be honest,' he admits. Nevertheless, he quickly made his mind up that he wanted to join. 'In Dead or Alive, all the guitar lines I was coming up with were being put in a sequencer,' Hussey remembers. 'In my own mind, I was a guitar player and it would have been good to be in a band where the guitar was the principal instrument.'

The prospect of regular touring, something he had never done in Dead or Alive, was also very attractive. 'I'd see my mates in Teardrops and Bunnymen and the Lotus Eaters go off on tour,' Hussey says. 'They had their names on flight cases. "I want to do that!"'

Eldritch phoned and offered him the job the next day.

In autumn 1983, when Hussey first met the Sisters, Andy Taylor had, to all intents and purposes, metamorphosed into Andrew Eldritch. 'I only ever knew Andrew Eldritch,' states Hussey. 'By the time I joined the group he was the same person off stage as he was on. I never met Andy Taylor. The persona was already all in place.'

Marx also recognises this change. 'That's one of the more interesting things I've heard credited to Wayne. I probably saw the old Andy . . . less and less, to be honest . . . Andrew did become more guarded, presumably as the stakes escalated and he felt he had so much more to lose. If you throw an ambitious outsider into the mix as well, Andrew was maybe wise to retreat behind the mask.'

Beyond the merely tactical, there were more profound reasons for Eldritch's transformation. The Leeds art school bands – the Mekons, Delta 5 and Another Colour especially – had approached being in a band as something far beyond the desire to make music, more as a mode of existing: the band as potent, world-making machine.* Kevin Lycett recognised the same impulse in Eldritch. 'Totally, for Andy. He *was* the Sisters of Mercy and that was his whole existence, completely so . . . Lifestyle is a slightly superficial word for it, but it is how he chose to make his way through the world. Life had been subsumed. There wasn't a beginning or an end of either of them.' The art school bands were rooted in socialist ideas of sharing the economies of production, Eldritch's were existential. Not for nothing did he once describe himself as 'Elvis meets Kierkegaard.'

The Sisters had chosen their new guitarist from a shortlist of one. An audition did not form any part of Wayne Hussey's recruitment. 'There's no reason we would have needed to hear him play live,' explains Marx. 'We were not a muso band or in need of any great technical proficiency. The fact he'd worked with more than one signed band suggested he could play anything we threw his way. That said, I do think we went over to Craig's at Hessle Terrace and got him to play through 'Temple of Love' once, more as lip-service to some sort of process than an audition as such.'

'He had lots and lots of equipment, guitars, acoustics, twelve-strings, pedals – even more than one type of distortion pedal,' Marx remembers. 'He had a "wardrobe", all these Worlds End

---

* The idea of the world-making machine comes from Gavin Butt in 'Being in a Band: Artschool Experimentalism in the Post-Punk Commons', which is collected in *Post-Punk Then and Now* (2016) which he edited with Kodwo Eshun and Mark Fisher.

outfits he'd bought during his time in Dead or Alive. It was like having a rich cousin you didn't know about suddenly turning up on your doorstep.'

'As soon as Wayne moved over to Leeds, we went out every night together,' recalls Adams. They took to calling themselves 'the Evil Children'. 'We were on a mission of destruction – of stuff and ourselves' is how Adams describes those weeks and the years that followed. A key shift in the band had been inaugurated. 'Wayne and I both drank and hung out. Andy and Mark did not come out very often. Mark didn't even drink tea or coffee. He drank water or orange juice,' Adams explains, with some degree of hyperbole.*

Previously, there had been one rock 'n' roll animal in the Sisters; now there were two. Marx believes that 'Craig did find his first close friend in the band with Wayne . . . they did seem to be in it for similar reasons. The more esoteric pursuits of Andrew and my confused punk ethos were of little or no interest. They went right back to rock basics – play hard and *play* even harder. I would say on the road that was increasingly how it became. In real terms, Andrew cut himself adrift every bit as much as I did.'

Hussey would never regard Leeds as his hometown, but he did appreciate the cachet that being in the Sisters brought there. 'When "Temple of Love" came out and went to Number One in the Indie Charts, I was enjoying the celebrity status and getting that much attention without really doing anything,' Hussey says.

---

* Adams' recollections, although they do reflect a very real demarcation in the band, are not accurate: Marx was by no means teetotal in this period. Despite plenty of evidence to the contrary, 'Craig would probably say, "Mark was on the Kia-Ora orange juice"', Marx surmises with some bemusement.

'It became clear how revered the Sisters were when you went out to the Fav, the Warehouse and the Phono.'

The years 1980 to 1983 had merely been the construction of a base camp; the real ascent would be made with Warner Music UK. Warner was the 'W' of WEA. Elektra and Atlantic constituted the other letters of that multinational conglomerate. Between them, they represented the home – posthumously in some cases – of Led Zeppelin, the Doors, the Stooges, the MC5, Devo, Roxy Music, Alice Cooper, Black Sabbath and Deep Purple.*

No one in the Sisters had qualms about aligning themselves with such a global corporation. Eldritch detested the barnstorming amateurism of Red Rhino (and the poor taste of Rough Trade); Adams was no indie purist, as his departure from the Expelaires had proved; Marx, despite his name, was not some anti-corporate ultra; and Hussey had already been on Sire and Epic.

As united as they were in this instance, there is little doubt that Eldritch and the band's lawyers, the illustrious firm of Harbottle and Lewis, had already considered the scenario of the band breaking up. 'The deal was weighted very heavily in favour of the last man standing,' says Marx. Indeed, Eldritch was the only named member of the Sisters of Mercy in the Key Member Clause. To all intents and purposes it was the usual multi-album deal: the big paydays were way down the line and the label had the option of not picking up the contract after each album.

---

* RCA Records and CBS Records both had discussions with the band in late 1983. RCA met the band in California in October and Muff Winwood, head of A&R at CBS came up to Leeds in December. The Sisters eventually signed with Warner and with RCA Music Ltd on 19 April 1984.

Warner's HQ was in Soho on Broadwick Street. The three most important people in the building were Rob Dickins, Max Hole and Paul Conroy. Dickins was in ultimate control as Chairman & CEO of Warner Music UK, Conroy was Head of Marketing and Hole was the Head of A&R, and therefore dealt most directly with the Sisters.

'Dickin Hole, I ask you!' quips Marx. If the old punk in him couldn't resist that bit of wordplay, he was taken by surprise at how supportive Warner were. 'They had given us the freedom to keep the Merciful Release identity and when they met with us all together there was never any suggestion of trying to dictate any future direction.'

Max Hole had been the Sisters' route in. He remembers 'going into a shop in Bedford, an HMV, and asking this weird singles buyer behind the counter, "So, any bands you're into on indie labels?" and he gave me "Alice" . . . I went to Leeds and saw them, I think at the Leeds Warehouse.' Hole was the one who pushed for Warner to sign the band. Other than setting budgets and completion dates, he felt the Sisters needed little shaping: 'All you needed to do was stand back from them,' he says.

Eldritch very much liked his new record company. At the time, he commented that, 'There are some pretty groovy guys working in London.' The feeling was mutual. 'I liked the music a lot,' Dickins says. 'I really liked Andrew and his iconoclasm and approved the deal.' Dickins has forgotten the minutiae of his business dealings with Eldritch but 'Andrew the man, the knowing sneer and that sharp, creative brain and his music are still crystal.' Hole remembers that 'Andrew was a remarkable character and I thought his imaging of the band was great. I thought they were potentially going to be a major act around the world.' Eldritch especially liked Hole. 'Big dollars, little flak,' he once summarised.

Dickins and Hole were in no doubt they had signed someone with star quality. The rest of the band – as the contract made clear – they could take or leave. Over the years both men would be on the receiving end of various postcards and sundry other vehicles for Eldritch's humour. One afternoon Dickins 'came back from lunch with Max and we went into his office and a note was pinned to his board: "A SNIPER'S RIFLE IS AIMED AT YOUR HEAD". Andrew had come in while we were out and left a very Sisters calling card.'

The early 1980s was a boom time for the record industry, and for Warner Music in particular. Not long before the Sisters, Dickins had acquired Warner's latest cash cow: Howard Jones. His album *Human's Lib* would go Double-Platinum while the Sisters were rehearsing in their Burley cellar. Foreigner, ZZ Top and Madonna also flooded the company with money at this time. There was no question that the Sisters were now through the looking glass and into a new world of opportunity.

Yet the immediate impact on the Sisters' lifestyle was not huge. Complex contractual negotiations prior to signing to a record label and a publishing company – RCA Music Ltd – racked up legal bills that took a bite out of the advance. 'We went on a wage for the first time,' Marx says, 'but in the same way as the initial advance was modest, we paid ourselves the absolute minimum.

The pattern had been set in our indie years to put as much as possible back into the Sisters machine."

Some of the advance was splurged in JSG, a music shop in Bingley, near Bradford. 'I bought a black Rickenbacker bass and a Marshall stack like Lemmy,' says Adams, 'Got it back to the rehearsal room: did not sound like Lemmy! Sold it.' With 'the money burning a hole in my pocket,' Marx bought a 'Fender amp which was pretty lousy as it turned out.' Hussey 'also added to his ever-growing arsenal,' Marx says. Eldritch's present to himself was a black Les Paul.

The Warner deal also prompted Eldritch to set up a Merciful Release office in London. The factotum appointed to run it was Nick Jones. The Sisters had first met Jones via Rough Trade, where he consolidated (in his opinion) 'the hottest gig booking agency around' with his partner Mike Hincs. Jones had been a fixture of the London music scene for nearly two decades. As a teenager, he had written for *Melody Maker*, including giving the Who their first review and 'after several years of mystical wandering' he 'resurfaced in 1975 to begin a six-year stint inside Miles Copeland's web of music companies.'

Not long after his time at Rough Trade ended, Jones found a copy of the 'Temple of Love' 12-inch on his doorstep in Notting Hill. 'I guessed it was a sign to make contact,' Jones surmised. 'A few days later, I was on a train to Leeds with directions to Village Place and an appointment with the Eldritch himself. Needless to say, the

---

* When they signed their recording and publishing deals, the Sisters of Mercy were paid £15,500 by WEA and Candelmaesse Limited (the music publishing wing of Merciful Release) received £15,000 from RCA Music Ltd.

bugger was asleep upstairs and totally unconcerned that I had arrived on time.'

Once Eldritch had surfaced, they struck a deal: as 'Front of House Day Manager' Jones remained freelance and would submit a monthly invoice. He sublet an office at 19 All Saints Road in Notting Hill from Troubadour, a tour management and services company owned by his friend, Reg Halsall.

At the time, All Saints Road was still the cultural heart of W11 and it maintained its status as 'The Frontline' in the local West Indian community's struggle against heavy policing. The crime rate was high and the street had something of a '"No Go" reputation, earned during the Notting Hill Riots [of 1976],' according to Jones. Troubadour's small suite – two offices and a kitchen area – was on the second floor of a four-storey corner premises. The door to Troubadour's offices was evidence of the kind of place All Saints Road was in early 1984. 'There was originally a steel security door,' says Halsall, 'but we had a break-in and it was bent in half. The police told us the guy did it with his legs because he didn't have any tools.'

Merciful Release took over the smaller of Troubadour's two rooms. This would soon be dubbed 'the Black Office'. 'It was never: "We're the landlord, you're the tenant,"' says Halsall. 'It was more of a joint venture . . . We got on really well; very good neighbours.'

It probably amused Eldritch that the Merciful Release office was only a five-minute walk from the totemic Powis Square location at which Nic Roeg and Donald Cammell had shot exteriors for *Performance*. 'When I'm rich and famous I've always wanted to buy that house in Notting Hill where *Performance* was set,' Eldritch once noted. For many young men interested in identity, rock 'n' roll and personae, the film is *the* key text.

'I knew Andy professionally as Eldritch not Taylor,' Jones says. 'I did not find him *particularly* unusual or any *more* autocratic than any other front man or woman I had met or worked with over the years. In fact, if anything, what *was* unusual (and refreshing) was to find an aspiring rock god who actually *knew* anything about the intricacies of the music industry . . . from contractual gobbledegook to corporate identity; from artwork to manufacturing records; from working the press to social climbing, from settling on a decent deal to avoiding a blatant rip-off. Andy had a bloody good grasp of what was necessary . . . to get shit done!'

The approbation did not necessarily go both ways. From what Marx could see, 'Nick Jones was great but someone who would infuriate Andrew. There was too much of the ex-hippy in him for Andrew to ever relax and trust him or just let him get on with the job.'

Troubadour's offices were just a three-minute walk from the flat Reg Halsall shared with Lucas Fox. Fox had been Motörhead's first drummer and had gone on to play in Warsaw Pakt. By the early 1980s, he was very much ensconced in the Notting Hill scene, picking up bits and pieces of studio production work, gigging with various bands and doing the occasional voiceover for documentaries. He also knew Nick Jones and could often be found on the second floor of 19 All Saints Road.

For Jones, working for Merciful Release was just a job, but Fox and Eldritch became properly friendly. Eldritch's considerable and obvious Motörhead fetish would have been more than titillated. Fox found Eldritch 'extremely intelligent and fun.' Both men fenced, were the sons of servicemen and spoke excellent French. Although Eldritch was an avowed Francophobe, Fox was proudly 'bilingual and bicultural.'

Fox found himself co-opted into the interior decoration of the Merciful Release office. 'Andrew's pretty precise: everything had to be black – matte black,' Fox says. 'He wanted me to build a sideboard down one side of the office to lay out artwork on . . . It had a false front on wheels to take books, which swung out. Behind there, they hid the guitars . . . I had to build a console to put the sound system in as well. *And* I built the desk and painted the damn thing black.' This bespoke desk also contained 'a slide-out mirror,' Jones says, 'specifically for chopping 'em out! For chrissakes!'

As soon as a telephone line was installed, the phone was also painted black. A rare departure from the colour scheme were 'the white satin curtains made to measure by Claire Shearsby,' Jones says. 'The office was stylish image-wise, ergonomically practical and right on budget!'

The office became another home away from home for Eldritch. 'He would crash out there from time to time when he was working,' says Halsall. 'He was a bit of a workaholic.' Fox also recalls that Eldritch 'actually did interviews in the complete dark with various journalists he wound up.'

Eldritch also spent a week of the Sisters of Mercy's hiatus producing an album for Salvation called *Clash of Dreams* at Strawberry. 'To us it was brilliant being there: proper studio, games room, kitchen and all that,' says Danny Horigan. 'We certainly weren't paying for it; must have been Merciful Release.' However, this time there were far bigger problems than a missing tooth. 'Everything took ages, partly because we couldn't play very well and Andrew was taking ages with drum sounds . . . When the red light came on, Mike [Hayes, the guitar player] would freeze. Eldritch did some guitars and backing vocals just to speed things up . . . it was a nightmare. I ended up doing vocals in one take.'

Eldritch did not like the results, and refused to release *Clash of Dreams* on Merciful Release. 'He kept fobbing us off,' says Horigan. 'At some point we realised he didn't want to put it out. He kept delaying it and delaying it. I don't think Andrew wanted his name on it."

By early 1984, the Sisters of Mercy had proper record and publishing deals, a new guitarist, new equipment and a London office with bespoke interior design. Now they just needed some new songs. When these finally arrived, the results were mixed.

The 'Body and Soul' 12-inch ('a vision of heaven with everyone on speed,' according to Eldritch) was recorded at Strawberry in March 1984. The original plan had been to knock 'The Scottish One' into shape as the lead track. Eventually it would become 'First and Last and Always', but at Strawberry the Sisters made 'an almighty mess of it,' in Marx's view. 'We worked for a while on the track with no vocal or idea in place for one. It meant Andrew fussed and added unnecessary elements to the arrangement, perhaps as a way of playing for

---

* Eldritch eventually dropped Salvation and left their album on the shelf. *Clash of Dreams* had a Merciful Release catalogue number MR 031 and was ultimately scheduled for March 1985 but was finally self-released by Salvation in 2014 after being 'rescued, revived and mastered' by the band.

time. It stopped sounding much like the band or the track I'd imagined.'

'The Scottish One' was mangled so badly that '"Body and Soul" was told to get its tracksuit off,' Marx says. Hussey had already demoed the music. 'I wrote it to order,' he says. It was his first attempt at writing what he thought a Sisters of Mercy song should sound like. 'I thought, "They like these kind of guitar-lines,"' Hussey recalls. 'It's not as good as the later songs where I felt more creatively free.'

'Body and Soul' also sounds like a hamstrung attempt to edge the Sisters towards the mainstream. It is neither musically, nor lyrically, prime Sisters. In fact, it was their least satisfying A-side since 'The Damage Done'. 'It's got a few decent moments but nothing significant at its heart really,' says Marx, 'but we had momentum and thankfully could survive the odd misfire.'

Fortunately, the EP also contained two excellent new Eldritch compositions. 'Train' harks back to the primitive, pumping and ultra-direct style of earlier Sisters songs and 'finally gave top billing to those Cramps and Vega influences,' Marx says. Eldritch had written good lyrics with ease: '"Take a walk downtown to where the victims go,"' Marx quotes, '"Take your shadow to the end, to the very last window." Come on boy, see how easy it can be!'

The best track is 'Afterhours', the first of Eldritch's American songs. It throbs and tingles, an evocation of the wee hours in Midtown Manhattan (a room in the Iroquois, to be precise), clammy with sex and amphetamine. It also contains one of his best riffs, this one an eruption of doom-laden, slow motion twang. To bulk out the 12-inch, the Sisters re-recorded 'Body Electric'. It was still a great song, but another version was redundant.

Eldritch would go on to complete only three of his own songs over the next two years. That he had virtually wrung himself dry can, in part, be blamed on the self-imposed burden of negotiating publishing and recording deals, and of setting up the Black Office. Eldritch, to all intents and purposes, had been managing the band. As the Sisters transitioned into the upper echelons, this was massively time-consuming and highly pressurised. Eldritch's stress levels rocketed.

Self-described as an 'intense young man . . . wound up by band things,' his nervous energy was being sapped. 'I don't relax,' he once observed. 'I suppose the only thing that stops me going completely insane is the kinds of dreams that you don't remember when you wake up.'

Eldritch did not go mad, but an almighty crash was coming.

15

Detroit's Finest

The first time Wayne Hussey played live with the Sisters of Mercy was a full six months after joining the band. This took place in the Tin Can Ballroom on the first floor above a strip club in Digbeth in central Birmingham on 7 April 1984. According to the other members of the group, not once in those six months had Eldritch rehearsed with them in the cellar of Village Place. Hussey recalls that, 'He'd just sit upstairs and listen.' Regularly Hussey would hear a voice from on-high shouting out: 'You're playing it wrong.'

'We were never that interested in trying the set, the running order and getting the end-to-this and the start-of-that organised or how the last two numbers would work,' says Marx. 'Did we know the songs, could we rely on each other to come in? That was our understanding of being gig-ready.' None of this required Eldritch to venture into the cellar. Also, because of the drum machine, 'we had to play everything exactly the same,' says Adams.

Three was the maximum the cellar could contain anyway. 'Good job we didn't have a drummer,' Hussey observes. 'We had a tiny little PA on stands and put the drum machine through that. Fortunately, all three of us just had little amps. We stood in the middle of the room nose-to-nose playing the songs.'

'Wayne was very confident and relaxed as a musician and . . . stepped into the role of band leader down in the cellar at Village Place,' Marx explains. 'It certainly wouldn't have bothered either me or Craig. It just represented a more easy-going version of what we'd grown used to.'

Hussey realised straightaway that he was vastly more technically proficient than Marx. Carving a space out for himself in the band was easy. Yet Hussey also knew how well his and Marx's opposing styles meshed and complimented. He enjoyed playing with Marx a lot. 'Mark's playing was ramshackle at times, but he had his own unique energy,' says Hussey. 'What he brought to the Sisters was unique. Technical ability can be learned but having something unique can't.'

Hussey had been a full-time musician for nearly a decade; highly adaptable, but nobody's cipher. 'When Wayne joined, we were playing that old set and it definitely started to change straight-away,' says Adams. 'He added things to those songs. It was an organic thing, changing as we rehearsed. Mark was teaching him the songs and he was adding in his little things.'

Although Marx found Hussey easy to like as a person, he was very aware that his own role within the band was being denuded, sometimes as a result of his own largesse. 'With his arrival I might have taken the opportunity to shed some of Andrew's guitar parts I'd grown tired of holding down,' Marx says. This was also 'a welcoming gesture . . . I thought he was too good to make do with the crumbs Ben had been living on.' If Adams now had a friend in the band, Marx had a rival. He was already frustrated, irritated and insulted by what he often saw as Eldritch's high-handed domination of the band they had started together and now he faced being sidelined by Hussey's arrival. 'It was no longer so clear-cut who was the lead guitar player within the band. That would become part of the narrative live – the better-sounding, better-dressed newcomer providing a better foil musically and visually for Andrew.' Nevertheless, he accepted that the Sisters were evolving and did not see Hussey's arrival 'as pushing me out the door.'

One of the lead parts that Marx handed over was 'Alice'. Whenever Marx played it, 'it really was hit and miss where my finger might land at the start of each cycle of the riff. I'm sure it drove Andrew to despair listening to me butcher it live.' Hussey was delighted to inherit it: '"Alice" is a genius guitar-line,' he says. 'All on one string – fantastic! Essentially my guitar style is quite lazy. I prefer to do as little work as possible for as much musical movement as possible . . . Don't move your fingers until you have to!'

The songs were not hard for him to play but Hussey came to respect them and Eldritch's abilities as a composer. Eldritch was evidently not a very good guitar player 'but sometimes when you're not a very good guitar player you have to use your imagination more,' Hussey explains. 'When I started rehearsing and pulling the songs apart, I started to realise how clever some of the guitar parts were.'

Eldritch, Hussey came to realise, was far from an instinctive artist. 'He didn't go for something that felt good right in the moment,' Hussey says. 'Andrew would spend days and days on a guitar-line. I think that's the academic side of him, that ordered part of his brain.'

Factoring in the Doktor and Adams, and Hussey knew he had joined a rock band of great musical potency. Playing in the cellar had given him an inkling, but onstage in the Tin Can it didn't take Hussey long to realise: 'This is special.'

Although the hiring of Hussey had been hasty, Eldritch was also sure he had made a wise decision. After the second song at the Tin Can, he told the crowd, with obvious self-satisfaction: 'This is Wayne' – and after a five second pause for effect – 'he's *very* good.' At later gigs Eldritch would refer to him as 'Brother Wayne', a comradely acknowledgement of 'the new boy', and an MC5 reference: Wayne Kramer had borne the same pseudo-religious title.

This was the fanbase's first sight of Hussey, onstage and off. They would get to know him well over the next year and a quarter. Dave Beer's reaction was typical of many who followed the Sisters: 'Ben was part of us, so when he went, it was a bit sad. And when Wayne came in, it was like: "Who's *this* dude? He's pissed out his head. Brilliant! He likes drugs. Wow! He can pull birds – even better. *And* he can play guitar. And other instruments."' The contrasts with Ben Gunn onstage were also marked in Digbeth. Where Gunn was rooted to the spot, Adams was surprised to see Hussey climbing the lighting rig during the gig.

It was clear the sound of the band had changed in those months in the cellar of Village Place, primarily due to the addition of Hussey. 'All these chiming, chorus and flanger-type sounds came to be the dominant feature,' Marx says, whereas he still mostly used reverb from the amp, a fuzz-box and a delay pedal. Adams' bass sound also became progressively cleaner, partly because he needed to leave more space for Hussey's richer sound, and partly because he was now playing through a decent amp and could rely on the edge from overdrive from that rather than just kicking his fuzz pedal on.

The Sisters' links to the Stooges, Motörhead and Suicide had therefore become more tentative during their hiatus. This would become even more apparent as more new songs – from both Marx and Hussey – came on stream and with the addition of a more sophisticated drum machine.

Some things had not changed – the God Squad still had their gymnastic manoeuvres. Not only were the pyramid-builders in action in Digbeth, but so was Rik Benbow. He spent several songs dancing upside down high above the audience, hanging by his feet from the ceiling latticework. Eldritch acknowledged this display by shouting out 'Rikki Benbow!' in the middle of 'Alice', in the manner of an MC announcing the entrance of a boxer into the ring.

Eldritch was now sporting an even longer beard, which gave him the appearance of an etiolated Jim Morrison. He shaved it off soon after the gig but left behind a pair of sizeable sideburns. This was a flagrant and radical gesture: sideburns were entirely anathema in punk and post-punk, unless you were courting rockabilly authenticity like the Clash. Eldritch was summoning up something far more contentious: post-'68 Elvis, Alvin Stardust and any man who played in a hard rock band 1966–1976.

Eldritch was not alone in using hair in his gestural repertoire: Hippy Craig was back. Adams took to the stage in Digbeth with shoulder-length hair. Over the coming weeks he could be seen onstage sporting hippy shades, Cuban heel boots and a battered 'straw cowboy-ish hat I bent and sprayed black'.

Adams also developed a taste for what he called the 'psychedelic, ridiculous stuff Wayne was wearing'. Hussey also wore shades onstage (and also off: prescription ones for his poor eyesight) and sported an unruly backcombed bird's nest hairdo that had got wilder as the weeks in the cellar had progressed. Marx had also added to his collection of second-hand and incredibly lurid shirts and women's blouses. As Eldritch pushed his Alvin Stardust fetish even further, so Marx was willing to play his part as Rob Davis, Mud's butch, dress-wearing guitarist.

The Sisters that re-emerged in 1984 had – visually and sonically – abandoned all links to punk: doom glam and psychedelicised heavy rock were now the order of the day.

For a band that had been in purdah for six months, there was remarkably little new material in their set. 'Body and Soul', 'Train' and 'Walk Away' – the latter with obviously draft lyrics – were the only additions, along with a cover of ABBA's 'Gimme! Gimme! Gimme! (A Man After Midnight)'. It was a great version, but very much repeating the anti cock rock statement of 'Jolene.' That and 'Train' would both be dropped from the set before the Sisters began their major spring tours of the UK and Europe. The paucity of material was a sign of the malaise that would grow into a full-blown crisis within just three months.*

Before that, Ruth Polsky had booked them in for some East Coast and Midwest dates. John Hanti was delighted to see the Sisters again. 'Of all the bands I've toured with,' Hanti says, 'The Sisters of Mercy are definitely my favourite . . . the Sisters of Mercy was a memorable experience for me on a multitude of levels.' One of those levels was conclusive and disgusting evidence that Marx now drank more than orange juice and water. He and Hussey fell asleep after cracking open the duty-free booze en route from JFK airport to their first show at the Spit Club in Boston. When they awoke, they were both covered in Marx's puke. Most of it was in Hussey's hair. Hanti, who was driving them in his van at the time, was able to keep this in perspective: 'We were all drinking very heavily and there was definitely more than one vomiting incident in my history with the Sisters.'

This one had consequences: Hussey needed to borrow money from Polsky to buy a hat to cover up the mixture of hair and vomitus – yet more headgear in the Sisters of Mercy. As well as Adams' flaking spray-painted 'cowboy-ish' number, there was the wide brimmed cattleman hat Eldritch had bought in Las Vegas the previous year. Only Marx would complete his time in the band bareheaded.

---

* The Sisters had also worked on Dusty Springfield's 'I Close My Eyes and Count to Ten' and Petula Clark's 'Don't Sleep in the Subway', which Eldritch was especially keen on doing. 'It seemed to have a lot of memories wrapped up in it,' Marx observes, 'but it just never sounded good. "Mandy" by Barry Manilow was more successfully attempted but was not able to dislodge "Emma" as the centre-piece ballad.' 'It's Over' by Roy Orbison was also considered.

Hanti – in spite of the boozing and the rat-slaughter with his van – was efficient and professional and, like Pete Turner, almost a decade older than the musicians in his charge. For Eldritch, Hanti was a fellow adult, rather than an Evil Child. 'I never had an altercation or butted heads with Andrew,' Hanti says, 'because he had respect. When I said something, he knew: "We got to do that." He trusted me.'

Both Polsky and Hanti were ambitious and had that combative zest that typified New York City, but where Polsky was a fan at heart, Hanti was all business. He liked that aspect of Eldritch too. 'He knew he had created a branding and an image that would relate: "OK, who's my audience and how do I reinforce that and develop my image as that guy: caustic, mysterious, dark clothes, the sunglasses?"' Hanti thought he recognised the difference between the young man and the marketable image. 'That was not the person I dealt with . . . I think they appreciated, especially Andrew, that this was me building my brand also.'

Unless they puked up in his van in front of him, Hanti had no interest in the band's recreational pursuits, so long as they were gig-ready: 'I didn't follow what the band did when they went off and did their own thing, I was never privy to it.' Hanti therefore missed Adams and Hussey attempting to snort crystal meth in the Iroquois; Hussey and Adams luring cockroaches into the semi-conscious Marx's mouth (also the Iroquois); Hussey's first 'American blowjob' backstage in Boston; his waterbed sex with a waitress from the Exit Club in Chicago; Marx's frontier gibberish that served as promo at local radio stations (half-remembered Blues Brothers and R. P. MacMurphy quotes were his speciality when

'The emblem of a macabre radical leftist cell': an early draft of the Merciful Release logo, tested out as the label of a 7-inch single, hence the hole and the glue stains.

The Sisters of Mercy on Belle Vue Road, Leeds, early 1981. *From left:* Craig Adams, Gary Marx, Andrew Eldritch.

'An extraordinary presence':
Claire Shearsby, the DJ and
sound engineer who was 'there
at the birth of it'.

The first of the second guitarists:
Dave Humphrey *(left)*, at the
Riley Smith Hall, University of
Leeds, 13 June 1981. Behind him is
Gary Marx with his infamous
orange juice.

The first great four-man line-up, at Leeds Warehouse, 28 January 1983. *From left:* Marx, Eldritch, Adams and Ben Gunn, plus the iconic 'Head and Star' painted on a kitchen blind by Eldritch.

From left: Gunn, Marx, Adams and Eldritch, almost all smiles, 1983.

'All bang and no whimper': the Sisters of Mercy live, 1983. *From left:* Eldritch, Marx, Adams, Gunn.

'High-energy proletarian
beefcake': Gary Marx
on stage, 1983.

The Sisters of Mercy during the Trans-Europe Excess tour: the Odeon, Münster, 1 September 1983. *Clockwise from top left:* Adams, Eldritch, Marx, Gunn.

'He resembled the louche – and probably sexually sadistic – leader of a biker gang in a Roger Corman exploitation film': Eldritch, the BZ (Berzelii Terrassen) club, Stockholm, 26 October 1983.

Wild mutation:
Andrew Eldritch on
the set of the 'Body
and Soul' video,
30 April 1984.

Not dark yet: test Polaroids for a *Melody Maker* photo shoot, London Docklands, 30 September 1984. *Top:* Eldritch. *Bottom, from left:* Marx, Eldritch, Adams, Wayne Hussey.

'Brother Wayne', London Docklands, 30 September 1984.

'Like a piece of
German theatre,
completely artificial,
totally knowing and
superb.' **Eldritch at
the Lyceum ballroom,
Black October tour,
Halloween 1984.**

'Philosopher King of Leeds 6': Andrew Eldritch in the sitting room of 7 Village Place, 6 March 1985.

Some kind of stranger: Gary Marx during his final gig with the Sisters of Mercy, Top Rank Suite, Brighton, 1 April 1985.

Eldritch, Hussey and Adams outside the Kolingsborg in Stockholm at the end of their gruelling final European tour together.

'Armageddon will be held indoors this year': Eldritch, Kolingsborg, Stockholm, 17 May 1985.

From left: Eldritch, Hussey and Adams at the Vikateateret, Oslo, 16 May 1985.

Left on mission and revenge: Eldritch at the Vikateateret gig in
Oslo, the controls set for 'BEACH' and 'REDEMPTION'.

Image © Raymond Mosk

drunk); yet more extreme reckless driving with Bryan Brain Damage in Manhattan; and Adams and Hussey pissing in the communal backstage beer at St Andrew's Hall in Detroit.*

Hanti also missed Polsky taking one of the best-known photos of the band. The Sisters 'had decided to do a bit of sightseeing around Detroit with Ruth . . . acting as our guide,' says Marx. 'We went to the original Motown building and some other landmarks.' This included the hairy Cass Corridor, the area of Midtown Detroit dominated by dive bars, drug dealers, strip clubs and prostitutes. While walking south on Woodward Avenue, the Sisters stopped to let Polsky take their photo outside the Sassy Cat, a porno cinema. Behind the Sisters, its hoarding declared that inside were 'Detroit's Finest Adult Movies'.

As well as an iconic photo, it is also the image of a band in the process of slow disintegration: 'The cracks were already there by then,' says Marx. 'In a way, the *Detroit's Finest* shot appears prophetic. I look the outsider, separate in any number of ways, without the leather and shades, shorter hair. . . I'm pretty sure I am hungover in the photograph . . . I remember being shivery and cold with only a thin T-shirt on under the big overcoat. I'm not even certain it is my coat.' However, Marx readily concedes that, 'It's a great photo of Andrew – about as handsome and cool as any picture of him up to that point.'

The relationship between Adams and Eldritch could be openly fractious. In New York City, at the Iroquois, 'I used to have to

---

* Marx's drunken radio routine would involve shouting 'It's OK, the government sent me' and various lines from *One Flew Over the Cuckoo's Nest* including: 'What are you doing here? You oughta be out in a convertible bird-doggin' chicks and bangin' beaver.'

share with Andy, which was a pain,' recalls Adams. 'I don't quite know how that happened. He used to drive me insane. He'd have the key and he would go out, so I couldn't do anything. So I'd go next door to Mark's room. One time, when I came back our room had got robbed, including Andy's Ramones plectrum, which he'd actually got from one of the Ramones. He was furious with me.' Adams' reaction was: 'I don't give a shit. You take the key, you take the consequences.'

'He used to lock me out, if he had a girl. I'd just go down to Reception and get the gaffer key. "This is my room. He's got the key. He's a wanker. He's locked me out and gone to sleep." And get them to open the door. He'd have put the chain on, so I'd just batter the door down.'

Even when both of them were in their beds, too wired to sleep, Eldritch also aggravated Adams (how intentionally, after the plectrum incident, is unclear):

'"Can I have a light, Andy?"

"It's your responsibility to get your own matches together. I have three matches because I shall be smoking three cigarettes this evening."

"Screw you, dickhead".'

The more they toured, the more Adams was infuriated by Eldritch, but in April 1984 – and for a good while yet – Adams was having a great time being in the Sisters and was not totally wound up by 'the little, niggling, stupid things'. He was anaesthetised against what he found to be the irritating aspects of Eldritch's personality. 'He was always on speed but I was speeding and a bit drunk and a bit stoned, so I think I could deal with it. A lot of the time I was really out of it.'

Throughout his time in the Sisters of Mercy, Adams never once laid a finger on Eldritch. All his anger and frustration were displaced onto inanimate objects. The Iroquois was not the first time that Eldritch found himself behind a door Adams was trying to break down. 'Oh dear. I could have a bit of temper, I suppose,' Adams summarises. Even when Eldritch lived on St John's Terrace, 'I tried to smash his door in and hopefully frighten the shit out of him. I used to go round his flat sometimes and do it. He used to let me in the bottom door and then I'd try to batter his door in upstairs. Why? Because he was a twat. He would act like an idiot:

"Why have you got to act like a dickhead?"

"Yeah, I've been awake for three days."

"No you haven't! I was round your house this afternoon. You were in bed!"'

None of this altered Eldritch's admiration for Adams' musical ability. 'He was the most rock solid bass player ever,' Eldritch has said. 'He'd only ever played bass with a drum machine, i.e. ours . . . He just naturally took to fuzz bass, which is an instrument and attitude all of its own. And he was bloody good at it.'

Adams in turn had deep respect for what Eldritch was doing with the band and found him highly effective. 'Without a doubt. You all knew something was going on and it was an exciting time.' The difference in leadership in the Sisters and the Expelaires was stark.

'But he was never a mate,' Adams says. 'He wasn't that sort of person.'

After Hussey joined, the Sisters dropped 'Temple of Love', their biggest hit, from their set, on the grounds that it was 'a ball-ache to play,' according to Hussey. Similarly, 'Gimme! Gimme! Gimme!' didn't last long because 'it was so bloody hard to do,' says Adams. Therefore only Americans and the Tin Can fans heard it live, along with Eldritch's various Scandinavian-flavoured set-ups: 'Got any Swedes in the house? This one is for the Swede in everybody' (Chicago); 'OK, Swedes, this is it' (New York). At the Danceteria show, Hussey and Adams momentarily abandoned any attempt to play it properly. Between the final two choruses, 'Wayne and me were sliding our guitars, strings down, across the stage to each other and back,' says Adams.

One Sisters fan had an unusual encounter with Eldritch right before the Danceteria show. Bob Beiner arrived late with some friends and 'went to the bottom floor of Danceteria. There was a little area, and there was Eldritch by himself in front of a big bucket of ice, his head down as if he was totally out of it. We walk over to him to talk to him and before we say anything, he looks up and says, "We're going on in five minutes."' Although he seemed utterly fucked, Eldritch's timekeeping was immaculate: five minutes later, he was onstage.

Alan Vega was a backstage visitor that night at Danceteria. 'He was wildly funny and could quickly take over a room,' says Marx, 'but he was drawn to Andrew rather than the band.' Vega was a huge influence on Eldritch: the cheap drum machine, the vocal style – especially the yelping and screaming – and a stage persona that had menace and toughness, but was also very camp. Hussey was especially intrigued by Vega's massive, rock hard bouffant hairdo. Vega was happy to pass on his secret: Aqua Supernet hairspray.

These were the last dates on which the Sisters ran the drums from four-track cassettes. This was another element of touring with the potential to irritate Eldritch. 'After the Philly show, on the way back to New York, I thought I had left the tapes at the venue,' Adams explains. 'We had to empty the van on the freeway; Grumpy was very pleased! I *hadn't* left them *and* we carried a set of spares just in case.'

Shortly after their return from the USA, the Sisters made a promotional video – their first – for 'Body and Soul.'

'The plan seemed logical and straightforward enough,' says Marx. '"The band are great live, so we'll have a performance video with them onstage." I don't know who had suggested the neo-classical pillars and the netting.' With those and the addition of fire and smoke, the video gave the impression of being filmed in a giant ashtray or on the set of *I, Claudius* after an airstrike.

'The worst part was that the stage was more like a catwalk,' says Marx. 'It had no depth to it at all, so you could only move within a very limited range side to side. If you had tried to move backwards or forwards you would have collided with the set or fallen six foot off the front of the stage . . . And then there was the actual volume of the playback we were working with, which hardly gave you the feeling of a gig. It was the equivalent of putting a small radio in the middle of a large function room.

'We'd already been warned that there could be a lot of standing around waiting while shots were set up. That was especially the case for "the backing band". The mainstream mentality meant there was a lot of extra time spent filming Andrew separately. He had his own rostrum in the centre of the floor so was able to do more than the three of us could up on the stage stood in a line.'

To enliven the proceedings – in addition to ingesting a large amount of amphetamine and alcohol – Hussey decided to mime playing his guitar with a violin bow, which undercut any intended seriousness.

'Andrew seemed to enjoy the process more than us,' says Marx. 'He surprised me by bringing his [black Les Paul] guitar along and miming in certain shots playing the power chords that feature on the track. It was all a bit odd and the day culminated in the scene with us stood on the edge of the fire, which the director had decided was going to be the closing scene of the video. He insisted that no one move a muscle when the song finished because he was going to be using some kind of slow dissolve on the image. All good until my feet began to burn through the very badly worn soles of my boots.'

The end product was categorically not worth the pain.

The day had further ignominy in store. Since the video was to be Marx's first time on TV, he had asked Kathryn Wood, his girl-friend, for some cosmetic products. 'She packed me off with these small amounts of foundation and blusher. Of course I got them mixed up and applied the blusher all over giving me this rusty orange face which stopped abruptly at my neck. Wayne did like-wise and then over the course of the shoot we kept topping up. I kept applying hairspray as well but all it did was compress my hair into this sort of mushroom shape.'

While this is not obvious in the video, it is all too apparent in a photo taken on the day that was used in *Smash Hits*. This became 'another one that regularly followed us on our travels for a year or more,' Marx laments. Flanked by Hussey and Marx's russet complexions, Eldritch – also in some kind of make-up and one of Hussey's hats – looks particularly sickly. Hussey appears to have deployed vast amounts of Vega-endorsed Aqua Supernet. Adams, in hippy shades and a shirt, originally belonging to Wood's father, that he had hacked the collars and sleeves off of – and sporting a quarter-hearted attempt at backcombing his hair – emerges the least scathed.

Two days after the video and photo shoots, the Sisters offered up conclusive proof that their powers of performance and visual presentation had only temporarily deserted them.

On 2 May, their largest ever tour began.

16

The Pilgrims' Progress

The Sisters' live dates – sixteen in the UK, twelve in north-western Europe – were known (according to the tour-books) as the British Pilgrimage and the European Pilgrimage respectively. These jaunts were also listed as The Body and Soul Train tour. Whether this was loose punctuation or a pun on the very groovy US music and dance show is not clear.

For these Pilgrimages Eldritch wanted to use a lot of smoke onstage. For that he needed a lighting designer. This was Phil Wiffin, listed as 'Brother of Light' in the tour-book. He was another of the 'Brid Mafia' (as Pete Turner refers to those with connections to KG in Bridlington) and was well known to Reg Halsall and Nick Jones because he'd been in charge of the lights on an Orange Juice tour. Wiffin knew nothing of the Sisters 'other than briefly meeting the band at KG when they were making "Alice" with John Ashton,' he says. 'It was an intrusion more than a meeting.'

When Eldritch telephoned him to discuss lighting design for the

Pilgrimages, Wiffin was immediately impressed. 'Obviously, he was after an element of mystery and dynamic. Expressionist lighting was an avenue he suggested I look down. It was a conversation with theatrical references . . . it was quite refreshing; I remember being excited about it. It wasn't just a rock 'n' roll thing we were doing.'

Wiffin contributed more than just lighting. Marx recalls that 'Phil was a good influence on the road: smart and funny, very calm. He could keep Andrew ticking over.'

Wiffin had studied set design and stage lighting at Mountview Theatre School in London before working for Opera North at the Grand in Leeds and other theatres in the region. Therefore, 'the organised chaos' of the Sisters tour was not his natural environment. 'It was a little bit of a shock to me,' Wiffin says. 'It really was punk. I suppose I liked the idea of having a bath of a night. It was all a bit rough and ready but there was a definite family. It was a very tight little group of people I was allowed into. You could feel it was close.'

Yet Wiffin was also in no doubt who the star of the band was: 'I only really had one focus: showing Andrew. That when he hit the microphone, his face was lit from below or from the side, never from the front, because he just did not like that. We had quite a specific light set-up, which he would be aware of. When he saw a light come on, he could put his face in it or move out of it. He knew he could make it more dramatic that way. The rest were in shadow with maybe a bit of backlight or floor light.'

Henceforth, thick onstage smoke became a signature of the band, part of Eldritch's drive to create an environment that affects 'you in that sort of bozo gut-wrenching heavy metal way'. This applied to him, as much as the crowd. That the smoke stank horribly also affected people viscerally. 'That led to the idea to add fruit-scented oil,' says Adams. Many Sisters gigs would smell strongly of strawberries. The regulars in the crowd became so attuned to the nightly ritual of filling the stage with smoke they could tell when the band was about to come on. 'We knew by the length of the "sssshhh" of the smoke machine, if it was going to happen,' says Dave Beer.

Kevin Lycett was a close observer of the Sisters on this tour because his video production company shot two gigs. 'I did it on U-matic with three cameras . . . but they were poor quality,' Lycett admits. The footage, now lost, might have been unsatisfactory but the band weren't: 'proper Sisters running on all four cylinders,' as Lycett puts it. He was especially impressed by the 'rebuilding of that barrier' between performer and audience, 'like a piece of German theatre, completely artificial, totally knowing and superb.'

Lycett also recognised that the Eldritch persona had also become even more developed – and necessary – as the band became more successful. 'If you carefully construct this persona, you're bulletproof, invulnerable. The "you" inside of that – it's like Iron Man when he's got his suit on . . . Shyness was a real driver,' Lycett says. 'Just because you are shy, it doesn't mean you don't want accolades, you haven't got an ego and you don't want to prove that you are really good.' The smoke was another layer of the disguise Eldritch needed. Amphetamine was another confidence booster. 'I'm pretty sure we had drugs every show, Andy and I,' Adams says. 'Maybe that was our little tot of rum before going over the top.'

Lycett had been invaluable to Eldritch's development as an artist during the Sisters' early days in Leeds. 'I owe a lot to him,' Eldritch has acknowledged. 'He encouraged me in my quest to learn a little bit about being in a band and scrimp and save for visits to the studio and keep hammering away at it . . . his encouragement never wavered.' By the time of the British Pilgrimage, Eldritch had long outgrown the need of the tutelage of the Mekons.

In spring 1984, Pete Turner was on tour with the Cramps, so did not mix sound, or function as tour manager, on either of the Pilgrimages. Richard 'Nipper' Bayes, the monitor engineer ('Brother of Feedback' in the tour-book) was promoted to 'Reverend Crewboss' in Turner's absence. Bayes was another member of the Brid Mafia. 'Nipper liked getting locked in flight cases and spun around for fun,' says Merb. 'Pretty much sums him up: hilarious guy.'

For the gig in Bristol, Wiffin and Bayes had to collect the sound system from the Ashton Gate football ground, which was hosting the final day of the evangelical preacher Billy Graham's *Mission England* crusade. Therefore, a crowd that had come to hear Cliff Richard sing and Graham preach, witnessed Bayes and Wiffin 'branded with Sisters of Mercy crew T-shirts and laminate passes' pass among them. 'The churchgoers . . . must have thought they were ecclesiastics,' Turner says. If so, they were lay brothers of a peculiar sort: black-clad and displaying a diagram of a flayed head and pentagram.

The new front of house sound engineer ('Brother of Noise') was Yaron Levy, a new addition to the Sisters' family. Levy was most definitely not part of the Brid Mafia. He was from Reading, but, as a Leeds United fan, 'couldn't have been any happier' to work for the Sisters.' Levy was fully aware that 'there is a difference between the North and the South. The North is much closer knit.' Like Wiffin, he was struck by the warmth of relationships within the inner circle. Levy's recreational tastes ('erring on the more hedonistic side of things') also made him a good fit with Horigan, Webb, Hussey and Adams – 'contemporaries with a similar mind-set,' as Levy puts it.

The only 'socialising with Eldritch was over a line of speed,' Levy says. 'He was very nocturnal . . . you wouldn't see him during the day until sound-check. After the show, we'd do our thing and weren't sure where he went.' Levy also instantly understood the power structure within the band. 'Coming in as an outsider, I saw him as the main protagonist of the Sisters of Mercy, the central linchpin. That had been established already.'

Levy also became aware of how fearsome Eldritch could be. 'I saw him as an intellectual person, and he used that as a weapon.' Levy witnessed one of Eldritch's interactions with a music journalist. 'He just proceeded to rip the guy apart. Like: "I'm not worthy of that question, you'll have to do better than that." He reduced the guy to tears with his intellect . . . And I remember thinking: "He's taking real pride in that." I don't think that was untypical.'

'Nothing like that was directed towards the crew,' Levy explains. 'There was a mutual respect that kept us together on a professional level and to some extent on a personal basis as well.'

Each night, the Sisters of Mercy went onstage to the coda of 'Sister Anne' by the MC5, providing a bierkeller oompah vibe, utterly at odds with what would follow. Even without Turner,

Sisters gigs regularly approached the Wall of Pain. The most notorious night on the British Pilgrimage was at the Electric Ballroom. 'There was a sound limiter with a flashing tube light which the sound engineer was supposed to keep an eye on,' says Wiffin, 'but it was never out of the red. It was a constant red noise all evening.'

Among the Electric Ballroom crowd was Dave Allen. Allen had learned his trade as a studio engineer with Martin Rushent at Genetic Studios in Berkshire and had just produced *The Top* for the Cure. Allen had no clue who the Sisters of Mercy were but 'I loved the gig,' he says, 'I thought it was incredibly powerful. I loved the swagger. I thought it must be great to work with this band. Drum machines – very controversial. Drummers give a focal point at the back, some spectacle – to see a band evading that was a very radical manoeuvre. I admired that.'

Allen had also previously engineered Dead or Alive's 'Misty Circles' and therefore knew Hussey, but he had no clue he was on the Electric Ballroom's stage that evening because of the density of smoke and Wiffin's lighting.

The tour-book listed the Sisters as: 'Mother Superior' (Eldritch); 'Six String Sisters' (Marx and Hussey); 'Sister Basso' (Adams) and Webb and Horigan as 'Sisters of Stage'. The other 'Brother', alongside Wiffin, Levy and Bayes, was Dave Kentish – mysteriously billed as 'Reverend Father'.

Kentish was another key element of the Sisters' touring set-up. He filled many roles but had initially been hired as a driver with his own vehicle. Compared to touring with Dave Hall or Steve Watson, Kentish's Dodge minibus was luxurious: fold-down bed at the back and some plush reclining seats. It became known as the 'Flying Turd' because of its brown carpeting. Turner recalls, 'It was a hellish thing to drive; it used to weave about,' especially with Kentish at the wheel. 'Andrew preferred me to drive when I could,' Turner notes.

Kentish was also most definitely not from Yorkshire. He had the air of a Cockney wide boy. 'He was like a character out of the film *Snatch*,' says Marx. 'He was a small fella, very fat – always wore a grey leather suit,' Adams recalls. 'Such a strange choice but fitted right in,' Marx adds. 'I don't know if he had any love or knowledge of music at all but he kept us on track, which became a thankless task the longer we went on. He could get a bit strong-arm when it was required.'

'He saw the Sisters as a vehicle to get on in the world,' says Levy, 'but he genuinely loved the band . . . He found some friends with the Sisters and would do anything to keep them happy.' Adams remembers that Kentish 'used to get lost constantly. Driving around Europe, we'd hear: "Chief, I don't know where I am!" If you got lost, you'd stop a taxi, tell it where you wanted to go and follow it.'

'Dave was more security and personal things, looking after the band production-wise,' Turner says euphemistically.

'He always had drugs,' says Adams. 'When we got to gigs in Europe, Andy would be like: "We've run out of speed! Who's going to go out and get some speed?"'

Adams would volunteer. '"I'll do it. I'll go and find somebody in the crowd."

'I'd disappear for about half an hour. I'd just go to Dave who was carrying them all in the van and buy them off him. Then I'd go back . . . "Got some!"

'How Andrew never clicked on that I was never going into the crowd, I was just going to Dave Kentish!'

The Flying Turd changed the dynamic of the band: crew travelled separately. 'It was such an evident loss of Danny and Jez when only the four of us travelled together,' Marx says. 'It immediately became Andrew and Dave Kentish sat up front, with Wayne, Craig and myself drinking ourselves silly in the back.'

The new dynamic quickly became 'us and him', a new kind of family, but this one profoundly dysfunctional: Eldritch as the cold and distant father, with the misbehaving sons in the back seats. It is not coincidental that Adams and Hussey refer to themselves as the Evil Children or that Eldritch called Hussey 'Young Wayne', although the guitarist is older than him.

At this stage the Sisters on tour also had the air of a grotesque school trip: Eldritch as the map-reading teacher in the front, puerile discontent fomenting behind his back. 'We had pea-shooters and we'd blow these little globs of paper at the back of his neck,' Adams says.

'One time Eldritch fell asleep in the front,' Hussey recalls.

'"Right, Craig, watch this."

'I put a cassette of "Careless Whisper" in and whacked the volume right up.'

Hussey mimics the blast of the opening sax riff. 'By this point, I was back on my bed in the back,' he notes with some glee.

Eldritch, shocked back into consciousness, was not amused:

'"You baaarstards, you absolute baaarstards."'

Adams' Eldritch impression is delivered in a drawling, slightly upper crust accent.

This was a miniature revolt against the distribution of power in the band. Onstage misbehaviour by Hussey or Adams could result in disciplinary measures by Eldritch. During the third gig of the tour at Manchester University, Hussey was standing on the monitor at the front of the stage, when Adams 'decided to give me a friendly kick and I fell off the stage,' Hussey says. 'I was lying on the ground among the audience. I don't know what hurt most, my pride or my back! Anyway, I picked myself up and continued the show . . . I had to go to the hospital afterwards.'

'Of course there was a post-mortem after the show,' Hussey recalls, 'and it was decreed by management, Andrew, that from now on the spirits and wine on the rider would not be delivered to the dressing room until just an hour before stage time.'

Marx's frustrations were sometimes apparent onstage. On the opening night in the Sisters' stronghold of Rock City in Nottingham, he played his Shergold Masquerader – the guitar he had used for nearly all his studio recordings and live work – for the last time.

'Towards the end of the encore I started smashing the guitar to pieces against the stage and the monitor wedges. I wish someone had filmed its death throes because I don't recall how it came to have its headstock snapped off completely. I think I did it pneumatic drill-style into the floor."

---

* Marx had come on tour with the one guitar he owned. After its demise, the Flying Turd 'detoured through Leeds and stopped off for me to buy a second-hand guitar from a pawn shop on Boar Lane.' Middlesbrough Town Hall was the first and last time it was used. 'Apologies to anyone at that gig – it was possibly the strangest sounding electric guitar I have ever heard. I can only assume I borrowed guitars for the remaining dates.'

This was probably a response to the first stirrings in Marx that 'we were short-changing people'. Sometimes he judged that the band were not always worthy of the adulation and devotion of the fans. 'Some kids were happy just to bum around but others had structured their entire year around Sisters shows and tours, using up their annual leave from work, spending whatever funds they had, and increasingly they were seeing diminishing returns.' During the British Pilgrimage, the set changed little for the entire three weeks: the same songs in pretty much the same order, very little of it new material.

Yet, the fan-base grew in number and intensity. The ranks of the God Squad swelled as it continued to draw recruits – primarily but not entirely – from the North and Midlands. It expanded to the extent that a splinter group, containing a new Plymouth contingent, developed.

There were also numerous other groupings and individual travelling hardcore fans outside of the God Squad's orbit. These included two young men from Goole in Humberside, who were naturally nicknamed 'the Goolies' (British slang for testicles), their true names now lost to history. Another group of fans, who followed Hussey when he was in Dead or Alive had transferred their allegiance to the Sisters. These included Maria Moore and her husband, Pat, and the Mullinder sisters, Rachel and Helen. With the addition of Julie Heyes, they would later dub themselves the Sisterhood, a name that would eventually – and in an entirely different context – spark open warfare between members of the band.

The Sisters played the entire UK tour with Flesh for Lulu as their support act. Avoiding proto-goth connotations was clearly not a priority. In 1983, Flesh for Lulu had been labelled positive punk by the *NME* and had been on the Batcave Tour with Specimen. Some of Flesh for Lulu were even regulars in the club itself.

James Mitchell, their drummer, remembers Eldritch as 'glowering on occasion, but when he smiled it was quite sweet. Wayne and Craig – nice people and fun, a *lot* of fun; Craig: a big puppy dog, with his Yorkshire accent . . . and his *Spinal Tap*-like rallying cry of "Where are the bloody women?"'

Eldritch and Rocco Barker, Flesh for Lulu's guitarist, had never met before but were unusually connected. Eldritch told Barker that 'one time he had been walking through a shopping centre in Leeds before he got the Sisters together and a bloke comes up to him. "Can I have your autograph? You're Rocco from Wasted Youth [Barker's previous band], aren't you?"' Eldritch told Barker that he pondered this for a moment 'and then said he was and signed it.'

It also emerged on tour that Barker and Eldritch were both good fencers, albeit via different routes. Eldritch had learned at private school in Middlesex, Barker through a scheme for underprivileged youngsters at his tough school in the East End of London. Hussey and Adams egged Barker on to challenge Eldritch to a duel. 'In sword fencing, the way you challenge someone is you swipe a glove across their face,' Barker explains. 'It's *en garde* and there's a lot of protocol. Somewhere along the line, Wayne or Craig found a glove and I went up to him.'

The ensuing duel 'was at a university' as best as Barker can recall. 'Andrew went home and got his fencing gear: the britches and the proper shoes and the knee-high socks, the thing that goes over your crotch. In his sword he had "Volpe" written on the inside of the guard. I fenced foil, the most popular, he fenced sabre, which is much more violent, slashing, a bit more swashbuckling. Not so popular, quite difficult.'

The duel had an element of class war about it: 'East End survivor stock' vs 'the definitely well-educated', according to Mitchell. Even though Barker was on a cocktail of illegal drugs (he was trying to kick heroin at the time) and had an injured leg (from jumping down a flight of stairs racing Adams and Hussey at a motorway service station), he had lost little of his natural ability. He had unusually excellent hand-eye co-ordination and had even made the Junior Olympic Squad as a teenager.

'When Nick [Marsh, Flesh for Lulu's singer] told that story it was: "Rocco fucking thrashed him." I didn't, but I did beat him. Just. He took it like a gentleman, but I sensed he really didn't like the idea of losing. Andrew was a funny fish. He was just very competitive in everything he did. Quite odd how he was.'

'Wayne and Craig were just regular blokes. We could buffoon about, be dickheads if we wanted to be,' Barker notes, 'whereas with Andrew there was that coolness about him. He was almost playing a part in a way . . . he had to keep up some kind of façade.' Barker sensed that being Eldritch was extremely hard work. 'It was almost a stigma in a way,' he observes.

The tour continued on into Europe without Flesh for Lulu. The

Sisters were in a better class of 'residential convents' than previously, but touring in the Flying Turd sapped both body and mind; drink and drugs frayed tempers and swung moods. The band's alcohol intake – Marx and Eldritch's included – rocketed on the Pilgrimages. 'It is no surprise there were flare-ups,' Marx observes. 'It is surprising there were so few actual fist-fights.'

One of the few instances Marx remembers was between Eldritch and Hussey. He has a recollection of 'Andrew and Wayne actually trading blows onstage at a club gig in Europe.' This was probably at the Hunky Dory in Detmold. 'Definitely less swashbuckling than the duel with Rocco,' Marx notes. 'This one involved guitar-versus-mic-stand with a few high kicks thrown in for good measure.'

The next morning Hussey woke up hungover on the floor of the Hunky Dory and was informed he had quit the band the night before after his spat with Eldritch. He had to scurry off and find the Flying Turd before it departed without him and reinstate himself.

Most confrontations were verbal. 'I was constantly leaving,' says Adams. He clashed with Eldritch in Brussels, quitting with the words: '"Bollocks to this. Jez, let's go grape picking in Greece."' Adams and Webb 'set off walking through Brussels, trying to find a train station, but just got bored and went back to the hotel.'

The Pilgrimages marked another definitive shift: the Sisters of Mercy now hurtled down, what Marx terms, 'the road marked carnal excess.'

'Even when the band had started to gain some profile towards the end of Ben's time, there was nothing remotely similar going on to what transpired once Wayne came on-board.' Hussey was not the lone sexual profligate, although he was the most voracious and indiscreet. The expansion of touring brought extra temptations, which both Eldritch and Adams seemed to make little effort to resist.

Marx 'did not want to have anything to do with that *Hammer of the Gods*[*] shtick,' not simply because he was in the early stages of his relationship with Kathryn Wood (one that endures to this day), but because he also suspected that Eldritch and Hussey were engaged in some race to the rock 'n' roll bottom. 'It really irked Andrew that Wayne seemed to be playing the archetypal rock star to a greater degree than he was . . . I found that competitive streak pathetic when it came to the on-tour behaviour.'[†]

Eldritch – with the arcane sense of morality that Rob Worby had noticed – nevertheless still managed to take issue with elements of Hussey and Adams' off-stage behaviour. He was most definitely interested in exploring his own degeneracy, but found much of Hussey and Adams' hedonism and general malarkey crass. Regularly, Hussey and Adams would find themselves on the end of a withering look (often over the top of Eldritch's sunglasses, in the style of a disapproving schoolma'am) or a verbal dressing down.

Eventually, Eldritch would become sufficiently nauseated by his own appetites that he would seek to withdraw from the beast-

---

[*] The 1985 book about the exploits of Led Zeppelin, as opposed to the low-budget 2013 action film.

[†] This is categorically not how Hussey sees the on-tour dynamic. 'I was never in a competition with Eldritch to be the most rock 'n' roll. That is not true.' What is accepted is that, 'we were all (Marx excepted) shagging some of the same girls.'

world of heavy touring. But in 1984 he and the Sisters of Mercy were at the zenith of their dissipation.

The Sisters played several great concerts in Europe, including at the Zeche in Bochum in West Germany (known as the 'Rock 'Em in Bochum' show to Jez Webb), the Paard van Troje in The Hague on Hussey's birthday and the Doornroosje in Nijmegen, which ended with a nearly twenty-minute-long medley of 'Ghost Rider' and 'Louie Louie'.

At the Melkweg in Amsterdam, Dave Allen was in attendance again, sat on top of the PA stack smoking hash. Yet he has a vivid memory of the gig. 'At the Milky Way, all the lights were up the whole gig, no dry ice, completely non-obscured. It was amazing, a really amazing gig . . . [Eldritch] held the audience spellbound.'

Allen was there because he was now 'on the band's radar . . . and the next step was to do a meet when they were on tour.' Allen 'flew out on the Saturday, stayed up late, got wrecked, had a great time. Had the roadies sleeping on the floor in my room because, as per usual, there weren't enough hotel rooms booked.' Allen remained intrigued by the Doktor. 'This was a drum machine in rock. What could it be? No rulebooks had been established.'

This time he was listening to an Oberheim DMX – the final iteration of the Doktor in this period of the band, and the first one to really merit the term 'drum computer'. Hussey, who had worked with one in Dead or Alive, became the Doktor's new handler and, often, programmer, which saved the band, in his words, 'having to get the manual out.' At the Melkweg, Allen witnessed Hussey 'kicking the tempo up or changing patterns on the DMX live while playing guitar.'

The Doktor made a huge impact on how the rest of the band played – and felt – onstage. 'We could have played that set in half an hour, if the drum machine hadn't restricted us,' says Adams. 'It held us back, otherwise we would have raced forward because of the old marching powder. It kept us at bay, but it kept that tension because we were always right on the edge of breaking out of the drum machine. It was like: "Come *on!*" . . . Trying to play "Emma" when you've done half a gramme of speed is like . . .' Adams then makes a sound indicating excruciating, delicious frustration. Some might consider a sexual analogy apt at this point.

The release came in the encore: some combination of 'Sister Ray', 'Ghost Rider' and 'Louie Louie', a medley of wild electrified industrial dance music. 'Once the main set was finished, it was like: "Anything can go now." We were not sure what we were going to play. We always got in the same way and then it was make it up as you go along . . . The best one we ever did was at the Milky Way: Wayne was playing on a windowsill, Mark was rolling about. That was just great.' Allen recalls Hussey playing his instrument while being carried around on Jez Webb's shoulders.

The last date of the Sisters' European tour took place on 6 June, the 40th anniversary of D-Day, in a club in a converted church in Maastricht. The crowd contained a group of Neo-Nazi skinheads. Eldritch was incensed when he caught sight of one of them in a Skrewdriver T-shirt. Marx 'chose to step down from the stage and play my guitar within the audience in a small area that cleared for me . . . It was hardly the first time I'd instinctively done something similar at a gig when there was trouble.'

Adams too was apoplectic. Lisa Levine had come on tour with him. She was Jewish and they had visited the Anne Frank House in Amsterdam together. When the Neo-Nazi at the front began Sieg Heil-ing, Adams had to be held back by Dave Kentish. Eldritch 'quickly took the decision to leave the stage in the hope we'd all follow and avoid things getting any uglier,' says Marx.

'We don't really feel like coming back and singing some more, while this man's got that T-shirt on,' Eldritch announced. 'We really don't want to hear any more about "white power", thank you. We just want you to take your shirt off.'

Backstage, Adams' rage did not abate, especially when he saw how 'freaked out and bewildered' Levine was. After a long debate, the band agreed their response: Eldritch and Adams would go back out and play 'Fix' as a duo. The song, which they had only played live once before – the night before in Nijmegen – was entirely apt. With the Neo-Nazis still in the crowd, Eldritch sang about love: 'for the party', 'for the nation' and 'of a genocide.' In Maastricht, 'Fix' was stripped of all its irony. Only the acid and the cold fury remained.

'It just seemed the most perfect response, completely compelling and off the scale for intensity,' says Marx. 'That was the pair I knew from way back in the F Club, when politics wasn't a notional, abstract thing; you put yourself on the line in a direct, physical, emotional way.

'Stripped of the studio version's layers and quasi-psychedelia, it was distilled down to the essence of the song, and those two men

– the thunderous, rolling, unshakeable bass riff, direct from Detroit, that handful of words, that voice . . . colossal.

'The few minutes listening to Craig and Andrew go back out and play "Fix" were among my proudest moments of being in the band – it meant so much. Firstly that the two people I'd built the Sisters with had the integrity and courage to make the stand, and secondly that within our repertoire there were songs that spoke so directly and forcefully.'

17

(After the Gramme)

Dave Allen 'got busted at Heathrow on the way back from Amsterdam for a half-smoked spliff.' By the time he was back home, minus £50 (the on-the-spot fine in the airport) and a lot of sleep, the Sisters had sent a fax to Warners approving him as their producer. Allen's 'baptism of fire' making the Sisters of Mercy's first album would shortly begin.

Allen was under no illusions about why he'd been chosen: 'The band had to pick *someone*. The record company weren't going to give a load of money to them to self-produce. Of *course* the record company is not going to give them carte blanche.'

The clock was now ticking. The band were on Warners' time, not their own. The label had scheduled them to record the album in June and July for an October release. Unfortunately, the Sisters did not have an album's worth of songs. In fact, there was not a single new song with properly completed lyrics.

The pressure to write, record and promote an album completely killed off the already faltering relationships between the original band lineup of Marx, Eldritch and Adams, and cost Eldritch his health. Over the next twelve months, he went further upriver, deeper into the heart of darkness. When the album eventually arrived it was deeply flawed, and it was questionable whether it merited the human toll it took to create it. The band was never to recover; the start of the recording process in June 1984 marked the beginning of the end for this manifestation of the Sisters of Mercy.

The severity of Eldritch's issues writing lyrics was in evidence during the recording of the Sisters' second and final Peel Session, two weeks after the European Pilgrimage. Of the four songs, one was their cover of 'Emma'; 'Poison Door' had music and lyrics by Marx; the draft lyrics to the live version of 'Walk Away' were only given a modest tidy up; and 'No Time to Cry' was recorded for broadcast even though it was woefully unfinished, instantly becoming the worst recording ever made by the Sisters of Mercy; it was clear there was no first verse or chorus, only 'an eleventh hour, scribbled-in-the-toilets-at-the-BBC lyric,' according to Marx. The repetition of snatches of phrases and an idiosyncratic vocal delivery – lots of falsetto and strange strangulated *basso profundo* – were an attempt to disguise this, but only accentuated the unreadiness of the song.

'Poison Door' (the title taken from a King Crimson lyric) 'represents the nadir of Andrew's writing: he actually sang someone else's words,' Marx notes, semi-humorously. Yet, on its own terms, the song was excellent – Adams thinks it should have been a single – and is an example of how emergency collaboration could rescue the Sisters of Mercy. Marx says he 'sang it as a guide for Andrew to learn how it went. That was recorded and he wanted to leave it on and maybe just add his voice here and there, which was either quite sweet of him or incredibly lazy. He came in and started singing and I instantly said: "Get my voice faded out." The result was one less lyric he would have to stress over.'

Nevertheless, when the Sisters went back to Strawberry in Stockport, they were still woefully short of functional material and Eldritch had no intention of sharing any lyric credits on the album.

He also appeared to be in the middle of consolidating absolute power within the band. Several weeks prior to the start of the album sessions, Eldritch had presented Marx, Adams and Hussey with a management contract, under the terms of which he would legally assume the role as sole manager of the band. Hussey and Adams signed it. Marx – once 'Captain' and 'T. C.' – was insulted in the extreme, and was still holding out on going into Strawberry. Hussey and Adams pleaded with him to sign, believing the band couldn't possibly start the sessions with a dispute hanging over them. Marx 'very, very reluctantly agreed to be shafted every bit as much as them,' thereby joining the ranks of 'Stupid United'.

Things also began badly for Dave Allen. On the first night in Stockport, he had to share a room with Eldritch (in what Hussey refers to as 'Mrs Miggins' boarding house'). 'Me and him had to share this frankly horrible twin-bedded room,' says Allen. 'You don't want to share a room with your artist, you want to get away from him,' but in 'standard rock producer-type mode', Allen still 'turned up with some grass.' While he got 'monged' and 'went off into weed/vodka paranoia', Eldritch 'laid awake all night on whizz.'

'It was extremely tense, sleeping in a room with someone who was lying fully clothed on his bed wearing shades,' Allen admits. 'It was a clash of drugs.'

Thereafter, Eldritch slept at Strawberry in a tiny office in the basement, which had a gold disc of 'There's No One Quite Like Grandma' by the St Winifred's School Choir on the wall. 'He was drip-feeding speed, almost like a coke spoon amount, a little bit on the end of a blade to keep him going,' says Allen. 'I told him: "You don't want to do that with speed, you'll have a collapse." Week Two, I knew. I'd been a speed freak. I knew what was going to happen: your nails get all bitty, it fucks your teeth, fucks your hair – it depletes the calcium in your body. I told him: "You don't want to drip-feed that speed, Andrew. It's not good for you. It'll end in tears."'

Allen, therefore, joined Mick Robson and Rob Worby on the roll call of producers with whom Eldritch had zero rapport. 'He could be *extremely* charming, when he wanted to be,' says Allen. 'In Strawberry, that was once in six weeks.' Instead, Eldritch marshalled the persona against Allen. 'I saw his eyes once in Stockport in six weeks,' he recalls. 'He was recording in shades. Shades at night. Shades in the day. Shades all the time. He looks totally different without his shades, like a funny, weasily little guy.'

Nor did Eldritch appear to have much music written. On the first day at Strawberry, he played a cassette of everyone's works-in-progress. 'Andrew sat bigging up all these tunes of mine and what he could see us doing with them,' according to Marx. 'Then it came to Andrew's – the first one of which sounded like his reinterpretation of the theme from *The Godfather* – and he starts getting all twitchy and dismissive of it and cuts it off before the end. He then spools through to the next one in a similar way: very weird, very unlike Andrew. He ended up by saying something to effect that they could be put on the subs' bench, but we wouldn't need them.

'I am still puzzled recounting this thirty-plus years later. I haven't got copies of those tunes so I can't categorically state they weren't stinkers but given we were a few songs short for an album, to just throw them by the wayside seemed bizarre.'

Nor was Eldritch able to employ his usual modus operandi at Strawberry: burning through studio time searching for 'not just for a little icing for the top but the whole supporting structure,' as Marx puts it. That was simply too risky now the band were beholden to Warner. Marx and Hussey already had lots composed, so 'he didn't feel the need to roll his sleeves up,' Marx speculates.

To all intents and purposes, Eldritch did not write any music for the album.* The only solo compositions he worked on at Strawberry were 'On the Wire' and 'Wide Receiver.' Only the first was completed and became a B-side. 'If "On the Wire" was to be his last shot for a while that was a decent way to go out,' Marx believes. That song and 'Poison Door' were both better than several songs that eventually made the cut for the album. 'Wide Receiver' was rightly left to wither forever on the vine.

'On the Wire' seems to allude to Eldritch's excesses – the 'clouds of dust erupting' – and to acknowledge the risks of his lifestyle:

---

* 'Possession' is the only track on the album for which Eldritch is credited as co-writer of the music.

'the ground comes up . . . too fast to meet you.' Yet the final words were full of hubris: 'On the wire,' he claimed, 'I will not fall.'

There were other, more technical, problems in the studio, too. Allen's first intention was 'to try to document what I've heard, so I need to get in something like a 3k PA in the studio, make a fucking big noise, mic it up from loads of different places and maybe I'll get something that kind of sounds like that drum machine in a club, like the Milky Way.' This approach – coincidentally the one taken at KG, albeit this time with a bigger budget – failed when 'on the third day, the studio engineer de-patched the whole studio,' Allen explains. 'He was diabetic and had gone into a catatonic coma-like state.'

Allen was convinced that, if the sessions continued to be problematic, Warner would throw him to the wolves, not the band they had only recently signed. He concluded: 'I'm going to fuck off the PA. I've *got* to get some songs down!' Allen also put pragmatism above any grand creative vision where intra-band politics were concerned. He enabled the band to work separately from Eldritch. 'He was basically sleeping all day and when everybody had fucked off, he'd get up . . . Craig and Wayne wanted to work in the day and go out and party at night. Mark would come in, do his parts and fuck off, like any rational person would.'

Had Adams and Hussey actually been partying, they might have been happier. Speed, cheap wine and the occasional takeaway were the limits of their decadence in Stockport. They passed hours of their considerable downtime waiting for Eldritch to write lyrics by watching Strawberry's selection of videos. This included sundry Cheech and Chong films; *Lace* – the epitome of a 1980s high-gloss trash mini-series, and a particular favourite of Adams – and two hardcore pornographic films, one featuring a male protagonist struck by lightning and rendered with a permanent erection.

When not in his improvised quarters, Eldritch could occasionally be found sprawled out on the floor of the basement by the TV, sheets of paper spread around him. 'It was hard to tell whether he was writing a new *War and Peace* or the next single,' Marx comments.

By the time of the Strawberry sessions, Marx had moved out of Village Place and was living in Wakefield with Kathryn Wood. He elected to commute from there, rather than endure Mrs Miggins'. One of his few outings into Stockport was a shopping trip with Adams to buy supplies so they could prepare food in the studio's kitchen. So meagre was their budget – or their imagination – that all they returned to Strawberry with was a large sack of potatoes. Marx was therefore presented with a choice between 'one or other of the two atrocious porn films, eating jacket potatoes and glaring at Andrew as he shuffled yet more papers, or escaping to some kind of sanity elsewhere [where] there might even be daylight!'*

The album was made by an utterly dysfunctional quintet.

'It was ships that pass in the night as far as the band was concerned. I was the link between the night shift and the day shift,' Allen continues. 'That disguised a lot of things . . . They were separate, so the flashpoints weren't there,' he says. 'The band could have blown apart. I kept that band together.'

---

* Marx therefore missed the earthquake that shook Stockport on 19 July 1984. A quake on the Lleyn peninsula, in north Wales, which measured 5.4 on the Richter Scale, was felt in Ireland, Wales and the North-West of England. It was the most powerful quake in post-war Britain.

Allen had no problems with the Sisters on the day shift. 'I thought Gary and Wayne were the most fantastic pairing. They had brilliant style, atypical but perfect, two different kinds of players but complimentary sounds: Gary played a Fender, Wayne plays a Gibson. Wayne's a formidable musician. Craig was so tight with the drum machine.'

Allen bore the brunt on the night shift with Eldritch. None of the other Sisters were 'subjected to the enormous number of hours I spent negotiating – if negotiating is the correct term – with Andrew,' Allen says, 'The meaningless bullshit dialogue, the interminable verbal fencing.' Allen faced hour after hour of what he refers to as 'Eldritch's multiple layers of intellectual doolally bullshit . . . the endless sophistry and rhetoric, the never-accepting-a-point and contrarianism. The whole whatever-you-think-I'm-going-to-think-the-opposite became a fucking nightmare.'

'Doing a vocal with him could be an extraordinarily tedious process,' Allen continues. 'You'd do a few takes: 'That's pretty good. Do you want to come and listen to it?"

'"Oh no, what's it like?"' (Allen impersonates Eldritch in a gloomy nasal voice, not unlike Peter Cook as E. L. Wisty).

'"It's really pretty good but we need you to come in and evaluate the take."

"What's wrong with Take 1?"

"What, specifically?"

"Yeah, specifically."'

Allen was incredulous: 'He's on the mic with a set of headphones, twenty foot away!'

'"Just come in and have a listen to it and see which one you think is better. I liked the last one."

"What was good about the last one?"

"I think you really got the lyric right, the tone of voice."

'And then you'd start analysing it out like that: fucking pointless. Pointless!'

Either this was Eldritch trying to kick-start his creative process or it was an attempt to disguise the fact that singing and writing an album's worth of lyrics were, at this point, beyond him. Instead, Eldritch reverted to something 'he could still do in his sleep: construct and win an argument,' Marx says.

Allen also regularly found himself 'stuck in the middle' of things he found 'fucking weird.' A case in point was 'the lead singer running down everybody in his band', complaining to Allen that '"So-and-so can't play guitar properly"' and that Hussey and Adams were using the kinds of drugs of which he did not approve. Allen was relieved that he 'didn't know enough to start being terrified.'

At Strawberry, differences in Marx's and Eldritch's background came to the surface. 'It was so apparent that my attitude to the large amounts of money we were spending was vastly different to Andrew's,' Marx says. 'I say "spending", but it was the wasting of money that offended me so much . . . To book recording studios and not record for days on end wasted thousands of pounds. A particular piece of equipment was sent up from a gear hire company in London, because Andrew specifically requested it. It sat there day after day in the control room, never coming out of its flight-case. At one point the engineer turned to me and said, "That fucking box is making more money sat there than I am." . . . The sums of money wasted equated to a year or more's wages for many of the people I knew, including my own father.'

What had once bound Marx and Eldritch together receded. Marx puts it like this: 'How is an exhaustive knowledge of the different ad libs on bootleg versions of "Ain't It Strange" by Patti Smith going to help you three or four years on when you're arguing about money?'

So little vocal recording was done in the initial Strawberry sessions that Marx and Hussey tried adding lyrics and vocal tracks to some of their backing tracks in order to break the stasis. Two of Hussey's songs gained titles: 'Garden of Delight' and 'Dance On Glass', the words for the latter Hussey 'had had hanging around for ages. They just seemed to fit that particular tune.' Of Marx's songs, 'The Scottish One' became 'Marianne' and another became 'Child of Light'.

This process triggered Eldritch into writing two sets of lyrics. Eldritch, it seems, adjusted the spelling of Marx's 'Marianne' and layered his own elaborate word game on top. This was to disguise how acutely personal the lyrics actually were: the singer was likely addressing a woman in Hamburg who refused to leave her boyfriend for him. Eldritch sang it right at the bottom of his range and sounded utterly exhausted, a drowning man crying out for rescue.

'Marian' certainly functions as the acme of a kind of lugubrious doom rock but is not to be taken entirely seriously. Its final and full title is 'Marian (Version)', indicating a crossword puzzle anagram, in this case of 'Marina', a short Eliot poem laden with waterborne imagery. A *Stingray* fan like Eldritch may even have had another Marina in mind. 'Marian' could therefore function as an elaborate joke, one sodden with its own watery images and puns, and not simply as a cry of desolation.

Eldritch rewrote 'Dance On Glass' as 'Black Planet'. Allen made the mistake of congratulating Eldritch on writing a powerful, ecologically aware song. 'It's not about ecology' was Eldritch's dismissive reply. 'Nothing to do with that. I *want* a black planet.' Allen was shocked: 'There's something quite inhuman about that.'

Indeed, 'Black Planet' proceeds from the assumption that global annihilation is looming and that the proper response is another kind of oblivion, best achieved after the sun has gone down – via sex and drugs, most likely. And if not global annihilation, then Eldritch was convinced, especially after visiting the USA, that the decline and fall of the American empire – including its Western European periphery – were imminent. Eldritch welcomed all sorts of obliteration.

Even these occasional bursts of progress came at a price. Eldritch had initially rubbished the work Hussey had been doing on 'Dance On Glass' and his music for 'Marian', rejecting the latter with, 'Nah, sounds like the Banshees,' according to Hussey, who had written and recorded it from scratch in the studio in a couple of hours. On hearing Eldritch's opinion, Allen thought to himself: 'Are you fucking mental, mate?'*

In contrast, Eldritch actually liked Marx's music for 'Child of Light' from the outset. In a rare moment of harmony at Strawberry,

---

* For detail on the creation of Wayne Hussey's music for these sessions see his autobiography *Salad Days*, especially Chapter 15.

they played the Gun Club's 'Mother of Earth' to Allen as a reference point. 'It was a massive favourite of ours and we saw something in its atmosphere and sense of space as being a useful guide,' Marx explains. Hussey to his great credit – and as much as he loved his effects pedals and his battery of guitars – realised there was little to add, except replacing the guitar arpeggios with piano. 'Child of Light' – 'Nine While Nine' in its finished form – is a rare Sisters track of the era, being redolent of the simplicity of its origins: Marx sat in his upstairs bedroom at Village Place playing his Shergold electric guitar, unamplified and untreated. It would remain the gentlest and sparest of the songs tracked at Strawberry.

It would take Eldritch nearly six more months to write and sing lyrics to.

Nevertheless, the lyrics for the Hussey songs indicated that Eldritch was emerging from the lyrical trough of 'Body and Soul', 'Walk Away' and 'No Time to Cry'. The clue to just how superb his writing would be for the album – in some cases among the finest lyrics in rock music – were evident in the Strawberry sessions on the track that would eventually become 'Some Kind of Stranger'.

Marx's music was also excellent. 'It's the only example during my time in the Sisters that I used a chord pattern as a starting point for any part of a song,' says Marx. This became the verse. Another chord sequence was layered over one of his 'usual one-or-two-string guitar-lines' and became the epic coda that would ultimately close out the album. '"If There Is Something" [by Roxy Music] makes use of that falling sequence, as does "China Girl" [by Iggy Pop], but it really would be a very long list if you started looking into it,' Marx explains. 'It's just something that has a great yearning pull between its changes and makes it ideal to cycle round and round and build on. It seems to function as a template to put your own stamp on fairly readily.'

The verse part of the song is a 'pattern that Andrew affectionately dubbed "Little Wing" because it shared something with that song and those other Hendrix ballads like "Angel". It's basically a chord sequence with a small embellishment which is what prompted the comparison, although any Hendrix pattern would have far more decoration and variety than I used.'

After weeks at Strawberry, 'finally, Andrew called me in one morning to tell me he'd put a vocal on the track. He was very excited and said he knew I'd love it, and described it as being like a cross between "Oh Yes You're Beautiful" by Gary Glitter and Roxy Music.'

Eldritch only had enough lyrics for half of the song, which he deployed over the falling chord sequence. They offered a further elaboration of Eldritch's moral philosophy: the world is a cold place, where words have little value and love is doomed. Therefore, one must seek out beauty and guard one's memories of it. Put another way: there's nothing casual about casual sex with strangers.

'Of course, it did sound fantastic,' says Marx, 'and the emotion sent shivers right through you – probably the most exhilarating moment within the entire album sessions for me. That just added to the frustration when it continued to sit unfinished for day after day.'

'A Rock and a Hard Place' also remained unfinished at Strawberry. Lyrically, it has its moments: sardonic, funny and utterly impenetrable. It seems to be at least partly about a New

York lover ('with her bangles and her reference') and is more than a little cruel, with Eldritch claiming, 'There wasn't a part of me that didn't want to say goodbye.' 'The Devil may care but I don't mind' would end up as the funniest line on the album, but who knows what 'down from igor' means, or why one line hangs unfinished: 'One from the church from the valley of the.'

Dave Allen was beyond frustrated by this point. 'We had working titles for the songs. One of them was "Down to E Like a Motherfucker", another one was "Shit on Your Chest" – which is probably a Noddy Holder reference. Another one was "The Horned One Stabs". I came in one day, went to work with Wayne, and Andrew had Tippexed out every single working title and put the real titles on,' Allen says. 'That was a very irritating thing to do. It's not wrong, but it is very irritating. Maybe that's being pissy, but at the time it was: "For fuck's sake, what's he done *now*? We've got to play all the fucking tapes just to find out what's on them."'

When the sessions ended, Allen gave Eldritch a lift back from Strawberry to the Black Office in his hire car. 'He said [again in a nasal, whiny Peter Cook voice], "I hate people who drive fast." A four-hour journey took two-and-a-quarter, 'to make sure I didn't have any dialogue with him whatsoever. He slept in the fetal position on the backseat.'

That Allen found Eldritch 'fucking irritating' is clear, but 'I liked him as well. It's difficult to explain: a pain in the arse but a really good artist . . . I knew I was in the presence of greatness. He's great. His lyrics are great . . . Eldritch always looks like there's something going on in there, an internal life. That's part of his charisma.' Allen continues: 'Of course he found singing difficult. Most artists do. And of course his voice is a construct, he doesn't actually speak like that. He's an octave higher when he speaks, so it's a thing he puts on. I'm not saying it's easy. He invented it. He made himself. I understand that no one's really super-confident about what they do, insecurities and the rest of it . . . but that can be part of making a great record. I was convinced from the outset that we were going to make some seminal thing that was going to be a reference point.'

For the six weeks the Sisters of Mercy spent in Stockport, there had been a heatwave. 'Amazing weather for Manchester. It didn't rain once,' Allen remembers. Eldritch had seen none of the sunshine, but despite six interminable weeks on the night shift, the seminal record was nowhere near finished.

After the failure of the Strawberry sessions, the Sisters went back to New York City to play two gigs as part of the New Music Seminar. Midsummer made the Iroquois additionally unsanitary. Cockroach-infested at the best of times, the heat brought new threats. Pete Turner was only partially sighted when he mixed the Sisters' sound at their New York gigs because 'some sort of insect had a chew of me. I got bitten on the eye and it all swelled up.'

The Sisters played twice: once at Irving Plaza with the Chameleons and the Danse Society and then three days later at the Ritz with Black Flag, a band that made the Sisters and Aswad look like a natural pairing. Their singer, Henry Rollins, hated the Sisters on sight: 'Of all the bands in the world . . . the Sisters of Mercy will be opening for us tonight. Smoke machines, all kinds of lights were brought in for them. What a crock of weak-assed shit they are.'*

The Black Flag fans at the front spat and jeered as soon as the Sisters came on. 'The best part,' Rollins concluded, 'was seeing the poor Sisters trying to maintain their pose with the front row trying to beat the shit out of the singer, swinging at his head and shit.' Marx summarised the gig as: 'Another night of music and bottles.'

While Black Flag were on, Eldritch was found slumped in a chair backstage, so pale and evidently fucked that a woman checked whether he was breathing and, when convinced he was alive, offered him a glass of water.

The tensions of Strawberry had been let loose before the gig: Hussey and Eldritch got into an argument when Hussey started badgering Eldritch about moving the band to the US. This was inebriated hot air, but Eldritch was so ground down he quit the Sisters of Mercy that night.

The rest of the band followed suit.

Each of them thought better of it and re-joined before the flight home.

When the Sisters returned to the UK to finish the album, they continued the slow process of breaking up for real. The next act of their disintegration took place at Genetic Studios, located halfway up a wooded hill, overlooking the glorious valley of the Thames. Genetic was an idyllic spot; the Sisters of Mercy made it hellish.

Also recording there were Lloyd Cole and the Commotions,

---

* Although the Sisters went on first at the Ritz, they had equal billing with Black Flag, as specified in their tour book. 'Check Front of House Security' was ominously – and correctly – also noted.

clean-cut regular fellows, who provided a marked contrast to the long-haired, drug-infested Sisters. The Commotions were staying in the residential cottages within the grounds of Genetic and could be spied in their pristine tennis gear or armed with a towel en route for a swim. The only evidence that Eldritch saw daylight in Berkshire are the photos taken, in the sun-dappled woods that surrounded the studio grounds, by Jill Furmanovsky.

Eldritch had arrived at Genetic at a time of maximum stress and pressure. He was approaching a critical moment in the whole Sisters project: four years in the making, this was the point at which it would stand or fall. On top of which, it was evident that his relationships with Marx and Shearsby were terminally ill.

Eldritch immediately began driving Dave Allen up the wall again. This time, Allen was on home territory. Genetic was Martin Rushent's studio, built in a converted barn on his property. He had produced *Dare* by the Human League there; Allen had been the studio engineer. Allen was therefore particularly unreceptive to Eldritch's notes on his production:

""This is just shit production."

"What's your idea then?"

"Jimmy Iovine."

"What's he done then?""

Allen had genuinely never heard of him.

"" 'Stop Draggin' My Heart Around' by Fleetwood Mac.""*

"" 'Gimme Shelter": when they did that at the Milky Way –

---

* To this day, Allen is no expert on Fleetwood Mac; 'Stop Draggin' My Heart Around' is actually a Stevie Nicks solo track produced by Iovine and Tom Petty.

"Rape, murder, it's just a kiss away." Er . . . I don't *really* fit that in the same bag as "Rhiannon" and Stevie Nicks,' he says. 'He wasn't being perverse – he actually wanted that. My analysis would be that he was trying to get a big slick MOR production out of me . . . Of course he wanted a big record. We all want that; I just didn't want a big record that's moronic."

Marx and Eldritch's relationship also continued to decline at Genetic. Major amendments to his music for 'The Horned One Stabs' (later retitled 'Amphetamine Logic') had disappointed Marx. Eldritch wanted 'the main verse riff . . . broken up to leave these gaps to incorporate Wayne's Duran Duran-inspired guitar . . . It made the part I was playing a bit worthless to my ears . . . I didn't like it but I saw the song as mostly just a good chorus anyway.'†

Another flashpoint was not even over one of Marx's songs: 'We'd lived with half a chorus for "A Rock and a Hard Place" for a long time before the second half came along,' he remembers. 'When it did, I viewed it as a lesser inclusion, an "anything-will-do-at-this-point" mentality. I challenged him over it . . . back then I expected him just to take it on trust. But trust was in pretty short supply by the time we'd been holed up in Genetic a while. Clearly, if you've been struggling to come up with lyrics for several months and have pushed yourself to the point of mental and physical exhaustion,

---

* Eldritch's taste for material by certain mainstream American artists had been amplified once he encountered them in its natural habitat: FM radio in the US. This would eventually manifest itself at vocal sound-checks. As well as 'Stop Draggin' My Heart Around', Eldritch often sang 'Racing in the Street' off of *Darkness on the Edge of Town*.' (Beethoven's 'Ode to Joy' was also in his repertoire.)

† Marx is thinking of 'Planet Earth' by Duran Duran, the guitar played by Eldritch's namesake, Andy Taylor.

the last thing you need is someone telling you they don't like the handful of lines you have got.'

The death throes of the Genetic sessions were 'the most difficult point in our time together: we had no way of talking to each other . . . We had been able to read each other so easily for so long that it had led to a complacency between us.'

Eldritch has put it like this: 'I'd never really talked to the guy. We'd always sort of understood each other perfectly just by looking at each other. It was a remarkable relationship; very good. And when – and I don't think it was me – at some point, he just started to glaze over . . . I'd look and he'd look and there'd be nothing. Then we had to start talking to each other, and we found at that stage, we'd never really done it and we couldn't do it. He'd moved to Wakefield and had a very different kind of domestic thing going all of a sudden, which seemed to be a lot more important to him.'

'Some Kind of Stranger' – primarily, but not entirely – a song about the sensual power of anonymous sex – seems also to memorialise the end of Marx and Eldritch's relationship, not least the title. Its opening lyrics describe how 'words got in the way' of 'what we had'. Marx was also convinced that the song contained a jibe at his inability to act on his own discontent within the band, instead lingering 'undecided at the door.'

'Some Kind of Stranger' was finally completed at Genetic. After two days spent on vocals, Allen reached the end of his tether. He arranged playback for Eldritch in the control room. 'I had two ashtrays on both NS10s [studio monitors] full of Isopropyl [an alcohol-based cleaning fluid]. And I timed it: just before he walked through the door, I torched everything, so when he came in, the speakers were alight, the desk was alight. Fucked it. That's how I pulled client approval on that track. We never did any more vocals on it after that.' Allen explains: 'He needed something *that* traumatic; it was just like he'd been out-madded. Isopropyl burns off, but it's a good party trick. That's how I avoided some interminable over-intellectualised discussion. The setting fire to the desk was: "I'm not putting up with bullshit – we fucking nailed it!"'*

One end product of this collective madness was that 'Some Kind of Stranger' emerged as the acme of Sisters' music, simultaneously witty – rather than funny – drawing on Roxy Music, Gary Glitter and Petula Clark's 'Don't Sleep in the Subway', but also devastating and brutally honest. As severe as Eldritch was with others, he was even more merciless towards himself. 'Some Kind of Stranger' is very beautiful, but also painfully excoriating. If there is an emotional equivalent of the flayed head in the Merciful Release logo, it is this song: brutal, wry and revealing.

Eldritch put himself through the wringer at Genetic. The final collapse when it came was physical, rather than mental.

'Genetic had a tape store and a chill out room,' Allen recalls. 'He made that room his own . . . Blinds down, cushions on the floor and doing the same kind of thing as at Strawberry: drip-feeding himself with speed and just getting sicker and sicker.' Eldritch slept for no more than an hour or two during the entire fortnight.

---

* Long before this point, Allen was affectionately known to the Sisters as 'Trolley', as in: 'He's off his . . .'. The pretended incineration of the mixing desk was just the most flamboyant of the many gestures that earned him the nickname. 'It is unclear whether he was simply reacting to the madness around him or he came pre-programmed,' Marx observes.

'He needed to stop sticking amphetamine sulphate up his nose,' Allen continues, 'get a bit of daylight and some food . . . He wasn't eating properly. You can't do that for weeks and live in the dark without Vitamin D.'

On what turned out to be the sessions' final night, Marx got word that Eldritch was going to sing and that he wanted Marx at the console when he did so. This role, once so familiar to Marx, had dwindled as Eldritch had become progressively more difficult and obsessive in the studio. Naturally Marx assumed that Eldritch had something substantial on the go when he heard his presence was required.

'It soon became clear he had little or no voice as far as I could tell from his initial attempts. Either that or he was so unsure of what he'd written that he was mumbling without a clear melodic shape in his head.' When Marx told him to step back into the control room, Eldritch complied. There was no 'bullshit dialogue' or 'verbal fencing' via the playback.

'He sort of bounced off the walls as he walked in and before he could ask how it was going or listen back to anything, I told him that I viewed it as pointless continuing. I made it clear that I didn't just mean continuing with that track, or for that evening, but with the planned sessions to finish the album. The fact that I didn't get a lengthy argument . . . gives an indication of how feeble he was at that stage. He slumped down and perhaps somewhere momentarily there was a sense of relief.' But, Marx continues, Eldritch 'quickly rallied enough to state that the decision to stop the sessions was mine and that I would have to be the one to break the news to the record company – the scheduled tour was dependent on the proposed release date and so on:

"'It's on your head."

"Fine."

"You know when I'm better I won't thank you for this.'"

This was Marx's last time in a studio as a Sister.

The sessions concluded with lyrics and vocals unfinished. Allen met with Eldritch on the final evening in the Miller of Mansfield, the eighteenth-century pub/hotel where the band were lodged in close-by Goring-on-Thames.

Allen was furious. 'During a lock-in I was fucking arguing with Eldritch: "You've been telling me for weeks you were going to get the lyrics. You haven't got them, have you? *Have* you?" And making him go: "I've not got the lyrics, Dave."'

That night Eldritch and Allen had to share a room again, Eldritch deciding to stay awake. 'Of course he did,' comments Allen, acidly.

'When I woke up in the morning, Andrew was there on the floor with this sort of curtain pulled over him. And he didn't look very well. I thought: "Oh fuck, he's ill." Obviously, he wasn't dead. He hadn't OD'd or anything like that. He'd just had some sort of hypoglaecemic collapse.'

Allen left Eldritch on the floor and drove to Genetic. 'I got them to ring for an ambulance.' He then called Warners. 'I had to take where the project was to the record company. They were paying for it. They were paying *me*.'

Allen accepts this sounds callous but 'the studio was about a three-minute drive away. He was breathing OK. He was just blue:

cyanosis. Realistically, at the time, he just needed a doctor and a stop. And to eat something.'

Eldritch was not looking for sympathy and none was forthcoming. Allen, Hussey and Adams found it easy to look on and let him pulverise himself. If Adams, Hussey or Marx had collapsed, Allen was sure Eldritch 'wouldn't have given a fucking fuck: "Another dead soldier. Get another one in." Military background . . . So, yeah, not a lot of love was shown. You get back what you give out.' Adams agrees: 'He wouldn't have cared if it was any of us.'

18

Too Dark to See

Eldritch's weight had dropped to a haggard seven stones. He was hospitalised and then placed under the care of a doctor in London who was seemingly aware of the nature of his drug intake and his utter disinterest in relaxation. As Eldritch has recalled, 'The doctor said "How do you relax?" and I said I don't. He said, "Well, wouldn't you like to be able to relax?" and I said no. And he said, "Take these."' Without the prescribed tranquilisers, another collapse was imminent. In the longer term, there was realpolitik: rather than abstaining, Eldritch would adjust his amphetamine use before his body informed him, 'No thank you. This has gone far enough. It'll end in tears,' as it had done at Genetic.

Dave Allen actually has significant regrets about his handling of the Genetic disaster. 'With more experience, I would have pulled the session weeks before. "This is madness. You're driving yourself into a hole trying to write these lyrics . . . Let's put a hiatus on it and reconvene in September."' As a producer, now in his sixties, who has transitioned from a father figure into a grandfatherly role for the younger bands and artists he has worked with, Allen 'feels terrible, guilty. I should have been more understanding or dogmatic about rest periods.'

The core problem was one not uncommon in Leeds: abject speed-freakery. 'For anyone who takes speed,' says Allen, 'it's all about disconnection of emotion. That's what they really like. You just become extremely clinical and logical, like you're playing chess with life and people are just numbers. You feel like you've got a super amount of energy. That's fine for painting and decorating or cleaning the house, but it's crap for art, especially music, which is about connection with emotions.'

All of Eldritch's best lyrics, regardless of how stylised or arcane, were highly personal. Until he could fully reactivate that connection there would be no album.

Before that could even be attempted, there were four festival dates booked for September. Good sense did not prevail: the Sisters elected to play them, even though Eldritch was obviously physically enfeebled. The first two were a split-site, two-day event in West Germany. The first of these 'Summer Nights' was in a muddy outdoor motocross arena in Westphalia – in daylight. It was so cold that the Glühwein vendors did excellent business. The Sisters were on a bizarre and incoherent bill with Blancmange, Rory Gallagher, the Waterboys and Frank Zappa. For Marx, it was 'really squalid, and a miserable day.' The weather and Eldritch's appalling physical condition were part of the grimness, but there was also the tiny and decrepit backstage caravan allocated to the band.

The night before, Adams had been given 'some pills by a German woman with a lot of rabbits. We were early on the bill, so I barely arrived back in time, saucer-eyed.' Marx 'was well and truly hammered when we came to perform . . . I was almost incapable of playing. At one point I broke a string and just wandered off mid-number back down the steps to the caravan where I'd left my spare strings – Lord knows how long I was gone, and if I ever replaced the string. I also remember needing to have a piss at some point and just going over to the back edge of the stage and relieving myself.' At one point his guitar cut out completely because 'he ran forward and pulled his amp over,' says Adams. 'He was at the front of the stage giving it some but there was nothing coming out of his guitar.'

After the second Summer Night at a former National Socialist amphitheatre on the Rhine, the Sisters cancelled their appearance at 'Les Nuits de la Saint Vitus' four days later at L'Eldorado, an historic art deco cinema in central Paris. This gave Eldritch two weeks' respite before the last of the festival dates: 'The York Rock Festival'. This festival was pure Wild West: the novice promoters, two guys in their early twenties (with financial backing from a Porsche-driving carpet-fitter), had booked the Racecourse, the biggest venue in the city, which held close to twenty thousand people.

As rough and ready as it was, the York Racecourse show was the biggest the Sisters had ever played. Adams and Hussey prepared by going down the Leeds Warehouse and staying up all night. When they went to Village Place with Jez Webb to collect Eldritch, they found he'd not slept either. Since Genetic, Eldritch had made adjustments to his lifestyle: food and daylight were back on the menu, but so were amphetamines and alcohol. Nevertheless, in the two weeks off between the German Summer Nights and the York Rock Festival, Eldritch had – by his recent standards – committed to a regimen of healthy living. He told one interviewer he had put on a stone and a half in weight and his blood pressure, heart rate and blood sugar level had all returned to virtually normal.

Adams arrived for the gig 'as high as a kite' and met his parents at the front gates of the Racecourse. The band did not travel in the Flying Turd; the Chameleons – below the Sisters on the bill – parked next to a 'shiny black van with heavily tinted windows that wouldn't have looked out of place in an episode of *Scooby Doo*,' recalls their singer, Mark Burgess. 'The side door of the van slid open. In my imagination, I heard a whoosh of air and saw a cloud of dry ice emerge from the interior.' Eldritch got out, circling the Chameleons' van, before approaching the driver's window. '"Nice van, man," he said. "It'd be better if it was in black, though," and walked off.'

Tony Mallett, one of the young promoters, confirms that Eldritch 'was indeed wankered' at the York Rock Festival. Part of the reason was that, before going onstage, he had been stuck in a broken lift with Mallett and a full bottle of Jack Daniel's. 'Three of us went in, only two of us came out,' Mallett quips. 'We were in there for fifteen or twenty minutes,' time enough for Mallett to be 'sure Eldritch had done a few bits and bobs prior.' The smoke from the number of cigarettes smoked in the lift 'hurried up the rescue teams.'

In daylight, and smoke-free, the Sisters were in clear view. There were repeated sightings of Eldritch grinning, 'completely wired off his tits and licking his lips,' as Jez D'Netto observed. Regardless – or because – of the contents of his own bloodstream, Eldritch had the nerve to introduce 'Alice' as being 'about how awfully bad for you barbiturates are.' Adams' bass cut out during the intro and the song was halted. 'You wanted the words as well?' Eldritch enquired, seemingly genuinely chipper to be playing in Yorkshire to what was effectively a home crowd.

The gig was disastrous. Marx's pedals and the Doktor were at their most temperamental and, while attempting to shimmy behind Adams, Eldritch got his mic stand caught on Adams' lead, unplugging him so roughly that he had to leave the stage mid-'Heartland' to get a fresh one. Hussey threw down his guitar and left the stage long before 'Ghost Rider' had finished. Marx saw out the 'chaotic and dismal set' and flung his guitar sideways over the PA stack. This was Danny Horigan's last gig as roadie and Merb's first; the baton was passed during a cavalcade of malfunctions, both human and technical.*

Worse was to come. Even without an album, the Sisters of Mercy still had 'Walk Away' to promote as a single. For the accompanying video, they decided 'not to offer any pretence of playing our instruments,' says Marx. 'Andrew had requested a laser which accounted for almost all the budget, so it's no surprise it is, again,

---

* The guitar Marx launched over the PA stack – unbeknownst to him at the time – landed on a steward doing security. 'The security guy set about looking for the culprit and become increasingly wound up by drawing a blank. He found himself in front of Ian McCulloch during his set and was a bit heavy-handed with some Bunnymen fans. [McCulloch] prodded him with his mic stand at one point and obviously became the new focus for his rage.' The festival ended with the out-of-control steward punching Ian McCulloch backstage.

dreadful. Given the imagination the band showed in other areas, it's alarming to think the best we could come up with was a series of shots where we all walk away from the camera. After the tedium of doing that for the umpteenth time we decided to dance and generally fool around.'

Marx also recalls that 'Andrew did this thing backcombing his hair to get extra height.' This was a mistake Eldritch has referred to as his 'Cliff Richard haircut'. His decision to sprinkle glitter and his inability to look secure standing on a travelator compounded the error. 'The person in those videos is my stupid twin brother,' he once commented.

The biggest error was not saving 'Walk Away', their best chance of a bona fide hit single, for the album release, instead squandering it as a gap-filler. 'Walk Away', like 'Body and Soul' failed to reach the UK Top 40 and get the Sisters on *Top of the Pops*.

Given the array of fuckups preceding it, the Black October tour of late autumn 1984 was a recipe for disaster: a fracturing band, containing a singer with a predilection for pushing himself past the limits of his endurance, on a gruelling six-week slog around the UK and Europe. The festival gigs, at a muddy German motocross circuit, a former Nazi open-air arena and a windy North Yorkshire racecourse, had not boded well.

Before embarking on Black October, Eldritch met Adam Sweeting of *Melody Maker* for pizza in High Holborn. Eldritch made no secret of the fact he had been sick. In the studio, 'people he engaged in conversation began to change colour and bend out of shape,' Sweeting recorded. Even back to his usual eight and a half stone, Sweeting observed that Eldritch still looked 'as overweight as a credit card and his complexion remains a brilliant white'. It was uncertain whether Eldritch could physically complete the tour. Nor was it at all clear that the band itself would make it to the end without a Ritz-style implosion, one that this time would remain unrepaired. It seemed there was every possibility that the Sisters of Mercy were in their humiliating last days.

Incredibly, much of Black October was a triumph. The Sisters played longer and more varied sets than on the spring Pilgrimages. Most of what would become the first side of *First and Last and Always* was a regular feature, mixed in with all the singles (minus 'Temple of Love' and 'The Damage Done'), plus 'Burn', 'Heartland', 'Emma' and 'Gimme Shelter'. A new cover – 'Knockin' on Heaven's Door' – as blackly humorous as it was magnificent, was played most nights and was regularly Hussey's masterpiece. In Manchester, he also played 'Stairway to Heaven' – fast and electrified – over the 'Ghost Rider' drum pattern. It was yet more evidence of just how good a guitar player Hussey was. If Eldritch wanted a version of the Sisters that could absorb great quantities of classic rock and still sound like the Sisters of Mercy, then the man at stage left would be key.

Although there was a musty sense of déjà vu as the band found themselves back in many of the same towns and same venues as previous tours – the Odeon in Münster, the Top Rank in Plymouth, Rock City in Nottingham, the universities in Sheffield and Manchester – there was evidence that the band were on an upward trajectory: they headlined the Refectory at Leeds university and the Lyceum ballroom in London for the first times. Sometimes, when they broke new ground the response could be rapturous.

Hussey remembered that in Colchester, at the University of Essex, 'we sold out and the crowd . . . went nuts.'

Their extended family and the support network it provided – critically absent in the studio – were restored during Black October and were essential to its successful completion. The key off-stage relationship was between Eldritch and Pete Turner. Visually, they were an odd couple: Turner, a giant who dressed like a trucker, Eldritch, small and skinny, perpetually in his rock 'n' roll regalia. Turner liked Eldritch enormously and thought he was in his natural habitat, despite the toll it was taking on him. 'He had star quality. It never occurred to me he shouldn't be there,' Turner says. 'Big Pete' and Eldritch were the two ranking adults on Black October. If Eldritch needed to discuss whatever was winding him up – and there would always be something – it was Turner he went to most often. If there was anyone Eldritch dropped the persona for, it was Turner.

Turner was quite aware that Eldritch had come on tour nowhere near fully recovered. Being the 'tour Dad', as Turner puts it, sometimes meant he had to put a metaphorical arm around Eldritch. 'Pete was very conscious of what Andrew was going through,' says Phil Wiffin. 'He wasn't well. The amount of drink and drugs that were going on, that creates its own stress . . . Pete would often try to get him to take a break, not mollycoddle him, but give him a shoulder . . . [but] Andrew was a difficult person to support. He needs it but he's reluctant to accept it. He was quite a difficult character in that time period . . . He was a quiet, shy guy.'

The importance of Jez Webb on band and crew morale was also vital. Eldritch has described him as 'an all round superhuman good guy . . . relentlessly cheerful and amicable.' Webb too was aware of the pressure Eldritch had placed himself under. 'Andrew created a character, a very cool persona that was very hard to let your guard down with. The more the band went on the more that character took over. He'd be as daft as us in the early years but I'm sure he became more aware as the band grew, what people expected of Eldritch . . . We all dipped in and out of living the Sisters thing, but for him it was 24/7.'

The gigs were often a potent mixture of adulation and contempt that created its own peculiar energy. Black October, even more than previous tours, seemed to pit the band against elements in the crowd. Someone swiped Eldritch's glasses off his face in Leicester; spittle and bottles were launched at them in Glasgow; spit alone in Cardiff, which especially infuriated Eldritch, who already had an irrational dislike of the Welsh, perhaps related to a head injury sustained in a Welsh playground as a small child. Eldritch often seemed genuinely irritated by people in the crowd. The head-master in him would often bark out, 'Shut up!', as if he was taking assembly. Sometimes there was added acid: 'We're not here for conversation, so keep it quiet' and 'We'll do the singing, you do the jumping up and down.'

Some of it was serio-comic stuff. Eldritch opened the Lancaster gig with, 'Let's get the heckling over with now. I can take it. Come on,' before tossing out his own invective: 'This one's for the bastards still playing pool. I can see you. I know who you are. I have your addresses.' His introduction of 'Heartland' as 'a song about roads and stuff; mainly stuff' was greeted with, 'Bollocks! You fuck-head!' Eldritch, obviously inebriated, shot back: 'I'm afraid, fella

. . . if you choose to carry on with that sort of behaviour, there will be retribution,' and after a pause for effect, 'of the *severest* sort.' However, sometimes Eldritch's threats sounded in earnest. In Nottingham he noted: 'Something we've learned in our many years is that the right hand is a horrible thing to lose; I'd retract yours, my man.'

Eldritch could also be self-deprecating. After 'No Time to Cry' in Stuttgart, he observed, 'I like the title better than the words' and after 'A Rock and a Hard Place' in Edinburgh, 'You'll get used to it. Not sure I will.' At Rock City, a member of the audience enquired about his physical health. 'I'm not anorexic, all right. I'm compact,' came the reply. The Doktor misbehaved so badly in Nottingham that 'Burn' began three times before being aborted, requiring the band to leave the stage to 'tend to our machinery,' as Eldritch put it.

Touring at the Sisters' level was still not without its hazards and the possibility of accidents and violence. 'There was a team effort to get from A to B, do what we had to do and then get out of there without getting injured,' recalls Wiffin. 'I got bitten on the leg at one show by a German guy as I was stood on a riser in front of him.' In Europe, there were instances of genuine danger. At the Schlachthof in Bremen, Hussey recalls Neo-Nazis 'chucking stones and rubble onto the flat roof. It sounded like a particularly heavy hailstorm.' They then got into the venue and 'fired a flare gun at us and it set fire to the backdrop,' Adams remembers.

Onstage during Black October the Sisters of Mercy were a potent rock band, but off it they were terminally divided. Hussey and Adams remained playmates but Eldritch and Marx separated themselves from them and each other. To Wiffin, the disintegration of the band was obvious: 'I was aware that the family was breaking down.' Hussey and Adams indulged their 'classic rock 'n' roll approach' as Wiffin terms it, whereas 'Mark would definitely gravitate towards the crew . . . and Andrew, if not with a woman, would disappear for a while or sit with me and Pete.'

Sometimes innocuous activities could become a mote in the eye. 'We'd go somewhere in Germany and Andrew would tell me what I needed to know about food,' Turner says, 'but he used to let the others get on with it. They had all sorts of weird food. That used to annoy Craig . . . that Andrew used to be able to order stuff and get what he wanted, whereas they would order pigs' heads – quite unpalatable stuff.'

An outbreak of pubic lice on Hussey and Adams also did not help relations within the band: 'Andrew refused to get into the vehicle with us,' Adams admits. Eldritch shunned the Flying Turd and instead travelled in the car with the crew. He insisted Turner call his wife, who was a nurse, to get medical advice and then acquire the necessary treatment from a chemist's. 'There was quite a posh lady behind the counter,' Turner recalls. 'There's a couple of friends of mine have crabs,' he told her. 'She gave me that knowing: "Couple of 'friends' of yours, sir?"'

Wiffin additionally suggested the wearing of shower caps as 'the correct health and safety clothing for dealing with crabs.' Adams and Hussey 'had to travel creamed up' (as Jez Webb puts it) in the Flying Turd in only their underpants and shower hats. They played the next sound-check in their entirely useless – as Wiffin well knew – headgear to peals of laughter from the whole crew.

Adams thinks he caught crabs when he had to sleep in Hussey's bed – he'd thrown his own out of the hotel room window. This was also the fate of a wardrobe on Black October and Marx claims responsibility: 'I was always fit but somehow managing to fling a wardrobe into a tree outside the hotel in Birmingham still astounds me whenever I'm reminded of that one.' Dealing with this also fell to Pete Turner. 'I had to go down the next morning and tell the landlord/hotelier: "Sorry, there's been a wardrobe broken."

'"No worries, I'll pop up and have a look."

'"Actually, you might want to go out into the garden . . ."'

As well as sound engineer and *de facto* tour manager, Turner functioned as the authority figure for the whole crew, which 'he ruled with a tough fist and heart of gold,' Merb says. Since Turner could 'pick up speaker stacks as if they were paper', it made sense to obey him.

Turner had no real interest in accompanying the band or crew in any after-hours fun. Ministering to the band's recreational needs was Dave Kentish's role; Kentish's background in security was useful should meaningful threats of violence be required. His handling of the Flying Turd could be equally unnerving. Merb recalls sitting next to him when he was 'driving from Bristol to Brum and watching him fall asleep on the M5 with me desperately trying to keep him awake.'

The band and crew consumed ever-more substantial amounts of drugs. 'There were people following us around in Germany providing us with amphetamine,' Yaron Levy recalls. 'There was one time – I think it was in Cologne Luxor – we'd had some crystal meth. It was cut into the amphetamine.' The ensuing paranoia and hallucinations were so strong that 'before the end of the show, Craig was already in the dressing room because he couldn't handle it,' Levy explains. 'We were surrounded by so much smoke, I just left my desk and walked off as well and joined him.'

Even among the bigger crowds the Sisters were attracting, the God Squad maintained their place front and centre, and on the guest list. 'The Sisters were a friendly lot, all of them,' says Jez D'Netto. 'Despite Eldritch giving out this persona, he was a nice guy. When we were there at sound-checks, he'd always come over and ask, "How are you doing? You alright?" He wasn't massively sociable but he would put in an effort for people who were making an effort to see the band.'

When D'Netto was waiting at Stoke railway station after the Hanley gig, the Flying Turd pulled up and he was invited in by Eldritch, who informed him: 'You can't be walking around Stoke at this time of night.' D'Netto ended up sharing a room with Eldritch. 'I was pretty off it and so was he. I remember him talking about how the quality of amphetamines had really gone downhill and about one of the Hell's Angels at Nottingham Rock City offering him a line on a flick knife.'

'I had to go to bed because I had work, so I asked him the time. Up to that point he'd been talking normally, but then [D'Netto adopts a slow, deep, posh voice] he said: "If I wanted to know the time, I'd have a watch and then I'd just worry about what the time was."'

As good as a lot of the gigs were, it was clear that being onstage was not some transcendental experience for Eldritch. Others might have that experience 'because basically they're bombed out of their

boxes,' he once noted, but 'I never step out of the confines of realising where I am and what I'm doing.' Partly this was his inherent
desire for control, partly it was nerves and but it was also because
'I'm aware that the littlest thing one does, it means something,
someone's going to take it away . . . and read something into every
little action, which is why we take care about every little detail . . .
I feel a great sense of responsibility.'

How he interacted with the lighting design was part of this for
Eldritch. He had long ago mastered slinking around bare stages,
but, with Wiffin, he refined the use of himself within the mise en
scène. 'Andrew needed the bigger canvas as a performer,' Marx
says. 'It wasn't an ego thing, it was just the things he was trying to
do required it to look and sound a particular way . . . I think even
early on he imagined a certain gesture he'd make with his arm
breaking the light in an Expressionist way . . . fine cinematic
details.'

On Black October, the band were carrying their own lights,
so Wiffin was able to push the theatrical lighting and use of
smoke even further. With a big rig in the larger venues, with the
smoke machines on full blast, the Sisters put on a rock show that
was rooted in the high contrast lighting of film noir just as much
as it was in rock's own psychedelic heritage. Not only did it look
great from the audience, it photographed brilliantly. Without TV
appearances, the photographs that appeared in the music press
were a key element of the Sisters' image-making and Eldritch's own
personal mystique.

The support band on the UK leg of Black October were Skeletal
Family from Keighley. The support slot was another example of

Eldritch's largesse to smaller bands. 'Andrew said the Psychedelic Furs had done them a favour, letting them support, so he was putting us up the ladder,' explains Stan Greenwood, Skeletal Family's guitarist. 'Andrew likes to have that reputation of being a bastard, but when you actually know the guy, he's great.'

Their bassist Roger Nowell (nicknamed Trotwood) had been the DJ when the Sisters played at the Funhouse in Keighley in 1982. There were other connections: Trotwood's then-girlfriend was a schoolteacher, who had taught Adams at Hartington Middle School. 'At the Leeds gig on the Black October tour, they were reunited,' Trotwood says. Backstage at the Refec, Adams, as much a handful as a touring musician as he was a schoolboy, walked into the dressing room and greeted his old English teacher with a very well-mannered: 'Hello, Miss Scatchard.'

Their debut gig in the Refectory was an especially big deal to Marx, Eldritch and Adams who had seen an array of famous bands there: the Clash, the Ramones, the Cramps among them. At the climax, during 'Sister Ray', Marx scaled the PA stack, clambered up to the balcony to where Kathryn Wood and his best friend Graeme Haddlesey were standing and handed his snakeskin-patterned guitar to Haddlesey, who (unlike Rik Benbow) could actually play the instrument. 'I think I just shouted "A" to him by way of musical instruction, or quite possibly, "fuckin' A", a reference to a catchphrase he'd know from *The Deer Hunter*.' Haddlesey thereby became the only guitarist to guest with the four-piece Sisters. Eldritch seemed to especially enjoy this particular piece of theatre.

Although it had made him unwell, Eldritch fundamentally

found being in the Sisters of Mercy deeply fulfilling. He had gone on Black October in an upbeat frame of mind. He told *Sounds*:

> If you want it to, being involved with music will enable you to use a very great deal of yourself; I mean, I could be doing a lot of other things, but I chose, a long time ago, to do this, because it looked like I could be a politician, an artist, a musician, a lyricist, a prat, be hated, be liked, die young . . . There's a lot of space there in which one can work. I've walked around for an awful number of years now, thinking I was God's gift to something, whatever it was, so I don't mind sitting here acting like some sort of ludicrous prophet. I figure that's my natural role, absurd though it is . . . I mean, I don't even go to the corner shop without figuring, 'Hey! Here goes Andy Eldritch to the corner shop.' This is, you know, some kind of a big deal to someone.

Eldritch was smart enough to realise that this was all at risk. Warner's patience, especially that of Rob Dickins, and therefore Max Hole's cheque-book, was not limitless. The Sisters could easily find themselves back toiling in the fields of independent music.

Leeds offered two clear examples: Virgin had dropped the Mekons after *The Quality of Mercy Is Not Strnen* and Polydor had dispensed with Music for Pleasure after *Into the Rain*. The Mekons thrived artistically but needed day jobs. Music for Pleasure put out one more album, *Blacklands*, and then threw in the towel. As the Sisters knew, life outside the major labels was hard graft with perilously fine margins. They had existed in that thin air for more than three years.

The Sisters' schedule for next six months was shockingly clear: finish the album and then go on tour again in early 1985 – an even longer one than Black October – in Europe, and then the USA, to support the album's release. In short, do whatever was necessary not to be dropped by Warners. Debilitating drug habits, intra-band squabbles, lack of a hit single, a large hole in the album budget (and in the label's release schedule) were all forgivable if the album hit. If it didn't, the band would be set firmly on the path to minor cult status and what Eldritch termed 'the chapeau shop' – *Spinal Tap* shorthand for a real job.

Eldritch was quite sure he didn't like the hours.

19

All the Clouds That Lour'd Upon Our House

After Black October, the band went back in the studio in an attempt to finish their album and meet Warners' new January release date. In reality 'the band' meant Hussey, Adams and Eldritch: the confrontations at Strawberry and Genetic had all but ended Marx's connection to Eldritch and the Sisters of Mercy.

When the Sisters reconvened at Livingston Studios in north London in November, 'it was a much easier session,' says Dave Allen. 'We didn't need to do any more guitars or bass or drums. It was just some singing and the mixing. We were evidently on the home straight. I thought to myself, "Let's see if we can get over this last kind of hurdle. I'm not going to have any more arguments."'

The presence of Tony Harris, the Livingston engineer, made a difference. 'Tony's a very bluff, no-nonsense, cheery, "have-a-cup-of-tea"-type of chap and very good at his job,' says Allen. 'He was a very good foil.' Eldritch responded well to Harris's obvious competence, warmth and lack of pretension. 'Tony would be: "Shall we go and do some singing then? Still got to sing it, haven't we?"' says Allen. 'I'd sit on the sofa and noodle it along, talk to Andrew, shoot the breeze, which worked really well because he's a lonely guy. He wants some company.' Allen remained oblivious to a more extraordinary possibility: that Eldritch *liked* him, and had done ever since first meeting him in Amsterdam.

The atmosphere was certainly much lighter than that at Genetic. Instead of pyrotechnics with cleaning fluid Allen 'had an infatuation with a thing called Zoids,' recalls Harris. 'These were self-assembly robot dinosaurs that were around at the time, many types that you collected. I remember that we had a piece of plywood across the meter bridge to have Zoid battles on while we were mixing! I also remember Bud, one of the studio cats, battling with "Tyrannozoid" one time!'

Unlike at Genetic, Eldritch laid down his vocals quickly. Songs which had remained incomplete for nearly six months were finished in Livingston. These were 'Nine While Nine', 'Possession', 'First and Last and Always' and 'Amphetamine Logic'. Taken together with 'Some Kind of Stranger' they represent Eldritch at a lyrical peak. He was physically damaged by the onslaught of stress and amphetamine overuse, but his gifts as a writer reached new heights. He became the epitome of the 'arrogant bastard who writes sensitive lyrics,' as he once described himself. 'It comes from the heart. The public person is the private person. It's all the same – with this album more than anything else . . . I was so shot when I wrote the lyrics to the album that there's no distancing of persona at all.'

'First and Last and Always' is Eldritch's 'My Way', an uncompromising statement of everlasting faith in oneself. It's an anthem to self-actualisation and sloughing off the dead skin of the past. 'Possession' is a warning from Eldritch to his audience not to treat him simply as their mirror. The masks he wore, the cryptic lyrics he wrote, the distance he created between performer and crowd were designed to draw the audience out, to give them the space to find themselves. 'Amphetamine Logic' is Eldritch at his most terse and vigorous: cavalier about his appetite for speed, and brazenly appropriating Eliot's 'The Love Song of J. Alfred Prufrock' to comment on the women who 'come and go' (where Eliot's are discussing Michelangelo, Eldritch's are 'talking about me like they know'). What nerve – or time pressure, or both – to rework a line from his favourite poet into a song about hoovering up whizz! Where 'Walk Away' and 'No Time to Cry' were evidently undercooked, 'Amphetamine Logic' was perfectly compact.

Desolate, brittle and beautiful, 'Nine While Nine' is a great and unrelentingly sad break-up song. Where 'Marian' conjured an elaborate fug of wordplay, 'Nine While Nine' is a kind of hard blues, a song of authentic heartbreak. Eldritch once admitted that he never cried. 'I had to teach myself at an early age not to. Many a time since I really wished I could.' Certain pieces of music could take him to 'the brink,' he admitted. 'I get as close as its possible *for me* to get.' 'Nine While Nine' is the sound of weeping – from a man who had no tears to shed.

Marx speculates why 'Nine While Nine' and 'Some Kind of Stranger' emerged as the standout tracks: 'Something in their mood and musical make-up could draw out a more emotive and powerful lyric . . . "Some Kind of Stranger" had such a power for me because of the contradiction and tension between the stately music and that worldview expressed in the words. I was imagining a new "Wedding March" and Andrew was busy burying the love song.' That Eldritch had decided to tackle the theme was not unexpected for Marx but 'the starkest of those statements did surprise me – I was way up close of course because I'd lived with Andrew and Claire. I don't think his idea of control necessarily meant he was afraid of wearing his heart, if not exactly on his sleeve, certainly somewhere about his person.'

That Eldritch had been delayed writing lyrics for Marx's music had been to their benefit. 'Whether that meant the various breakups/downs were in a more advanced state when he was completing the final batch of songs and that prompted the outpouring, I couldn't say. If he was working through his farewells to Claire and, to a lesser extent me, he might have felt a greater sense of urgency by the time he wrote "Nine While Nine" and "Some Kind of Stranger".'

Even at the mixing stage Eldritch was still referencing Fleetwood Mac and 'wanted a really clean hi-fi sort of sound,' says Harris. Eldritch, in his usual manner would fiddle with the minutiae of the mixes for aeons. 'Dave and I kept out of it,' says Harris. 'Eldritch would spend hours equalising the drums in particular, listening at a very quiet level. Then we would reappear and correct everything.'

Allen's work on the album finished at Livingston. He had found working with Eldritch an ordeal but also fascinating and rewarding. 'Basically, he was an extremely difficult person but we made a bit of art: fucking hard to do, that.' He continues: 'Eldritch is the master of bullshit . . . but there's no denying that he has an artistic integrity.' Allen remains impressed that Eldritch 'number-crunched a complete identity . . . and made his own legend.'

Allen might have finished work on the album but Eldritch had not. The release date for the album was pushed back again, from January to March. Warners wanted the German studio engineer Reinhold Mack to remix the album; Eldritch spent some of December 1984 with Mack at Giorgio Moroder's Musicland Studios in Munich. Eldritch naturally hated what Mack was doing, since he wanted to remix the album himself, and the interlude in Munich was cut short after only four tracks. None of Mack's mixes appeared on the album.

Eldritch was only able to remix four tracks in time for the March release: 'A Rock and a Hard Place', 'Black Planet', 'First and Last and Always', and 'No Time to Cry'. Harris remembers Eldritch needing to find a mastering engineer, 'who'll add back all the midrange I've EQed out.' Eldritch had also decided to remix a single version of 'No Time to Cry' at Eel Pie Studio on the Thames.

More productively, he also recorded two new songs with Hussey ('Blood Money' and 'Bury Me Deep') for B-sides. Hussey felt he and Eldritch edged slightly closer during the recording. He calls it 'the high point' of their relationship. When Marx had visited them in the studio 'at the request of Craig, who was trying to act as bridge-builder', Marx noted that, 'Andrew and Wayne were playing out some weird bromance.' Although this is almost certainly over-stating any affection between Eldritch and Hussey, the nadir of their relationship was more than half a year in the future.

Eldritch spent Christmas 1984 in Rome. There, he met up with Daniela Giombini, who had interviewed him in Munich the previous month with Romano Pasquini for the *Tribal Cabaret* fanzine they ran together. On Christmas Eve, Giombini and Eldritch visited the ancient Etruscan necropolis, the Necropoli della Banditaccia, in Cerveteri to the north-west of Rome. The visit ended in an argument when her car sank into muddy ground and she and Eldritch had to travel back to Rome by coach.

Nevertheless, both Giombini and Pasquini liked Eldritch and enjoyed his company a lot: 'a very sweet person . . . great culture, great conversation,' is Pasquini's summary. They interviewed him again for *Tribal Cabaret* during his Italian respite. All kinds of ideas spilled out. Eldritch told them that 'after the world tour that will follow the release of the album I'll leave the group . . . I'm going to stay just as a manager . . . I can't be both the manager and the singer.' This was obvious fantasy – the Key Member Clause alone made it so – but it was underpinned by genuine disenchantment with being in the band: 'I have no time for myself and the things I'd rather do, such as learning how to play the guitar.' To lighten his spirits, Eldritch conjured a light at the end of the tunnel: 'I've already contacted Patricia Morrison and Alan Vega to form a supergroup before the end of the year.'

In February 1985, Eldritch emerged from his long winter to promote *First and Last and Always*. The months finishing the album had damaged him: a studio, it seemed, was just as brutalising an environment as the road. Eldritch still looked really ill. It was hard to believe he was still twenty-five. With his now-battered Vegas hat, even larger sideburns, and draped in the black cloak gifted him by the Gun Club, or his knee-length crushed-velvet coat, Eldritch looked like a consumptive gentleman-assassin in a Spaghetti Western.

Eldritch's presentation was typically overdetermined and playful, but the hat was also a dreadful necessity; perhaps due to an excess of stress and amphetamine, his hair had begun to fall out in clumps. He had grown what remained longer, and added the hat to hide the bald patches. If the hat is iconic of anything, it is as an emblem of Eldritch's sickness, and his nerve. The image he created in 1985 – and discarded as soon as he could – has endured and, partially at least, defined him and the band. It is certainly not the epitome of cool, as some would like it to be. If Eldritch's malady became known – photographed, even – it would be met with an onslaught of cruelty at concerts and in the press. As if the fate of *First and Last and Always* was not stressful enough, for months on end in 1985 Eldritch risked the vicious public dismantling of his image. Whatever character flaws he may have had, lack of courage was not one of them.

In interviews, Eldritch was open with journalists that he was poorly, but was selective in the information he fed them. He told one that he spent Christmas in Rome dosed up on morphine. For another, he made sure his tranquillisers were in plain sight. The pills were necessary, Eldritch explained, because 'there isn't a detail of life or anybody else's life that I can't get severely worked up about, given the slightest opportunity.'

Eldritch also wanted it to be known that there had been no sea change in his consumption of other pharmaceuticals. 'So I've calmed down a bit although . . . I enjoy it so much, being strung

out for a very long time . . . I'm told you can't do it for *that* long.'
Eldritch spun his calculations as a sort of existential game: 'Even
I've not decided how far I'm prepared to push it . . . I was told last
year, you can push it to this extent and you'll die before '85 is out,
or *this* extent and you'll die before you're twenty-six, or *this* extent
and you'll live but be very unhealthy, or *that* extent and you'll get
by fine.' He portrayed being in the Sisters of Mercy as a calculated
risk: 'I'm very aware of how fast the blood's going around and how
high the sugar level is because I've been forced to be aware of it.'

At other times he postulated: 'None of the songs on the album
are about being a victim of one's own pleasures except in the case
of getting emotionally involved with people who aren't very good
for you.' This was very Eldritchian: seemingly revealing but actually oblique. As was the admission that there were 'twelve fresh
lemons I have to have every night on the next tour.'

Eldritch even offered up the possibility that he might be on
some death trip, shackled to his persona, Frankenstein being
destroyed by his Monster: 'I've spent so long doing this that I can't
distance the two . . . once you become Eldritch with a capital E,
that's it, *doomed*.' He speculated that there could be a point at
which he would 'probably just keel over.'

This was theoretically possible, but fundamentally a pose.
Eldritch found nothing interesting about rock 'n' roll self-destruction: 'Greatly overindulged in,' he also said. 'Also, most of them
don't seem to do it with a great deal of style. There was this French
poet called Gérard de Nerval who hung himself in a Paris street –
from the underneath of a street drain, with a pink ribbon. I mean,
that's fair enough. But choking on your own vomit or turning blue

in other people's bathrooms doesn't seem like a good idea.' Nor did turning blue, wrapped in a curtain in a bedroom at the Miller of Mansfield.

Using the majestic plural, Eldritch explained the costs of his quest for fame: 'We've sacrificed a great deal of our lives for this. We've sacrificed ourselves business-wise, personally, domestically . . . we've trashed our lives and we're not about to sell that short.' He was as determined as ever to make it, to 'get into big school' as he termed it.

Eldritch's body might have given way, but his mind remained intact. Boyd Steemson had stayed friendly with Eldritch ever since Oxford. While he was concerned to see Eldritch's health decline, he 'was conscious that he was moving forward . . . I would have been far more worried had he ended up being a junkie. I thought that mentally Andrew was strong enough and had enough resilience. The thing that would have worried me, was if there'd been evidence of some mental collapse, and there wasn't.' Dave Beer makes a similar observation: 'He was a bit like an old man back then: he was very frail. But strong – like he works in, not out . . . he was very interested in his own thoughts, more into his inner space.' Behind the persona, the original person that Steemson had known since Oxford was still very much present.

There was also evidence that Eldritch's sense of humour was undiluted. When the subject of mortality was raised in an interview for *Sounds*, Hussey interjected that 'It's difficult to comprehend sometimes. Dying. Being dead.'

'But you lived in Liverpool for how long?' Eldritch archly enquired.

Eldritch's increased contact with the music press enabled him to refine his public image. His self-presentation in newspapers and magazines was as deft as Sisters videos were ham-fisted. 'My brain works quicker than my mouth, and that's an advantage,' he told *Sounds*. 'I'll always pause before I say something if I think it's important. I'm not the sort of person who'll just, like, gush.'

Eldritch therefore carefully injected various supplementary notions into the discourse around him and the band. Some were central – for example, he classified people 'into us, them, and people I don't talk to,' – but a lot were frivolous. Eldritch revealed that he would like to develop telekinesis 'to demolish Liverpool just by thought-power'; that he had five autographs (Tony Blackburn and the Ramones), and that he wanted to mash up two of his favourite programmes – *On the Buses* and *Doctor Who* – by casting Reg Varney as the Time Lord.

A reader of the UK music press would have further discovered that Eldritch supported Manchester United; his Francophobia extended to Wallonia ('The French half of Belgium can go fuck itself!'), but not to young French women, whom he would levitate to safety before obliterating their homeland. There was plenty more in this vein. Eldritch announced he liked Detroit enormously because of 'Motown, the MC5 at its urban wasteland'; he was a fan of the Leeds chansonnier Jake Thackray and he appreciated 'how beautiful napalm is.' His pronouncements could be mordant, infuriating, witty, often smirking but he was rarely, if ever, dull.

The persona was finely honed by 1985. It could strike awe into fans and intimidate journalists, but it could not ward off jealous men. The Armageddon '85 tour (posters made the announcement that 'Armageddon will be held indoors this year') began in Glasgow with Eldritch wearing a large dressing over the left side of his face. The previous night at the Warehouse in Leeds an assault had left Eldritch with cuts on, and around, his eye. Whether this was the direct result of a broken glass being shoved into his face, or a punch that shattered his sunglasses – or both – is unclear, but the damage required a trip to the casualty department of Leeds General Infirmary. The motive was common-or-garden: 'an enraged ex-boyfriend' (as Eldritch has hinted) of a Leeds woman, with whom he was a having an affair or manoeuvring to begin one.

Although Eldritch had been lucky – he could easily have lost the sight in his left eye – the violence was unnerving and added to his already keen sense of paranoia; before the year was out, Eldritch would leave Leeds and the UK.

For Andrew Eldritch, the rest of 1985 would be unrelenting, perpetually testing the limits of his physical endurance. In that time, the Sisters of Mercy would die and a new, very different version of the band would be reborn.

20

Waiting for the
Summer Rain

The same day as the assault, 'No Time to Cry', the least interesting song on *First and Last and Always,* was released as a single. It sold less than 'Body and Soul' and 'Walk Away' and disappeared from the UK charts even before the UK leg of Armageddon '85 was finished.

The accompanying video, ostensibly shot as a mock live performance in the Electric Ballroom was, at best, serviceable. It was, therefore, a massive improvement on its predecessors. Marx was in a sour mood during the shoot, well aware that he was in the closing chapter of his time in the band and clearly feeling he had been supplanted by Hussey. 'Whether planned or otherwise, it was the first time I remember Wayne sticking so closely to Andrew's look in his choice of clothing,' he says. 'The director instantly picked up on that and made the video largely about the pair of them.'

Three days into Armageddon '85, *First and Last and Always* was released, nearly nine months after its recording had begun. The reviews in the UK music press were largely dismal. *Sounds*, usually supportive of the band, was the most dismissive, calling the album an 'over-produced and over-dramatic outing' and the *NME* railed against the 'mockdespair [sic], rock theft and semi-glam appropriation of Joy Division.' *Smash Hits* called it 'a cross between Bauhaus and Siouxsie and the Banshees.' *Record Mirror* described it as 'sung through a tunnel darkly' and further suggested the band was performing a 'useful social service . . . for angst-ridden teen people' who might otherwise turn to suicide, witchcraft or 'trying to look like Lou Reed when you live in Bridlington.' Of the three big weeklies, only *Melody Maker* raved, claiming the Sisters 'have successfully accumulated a startling array of timeless jewels', but still called it 'music to hum over the three-minute warning.'

Every member of the band had misgivings about the album, not just because of the miserable experience of making it. Eldritch strongly disliked the sound of his voice on the record; Marx didn't really like the final versions of half of the songs, including some of his own; Adams regretted losing the dirt and immediacy of his bass sound; Hussey, the most present musician on the record, was the least ambivalent. 'For me, it's an eight out of ten . . . My only reservation probably would be that it's not a particularly great sounding hi-fi album, but there are other qualities that more than make up for it.'

However, *First and Last and Always* was a crushing disappointment for many Sisters fans when it came out. Boyd Steemson – by this point being groomed as Nick Jones' successor in the Black Office – says: 'It should sound enormous, it should just roll out of the speakers . . . but it's like listening through a seashell, you have to infer everything . . . You know it's a big record that ends up sounding like some fart in the bottom of a dustbin. It reminds me of *Raw Power*, a drug-addled production that sounds fucking awful.'

Those who think *First and Last and Always* sounds enfeebled usually point the finger at Dave Allen. Steemson instead blames Eldritch at the mixing stage. 'You can rescue a lot . . . it would have all been there on the twenty-four tracks, but I think his ears were just fucked by amphetamine; there was a whole bunch of stuff he couldn't hear.'

For some fans, *First and Last and Always* was the last straw. The album sounded nothing like the early songs that had hooked them in in the first place. Hussey concedes that musically, 'it's definitely lighter and more colourful than previous TSOM singles and EPs, but I believe it was the record the band wanted, and needed, to make at that particular point in time.'

The Sisters' debut album was therefore far from an instant classic, but time has proved Hussey correct. *First and Last and Always* is now adored far more than when it was first released. Over thirty-five years on, it has acquired devotees across generations and continents. Dave Dickinson in *Extra Kerrang!* was the lone voice at the time who sensed its importance and long-term impact. 'To find a band so acutely in tune with everything you have ever felt or known, feared or desire is something akin to a revelation . . . *First and Last and Always* . . . is the single most powerful piece of music I have heard for some considerable time – perhaps since I first encountered *Heroes* or *Berlin* or even *Desertshore*.'*

* The intensity of Dickinson's prose was at odds with the accompanying photo, in which Marx wears a long, curly blonde wig he had sourced from a women's clothing shop in Wakefield. It was an attempt to reference Dee Snider and make a Twisted Sister visual gag.

Marx is more circumspect but still recognises its power: 'As a collection of songs I don't know if it ranks up there with *Blood on the Tracks* but there's some open-heart surgery going on there.' *First and Last and Always* is unquestionably best when it functions as an emotionally heavy record. Eldritch's voice and lyrics were not those of a young man. The best songs on *First and Last and Always* had such an air of seasoned cynicism – or hard-won realism – that they would make particularly excellent covers for much older, hard-living men and women of the world. Marianne Faithfull, entirely aptly, was once in the frame to cover the title track. It's easy to imagine Nico singing the whole thing.

The rehabilitation of 'Nine While Nine' is emblematic of the longevity of *First and Last and Always*. This 'deceptively potent song' (in Marx's words), once often regarded as an insubstantial, lesser Sisters track now stands as the peak of Eldritch's lyric writing and vocal delivery, and of Marx's writing and playing. A song that meant so much to the two men at the heart of its creation, has now been embraced by many Sisters fans as the finest track on the album. It is also Adams and Hussey's favourite song on *First and Last and Always*.

Yet Dave Allen is right when he says that '*First and Last and Always* is not a masterpiece, it's a template. Many people have imitated it.' Allen had succeeded in making his seminal record after all. 'It's pretty hard to do that: make a breakpoint in music and move anything on,' he says. Hussey agrees: 'There'd been nothing else quite like it before.' *Sounds* (with some odd wordplay) was especially wide of the mark in this regard: 'No generations will breed from this diamond.' At least *Melody Maker* had some inkling:

'God forbid, but these songs are almost explosive enough to launch a gothic revival.' The Sisters of Mercy's debut album became one of the defining documents of an entire global subculture.

Within days of its release it was clear that the album had sold well enough to lift any pressure coming from Warners in the UK, but on Armageddon '85, it was a zombie band on tour, the living dead in a Flying Turd.

The tour ground on with only one functional relationship within the group: Adams and Hussey. Marx could handle the physical demands of touring but 'the mental strain was the real problem,' he says. 'You can only tour with no-one talking to each other so many times.' Eldritch was also seething with resentment: 'I was killing myself on the road and nobody was really saying thank you . . . I almost dropped dead during the recording of the first album and the band didn't thank me, maybe they were trying to tell me something.'

As shattered as the band was offstage, Adams was aware that 'the rock 'n' roll was good' on it. The band was terminally ill but, paradoxically, sounded in peak condition. Armageddon '85 in the UK was definitive Sisters: the full two-guitar band playing most of *First and Last and Always* interspersed with fine older songs like 'Train', 'Body Electric', 'Alice' and 'Floorshow'. They still did the same covers from Black October too, typically ending with the Doktor battering its way through 'Sister Ray' (and/or its analogues 'Ghost Rider' and 'Louie Louie'). The Sisters' set effectively documented the band's five-year journey.

Most of the Armageddon '85 concerts offered a counter-argument to the image of the Sisters that had set fast in the UK music media: gloomy, dour and appealing mainly to depressed adolescents. There was nothing morose about the audience, which was usually in a kind rapturous Brownian motion. The ludicrous amounts of smoke, Marx's shirts and Eldritch's sideburns were surely counterpoints to the gravity of the songs. In his black hat, jacket, shades and sideboards Eldritch looked like a high plains Blues Brother.

Although touring behind a major label album, the logistics and personnel were little changed. Nigel Holbrough replaced Phil Wiffin but the crew was essentially the same small group: Turner, Levy, Kentish, Merb and Webb, but with Brian 'Dub' Smith added as driver ('hedgehog crusher', as the tour-book billed him). Reg Halsall still managed production from the Troubadour office. The tour-book listed Levy, the monitor engineer, as responsible for 'hearing aids', Kentish was euphemistically termed 'Procurement Director' and Eldritch was a 'consultant' specialising in 'wind ups'.

One of the surprises of Armageddon '85 was how well Eldritch and Holbrough got on. 'Andrew took a shine to him,' says Levy, despite the fact that 'Nigel was a big dope smoker . . . an archetypal hippy wearing purple corduroy flares with long ginger hair and beard.' The light show was Wiffin's design, but even without him present (he was working at the BBC), Eldritch was still able to push his taste for smoke to extremes. The stage was often so foggy, that even for Levy by the monitoring desk, 'there were some nights where I couldn't even see Craig – and he was closest to me! It was crazy.'

For the support band on Armageddon '85, Eldritch chose the Scientists, a brilliant amalgam of Suicide, the Stooges and the Gun

Club. If Eldritch felt they were kindred spirits, the Scientists for their part did not recognise any shared DNA between themselves and the headliners at all. This was a mark of how little the Sisters of 1985 resembled the 1982/83 iteration of the band. 'Certainly, any influences of the Stooges were far from obvious,' says Leanne Cowie, the Scientists' tour manager and future drummer. 'I wouldn't have made that connection listening to their music . . . My overriding memory is of black – black clothes, black hair and goths!' Tony Thewlis, the guitarist, felt the same: 'I certainly had no knowledge of them at all . . . They weren't on our radar at all. We weren't into or interested in the goth scene in the slightest.'

After the Leeds gig on Armageddon '85, the Scientists were offered Adams' house on 'Betty Street' (Elizabeth Street) as a place to stay. 'We had a few drinks and Craig showed some of his videos of Leeds United fan violence,' Thewlis recalls. 'Leanne had an actual room to herself, but she had to climb over piles of furniture and equipment to get to the door. The rest of us slept on the living-room floor.'

'What they forgot to tell us,' remembers Boris Sudojvic, the bassist, 'was that they had a pet snake.' The snake was quartered, like the Scientists, in the living room. It was a rat snake belonging to Steve Watson and usually resided in a glass tank. 'They assured us it was safe,' says Thewlis, 'and being winter, was semi-hibernating and had hardly moved from its curled-up position for months. They didn't have enough blankets for all of us, so we had to have the heating – was it a gas fire? – on all night.' Thewlis remembers 'finally dozing off and a few hours later waking up and being alarmed to see that, thanks no doubt to the sudden warmness of the room, the snake was moving about . . . I woke up the others, worried that it might get out of its tank, but Boris was confident that the glass lid was too heavy for it to push it off. Eventually we got back to sleep only for me to then roll onto an electric plug, which dug into my neck. I went from being horizontal on the floor to being up on the windowsill in about 0.0000001 seconds.'

Thewlis had got off lightly. Adams remembers that the snake was a menace to him, Webb, Watson and any visitors to Betty Street. 'That snake man! We would all be stoned and then someone would realise the snake was out. It was fast and mean and bit you if you did not get up the stairs sharpish.'

Betty Street indicates just how little five years of being in the Sisters, even with the deal with Warners, had changed the lives of the band. Certainly, they had come off the dole and had better riders and hotels on tour, but Adams, Hussey and Eldritch still lived in small, shared houses in the cheap part of Leeds.

Adams was his usual gastrically unsteady self on Armageddon '85. At the King's Hall in Blackburn during 'Sister Ray', Adams leapt off the top of the stack of amps at the rear of the stage but 'it shook him up so much when he actually jumped to the floor, he threw up,' Marx recalls, 'then started rolling around in it.' Hussey has a different version of this story, which additionally has Adams vomiting over the audience.

If true, very few people would have been affected. 'Don't worry, we aren't going to take it out on you because the rest of Blackburn didn't show up,' Eldritch assured the crowd, before dishing out various *bon mots* to hecklers: 'One at a time! You with the yellow flares!' as if he was holding a press conference or chairing a debate. 'Look, there's a bus that goes now from out there, and you'd be advised . . .' he felt was sufficiently hard-boiled that he didn't feel the need to finish his sentence. With so few in attendance, the Sisters risked delivering a very literal reading of 'Stairway to Heaven'. Eldritch got through the first verse before abandoning the song with an 'etcetera', either to indicate how ill-judged the attempt was, or that he'd forgotten the words.

In post-punk Britain in 1985, showing any love to Led Zeppelin was taboo. 'Stairway to Heaven' was attempted just once, but every night the Sisters came onstage to 'Kashmir'. Eldritch wisely chose the pages of *Extra Kerrang!* to confess that, 'It's about time someone got up and said something as crass as: Led Zep – ace!' The acknowledgement of Zeppelin by the Sisters is a key milestone in the re-incorporation of long-haired, denim-and-leather heavy rock into the – so-called – alternative music scene in the UK.

The group's reverence for glam rock and Eldritch's Bowie fetish were hinted at in the new props the Sisters had brought with them on Armageddon '85: two glowing white discs with red 'Head and Star' logos that poked above the amps at the back of the stage. These referenced the two *Aladdin Sane* lightning bolts that Bowie had projected behind him at Hammersmith Odeon the night he killed off Ziggy. The Sisters' props were as DIY as the painted kitchen blind they once used: cheap hardboard with a round hole cut in it, covered in cloth, with a light bulb fixed behind.

Among the usual fun and games, there was also sublime drama. Eldritch opted to perform 'Nine While Nine' – his intimate goodbye to Claire Shearsby – in public. It was played twice during Armageddon '85, once as an encore in Newcastle and once in Leeds. The first was a dress rehearsal, the second was the opening and the closing night: the Sisters of Mercy never played 'Nine While Nine' again. Leeds was Shearsby and Eldritch's hometown – his by adoption, hers by upbringing.* Leeds had made them a couple, the Sisters into a band and Taylor into Eldritch. The Refectory of the university therefore played host to a hugely symbolic piece of theatre. The first band Andy Taylor had seen there was the Ramones, six and a half years previously. As he stood on the same stage as his idols, it would have been clear to Eldritch what he had achieved. And what he had lost along the way.

Claire Shearsby was in the audience that night. Obscured by smoke, sunglasses and a cowboy hat, Eldritch delivered his most lyrically open and highly personal song. The irony was thick but as a connoisseur of melodramatic sixties pop, Eldritch was fully aware that high camp was an excellent mode for crushingly sad songs. Dusty Springfield or Shirley Bassey had performed emotionally shattering numbers disguised in their wigs and gowns and heavy make-up.

History does not record how many broken hearts there were in the Refec on that Saturday evening in mid-March 1985, but if there was one, it was Eldritch's.

Gary Marx, meanwhile, did not complete Armageddon '85.

---

* Shearsby was born in Maidenhead, Berkshire, and moved to Leeds when she was six.

Before the tour, Marx and Hussey had gone to Parkside rehearsal studios off the Armley Road in Leeds 'to do some rough demos in the post-album period when we were expecting to split up,' Marx recalls. The intention to dismantle the group, leaving Eldritch on his own, was so far advanced and in the open that a meeting was arranged at the London office of the band's solicitors, Harbottle and Lewis, with all four members present. The plan fell apart when the Evil Children talked themselves out of quitting the band along with Marx. Their logic moved rapidly from: '"Why do we need to do that as well?"' to '"That ain't gonna happen",' says Adams. The decision to renege was made in the long hours of a National Express coach journey up the M1: 'Wayne and I were bolloxed up, talking rubbish to each other and working something out,' says Adams.

'I was ambushed sometime slightly before that meeting,' says Marx. He had sufficient advance warning to prepare himself. 'I went into the meeting wearing sunglasses. I did this deliberately as an act of self-preservation, fully believing the outcome of the meeting would be deeply upsetting and I didn't want them to be able to see my distress . . . at the devastating news being made official. Of course, the outcome was the same, I just managed to preserve a modicum of dignity temporarily.'

To all intents and purposes, he had been fired. He therefore endured the UK leg of Armageddon '85 as an ex-member of the Sisters of Mercy.

His time in the band was legally ended by Harbottle and Lewis on 20 February 1985. Knowledge of his departure was kept within a small and tightly closed circle: the band, their lawyers, the label and a handful of close confidantes.

Marx was appalled that Adams and Hussey 'hadn't had the balls to leave when I did . . . My relationship with all three of them was completely shattered . . . If anything I felt more animosity towards Craig and Wayne than I did to Andrew. As badly as our relationship broke down there was still great loyalty there somewhere. He made a lot of plays to make me stay, it's just I didn't always see them for what they were.' He concludes that 'anyone who was genuinely ruthless and looking to fast-track their career would have shown me the door a whole lot earlier.'

That Marx had left the band only became apparent to the God Squad on the final night of the tour at the Top Rank in Brighton. 'The rumour had gone around that it was going to be Mark's last gig,' says Jez D'Netto. This was so shocking that it still registered despite the state D'Netto was in. 'I was so wasted I thought the gig was in London. I didn't know it was in Brighton. To me the South was the South, it just blended in.'

'There was a change in the crowd in Brighton and it went really sour that night,' recalls Martin Lambert, a young Wakefield recruit to the God Squad. 'Dave Beer, who was normally so full of beans, was very aloof, didn't want to engage in normal chit-chat. I looked about and other people looked really pee'd off. Can't remember who came up to me: "Have you fucking heard? This is it. Mark's last gig." People seemed to be getting more and more revved up towards the end of the gig: no one was really talking to each other, the pushing and shoving got a little harder, a torrent of abuse at Eldritch, beer thrown at him. He looked a little bit shocked, to be honest. His children had left him. There was real anger and resentment.'

If Marx was in mourning during his last gig in the Sisters of Mercy he did not dress that way. He elected to play in a bright orange shirt that was ruffed at the cuffs and its V-neck. The shirt had been made for him by Joolz, the punk poet, first introduced to him by Rik Benbow. 'She offered to make me a shirt and I requested one based on something I'd seen Jimi Hendrix wearing in a photo . . . It didn't especially suit me (not many people can pull off orange and frills) but there was a certain savage, self-deprecating humour in that – I was not in any way Jimi Hendrix!'

During the gig Eldritch did not once acknowledge that Marx was leaving the band. The gig culminated with Marx climbing on top of the speaker stack and hurling his guitar into the crowd. With the rest of the band still playing, he went back to the dressing room. 'We used to take a cheap football around with us on tour and that was in the dressing room,' Marx recalls. 'I stood alone playing with the football: juggling it, practising turns and kicking it against the wall. I did it over and over again with the music still pounding from onstage, lost in my own world. I did it without thinking, but when I looked back on it years later, I realised it was something I'd done repeatedly through my childhood and adolescence, especially at the bleakest moments. Everything else was beyond my control, but the ball went exactly where I wanted it to.'

'I remember the drive home,' says Martin Lambert. 'We got out at the services near Sheffield to stretch our legs, everybody had cramp . . . We were left with eighteen, twenty of us in a circle, somebody's opening a tinnie of Colt 45, somebody's lighting a cig. It was so weird: everybody knew each other so well but nobody had anything to say to each other. People were just kicking rocks on the tarmac, looking at the floor. Nobody wanted to make eye contact. This was the end: no Mark, no Sisters.'

Many of the Wakefield contingent took Marx's departure personally because he and his girlfriend Kathryn were their friends. Some of them – Beer and Lambert, as well as Merb – remain so to this day. Marx is godfather to Dave Beer's son. 'Mark's the most upstanding guy I've ever known,' Beer says. 'To sum him up in one word: beautiful. He is a beautiful human being. Honest, reflective, balanced. The best friend anyone could have and what happened in the band was outrageous and heart-breaking. The band ended when Mark left . . . Losing that band was like losing a child.'

Marx had one final duty to perform in the Sisters of Mercy. The night after Brighton, the band were booked to play two songs live on the venerable BBC music show, *Whistle Test*.[*]

During rehearsals, Marx and Eldritch found themselves momentarily alone together in the dressing room. Any conversation was 'particularly stilted, with me making all the running,' says Marx. To

---

[*] Wayne Hussey has recounted on several occasions that he fired Marx on a phone call he made from the Columbia Hotel in west London not long after *Whistle Test*. This cannot be an accurate memory. The letter from Harbottle and Lewis with the date of termination of Marx's time in the band and the financial terms on which he would participate in the UK leg of Armageddon '85 is clear. If Hussey made a call to Marx's home in Wakefield from the Columbia at this time, Marx assumes it was to confirm he 'wasn't doing the European dates. Either that or it was purely to tie up some practicalities – where my equipment was, etc.' Not that Marx remembers any such call. Nevertheless, 'the notion that he fired me is just ridiculous.'

In Hussey's version, he had to make the call after being given a him-or-me ultimatum by Eldritch. 'I think it's always come across to some faction of Sisters fans that I sacked Mark,' Hussey says. 'I was keeping the fucking band together.'

ease the atmosphere, Marx commented on the superiority of Dan Aykroyd and John Belushi's comic timing to that of co-presenter Steven 'Seething' Wells, who had been running through his comedic links for the show. 'It was just a stupid thing really,' Marx says, 'deliberately trying to shoehorn a reference into the conversation, that harked back to happier times, the pair of us sat watching *The Blues Brothers* on an old VHS and quoting the best lines ad nauseam . . . On one level, it was a clumsy attempt to say thanks for the memories, I guess.'

At the fourth time of asking, the Sisters of Mercy finally looked good on TV: all they had to do was re-enact their stage show.

Nevertheless, disaster nearly stuck. With seconds to go before the Sisters were to open the show with 'First and Last and Always', Marx's guitar stopped working, just as the Doktor's kick drum heralded the start of the live broadcast. After eight bars, Marx was supposed to come in and play the lead riff.

'Wayne knew Mark was in trouble,' says Adams. 'Where Mark was supposed to come in, Wayne came in. And I played Wayne's line. Then we swapped over . . . It was just a case of thinking on your feet. As soon as we knew he wasn't coming in, we knew instantly what to do, just got it straight away. Keep count and just play anything where Mark was supposed to be so we knew where the hell we were.'

During this, the director cut to Marx as planned in rehearsal but all he got was a fifteen-second shot of the guitarist cradling his fretboard and chewing gum and Dave Beer in a cowboy hat rearing up out of the smoke in the background. During Hussey and Adams' improv, Beer and Jez Webb had been scurrying around behind the backline trying to fix the problem with Marx's amplification.

'Then Mark came back in and we got away with it,' says Adams. 'A hairy scary moment,' says Hussey, 'but a mixture of youthful bravado and a few hefty lines of speed beforehand saw us through.' Eldritch had also needed his tot of rum before going over the top and facing the cameras: 'I was in such an altered state for our only live television performance that I honestly cannot remember a single thing.'

Beer was standing in for Merb, who watched the *Whistle Test* performance in Leicester Royal Infirmary. He had dropped out of Armageddon '85 with acute appendicitis and needed an operation. Marx had a message for him. Written on his fretboard in Tippex was 'Surfin' Merb'. Even after he had recovered, out of loyalty to Marx, Merb never roadied for the Sisters again.

Marx's final seconds in the Sisters of Mercy were played out over the end of 'Marian'. As the Doktor came to a halt and Eldritch's voice faded away, all that was left was the sustain from Marx's EBow. As Eldritch bowed deeply – to whom is not known – Marx walked back to his amp, which had begun to feed back. This was the last sound made by the Sisters of Mercy as a four-piece band.

The Sisters of Mercy did not play 'Some Kind of Stranger' that evening. This would have been the most fitting acknowledgement of Marx's departure. What Eldritch and Marx had started together in the Sisters of Mercy had begun inauspiciously with 'The Damage Done'; 'Some Kind of Stranger', the end of their recorded output together, was brilliant. It's Marx's favourite song on *First and Last and Always*: 'Does it work as an album closer and more broadly my swansong? Yes . . . hell, yes,' he says.

21

Non-Alignment Pact

In the midst of their slow death, the Sisters had achieved much of what they set out to: their album had cracked the Top 20 in their home country, they were a solid live draw across the UK and Northwestern Europe and they were well placed to make further inroads both there and in North America. Dave Beer speaks for many when he recalls the *Whistle Test* performance with a mixture of sadness and awe: 'They'd really got there by this point. Think where they could have gone.'

Adams and Hussey thought exactly the same thing. Their decision to stay was the cold calculation of ambitious men: Adams did not want to repeat the Expelaires' error by turning his back on a major label deal and Hussey had no desire to go back to square one. He'd been there too often. He was the furthest advanced in his career that he had ever been in the seven years since he'd left his parents' house in small-town south Gloucestershire with the express intention of becoming a successful musician in Liverpool.

As infuriating as they found him, remaining hitched to Eldritch made better sense to Adams and Hussey than quitting with Marx. The release of the biggest record of their careers and the ensuing months of touring were far too appetising a prospect.

Furthermore, other than being onstage with Eldritch, Adams and Hussey could largely avoid him on the road. 'I didn't have to deal with him very much,' explains Adams. 'He always sat in the front seat when we were travelling,' and when not in the van, Eldritch avoided his band-mates. Adams and Hussey also naively still held out the hope that things would improve within the band with Marx gone.

There were ten days between *Whistle Test* and the start of the five-week European leg of Armageddon '85. This was plenty of time to adjust to Marx's departure. 'Let's put it this way, they weren't the hardest songs in the world,' says Adams. 'For me it made no difference, I was playing exactly what I was playing already. Wayne had more difficulty. He was covering but most of it he was already playing anyway.' Those ten days also included a trip to Munich to mime along to 'No Time to Cry' on the TV show *Formel Eins*.

The tour that followed was the Sisters' longest yet and took them to familiar venues and cities, like the Paradiso in Amsterdam and Alabamahalle in Munich, but it also included a proper Italian tour and their first gigs in Switzerland and Norway. Germany was still the most fertile ground. Hussey, with only a little exaggeration, told a fanzine the band had received 'a Duran Duran-type reception' there. The rumour that 'Marian' was directed towards a woman Eldritch had not been able to pry away from her boyfriend was given credence by the song's omission in Hamburg from its usual place between 'Body and Soul' and 'No Time to Cry' in the set-list. When the crowd were still calling for it later, Eldritch dismissed the requests: 'I hate to see a grown man cry, especially when it's me.'

'I'm sure we were fucked most of the time' is Adams' summary of that tour. Amphetamine was indeed plentiful. Munich provided one of many examples. 'We were leaving Germany and coming back a few days later,' says Yaron Levy. 'We had this speed with us: "So what are we going to do with this? Leave it with the promoter or do we do it?" There was a quick discussion. There was this full-length mirror. We laid it horizontally, broke the speed into however many there were of us and did this six foot rail.' A photo exists of Eldritch in hat and shades and Adams bent over the mirror grinning at the camera. 'What would you do if you had six foot of amphetamine in front of you?' enquires Levy by way of explanation.

The ongoing affinity between the Sisters and metal were apparent in Zürich. Tom G. Warrior and Martin Ain from Celtic Frost went to the gig at the Volkshaus. 'It was the loudest concert I've ever heard in my life,' recalls Warrior. 'It was so loud that you had to leave the hall periodically because it was so painful. But at the same time we witnessed something that we had never witnessed before . . . that heaviness, that darkness, that volume; it was amazing.' By contrast, Hussey and Adams were later witnessed dancing to Simple Minds at the Big Apple Club, an alternative club on the outskirts of Zürich.

The levels of self-destruction and violence seemed to ratchet up a notch. Jez Webb celebrated his twenty-first birthday in Milan. 'I ended up at a house party with Wayne and then somehow running around the streets of Milan, trying to set fire to mopeds. What idiots . . . I think a hoarding near the hotel finally caught alight. We scarpered back to our hotel room. . . listening to sirens and hiding under the covers, in case Pete [Turner] came to give us a clout.'

Also in Milan, Adams and Turner were on their way back to their hotel one afternoon when an ambulance passed them. Turner was immediately suspicious, telling Adams that if the ambulance turned left, there was trouble. 'The ambulance turned left,' Adams notes. 'When we went round the corner, it was parked outside our hotel.' Hussey had waterboarded a fan he found irritating with vodka.

There was another hospitalisation during the Oslo concert. During 'No Time to Cry' Eldritch threatened a spitter: 'Do that once more and I'll have you . . . with the microphone stand.' The Norwegian was drunk and shouting 'Bauhaus!' which would have annoyed Eldritch only slightly less than the gobbing. When it continued, Eldritch kept his word and used the stand on him like he was harpooning a whale. 'Craig clocked what was going on,' says Levy (who could see through the smoke at this point). 'He moves over centre stage and while he's rocking backwards and forwards, he's hitting the guy on the head with his headstock. And then Wayne's: "Hello, what's going on here? I'm having some of this," and he just starts putting the boot in. The three of them laying into this one poor guy.'

Standing by his monitoring desk, Levy wondered: 'What the fuck are you guys doing?' He now ponders: 'Was that the one where the police were involved?' Adams confirms that 'the police came, not much happened. Dickheads get what they deserve . . . We probably had to apologise.'

'Oslo got rained off pretty much,' was Eldritch's view of the band's first visit to Norway. The gig required a thousand-kilometre detour between two Swedish gigs and only 211 people, by Eldritch's reckoning, showed up. 'We thought that Oslo was a capital city until we went there,' he deduced. This experience – plus sputum – was so unedifying that Norway was added to his national and urban shit-list that already included France, Liverpool, Wales and sleepy English cities like Peterborough and Ipswich.

Oslo was bookended by gigs in Gothenburg and Stockholm. The first was on Eldritch's birthday which accounted for the updating of the lyric of 'First and Last and Always' to 'twenty-six years of ever after, ever more, more, more', that the band came on two hours late and that Eldritch was sufficiently discombobulated to introduce 'Gimme Shelter' as 'Body Electric.'

The Swedish gigs featured Eldritch banter with the crowd which straddled the customary line between amusing and corrosive: a shout for '1969' was met with 'You're sixteen years too late'; a cheer over the drum intro to 'Gimme Shelter' was met with 'You don't know what it is yet, chicken-shit'; and most bizarrely, since he was on the south-west coast of Sweden at the time, 'Hey, English, why you no play "Temple of Love"?' was delivered in a kind of Italian accent.

There was, however, real venom directed from the stage during the Swedish gigs. In Gothenburg, Eldritch became so exasperated by the duration of Hussey's guitar solo during 'Knockin' on

Heaven's Door' that – as it entered its fourth minute – he exited the stage saying, 'Wake me up when it's finished,' leaving Hussey and Adams to complete the song as an impromptu instrumental. When Eldritch returned for an encore of 'Train', he reassured the crowd: 'It's alright, this one doesn't have a guitar solo – much.' On the final night of the tour in Stockholm, Hussey assumes he was the target of another Eldritch barb, this one during 'Gimme Shelter': 'After forty nights, he still fucking gets it wrong . . . please, send out a new one.' Eldritch's temper was as frayed as some of his clothing. His blue jeans were disintegrating and his elbows showed through the large holes in the black jumper he wore offstage.

There was further photographic evidence of how gruelling the tour was. At Gothenburg docks, while waiting for the ferry back to the UK, Adams snapped Webb and Eldritch in the van. 'I've got a photo of Little Jez sat in the vehicle and he looks like he's just going to die but Eldritch is behind him in the van and he looks horrible, absolutely bolloxed.' Webb puts it like this: 'I look like death warmed up . . . and Andrew in the background, just looks like death.'

Adams' memory is of Eldritch 'moaning continually about every little thing' during Armageddon '85. Five weeks of amphetamines and the associated crashes and mood-swings would account for a lot of that. 'You get into the routine of working certain hours and being very up when you're up and being deeply down as possible when you are down' was Eldritch's summary of touring. He was ill, utterly exhausted and fed up to the back teeth with being on the road again – his third time in twelve months. 'I like the idea of concerts,' he has said, 'but tours? That's something else. Night one you haven't got your act together. Night two your voice is fucked. Night three you're already going through the motions. Night four you're trying to stand stationary and stop slavering and, by night five, you're resorting to the old you-know-what just to keep going. From then on it's downhill all the way. It's that hideous rollercoaster ride that turns you into a beast. There are some people that function very well in the beast mode, but sadly I'm not one of them.'

The sheer daily squalor of touring had long ago begun to grate on Eldritch. He was first and foremost intellectually fussy, but, even so, he was sufficiently finicky to object to the demands made on his personal hygiene. This was 'one of the reasons he didn't want to tour,' Boyd Steemson believes. 'There was enough of the bourgeois left in him for it to be problematic.' The Sisters were not alone in being a grubby and smelly band on the road. This state of affairs would degenerate to the point where – for Adams and Hussey – a change of underwear meant turning their underpants inside out.

. Long before he got to Sweden, Eldritch had had enough of being 'in an all-boys together, all singing, all dancing, all farting in the van rock 'n' roll band . . . I find the rock 'n' roll lifestyle so debasing. And it's easy to slip into.' In the 1990s, he would develop an equation that summarised his approach to successful touring: since it was impossible to 'feel like a person . . . you have to do it in a way that makes you feel like a rock 'n' roll star' and then 'try to get over it once you get home. You have to go with the flow to make it work and that requires quite a lot of self-abuse.' On the road in 1985, it seems Eldritch felt neither like a rock 'n' roll star, nor a person.

Nevertheless, all three of the Sisters of Mercy talked optimistically of continuing as a trio. They were unanimous in having no intention of replacing Marx. Hussey told a Swiss radio interviewer that 'I think what will happen is we'll keep the basic nucleus for recording and writing, to the three of us, and then see . . . the tour so far has been going very well with just the three of us, there's enough noise with the three of us.' Eldritch told a Belgian journalist, 'Wayne is covering both guitar parts. He doesn't make the same "noise" at all as him [Marx]. He's more one-dimensional and dynamic. I think that the songs will benefit from this in the future.'

In reality, the departure of Marx had solved nothing. Eldritch openly speculated about this during an interview with Federico Guglielmi at the Sisters' gig in Rome in May. 'I'm tired, I'm not feeling well . . . there are just three of us in the band, but I think by the summer that will be reduced to one; the current lineup is quite united, but I don't think that working in this way is the best thing for me. Over the last five years I have learned to make records, release them, to design the covers, to manage the band, and I've found it much more satisfying than just "being in a band."'*

Eldritch also told Guglielmi that after the group ended he would embark on a solo career, and that the way *First and Last and*

---

*   Guglielmi and Eldritch talked for two hours in one of the dressing rooms of the Cinema Teatro Espero in Rome. At the end of the interview, Eldritch gave Guglielmi 'two gorgeous handcrafted books with all the lyrics of the Sisters of Mercy in.' Eldritch wrote in one: 'a Frederico (sic), il miglior fabbro'. This referred to T. S. Eliot's dedication to Ezra Pound in *The Waste Land*, which was in turn drawn from the *Purgatory* book of *The Divine Comedy*. In the second book of lyrics, Eldritch referenced Dante again, this time *Inferno*. Instead of 'Lasciate ogni speranza o voi che entrate' ('Abandon all hope, you who enter', Eldritch wrote 'Lasciate ogni speranza o voi che partite' ('Abandon all hope, you who leave'). What Eldritch might have meant by this alteration is not clear. These gifts from Eldritch are 'among my most precious things,' Guglielmi wrote in 2013.

Always was written was an aberration. 'In the last two years I have been very busy dealing with practical management matters, so I left Gary Marx and Wayne Hussey to write the music for the songs . . . I do like to write and I can't wait to start again. After a tour I love to sit on the couch with a guitar in my hand, in front of the TV, with my girlfriend and my cat beside me – I am completely happy doing that. After a while though, the frenzy begins again and there's another tour. However, I promise you that after these dates, I'll not be back out on the road for quite a while.'

This was not a promise Eldritch had shared with Hussey and Adams. They expected to be back touring behind a new single within the year. It was a promise Eldritch had made to himself.

22

Twilight of the Idols

Once the European dates were over, Eldritch replaced Nick Jones with Boyd Steemson in the Merciful Release office.

Since graduating from Oxford, Steemson had done various 'hapless jobs', including sitting 'on a chair in the Courtauld Gallery reading Proust, ostensibly guarding paintings; stopping little old ladies with sticks punching holes in Monets.' He was on the verge of becoming a civil servant in the Export Credit Guarantee Department when Eldritch offered him alternative employment in Notting Hill.

Steemson had observed Jones at work for a couple of months and thought him 'a really nice hippy, slightly confused, very amiable; not ideally suited to dealing with Andrew.' Jones (in the third person) insists that 'there was *not* a huge clash of personalities between Nick and Andy . . . We went upon our separate ways quite amicably.' Jones set up KARBON records in an office one floor below. 'Out of the black and into the sunlight!' he says. The

Sisters of Mercy and their music 'had no lasting impact' on him. 'Drum machines just don't *swing* . . . for me . . . maaan!'

Other than his time shadowing Jones, Steemson had no experience in the music industry whatsoever. His qualifications were his enduring friendship with Eldritch and his obvious intelligence: Eldritch referred to him as the brightest person he knew. Eldritch felt that if he had managed to learn the music business from scratch, then so could Steemson.

Steemson was in situ in the Black Office when work began on the Sisters of Mercy's most idiosyncratic and ambitious concert yet. It was scheduled for 18 June 1985 at the Royal Albert Hall in London. Before that however, there was a short US tour to complete.

When Rob Dickins and Max Hole signed the Sisters to Warner in the UK, Howard Thompson had been delighted. As Vice-President of Elektra and Head of A&R, he was able to pick up the Sisters for free in the USA. 'Often, bands signed to labels for the world in the UK never got an American release,' Thompson explains. The embrace of an illustrious and hugely powerful American record label was yet another dividend of Eldritch's 1981 meeting with Thompson in his Soho Square office.

'An Elektra release *meant* something,' says Thompson. 'Elektra was a good place to be at that time. Apart from its extraordinary history, it was a label seen as very artist-friendly, working with bands that you wouldn't find on most other majors . . . Elektra was building a reputation for being the cool label to be at. Our A&R and Marketing departments were hot.'

In other key respects, the Sisters and Elektra were also a great fit. 'I think Andrew was happy to be at a place that wasn't going to tell him what to do,' Thompson says. 'Two of my favourite people work A&R for Elektra, East and West Coast,' Eldritch commented at the time. One was Thompson, the other was Steve Pross, who had put out 'Alice' and later Merciful Release records through Brain Eater. '[I] was not cool, like Andrew, just a nerd music enthusiast,' Pross says. 'I definitely liked him. He had such a clear vision as an artist.'

By the time Elektra put out *First and Last and Always*, Thompson had known Eldritch for four years. His approbation had not diminished: 'Andrew was fantastic: smart, biting, funny, kept you on your toes.' In fact, Thompson liked the whole band. 'The Sisters were brilliant. All of them,' he states. 'I always enjoyed hanging with them, professionally and (occasionally) socially,' – even though one member of the band was especially tactile. Thompson was in the bar of JFK airport when he encountered Wayne Hussey for the first time. 'I vaguely remember him trying to bite my ankles.'*

Eldritch was fully aware of how vital being attached to a major label was in the US. 'It is no good resigning yourself to an independent state, especially in this country, because you can't get distributed and you can't reach everybody, and you can't get on TV. Stuff like that can really mean a lot to a band.' Therefore the band began their promotion of *First and Last and Always* in the US with an attempt to get on television by making a video for 'Black Planet'.

For this, Elektra hired the Monkeemobile from its designer George Barris. On location near the Port of Los Angeles, the car's

---

* Adams admits that he was also 'biting Howard Thompson under the table at JFK.' He and Hussey 'were drunk as skunks. Howard was talking to Andrew and being all serious, so things are required sometimes.'

minder, Robert Webb, was unnerved to discover that the director wanted Eldritch to drive it. Eldritch's skills might have been sufficient in a station wagon on interstates to Las Vegas, but in an illustrious custom vehicle in proper traffic – on camera – was a different matter. 'So, it was agreed after some discussion to give Andy a driving lesson,' Webb recalls. 'Oh, Gawd. The first turn he made nearly took out the front right quarter panel on the car . . . He struggled and apologised for not knowing how. He explained that he had always been poor and did not have a car. No one in the band had a car.'

Webb, who was well over six foot tall, had to double for the much shorter and skinnier Eldritch when the director shot the driver from behind. 'I slouched in the driver's seat with my legs spread out under the dash. I wore a women's long hair black wig, Andy's jacket and hat. I nearly split his jacket in the back and his hat felt like one of those little organ grinder monkey's hats on my head.' Webb also noted that Eldritch was 'very pale, almost clear . . . He really needed some sun,' correctly guessing that 'his lifestyle must have kept him out only at night.'

The Sisters' US tour of May/June 1985 was much shorter than Elektra would have wanted – only three dates on the West Coast, two in the Midwest and two on the East Coast. It began at Fender's Ballroom in Long Beach and passed largely without onstage incident. The exception was at Cabaret Metro in Chicago when a woman from the crowd got onstage and grabbed at Eldritch. According to the booklet that accompanies *Silence Is Platinum*, a bootleg recording of the show, Eldritch 'fell backwards under her weight but came around to knock her on her ass with the mic-stand' before leaving the stage, thereby ending the concert (the recording seems to indicate an interrupted final song).

The encroachment onto the stage was both gross impertinence and, after the assault in the Warehouse, unnerving. The barrier the Sisters created between themselves and their audience was not just a theatrical one: audiences, like dogs, could turn on you. In this era, Eldritch claimed he played concerts with an iron bar concealed up one of his sleeves.

In New York, when the Sisters headlined the Ritz, John Hanti was back in his backline rental/sound engineer/tour manager role. Eldritch had given Hanti instructions that he was not be disturbed before the band went on for their biggest ever New York show. When Michael Alago from Elektra's A&R department arrived with a heavily muscled bodyguard and tried to get into the dressing room to see Eldritch, Hanti enforced the ban. Alago – highly likely to have been out of his gourd on ecstasy – 'spit on me,' claims Hanti. 'As I went to grab him, the bodyguard stopped me: "You really don't want to do that, John."'

The threat had as much to do with Alago's industry power at that time, than the possibility of violence: Alago had signed Metallica, he was buddies with the son of Bob Krasnow (CEO and Chairman of Elektra) and had booked and promoted shows at the Ritz for Jerry Brandt, its founder. Eldritch was sufficiently politically aware: no matter how tired or nervous he was about the show, he assented to meet Alago.

Sometimes, however, Eldritch's political skills could be found wanting. 'Andrew had a very bad relationship with Bob Krasnow,' Steemson explains. This was the case from their very first meeting.

Andrew 'looked a bit of a state and Krasnow said something along the lines of: "Hey, guy, here's a dollar, go and get yourself some fucking clothes." As you can imagine that stayed with Andrew. That really determined his relationship with Elektra, Howard's best intentions notwithstanding.'

'I set up the [Krasnow–Eldritch] meeting,' confirms Thompson. 'Something coloured Bob's attitude towards Andrew. I thought Bob would appreciate Andrew's artistic vision and that, together, they would have a few things in common and be able to engage each other. Bob had signed and worked with Beefheart, Devo, George Clinton, T. Rex – a slew of incredible, unique artists that didn't fit any mould. Wouldn't you want to pepper him with questions? I thought Andrew would realise that his success in the US depended, somewhat, on Krasnow.'

Thompson doesn't believe that 'Andrew's sartorial appearance was the reason the meeting was a bust. It had to have been more and, if it wasn't, perhaps Andrew should have realised exactly what was at stake.' Perhaps Eldritch could no more resist being an awkward bastard cluttering up an Elektra office in 1985, than he could a Rough Trade one in 1981.

Along with headlining the Ritz, another sign that the Sisters had moved up a notch in the US was that they stayed at the Gramercy Park Hotel, which was significantly less squalid than the Iroquois. Alan Vega was a resident at the Gramercy Park. One evening, Eldritch painted his nails red and hung out with Kevin Patrick, also from Elektra's A&R department, in Vega's room. Thompson photographed the three of them in front of one of Vega's wall-mounted light sculptures.

At the Gramercy Park Hotel, Eldritch presented Thompson with a full track listing of the Sisters' next album, entitled *Left on Mission and Revenge*. Eldritch had torn off the back of the breakfast menu and written the titles out: Side One: 'Second Nature', 'Torch', 'Giving Ground', 'Pillowtalk' and 'Heaven on Earth'. Side Two: 'This Corrosion', 'Ritual', 'Driven Like the Snow', 'Mission' and 'Bury Me Deep'. Eldritch even indicated that 'This Corrosion' and 'Driven Like the Snow' would be the singles. The 12-inch of 'This Corrosion' would include 'Wide Receiver', 'Dominion' and 'Garden of Delight'. The 12-inch of 'Driven Like the Snow was to be accompanied by 'Avalanche' (Part I and Part II) and 'Untitled'.

With the exception of 'Garden of Delight', for which Hussey had provided the words and music, and 'Wide Receiver', which had been attempted at Strawberry in 1984, none of these songs had yet been written. Nevertheless, Eldritch was consistently clear about what the album was to be. He gave exactly the same track listing to Daniela Giombini and Romano Pasquini, the Italian fanzine mavens, when they visited him in the Black Office in August 1985. As Kevin Lycett had noted, Eldritch's version of artistic practice was to work from ideas; songs came later.

However, Eldritch did not have some intricately worked out vision, which he then engineered in the manner of a grand strategist. The upcoming death, disappearance and rebirth of the Sisters of Mercy played out so well for him that the temptation might be to assume he planned it all: the master of puppets, puller of strings. As Steemson puts it: 'Andrew has an idea and it's a theoretical idea and there will be circumstances in which that idea can be deployed. And the fact that that idea can be deployed does not mean that those circumstances were planned or prearranged.' The end-products of those protean ideas, which were written out on a Gramercy Park Hotel breakfast menu were 'deployed' at various points during 1985, 1986, 1987 and 1988.

Nor should the track listing be seen as a smoke and mirrors attempt to pacify a label that was disappointed in the band. 'I never saw it like that,' says Thompson. 'Relations between the band and the label (whether Elektra, or Warner in the UK) were good then . . . You gotta admit, *Left on Mission and Revenge* is a great title and *very* Sisters! Seemed perfectly genuine at the time.'

Furthermore, Thompson rated *First and Last and Always* highly. '"Black Planet", "Walk Away", "Marian", "First and Last and Always" . . . what's not to like? We got a bit of college radio, got them on MTV with that silly Monkeemobile video and – with Ruth's tireless efforts – set them up nicely [for their second album] . . . There was never any doubt Andrew was going to do another album, as far as I was concerned. These were days when it took two or three albums for a band to make its mark.'

The stay at the Gramercy Park Hotel featured an incident in which Hussey and Adams seemed once again to have found the limits of Eldritch's degeneracy. The three Sisters had been booked to do an interview in Eldritch's room for one of New York City's X-rated cable shows. Hussey and Adams, in their underpants, had a rubber sex doll with them. 'Eldritch walked into his room, saw it and walked straight back out again,' says Adams.

In 1985, for a band that had never toured the USA to the extent they did in the UK and Europe, there was a sizeable audience for them to tap into. John Hanti saw this first-hand. 'On the last tour,

I handed Andrew an envelope with a little over $15,000 in cash right before they got on the aircraft: "This is what's left over after all the expenses, man." I think he was somewhat amazed. I went out on a high note with them.'

This was one of Hanti's very last official duties. 'Even the bad experiences were fun,' Hanti recalls of his time with the band. 'The worst situation I had to deal with was when I had to intervene to prevent Craig and Wayne being arrested in an airport for drunk and disorderly conduct. I think the band knew I gave them as much rope as I possibly could . . . We were never late for an interview or a gig, we never missed a flight. I'm no saint. I was pounding vodka just like Wayne and Craig. We would start drinking at six-thirty, seven in the morning and that wouldn't end till we went to bed at night. We loved drinking and we loved having fun.'

'Nice lads, sweet kids,' is how Hanti, somewhat incredibly, remembers the Sisters of Mercy.

On one occasion, jollity led to injury. 'I'm a stocky guy and in those days I was pretty strong and we used to horse around,' Hanti explains. 'We were laughing our asses off and I said, "OK, you two, that's it", and I grabbed Wayne around the waist with my left arm and Andrew around the waist with my right and I hauled them off . . . Andrew, you know, if he weighed one hundred pounds soaking wet . . . he was always so thin and fragile. Unfortunately, I bruised Andrew's rib. I must have squeezed too hard but that's the kind of relationship I had with them. How many people in the world would think about scooping up Andrew Eldritch? He didn't even indicate that he was hurt till a little while later: "Oh, my rib is killing me."'

Hanti cannot remember exactly when or where this incident happened – but Eldritch was complaining of a cracked rib when the band played at the Royal Albert Hall ten days after their show at the Ritz.

The rib was just one aspect of Eldritch's crumbling health and mood. A journalist from the *East Village Eye* noted 'his clipped sarcasm and reluctant monotone and the sunken craters that pass for his eyes. Eldritch has apparently taken too much speed and too much pain. He's had one trauma too many. He never smiles and when asked about his family or his past, the face grows a little grimmer and the communication a little weaker. He is a bitter and miserable man.'

In another New York interview – this one with the *Rockpool* magazine – Eldritch made a significant announcement: 'We've got one final date in Britain and it'll be Gary's last. A sort of Memorial Day in more than one way.'

While the Sisters were away on tour, Marx had been approached to play the Albert Hall. 'I believed Brighton to be my final gig and was resigned to that,' he explains. When offered the Albert Hall show, he 'initially turned it down without hesitation.'

Marx doesn't remember who called him 'but the words were in essence Andrew's. The situation was explained to me, and went something like this: things had moved on apace since my departure and Andrew had decided the band as such would cease to exist. Wayne and Craig would continue as session musicians only with no stake in the enterprise and be used as and when Andrew saw fit. For that reason he wanted to film the band and document the end of that stage of the group's existence for posterity. He felt it was only fitting that I should be invited back to participate in that.

'The concert must have been announced regardless of my decision and so speculation began, surrounding my participation in full or part. It was reported back to me that a prominent member of the Sisters' most loyal fans had stated he would commit suicide at the Albert Hall if I didn't play. It sounds ridiculous with so many years' hindsight to imagine I could have taken that threat seriously, but I did.'

Marx describes what follows as 'a horrible mess for me . . . I'd have been far happier if Brighton had been the last word, without the ugly footnote. It was a source of considerable embarrassment and regret for me – all I can say in my defence is that emotions were running incredibly high back then.'

After the Sisters returned from the USA, Marx was invited to Parkside Studios to rehearse in the final run-up to the Albert Hall show. As a condition for playing the gig, Marx insisted the band play 'Heartland', dropped from the live set since Black October. According to Marx, it was at this point that Eldritch rescinded the invitation to play the Albert Hall.

'I don't even know if I played a note in rehearsal,' Marx says. 'In front of Wayne, Craig, Pete Turner and the rest of the crew, Andrew told me that he couldn't risk me taking part in the show when it was clear I wasn't behaving rationally. The very fact I'd tried to impose my conditions on the material we would play had convinced him that I was no longer the man he'd known, and that he couldn't trust me. It was deeply wounding, not least to my pride, because I really shouldn't have gone back at all. I broke down and was tearful, I remember jabbering on about some bizarre childhood event, which doubtless only served to prove Andrew's point – the man is on the verge of a breakdown. I wasn't . . .'

For Marx, 'the whole episode left a bad taste for years . . . I'd been so exposed in front of all those people I loved and respected. I'd managed to bluff it out behind my shades in the office at Harbottle and Lewis when my fate was sealed; I'd slung my guitar and kicked a football against the wall in Brighton, but I had nothing left to hide behind in that dingy room in Armley.'

Marx concludes that 'Taylor and Pearman were friends but Eldritch and Marx never were. It was purely a name change for me, but clearly signalled something far more profound for Andy Taylor. I suspect friendship was viewed as a weakness in the eyes of the weird and hideous Eldritch. That we survived as long as we did suggests there was some internal struggle going on for him, but there seems little doubt who won out.'

23

Life Out of Balance

Exhaustion, paranoia, bandaged ribs and a longstanding expertise in verbal and emotional violence could account for what Marx experienced as a vicious dismantling by his old ally in Armley. The greater the strength of the former bond, the more savage, it seemed, was Eldritch's rage. What happened later that year and on into 1986 was just as merciless but lacked the outright and up-close brutality of Parkside.

The events in Parkside say much more about Eldritch's sense of betrayal, his need for displays of power and his anxieties about the intricacies of the Albert Hall extravaganza, than they do about any intentions Marx had to spoil or steal the show.

There was indeed much for Eldritch to fret about. The Albert Hall show had been weeks in the planning and was the most logistically and conceptually ambitious Sisters concert to date. The presence of a film crew was an added pressure.

The Sisters of Mercy themselves were just one element of the entertainment Eldritch had designed. In lieu of a support band, a member of the Royal College of Organists was to play 'Freebird' by Lynyrd Skynyrd and then some pieces by Messiaen. There was also to be a screening of a section of Godfrey Reggio's experimental documentary, *Koyaanisqatsi*. Eldritch had designed a range of promotional posters, the best of which adapted a photograph of the high and mighty in the Royal Box to mimic the cover artwork of *First and Last and Always*.

Eldritch billed the concert as 'Altamont: A Festival of Remembrance', conflating the Rolling Stones' murderous 1969 debacle with the annual ceremonial commemoration of British and Commonwealth war dead. Eldritch's denouement, 'The Scattering of the Ashes' – the dropping of strips of glitter from the dome of the Hall – was in imitation of the poppy petals that are released during the actual Festival of Remembrance. As someone whose own family was, in his words, 'almost completely used up as cannon fodder in two world wars' and who gets 'sad beyond words when I think about the First World War,' the humour in Eldritch's staging was obsidian black.

The other death being commemorated that night was the current version of the Sisters of Mercy. The condemned three-man line-up played a set that cleaved very closely to the one they had honed in Europe and the USA. 'Fix' was a pointed addition. Delivering it inside one of the great monuments of British High Imperialism proved irresistible. Hussey played 'Knockin' on Heaven's Door' exquisitely that night. It would serve as a requiem for the band: Adams, Hussey and Eldritch would never play live together again.

As well as being a first-rate rock 'n' roll show, the Sisters of Mercy at the Albert Hall was deeply iconoclastic, hugely symbolic and, at times, more than a little funny. It also flirted with disaster. Hussey was so hungover he could barely make it out of his hotel room for sound-check; he had caned it the night before with Ian Astbury and Lemmy at a Damned gig at the Hammersmith Palais, the low point of which was being told to fuck off by an equally pissed Jimmy Page. A top-up of speed straightened Hussey out sufficiently to play the gig. His poncho and Phil Wiffin's lights helped him sweat any remaining booze out.

While the band were jubilant about their performance, Wiffin and Boyd Steemson ended their evening lamenting what might have been. 'How do you fill the Albert Hall with three people? Answer: make them fifty-feet tall,' says Steemson. 'For the first few numbers, we were just going to light them from behind and just have huge silhouettes on this front gauze hanging in front of the stage,' Wiffin explains. This was immediately abandoned because 'the audience was pulling on this drape so much we had to fly it out.'

The grandest design concept also came to nothing. 'It would be like looking down into a valley on a misty day,' recalls Steemson. 'You'd see this sea of fog and at the end of it, these huge figures looming . . . reversing the band covered in smoke, the audience would be covered in smoke.' To achieve this, 'big film and TV wind machines were installed in the private boxes around the hall,' Wiffin explains. 'At any given moment, I could fill the Albert Hall with smoke.' Instead, he and Steemson ended up arguing with fire officers backstage while the band were playing.

'None of this stuff – *none* of it – happened at all,' says Steemson. 'We were so upset, really, really miserable, in absolute despair.'

'In the end, it just ended up being another show,' Wiffin concludes.

To film the concert, Eldritch had employed Mike Mansfield, well known to the Sisters as the host and director of the children's music show *Supersonic*, on TV during their teenage years. Wiffin knew Mansfield would have problems with the light levels during the filming but 'I wouldn't have got away with doing another light show,' he says. 'That's not how Andrew wanted it. He just wanted the same show.' A lot of the footage was therefore unusable and a nightmare for Mansfield to edit. In the finished version (eventually released as *Wake)*, 'you can see that sometimes the lighting states aren't from the number they are supporting,' says Wiffin. 'They used the brightest lights to pad it out and a lot of effects to liven it up."

In another gesture of wickedly bad taste, Eldritch hired Hell's Angels as security at his Altamont memorial. These were the Mofos from Rock City in Nottingham. The management of the Albert Hall point-blank refused to allow them to police the venue. 'The Angels were only allowed to secure the backstage area,' says Pete Turner. 'That was quite funny: there was a Hell's Angel on *every* door.'

The Sisters had also been hoping for a mounted escort of Mofos

---

* Mansfield's signature in the 1970s had been garish and trippy post-production video effects when he shot bands in performance. The Sisters were not disturbed by that at all. 'We wanted all that solarisation,' Adams says. 'We wanted it *all* like that: more of that solarisation! More. More. The staggers where it went super-psychedelic – we *wanted* that.'

from their hotel, the Tara in Kensington, to the venue. Adams thinks the squadron of cycles didn't materialise because the Mofos 'would have needed permission to wear their colours on another chapter's turf.' In fact, Steemson had rung them up beforehand to make the arrangement but found the genuinely fearsome Mofos extremely reluctant.

'"So are you coming down on your bikes?"

"Oh no, we don't know where to park them and we're a bit afraid of them being stolen."'

Also, the show itself lasted much longer than Eldritch intended. Lemmy was again implicated. In Eldritch's mind, the current phase of the Sisters of Mercy had finished when he left the stage after 'Train' with an emphatic 'Thank you . . . and goodbye.' He therefore refused to heed the audience's calls for an encore. 'He was complaining about having hurt his rib,' Steemson explains. 'Lemmy wasn't having any of that . . . he was backstage with this fucking knife, waving the bloody thing around.'

'Lemmy was shouting at Eldritch in the backstage,' Adams recalls. '"What's fucking wrong with you? These people are your fans, man. Give them one more. For fuck's sake, don't be such a pussy." Adams was delighted to see one of his heroes goading his lead singer. 'Wayne and I wanted to go on but Eldritch was, "No, no, this is the end blah blah blah."'

Eldritch needed more than strong words to get him to go back out. The blade – thankfully the only knife deployed during his Altamont memorial – was loaded with speed and proffered to Eldritch. It was an offer he wanted to refuse, but the band went out and did 'Ghost Rider' and 'Louie Louie' anyway. A significant portion of the audience had already left the venue, the house lights having been up for some time. Eldritch's planned valediction had been scuppered.[*]

The afterparty stretched across London. Jez Webb left the Albert Hall 'in the back of a black cab with Andrew and Craig . . . doing lines of speed with Lemmy, heading to the St Moritz bar in Soho for a few after-hours beverages.' Adams reckons he went to Dingwalls as well, before the Mofos joined the band for 'a bit of a drinkathon in the Tara.' This was 'quite a posh hotel, but it must have looked like a biker convention.' The Mofos, the Sisters and their crew 'were really, really well behaved. It was amazing,' Adams stresses.

Steemson confirms that decorum was observed: 'I was chatting to one of these Hell's Angel blokes in the hotel after the gig. There was a travelling salesman pissed out of his head being really intrusive. I remember him being thrown out of the hotel by the night manager who then apologised to the Hell's Angel, hoping that his evening hadn't been ruined.'

The three-piece Sisters of Mercy still needed to perform for the cameras one more time. The band had to re-shoot the 'Black Planet' video in Los Angeles because the original footage had been destroyed, 'ruined in some sort of film laboratory accident,' says Robert Webb, there again to chaperone the Monkeemobile. Eldritch was still barred from driving it. The final footage is evi-

---

[*] Marx spent the day of the Albert Hall concert, his twenty-sixth birthday, 'perfectly happily' in the Black Swan in Wakefield, his adopted hometown. 'Needless to say, there was no ritual suicide during "First and Last and (Fucking) Always". Such was the nature of a Sisters show back then, with the wall of sound and all the dry ice, that a host of perfectly knowledgeable people believed I was present and playing anyway.'

dence that he and the crew blithely ignored any such interdiction. Hussey 'was terrified in the back of that car with him driving. He had to drive up close to the truck in front with the camera – at speed – and keep the same distance.' Hussey knew Eldritch didn't have a licence and until that moment had no evidence that Eldritch could actually handle a motor vehicle.

After the shoot, Webb drove the band back to the Tropicana Motel on Santa Monica Boulevard. Eldritch was 'all pumped up . . . and wanted to go out!' Webb recalls. It was a Sunday and, since LA would be subdued, he suggested driving to Tijuana, the notoriously sleazy party city over the border in Mexico. Eldritch seemed enthusiastic and 'went into his hotel to talk about it with his buddies. Maybe they told him to ditch the car guy, they had visa problems or they were all just too tired. He never came out.'

Hussey and Adams had turned down Eldritch's offer. He was also mortified to find they were planning to go to Disneyland the next day. Eldritch therefore went to Mexico with John Hanti instead. This has become a legendary lost weekend, after which Eldritch came back 'bleary-eyed and walking funny', according to Hussey.

Eldritch would mythologise this as an emblem of the band's break-up: 'I went to Mexico for the day and the other two couldn't think of anything better to do than go to Disneyland. And when I got back from Mexico a week later, having got somewhat . . . uh . . . distracted, I thought, "God, what are these people whinging about, really?" They just got so feeble.'

'Tijuana was us sitting around drinking tequila and beers,'

Hanti says. 'I don't remember any "Tijuana Experience" . . . I was down there to keep an eye on Andrew. Do I remember us being debauched? No.'

The band then flew to New York. Hussey and Adams separated themselves from Eldritch and spent several weeks living in Lisa Levine's Mercer Street studio apartment, which she shared with Jenny Foster and their friend Debbie.*

In New York, there certainly was debauchery. Mostly it was narcotic. Who consumed what, with whom and where is explicably hazy. Hussey remembers wandering Lower Manhattan with the girlfriend of Billy Idol's guitarist Steve Stevens and wanting to strip naked, not because he was randy but because of the burning itching induced by the ecstasy he was on. Levine recalls Adams refusing to shower after being up all night on speed because he was paranoid about having a heart attack in the bathtub.

On the day of Live Aid (13 July 1985), Hussey and Adams, according to the latter, 'accidentally took heroin'. Hussey stayed in the Mercer Street apartment and was appalled to witness Jimmy Page on TV 'looking almost as dishevelled as when I'd met him just a few weeks before . . . visibly dribbling down his front,' while Adams went to 'a mini-Disneyland in New Jersey'.

This was Six Flags Great Adventure, not far from Trenton. Adams, Levine, Bryan Christian, Foster and Debbie, 'thought that on the day of Live Aid, there'll be nobody about.' They were wrong. The park was full of African-Americans not remotely interested in

---

* Foster's band Mr Mehta had supported the Sisters at the East Side club in Philadelphia in September 1983. Her relationship with Eldritch (alluded to in 'A Rock and a Hard Place') had been over for a year by this point.

watching the very white Live Aid. Adams and friends were additionally conspicuous because as 'we were queuing to get on rides, we were smoking these little spliffs. When this securi-cop came over, the black people went: "It's the punkies, they're all smoking weed!"' The weed was confiscated, even the part of the stash 'Debbie had pushed down her bra.'

Adams also had a couple of small white tablets with him. 'As we were leaving Great Adventure, we took it in the car. We thought it was ecstasy and then the next thing we were all smacked out. It was quite obviously smack. When we got back to the apartment Wayne was: "Oh my God, what the hell was that stuff?"' Even the Evil Children had now had enough. They soon flew back to England.

After the 'Black Planet' shoot – and a sign that the Sisters of Mercy were in semi-retirement – Eldritch grew another of his periodic beards. After the tortuous year he had had, Eldritch now began a long period of recovery. Some of that recuperation was in Los Angeles with Patricia Morrison. She would be a significant part of the next phase of Eldritch's assault on the mainstream.

Eldritch also turned his attention back to Merciful Release, which had no bands on its roster at the time.

Eric Mansfield from the Tyne valley, west of Newcastle, had returned home after college in Kent and made demos of four songs: 'Mexico Sundown Blues', 'Edie Sedgwick', 'Johnny Goodbye' and 'Dance'. Mansfield (using the stage name of James Ray) sent his demos to the Merciful Release office. 'About two weeks later I came home,' he says, 'and my mother said I had had a telephone call from a "very well spoken" Mr Eldritch wanting to speak to Mr Ray . . . I called their office, only to hear a message saying it was closed until the "Glorious Twelfth". Sometime between then and 12 August I received a "Tune in, turn on, burn out" postcard from Eldritch saying he loved "Mexico" and "Edie".'

Mansfield's first meeting with Andrew Eldritch was 'a remarkable experience . . . The office Andrew and Boyd rented was a small one, and everything I could see was black; the table, the chairs, the closed blinds, the phone appeared to have been painted black. The only light was from a black, Anglepoise lamp on the desk, which was positioned to cast more light down rather than into the room.' Mansfield describes Eldritch 'sitting behind the desk . . . suitably dressed in black, wearing his trademark black hat and sporting a black beard and shoulder-length hair, and of course his Ray-Bans. Due to the theatrical lighting and hovering Marlboro smoke the only visible part of his face was his sallow cheeks . . . The impression I got was an amalgamation of Don Corleone, Colonel Kurtz and Roky Erickson. It was funny.'

Less funny was that the more he met him over the next few months, Eldritch also seemed 'very tramp-like . . . Andrew wasn't drinking during this time but he chain-smoked and hammered the sulphate like he couldn't function without it. He said he detested junkies but that's what I saw.' Eldritch was also definitely behaving a little eccentrically around this time: 'Andrew slept in the office for months in the middle of 1985 . . . on a mattress made of cardboard boxes,' recalls Steemson.

The Sisters had dates booked in Japan for early 1986, but apart from that there was no imminent prospect of live work. This was especially intolerable for Adams. To sate his need 'to go out and play live and have a laugh' Adams formed a low-rent Leeds supergroup called the Elvis Presleys From Hell. 'We played at one of those all-dayers at the Royal Park [a large Victorian pub in the Hyde Park area of Leeds],' Adams says. 'We used to do covers. John [Burman] from the Batfish Boys was on guitar, Mick Brown on drums, me on bass and Grape sang. We were sometimes called Shirley Bassey's Tragic Daughter.' One of the Elvis Presleys' few out-of-town gigs was 'at a working men's club in Bradford on a Saturday night.'

While Adams was enjoying himself in West Yorkshire, Hussey was having a miserable time in Bramfeld, a quiet residential quarter of Hamburg, where he was sharing a house with Eldritch. 'I went there thinking it was going to be in *Hamburg*, thinking we could go off into the bars at night. I didn't know it was in boring, suburban Hamburg, ten kilometres out. I got to Hamburg and it was like: "The taxi's going the wrong way!" At that time there was no cable TV. Eldritch just had a bunch of videos all in German and he was watching German TV. We had no transport. It was a long, long four weeks, I can tell you.'

The Bramfeld experience rubbed salt into Hussey's wounds. Over the previous year, he had written and demoed an album's worth of songs. In Hamburg, Eldritch rejected every last one of them. Eldritch would later insist this was a matter of quality control but it was just as much a power game, to determine whether Hussey would tolerate being relegated back to the role of a sideman rather than a writing partner. In the short term, Hussey did tolerate it: 'I was prepared to go along with it at that point with Andrew to see where it went.'

It went nowhere. It was clear that Eldritch had no intention of making *Left on Mission and Revenge* in the same manner as *First and Last and Always*. 'He gave me this bunch of demos to work on,' says Hussey. 'They were really ponderous, really skeletal, no dynamic. I'm old school: intro, verse, chorus, bridge, re-intro . . . there was none of that. It was basically one sequence over and over again. What I was given was a bassline:

'"What do you want me to do?"

'"Put some guitar and keyboard on."'

Some of the titles from the Gramercy Park breakfast menu were there in Hamburg in embryonic musical form: 'Torch', 'This Corrosion', 'Dominion' and, under another title, the song that became 'Lucretia My Reflection'. Everything was in such early draft form that Hussey cannot say for sure what else he worked on.

Nevertheless, the origins of *Floodland* [the Sisters of Mercy's second album and Eldritch's biggest success] were already apparent. It would take another two years of tinkering in Hamburg and Hull and then studios in New York, Bath, Manchester and London for a finished album to emerge. It is even possible that *Floodland*'s roots are in the demos that Eldritch would not play on that first day of the *First and Last and Always* sessions at Strawberry. Perhaps the track that reminded Marx of the theme from *The Godfather* later mutated, was recorded and was eventually released; it is not uncommon for Eldritch's songs to gestate for months, even years.

Eldritch's dawdling and lack of pragmatism in Hamburg seemed at best bloody-minded, at worst a deliberate head-fuck. Hussey had a batch of tunes ready to go and would have been content with four or five of them being included on the next album. He wanted to build on the momentum of *First and Last and Always* and was convinced that a second album on that template would be huge. Instead he was being tortured in suburban Hamburg.

Six months after Hussey had backed out of quitting the band with Marx, Adams would present him with another opportunity to leave. This time he would take it.

24

Eldritch, Wrath of God

Eldritch and Hussey returned from Hamburg and reconvened with Adams in Leeds. 'Eldritch had blocked off this really long period in Parkside,' Adams explains. 'He wanted us to rehearse for like fourteen hours a day for the next album.' Adams' immediate thought was: 'This is just a crock of shit. I'm not doing this. If he's not going to tour, I'm not going to sit in studios doing crap like this.'

Adams did not complete the first day in Parkside. 'It didn't take much to light the blue touch paper,' says Hussey. 'Craig threw his bass down and walked out.' The final straw for Adams was either – depending on the version of the story – being asked to play the bassline for 'Torch' or for an ultra-fast version of what would become 'Lucretia My Reflection'.

Eldritch had also rejected all of Adams' demos in the same way he had Hussey's, and yet did not really have much evidence of his own songs. '"Where are your demos, Andy?"' Adams asked. 'He tapped his head with his forefinger: "In here."

'"Screw you! Bullshit!" Utter rubbish: probably meant he's got half a guitar-line, which he wanted someone to finish,' Adams concluded. 'He didn't want to play live any more. He didn't want to do anyone else's songs except his. Wayne and I had loads of stuff from way back, all on demo tapes. He just did not want to do any of it. What's the point in being here? I was like: "Screw it. I'm off." So I walked out. Game over.'

'But there was also the cumulative thing of him just being annoying. Like making shit up on the spot: "I've got a master-plan." "Really? And, what, the master-plan is just make it up as you go along? And just say stuff and hope for the best?" I didn't want to do that. There were other things I thought I could do. And it turns out there was.'

'When Craig left,' says Hussey, 'I remember Andrew turning round to me and saying: "Well, we've got rid of the driftwood now." I remember those exact words.'

That evening Hussey went out in Leeds with Adams.

'"You sure about this?"

"Yeah."

"OK. In that case, I'll leave with you."'

Hussey went round to Village Place the next morning and told Eldritch he was 'leaving as well and was going to form a new band . . . He asked me at that point, if I would still play on the next record. I'd been a sideman, so: "If you want to pay me to play guitar – fine. I'll come and play guitar on your record." But I didn't want to be in a band with him any more.'

'The bottom line was that Eldritch and I didn't get on great at a personal level,' Hussey says. 'It was not a relationship for the ages.'

Hussey did not necessarily need the friendship of those he worked with any more than Eldritch did, but he couldn't endure Eldritch's dismissiveness and *froideur* any longer. He liked Adams and Adams liked him – and his demos.

Eldritch was not the first abrasive front man Hussey had worked with; Pete Burns of Dead or Alive could be spectacularly rude and egomaniacal. But Burns at his worst had been much easier to deal with than Eldritch in his current imperious phase. 'Pete was a bitch and he was a gay bitch. Andrew was not a gay bitch but there was no warmth in him,' Hussey says. 'Pete, no matter what, could be really, really warm and loyal and I felt he had an awful lot of respect for me, for what I brought to him, to Dead or Alive . . . Eldritch, I never felt he really respected me or valued my input. We need some kind of validation in what we do and I never got that from Eldritch."

Hussey and Adams had not planned or co-ordinated their exits. Adams' storming out of Parkside was impromptu. He and Hussey had no strategy in place at all. They had quit with no thought about who would be in their band, no clue about management and no sense of Warners' reaction. They, at least, did have songs.

Nor did Eldritch have a clear strategy. Without a band, he now had to deploy one of his amorphous ideas. He chose the one he had outlined in Rome in May 1985: he would be a kind of solo artist.

For the first month or so, the split – between Hussey and Eldritch at least – remained amicable. Hussey was quite civil in an

---

* James Ray once told Eldritch that he didn't particular like Hussey's songs or his playing on *First and Last and Always*. Eldritch – much to Ray's surprise – informed him that Hussey was 'the best thing to happen to the Sisters.'

interview with the *Mass Murder* fanzine, in which he correctly identified two trends in the new Eldritch material: 'The stuff Andy's
doing now is softer and slower' and there was also 'music you can
dance to . . . I'll reserve judgement on what he's doing until he's
finished. He'll pull something out of the bag – he always does.'

Adams and Hussey persuaded Max Hole to pay for some studio
time for them to start making demos at the Slaughterhouse in
Driffield in East Yorkshire. They also persuaded Mick Brown of
Red Lorry Yellow Lorry to drum. Hole and Dickins hated the
demos, especially Hussey's singing, and refused to fund their completion. To make it even clearer they were not really interested in
any band Adams and Hussey might put together, Hole and Dickins
had a very long list of singers they might want to consider, including Sal Solo of Classix Nouveaux, Gavin Friday of the Virgin
Prunes, and several tuppenny ha'penny London goth bands.

Hole and Dickins were clearly backing a different horse. While
Eldritch remained under Warners' wing, Adams and Hussey were
effectively being cut loose. They had to borrow money from
Adams' father to finish their Slaughterhouse demos.

Still with no prospect of live work, Adams had the option of
playing bass in the Dead Vaynes, Leeds' answer to the Dead Boys,
with – as the name also suggests – a massive dose of Thunders-
worship added to the mix. The band was fronted by Steve Hulme
(aka Stevie Vayne or Stevie Dead Vayne), the most un-Eldritch-like
figure imaginable, save for a gargantuan appetite for amphetamine.
Forethought, planning and crafting of presentation, 'there was
none of that with Stevie Dead Vayne,' Adams says. Despite – or
maybe because of that – Adams agreed to go on a tour of Holland

with them. With Vayne leading the line, this jaunt was 'complete madness'.

'After the first show in Holland, Stevie was sitting in the front of the van and passed out,' says Adams. 'Mick [Ingham aka Prince Michael Vayne] opened the door to the van and Stevie fell out and broke his collarbone. Most people would cancel the tour. No. We gaffer-taped him into his leather jacket. And then for the next show, he was heavily sedated. He would sit on the drum riser and sing, and the drummer would be at the front. We were based in a wood in a holiday chalet with bunk beds in. We drove back there every night, sometimes on acid, sometimes not. Just madness. I had a great time doing that tour . . . It was fun because you were dealing with people who wanted to have fun and not sticking their head up their arse. Eldritch was constantly moaning and whinging about everything, so it was a breath of fresh air to be out with people who actually wanted to be out touring.'

Eldritch believed that he had an agreement with Hussey and Adams that 'no one would use the name [the Sisters of Mercy] when the band went its separate ways.' Hussey, too, was under the impression that 'Andrew wanted to start making songs as himself, and to kill off the Sisters.' It was therefore a deliberate provocation, desperation or bad faith – all three rooted in the need to get some career momentum going – when Hussey began 'putting together cassettes of demos and the Slaughterhouse recordings [and] labelling the tapes as "the Sisters".' Hussey claims this was 'for convenience sake . . . more as reference rather than with any real intent of permanently using the sobriquet.'

When Eldritch found out, Harbottle and Lewis were called into action: the truce between him and Adams and Hussey was over. Nevertheless, this was seemingly the end of the matter. Adams and Hussey simply could not legally call themselves the Sisters, no more than they could call themselves the Sisters of Mercy.

Eldritch had other pressing issues. He had no band, not much evidence of finished songs of his own and no intention of touring. Hole and Dickins were, naturally, concerned. 'Andrew had to convince that there would be songs and at some point there would be a band,' says Boyd Steemson. 'Patricia was mooted, pictures thrust under executive noses.' Their reaction, according to Steemson, was: 'That would work.'

The second necessity was for Eldritch to produce some proper demos. By December, he had made versions of 'Ritual', 'Torch' and 'Giving Ground'. 'Torch' was a successor to 'Bury Me Deep' – slow and sparse, a mutant English folk song juxtaposing acoustic guitar with the thwack of the Doktor. 'Ritual' was kin to 'Blood Money', both containing driving electric guitar daubed in liturgical organ.

'Giving Ground', however, showed how far Eldritch was prepared to move away from the rock idiom altogether, sideline the guitars and indulge his John Carpenter fetish. Eldritch perhaps saw the Albert Hall show as evidence of the limitations of the guitar-bass-drums iteration of the band. The gig had not been a sell-out and the plan to announce a second night was never realised, further reasons for Eldritch not to want to make 'First and Last and Always 2'.

With Patricia Morrison on board, some demos complete and the execs at Warner sufficiently encouraged, Eldritch began making the first James Ray and the Performance single, 'Mexico Sundown Blues', with 'Edie Sedgwick' as the B-side, in December 1985. The band was Ray and Carl Harrison, supplemented by a saxophone played called Franky. 'We signed the contracts on New Year's Eve while in Fairview Studio near Hull,' says Ray. 'We spent the thirtieth and thirty-first of December recording the sax until Franky had had enough and said he needed to go back to Newcastle for the New Year's Eve celebrations.' Eldritch kept Ray and Carl Harrison working, 'although Andrew did let us have the alcohol from his Fortnum & Mason hamper.'

Unbeknowst to Eldritch, Hussey and Adams now had a manager (Tony Perrin from Sheffield, who had managed Artery), financial backing from Dave Hall (who had made a fortune in flyposting since he stopped driving the Sisters) and an offer from Hussey's friend, Billy Duffy, to tour as support band for the Cult through Europe.

Boyd Steemson recalls being in 'the Royal Bank of Scotland in Notting Hill Gate and I run into either Craig or Wayne:

'"We're going to do this band. We've got Simon Hinkler from Artery, Mick Brown from Red Lorry Yellow Lorry."

"Oh. What are you going to call yourselves?"

"We're going to call ourselves the Sisterhood."

"Oh."'

Hussey explains the choice of name as follows: 'With the Cult tour fast approaching we needed a name for our band . . . we decided to antagonise the bugger by going out as the Sisterhood, the name by which a group of fans had called themselves while following the Sisters of Mercy. I knew perfectly well that it was an inflammatory and provocative act and would, once and for all, demolish any bridges between me and Andrew.'

'So I ring Andrew up,' continues Steemson, 'and I say, "Andrew, I just bumped into Wayne and he's going to have this band called the Sisterhood."

'Andrew just went: "No! That's the fan-club, they're not having any of that."'

Yet, it seemed there was nothing Eldritch could do about it. Hussey and Adams now had their own lawyers, who explained that 'He couldn't sue us, couldn't force us to cease and desist,' says Hussey. 'We knew we had not done anything illegal by using the name. Morally it was maybe another matter but we didn't bother ourselves with such trivial and ethical considerations.'

The Sisterhood announced their debut concert would take place in London on 20 January.

'Well, what are we going to do about that?' Steemson asked Eldritch. 'We're probably going to have to release a record because you're not going to play. There's just you.' In no way could this be under Warners' auspices; any record would have to be on Merciful Release.

Steemson and Eldritch therefore made a recording of 'Stop Draggin' My Heart Around'. It was 'just drum machine and Andrew singing "Stop Draggin' My Name Around", which fades into "Rhiannon",' says Steemson. 'It's very good. I sort of mumble at the beginning – the lead vocal – and then Andrew does the singing.'

'The rarest of Andrew records are the acetates made of it,' says Steemson. 'Probably only Andrew and I and the guy in the cutting room have heard it.'

The record was unreleasable: Eldritch's contract with Warners forbade him to sing a lead vocal on a record for another label. According to Steemson, 'Andrew had a rather legalistic view of "lead vocal" as the first vocal you heard, not the most prominent. That didn't wash.'

This left the option of releasing one of Eldritch's demos. 'So the idea was to just shove out an instrumental,' Steemson says. 'Giving Ground' from the December demos was chosen. Ominously, this was the one Max Hole had heard and liked and expected to become a future Eldritch song complete with lyrics.

In early January 1986, with the Sisterhood's debut show in London imminent, Eldritch went to Germany, leaving the 'Giving Ground' tapes with Steemson in the Black Office: Eldritch had a meeting set up with Werner Herzog.

After *First and Last and Always* had been completed, Eldritch had written down a list of possible producers for the second album. At the bottom was Werner Herzog. 'In the A&R department the administrators were very sweet and sent out letters willy-nilly,' Steemson explains. Herzog, one of the greatest directors of the German New Wave, best known at the time for *Aguirre, Wrath of God* and *Fitzcarraldo*, had no experience making records. Nevertheless, when he received his letter from Warner's A&R department, he expressed an interest in producing Eldritch's next record.

Herzog rang up the Black Office. Steemson took the call.

'I love your films, your whole approach to things . . . blah blah blah. But have you produced a record before?'

'He was so polite: "Well, I have worked very closely with Popul Vuh on soundtracks and in a year's time I'm going to go to Bayreuth to prepare a production of *Lohengrin*."'

'Outrageous really,' is Steemson's summary of the conversation.

Steemson arranged for Eldritch to meet Herzog in his office above the Arriflex camera factory in Munich.

"'Boyd, how will I recognise him?"

"Don't worry, he'll recognise you."

"No, no, I'm concerned about this. What does he look like?"

"Well, he always dresses in black."

"Tell him I will be dressed in black also."'

In Munich, the black-clad Herzog and Eldritch enjoyed each other's company. They discovered that they had a mutual interest in the Malvern Hills. 'Herzog's very interested in ley lines and Andrew has this thing about Elgar,' Steemson explains, 'but Herzog wanted to go camping along the ley lines to get inspiration.

'Andrew is no camper.'

In the midst of this, Warners' A&R department received a post-card featuring a photograph from the 1973 International Birdman Competition – a winged human leaping off a pier. On the reverse, Herzog announces that 'Andrew and I are brooding over a possible cooperation again today.' A message is added in Eldritch's instantly recognisable handwriting: 'So – still so dark (all over Europe): $1m in Peruvian currency NOW, or we turn the lights on.'

While Eldritch and Herzog were crafting such missives in Munich, Steemson was in possession of the 'Giving Ground' instrumental in London. 'We can't just put out an instrumental; we've got to have a proper song,' he thought. 'I couldn't get in touch with Andrew, so I thought I'd better write some words and called up Eric Mansfield.'

Eldritch, Wrath of God

'Giving Ground' was played to him over the phone 'so I could familiarise myself with it before going into the studio . . . The recording of "Mexico" was put on hold and I was sent to a studio in London . . . which is where I met Lucas Fox, who was to produce the vocals.*

'I got called into the Black Office,' says Fox. 'I only lived around the corner at 244 Westbourne Park Road. A case of: "Here's a tape; here's a singer."'

'Boyd . . . gave me a sheet of words, which he proudly announced he had written,' says Ray. 'So the first part of the . . . recording was me trying to find a melody in a tune I didn't really like, for words that I had no idea what they were about.'

In double-quick time after the recording session, Steemson arranged for a lacquer to be cut, a single pressed via MayKing (a short walk from the Black Office in Notting Hill) and distribution through Red Rhino in York. 'Andrew hadn't heard the single until he came back,' says Steemson. 'It may actually have been in the shops.'

'Andrew called me at home to say he had heard the finished track and said I sounded like an angel,' Ray recalls.

The single was released on 20 January 1986, the same day that Hussey and Adams played their debut concert in London as the Sisterhood.

When Max Hole found out about the 'Giving Ground' single, 'he was quite upset,' Steemson notes with some considerable understatement.

---

* Ray's recollection is that it was Eldritch who called him and played 'Giving Ground' over the telephone.

371

'"Who the fuck's singing on it?"

"It's not Andrew."

"Which song is it? Not that really great one."

"No, it's not 'This Corrosion'."'

'He was fine with that and "Giving Ground" did sort out the name,' Steemson observes.

With Eldritch the first to release a record as the Sisterhood, Hussey and Adams could no longer use that name themselves. A radio session for the *Janice Long Show* on BBC Radio 1 on 10 February was broadcast under the provisional name of 'the Wayne Hussey and Craig Adams Band.' By the end of the month, they had settled on the Mission as a name.

'Giving Ground' sold so well – a Number One in the Independent Charts – that Eldritch decided to make a second Sisterhood single. He too had an eye on cash-flow. Even though the Sisters of Mercy were deceased, he still had the Merciful Release operation to fund.

Lucas Fox and James Ray would therefore spend weeks with Eldritch in Hull working on 'that really great one'.

25

Poison

'Andrew had a skeletal demo of "This Corrosion", more like a bag of bones, and a few lines of written lyric,' says Ray. 'We started recording the vocals at Fairview – the same few lyrics over and over and over again in various styles . . . he had me singing in various guises and styles. He wanted it pretty camp.'

'Sing it like Frank-N-Furter would,' was one of Eldritch's directions. This was pure Bowie. During the recording of *The Idiot*, Iggy Pop had been instructed to sing like Mae West, one of Bowie's many seemingly bizarre approaches to getting a vocal performance.

Eldritch also had a go at singing 'This Corrosion' at Fairview. 'Andrew's vocals were supposed to be a guide,' Ray says, 'but I think it was a case of the blind leading the blind at that point, as no one seemed to know what the track was supposed to be doing.'

A change of studio and city did not lead to any great leaps forward. 'I came down to London for six days to work on "This Corrosion",' says Lucas Fox, 'but Andrew only gave me one verse.

If he had more, he refused to give it to me, which was typical Andrew.'

'I sang while in a dress, naked (whisky required), drunk, naked and drunk,' says Ray. 'Luckily, the vocal booth in the London studio was under the control room and out of sight, as I was probably naked when Andrew and Patricia turned up for the first time. While recording the vocals, I was expecting Andrew to be working on the music and more lyrics but as usual he wasn't too forthcoming. I grew particularly bored with the whole process and just wanted to get on with finishing *my* record.'

'Six days just on the vocals was arduous,' says Fox. 'Six days just doing that same verse. It was a nightmare for him [Ray]. And it wasn't that much fun for me either. And then we went back off to Hull where some more lyrics appeared and then we started crafting the thing together. There was a hell of a lot of potential for that song from the beginning, which is why it was possible to do so much with so little.'

Sounds reported on 20 February 1986 that the Sisterhood would have a new 12-inch EP called *This Corrosion* in the shops soon, 'featuring the same line-up but with the addition of a mysterious and so far undisclosed American vocalist.' This was Alan Vega.

When Vega played at Leeds university on 4 February, 'we borrowed a BBC portable tape recorder, a small reel-to-reel, and took the train from Hull to Leeds,' says Ray. 'Backstage at the sound-check Andrew asked Vega if he would contribute some vocals to "Giving Ground" and he obliged. Headphones on and mic in hand, he spent about four minutes moaning and grunting onto tape.'

Some of this recording would appear on an extended version of 'Giving Ground'. 'I brought up a reel of two-inch tape to Hull and made a copy of "Giving Ground", sliced it up into pieces,' says Fox. 'We went through a whole box of razor blades. We had pieces of two-inch tape all over the control room with chinagraph marks on: "verse", "chorus", "verse two" etc.'

Ray summarises the extended 'Giving Ground' as 'just an edited version of the single with me singing and Vega's mumbling dropped in.'

Fed up, Ray went home to Tyneside but Fox and Eldritch soldiered on, week after week in Hull. Whether they were working on a Sisterhood single or treating Fairview as a demo studio for the next Eldritch album became less and less clear. The deadline for the Sisterhood's second single came and went.

Whatever they were up to, 'I got to know Andrew well,' says Fox.

'If he hadn't got the sound right he couldn't advance at all. So we would spend literally the whole night working on a bass sound until he was finally satisfied. Andrew was incredibly difficult because he was so centred on his own way of doing things. He was definitely a control freak.'

Fox suspected that Eldritch was trying to provoke him and create a process that resembled 'a good old fashioned joust, sabre-rattling around the studio,' but that never transpired. Fox found other ways to communicate with Eldritch.

'We'd use codes between me and him. He'd go: "Where am I?"

'"Well, you're still slightly outside the harbour as far as I'm concerned, now bring the ship in. We're close but we're not quite there yet."

'We'd have these bizarre discussions late at night . . . It was faffing, but it's a fine art . . . I basically became his foil, playing ping-pong with him, constantly keeping him flowing into doing stuff. I ended up being more of a sounding board than doing actual production.'

This, what Dave Allen called 'noodling along', worked well with Eldritch. As much as he thrived on conflict and rancour in other environments, in a studio, as Ken Giles and John Spence had found, a softly-softly, patient approach allowed Eldritch to find out what he wanted.

In fact, there was a relaxed atmosphere both inside and out of the studio in Hull. Eldritch did not isolate himself from Fox, as he had done from Allen at Strawberry and Genetic.

Fox and Eldritch kept the same hours and had lodgings together in town and would take a taxi to and from Fairview together. 'He used to do *The Times* crossword before "breakfast" every morning,' Fox recalls. 'Actually, we went to bed after breakfast and got up at four o'clock in the afternoon to go into the studio for five or six, eating saveloys and chips or fish and chips on the way in and then working through the night. I was not on amphetamines at the time, but I'd done so many over-nighters with Lemmy that I don't have much of a problem staying awake and concentrating, as long as I eat.'

Fox describes his work with Eldritch ('the strangest session I've ever done') as 'six weeks of being a kind of sidekick, psychoanalyst and psychic, to make all these ideas come about. Andrew was an interesting guy to work with. It was an entirely different approach to recording and music.'

Steemson agrees that Fox was 'exactly the right kind of personality' to work with Eldritch. 'Comfortable in his own skin, articulate, clever. Somebody with a broad cultural outlook, somebody
that Andrew would enjoy talking to.'*

Fox describes himself as 'a strange fruit. I've managed to work
with a lot of alpha males without threatening them and without
being subservient . . . I don't need to prove I'm in competition.
Andrew and Lem were those alpha males in certain ways, but both
of them are much more complex than that.'

'This obsessive nightly hunt for the ideal sound was what helped
Andrew soothe his nerves . . . One of the things he told me is that
he had a memory where he couldn't forget anything, like [Benedict]
Cumberbatch in *Sherlock*. Therefore it was quite painful for him
because he took in so much information that he couldn't get rid of
in some ways.'

Hussey, Adams, Mick Brown and Simon Hinkler had three UK
shows booked for the end of February/beginning of March 1986.
Although they had already decided to call themselves the Mission,
shows were still advertised as the Sisterhood, despite the band
having lost any legal right to use the name. At the first gig, at the
Electric Ballroom, 'Ian Astbury and Billy Duffy joined us onstage
for an extended encore,' says Hussey. 'It was rumoured that
Andrew was in attendance, but he didn't make his presence known

---

* Fox and Eldritch had remained friendly since their bespoke interior redecoration of the
  Black Office. Fox was the Scientists' stand-in drummer on the UK leg of Armageddon
  '85. On the final night of the tour at Brighton Top Rank, Eldritch asked him to sing
  the encore of 'Knockin' on Heaven's Door' with him.

to us and would no doubt have slinked away when Astbury starting chanting "Eldritch is bald" over and over.'

The Mission were due to play at Leeds university on Saturday, 1
March, 'but the show was cancelled due to an injunction served on
us by Andrew's lawyers,' Hussey continues. 'Which made it all the
more extraordinary when, the very next night, he turned up again
in the audience when we played at Birmingham Powerhouse,
apparently commenting to a mutual friend how good he thought
the songs were; the very songs of mine he had rejected in Hamburg
the previous year.'

In the Mission's tour-book for these dates, the cast-list included
this:

Craig Adams – ex-The Sisters of Mercy

Wayne Hussey – ex-The Sisters of Mercy

Pete Turner – ex-F.O.H Engineer, The Sisters of Mercy

Yaron Levy – ex-Monitor Engineer, The Sisters of Mercy

Phil Wiffin – ex-Lighting Designer, The Sisters of Mercy

Dave Kentish – ex-Security/Driver, The Sisters of Mercy

Trina Wilson and Reg Halsall – ex-Production Co-Ordinators,
    The Sisters of Mercy

THIS TOUR HAS NOTHING WHATSOEVER TO DO
WITH A BAND CALLED THE SISTERS OF MERCY

As well as being a kind of legal disclaimer, this gives an inkling of
the bitterness felt by Hussey and Adams about the fact that
Eldritch could alone define himself as the true claimant to the
Sisters of Mercy's legacy and enjoy all the concomitant advantages.

Although Eldritch had made demos at Fairview under his own name, Steemson doesn't think 'there was ever a question of deactivating the name the Sisters of Mercy, not seriously by Andrew.'

In part, Eldritch had gone to war with Hussey and Adams to protect his brand. Yet, Lucas Fox saw first-hand how genuinely surprised, how shocked Eldritch was by what he considered to be Adams and Hussey's betrayal. 'There's a parallel between that and when Lemmy got kicked out of Hawkwind,' Fox says. 'There was a similar atmosphere . . . I think Andrew was working himself through a lot of grief and anger from the Sisters of Mercy split-up. He was feeling pretty embittered.'

The process was also one of physical recovery. 'The hair grew back. The hat came off,' as Steemson puts it. One day in the studio, 'he disappeared for half an hour into the bathroom,' remembers Ray, 'and later emerged clean shaven with shorter and freshly dyed hair.'

Eldritch no doubt found the speed and effectiveness of Hussey and Adams' endeavours galling. 'They just got on and did it and became big, quickly,' says Steemson. 'They were able to use all the momentum of the Sisters and they had someone who was unproblematically up for it, somebody who could write a tune, which was the reason Andrew worked with Wayne in the first place. There was a vacuum, which Wayne was able to fill very effectively.'

The Mission's first single, 'I', which featured 'Serpent's Kiss' as the A-side with 'Wake (RSV)' on the B and 'Naked and Savage' on the 12-inch was the biggest selling independent single of 1986.

Max Hole and Rob Dickins still didn't like the Mission's music and didn't for a moment regret letting them go, but 'there was real frustration at WEA,' says Steemson. Over a year since *First and Last and Always* had come out, there was no sign of a WEA record from Eldritch. Hole, good A&R man that he was, had spotted the potential of 'This Corrosion' even from the 'skeletal . . . bag of bones' demo. He was expecting it to be the track that would re-launch Eldritch and the Sisters of Mercy.

Eldritch was about to turn Warners' frustration into boiling rage, while Adams and Hussey would feel the knife twist once again.

'We had a problem with the publishing company, RCA Music,' Steemson explains. 'They hauled me in and basically said, "We're going to take up the option but there's an advance that is due with us taking up the option and we're going to divide it between Wayne and Craig and Andrew."

'"Andrew is the Sisters of Mercy and it's the Sisters of Mercy's publishing deal. Why are you giving them half the money? Why are you going to do that?"'

Steemson then had the 'contract stuffed under my nose.'

'"If you have a look at the contract, it is not the Sisters of Mercy that are signed to that publishing deal. The Sisters of Mercy aren't mentioned. It's the individuals. The only thing you need to think about is the minimum commitment that needs to be delivered."'

This 'minimum commitment' was an album. Eldritch did not need to be singing on it, nor did it need to be released by Warners. 'That's why *Gift* was done because we needed the money and we were fucked off with RCA Music,' Steemson summarises.

Even after weeks at Fairview, Eldritch did not have an album's worth of tracks. 'This Corrosion', on which the most time had been spent, was not up for grabs. 'Dominion' was also ring-fenced, as were 'Torch' and 'Ritual'.

This left a trio of incomplete songs in the John Carpenter mode: the extended 'Giving Ground', and the tracks that became 'Colours' and 'Rain From Heaven'. 'Jihad' and 'Finland Red, Egypt White' were written from scratch at Fairview. They are of a piece in their intention: the use of images of (holy) war and munitions as part of the offensive against RCA Music and Hussey and Adams.

'For "Jihad", I think Andrew was looking for something quite audacious,' says Fox. 'One of his and my favourite tracks we vaguely discussed was "Kashmir". There was something we could do with that using Arabic melodies – a bit "Kashmir", a bit Stones' Morocco-era.'

In this way, 'little bits of the demos get siphoned off, but a whole bunch of other stuff comes in,' as Steemson summarises the process of creating *Gift*. 'For Andrew what was really kind of refreshing was the need to whack something out quickly and for it not to be a Sisters of Mercy record, I think he found it quite liberating. *Gift* was cobbled together very, very quickly.'

Other than Ray on 'Giving Ground', the lead vocals are Fox's. 'Andrew liked my voice . . . I'd done a lot of voice overs . . . so he put me behind the mic and then guided me through the tonality he was looking for.'

Eldritch only had a few lyrics: 'Colours' had one verse, 'Rain From Heaven' had two. 'Finland Red Egypt White' featured Fox quoting from a book about NATO ammunition that Steemson had found in Laurence Corner (a now-defunct military surplus store) on the Euston Road. Steemson read passages over the phone to Eldritch at Fairview, who transcribed.

'Two, five, zero, zero, zero' – the size of the publishing advance in pounds sterling, the words that open *Gift*, were spoken by Patricia Morrison. She also joined Fox and Ray to form the Chorus of Vengeance to sing backing vocals on 'Rain From Heaven'. Ray, to his continuing frustration, had come to the studio to finish 'Mexico Sundown Blues', but had been co-opted yet again into an Eldritch project.

As with 'Giving Ground', *Gift*'s journey from studio to shop was quick.

Steemson went to RCA Music with a copy of the album.

'Andrew has delivered the minimum commitment with this record,' he announced.

'They were extraordinarily upset. They immediately dropped Andrew. They didn't take up the option – through fury.'

But they did pay Eldritch £25,000.

Then, with a considerable amount of mischief, Steemson went to Broadwick Street and told Max Hole that Eldritch had completed an album.

Hole was delighted that Warners finally had material from Eldritch to release.

'"When can I hear it?"

"Well, you can go to HMV and buy it."'

'My God, he was upset. So, so angry with everybody concerned,' Steemson recalls. 'He had defended Andrew and let Wayne go, realising he couldn't have the two bands on the same label.'

Hole expressed this to Steemson as: '"I stuck my dick in a

fucking door for you!" He was apoplectic. His major concern was:
"Is that fucking 'Corrosion' on it?!" He thought "Giving Ground"
had potential, even though he only heard an instrumental version,
so hated the idea of something that was even more commercial
being thrown away. He became slightly less apoplectic when he
discovered that "Corrosion" wasn't on *Gift*.'

'That was the point at which the relationship with WEA restored
itself,' Steemson continues. 'The record company took the view
that this may have been subversive, but it kept the profile going
and that something that might relaunch the band properly hadn't
been used up.'

Eldritch then had the extraordinary idea of sending the demo of
'This Corrosion' to Jim Steinman, the superstar songwriter/producer,
best known for his gargantuan work with Meat Loaf and Bonnie
Tyler. Jimmy Iovine, it seemed, was now too lo-fi for Eldritch.

Even more extraordinarily, Hole thought this was a good idea
and expected Steinman to agree to produce it. 'Max to his credit,
shoved the demo on Concorde and got it over to Jim,' Steemson
says.

Hole was right. Steinman liked 'This Corrosion' a lot and agreed
to produce it. Dickins also 'loved the song but thought it was
unnecessary to spend that kind of money, but Max was adamant,
so we went with it.'

Six months later, in late January 1987, Andrew Eldritch was in
the Power Station in New York City* with Jim Steinman making

---

* This was on a completely different level, in terms of prestige, to the recording studios
Eldritch had previously worked at. Bowie's *Let's Dance*, Springsteen's *The River* and
Madonna's *Like a Virgin* were all recorded at the Power Station.

'This Corrosion'. The second Martin Luther King Jr Day was observed, and the New York Giants defeated the Denver Broncos in Super Bowl XXI while they were doing so.

In the studio with Eldritch and Steinman were Patricia Morrison, a host of crack session musicians, six backing singers and a forty-piece choir. They were trying to make a something that Eldritch described to Steinman as needing to sound 'like a disco party run by the Borgias.'

'And that's what we got,' Eldritch concluded.

A new phase in the history of the Sisters of Mercy was being inaugurated.

EPILOGUE

Ozymandias/Songs of the Free

'We live, as we dream – alone . . .'

Joseph Conrad (1899) and Gang of Four (1982)[*]

'This Corrosion' and *Floodland*, its accompanying album, propelled Eldritch far beyond the levels of success he had achieved with Marx, Hussey and Adams. With Patricia Morrison now an active member of the Sisters of Mercy and with the full weight of WEA behind him, Eldritch orchestrated a media onslaught that filled the vacuum created by his refusal to tour a hit album. Now, for the first time in Sisters history, a sequence of big budget and highly effective promotional videos were unleashed.

After 'This Corrosion', Eldritch recorded more remarkable

---

[*] Conrad in *Heart of Darkness*; 'We Live As We Dream, Alone' is the eighth track on Gang of Four's 1982 album *Songs of the Free*.

songs, among them 'Dominion/Mother Russia'; 'Lucretia My Reflection'; 'Never Land'; '1959'; 'Vision Thing'; 'More'; 'Ribbons'; a reworked 'Temple of Love' with Ofra Haza and, five years after he had first sung it, his version of 'Emma'.

When Eldritch began touring again – behind the *Vision Thing* album in 1990 – there was a large audience waiting for him on both sides of the Atlantic. Although a poorly promoted 1991 tour with Public Enemy stalled him in the USA, his rise in Europe continued unabated during the early 1990s. It took him into arenas and onto the tops of bills at huge festivals.

His ascent had taken him from the 'oversized toilet' on Call Lane as 'our version of the Fall' to genuine pop and club hits; from smudgy fanzines into international TV studios; from a bedsit on St John's Terrace to a mansion overlooking the Mediterranean.

Eldritch became a star.

Yet, some things did not change. Eldritch remained Eldritch: albums barely completed on time, brutalising tours, line-ups rent asunder, massively expensive singles, feuds with record companies, friendships incinerated, romantic chaos, the recourse to lawyers.

Eldritch speculated about his future stardom to the *NME* in early 1985: 'There's got to be a good way of doing it . . . It's brazen self-confidence, in a way that doesn't upset the people you like – and annoys the fuck out of people you hate.' Perhaps in his mind he achieved this, perhaps he would admit to failure; he certainly upset people who liked him. Patricia Morrison was one. Those aggrieved – or just very disappointed – also included almost everyone at Merciful Release and WEA.

When Eldritch was in the wood-panelled splendour of the

Power Station in Manhattan making 'This Corrosion', he had already passed the mid-point of his recording career. It had been a seven-year slog from 'a shed in Wortley' to West 53rd Street in Manhattan, but in January 1987 there were only six more years of Sisters of Mercy records remaining.

Eldritch spent most of the 1990s withholding his labour in order to effect his release from his recording contract with East West Records, the newly created subdivision of WEA onto which he had been moved in 1990.

Eldritch went to the mattresses for so long and so bitterly, that even when Max Hole (who headed East West) had moved on to Universal International he kept a photograph of Eldritch on the wall of his Los Angeles office. 'People see that picture of Andrew,' Hole once explained to Boyd Steemson, long after either of them had any association with Eldritch, 'And they ask me why the fuck have you got that photograph of this – at best – middling artist on a *different* label, when you're head of Universal? Why not a photograph of Mick Hucknall, who was the great success? What I tell them is that it's to remind me of the most difficult bastard I ever had to work with. I look at that and I think nothing could be as bad as that.'

More moderately, and more recently, Hole has put it like this: 'I worked with him for a long time. He was interesting, difficult, talented . . . Andrew was both the remarkable plus and the minus [of the Sisters of Mercy].'

Steemson puts it like this: 'You have to work really hard to get dropped as a recouped artist, even harder than to get sent down in the late seventies from Oxford. Andrew had always been a contrarian

. . . holding out and being unreasonable, and somehow your unreasonableness is the thing that makes you distinctive . . . His contrariness became pretty self-destructive.'

The Sisters of Mercy's contract with WEA was terminated in 1997. Eldritch never signed to another label.

In terms of released recordings: nothing beside remains.

Steemson imagines that Eldritch could have gone on to have a career like that of David Byrne or Nick Cave.

Gary Marx, with only a modicum of hyperbole, thinks Eldritch could have been able 'to make his own genre-defying music, but also collaborate and produce other artists, whether in the mainstream or the avant-garde. He could do his John Carpenter-style soundtracks, explore his graphic art more fully, write, deliver his [Richard] Dimbleby lecture . . . I don't want to use the term "Renaissance Man" in relation to Andrew, but certainly he looked to be heading for a role which made fuller use of his multiple talents.'

Instead, Eldritch achieved almost none of this. Other than for annual or bi-annual tours and festival dates, he has withdrawn ever more into the private sphere. There is no evidence he has any regrets. Eldritch keeps his own counsel, as perverse it might seem to others.

'I don't make music for you. I make it for me,' is one of his pithier summaries of why small batches of songs are written, recorded, digitally tinkered with and played live, but not released. 'There's a difference between being a musician and being a pop star,' is another.

Yet through his middle age and into his sixties, Eldritch has written some of his best lyrics, among them 'Show Me', 'I Have

Slept with All the Girls in Berlin', 'Crash and Burn', 'Far Parade' and 'Eyes of Caligula'. Some of these can be heard in songs at concerts, some are in files on one of his computers. The need to be creative remains; the introvert's willingness to engage in 'simply preening' has faded.

Therefore, it is also possible that over the last three decades Eldritch has made a different kind of journey upriver: this one a reversion to being Andy Taylor. ('Whatever happened to him?' Marx wonders. 'He was a nice kid.'). Perhaps 'Eldritch' is a skin Andy Taylor shed years ago, a vessel no longer needed.

Alternatively, Marx speculates, 'By the time you've worn a mask for thirty years or more what difference does it make if it is a mask?'

The collision of Andrew William Harvey Taylor – and his persona, Andrew Eldritch – with rock 'n' roll defined the Sisters of Mercy and has eclipsed any of the relationships he has had with various band members. The dialectic between Eldritch and his art – whether creative or destructive – has beguiled and bewildered for forty years. It has required stamina from those that have witnessed it: Eldritch has sometimes been a wilful custodian of his own legacy.

Even at its most fecund, the relationship between Eldritch and rock music has been an uneasy one. In his interview with the *NME* in March 1985, Eldritch observed that, 'The most unlikely people end up being stars.' There were aspects of himself that he surely recognised in this: the shy intellectual, 'an unprepossessing youth' with no musical pedigree, an adult by the time he stumbled into playing in bands.

John Keenan, the man who created the swamp out of which the

Sisters of Mercy first crawled, recalls Andy Taylor in the late 1970s as: 'Long, greasy black hair, glasses, skinny . . . he was the last person you'd imagine becoming a rock star . . . I still find it amusing that for years his picture was on the bedroom walls of fourteen- and fifteen-year-old girls and he was idol worshipped. C'mon, it's *Andy Taylor*!'

Yet Keenan also recognised the grit and the idiosyncrasy that would serve Eldritch well in the Sisters of Mercy. 'People took the piss out of him because he was always acting the rock star . . . [but] you did notice him; he was not like everybody else [but] nobody ever dreamed . . .' Keenan trails off. 'But fair play to him, he really pulled it off and showed everybody. I think he's amused by it himself. He's probably as amazed as the rest of us that he's gotten away with it this long.'

The people who knew Eldritch best in Leeds are less surprised that he became a significant artist. 'He's quite an extraordinary person,' says Claire Shearsby. 'Very determined, methodical, with a superior intellect . . . He was very determined to be successful. That was quite clear from early on. He put the hours in, definitely. He was fairly ruthless; you have to be.'

'I would estimate that Andrew was ninety per cent likely to go on to achieve greatness whether or not he had met me,' says Gary Marx. 'He was always brimming with self-belief. He had a sizeable ego long before he'd rebranded himself "Eldritch" . . . It seemed to be the result of that kind of privileged education where it's perfectly normal to believe you're going to be Home Secretary or Poet Laureate.'

The young Eldritch certainly expected to make his mark on the world. That it has been as a musical artist may well still surprise him, as Keenan suspects. Although Eldritch has often found being a worker in song gruelling, it is unlikely he could have found an occupation that fit him better, not simply because it has allowed him to do what he damn well pleases for the majority of his adult life and avoid anything he might consider 'a proper job' since the late 1970s.*

At the height of his productivity, Eldritch's abilities as a lyricist, writer of riffs, producer, graphic designer, singer, live performer – and talker – were unassailable. Yet, they were just elements of an even greater talent: Eldritch created such a vivid and perfectly articulated version of himself that he conjured an entire worldview into being. It connected directly into the consciousness of young people – and even the not so young – in their quest to create their own self-images and develop intellectual lives. Great songs alone cannot explain the hold Eldritch continues to exert over his fans. Perhaps he could be a bit of a shit and even on occasion 'a prize tool' (as an exasperated Marx once referred to him), but Eldritch to this day remains a heroic and important figure to many, and rightly so.

Eldritch, of course, was lucky too. He decided to become an artist during one of the great golden ages of music: 1978–84, the post-punk era. Eldritch was part of that explosion of highly idiosyncratic performers fully exploring their own aesthetic in the considerable freedom punk and its aftermath afforded them, initially unencumbered by commercial imperatives. Keenan likens

---

* Therefore 'BEACH' is one of the two capitalised words on the landing page of the Sisters' official website. That the other is 'REDEMPTION' might indicate that, like so many (to quote that 'boring old twat' Lou Reed), Eldritch was saved by rock 'n' roll.

Eldritch to one of the most pungent of those artists: 'Andrew reminds me of Genesis P-Orridge – showmen, the power of suggestion, a bit of charisma, a bit of kidology.' Eldritch is much less of a controversial figure than P-Orridge, but just as much an extremist.

Eldritch also arrived in Leeds at a perfect moment. So much of the city was dying just as its musical culture was peaking, in both its art school and townie forms and as host to scores of touring acts. In the clubs and halls of Leeds, Eldritch experienced – with maximum intensity – hundreds of gigs during the great wave that punk had let loose. Without that, and without being directly injected into the epicentre of the city's music scene by dint of being Claire Shearsby's boyfriend, there could have been no Sisters of Mercy.

Leeds also offered him specific examples of how to operate as an intellectual in rock music. He knew the Mekons personally, but in the ability to fuse theory and abstraction with the visceral power – and the groove – of guitar, bass and drums, the Sisters of Mercy were more the heirs to Gang of Four.

On the cusp of his ascent to stardom, the former Village Place trio of Eldritch, Marx and Shearsby were, after a fashion, reunited in the Warehouse in Leeds: on Monday 6 July 1987, Marx's post-Sisters band, Ghost Dance, headlined. Shearsby was their regular sound engineer by this point.

Early in the evening, with the band in the dressing room prior to going onstage, Shearsby told Marx 'she had a pre-release copy of Andrew's new single and she was going to ask the DJ to put it on over the sound system.'

Marx heard 'This Corrosion' for the first time the way he had first heard 'Temple of Love': through a doorway. 'I stood on the steps of the dressing room leaning out to try and get a better listen. Both Claire and I knew it was staggeringly good and likely to be his real breakthrough. If people had been tempted to think he was a busted flush, "This Corrosion" was two fingers shoved right up in their faces.

'Claire had no doubt played the track at home before, so already knew some of the words, and was singing along as the outro continued to build and build. I caught her eye; it was a sweet exchange. Other people in the cramped dressing room looked on nervously wondering how I might react when it ended, *if* it ever ended. Claire knew I would react much as she was going to – a look, a smile; if words were used, they weren't needed.'

Afterhours

Craig Adams left the Mission in 1992. A stint in the Cult followed. In 1999, Adams joined the Billy Duffy/Mike Peters project Coloursound, later playing in Mike Peters' solo band and then the reformed Alarm, before leaving in 2018. Adams returned to the Mission for 25th anniversary shows in 2011 and has remained in the band ever since. He is also currently in Spear of Destiny, which he joined in 2005. He lives near Washington DC with his wife Kristy and their animals: cats Dr Evil and PuttPutt and a black and tan coonhound called Jolene.

Michael Alago left the music business in 2004. He is now an author and photographer. In 2020, he published a book about his life and work, *I Am Michael Alago: Breathing Music. Signing Metallica. Beating Death*. He is also the subject of the documentary *Who the Fuck Is That Guy?*

Dave Allen has continued to work as a record producer and engineer, including with the Cure, the Chameleons and the Mission. About his time with the Sisters of Mercy in 1984, he comments: 'You only get so many seminal albums in a career so I am duly grateful to have at least one. I have learned a lot since then and now understand that only ignorance can take one through some of the difficulties that life offers.'

John Ashton: Since leaving the Psychedelic Furs in 2007, Ashton has been involved in music production. In 2014 he released a collaborative album under the name of Satellite Paradiso. He also plays with Mercury Rev on occasional side projects and has served as the music producer for an independent movie called *The Dwarvenaut*. He lives in upstate New York.

Tom Ashton moved to the USA after the March Violets ended in 1987. He founded SubVon Studio where he records, mixes, remixes and masters the music of 'other dark and likeminded artists'. He played guitar in the reformed March Violets between 2007 and 2015. They released their debut album, *Made Glorious* in 2013.

Stephen Barber is now a writer, and the author of eight novels and twenty-plus non-fiction books. He is also a professor of art at the Free University, Berlin, and at Kingston University, London. He wrote about the Leeds music scene of the winter of 1978 in his book *White Noise Ballrooms* (2018).

Rocco Barker lives with his wife, TC, and twin boys, Rocco Junior and Caesar Sid, 'on the shady side of sunny Notting Hill.' He is also 'in a state of RetoX with Wasted Youth' and is a craftsman/eyewear maker.

Jim Bates: After being the bar manager of the Faversham and DJ on Monday nights at Le Phono, he became a nurse at Leeds General Infirmary.

Dave Beer became a major figure in UK dance music as promoter, producer and re-mixer. He was honoured as a son of Leeds by Leeds City Council for the cultural and economic contributions his club night, Back to Basics, made to the city. Beer continues to make music and be a 'purveyor of good times'. He lives in Leeds.

Rik Benbow went on to work in the music business as a stage manager, including at the BRIT Awards, the MTV Awards, on *Top of the Pops* and on tour with Iron Maiden, George Michael, Take That, Coldplay and Massive Attack. He is married with four daughters and lives in Sussex.

Andy Booth is a lawyer in Manchester and 'looks after the great and good, young and old, of the Manchester music scene.' He still plays guitar for the Cassandra Complex, who retain a following in Europe.

Chris Bray (Frater Marabas) moved the Sorcerer's Apprentice shop from Burley to Hyde Park Corner in Leeds, where the premises were firebombed by Christian extremists in 1989. The shop later returned to the original Burley Park Lodge Road location. It now appears to be closed for business.

Mark Burgess continues to tour extensively as Chameleons Vox. He is currently working on a sequel to his 2010 memoir *A View from a Hill*.

Graham Cardy died in October 2020.

Chris Carr is still active in PR and management consultancy in the music industry, working with Delta PR and also independently as a manager.

Nick Cave: In 2017, Cave became an Officer of the Order of Australia 'for distinguished service to the performing arts as a musician, songwriter, author and actor, nationally and internationally, and as a major contributor to Australian music culture and heritage.'

Bryan Christian ('Bryan Brain Damage') became a successful sound engineer. He lives in New York City.

Adrian Collins is retired, lives in Plymouth and has an allotment. He remains passionate about politics and music. 'Politics is depressing these days: right wing governments have sway and I fear for people. Music is more uplifting.'

Ali Cooke co-created the Back to Basics club night in Leeds with Dave Beer. They also recorded together under the alias the God Squad. Two of their songs 'Beans' and 'Floored' sampled the Sisters of Mercy. Cooke died on 12 March 1993.

Mark Copson (Johnny Copson) continued in Music for Pleasure until the band ended in 1985. He then sang in the Danse Society off-shoot, Johnny in the Clouds, who recorded an unreleased album. He lives in Burley.

Simon Denbigh: As his time in the March Violets was ending in 1985, Denbigh formed the Batfish Boys. He fronted that band until 1990. He was 'Nurse to the Doktor' (the operator of various drum computers) on the Sisters of Mercy's tours from 1997 to 2012. He sang in the reformed March Violets until 2015. In 2016, Denbigh suffered a stroke and began a long period of recovery and rehabilitation.

Rob Dickins was Chairman of Warner Music UK until December 1998. He became a Commander of the British Empire (CBE) for services to the UK music industry in 2002. He has chaired the National Museum of Childhood, the Theatres Trust and the British Architectural Trust at the Royal Institute of British Architects. He has also been a Trustee of the Victoria and Albert Museum and the National Portrait Gallery.

Jez D'Netto now lives in Tuscany and runs vineyards and olive groves. He makes wine and enjoys gardening.

Martin Docherty: After he finished tour managing, stage-managing and promoting, Docherty set up his own clothing business supplying band merchandise. This developed into RAW clothing, which imports environmentally friendly cotton garments. He now lives in Wallington in south London and builds interactive websites.

Andrew Eldritch (Andy Taylor) is the singer of the Sisters of Mercy and a consultant to the trust The Sisters of Mercy Limited. He has described the Sisters as his 'Saturday job'. What he does the other six days of the week is by no means clear. He has suggested that it involves playing with cats, watching films in non-English languages, reading books, listening to cricket on the radio, drinking and tinkering on one of several computers. This sounds not unlike his first years in Leeds. At the time of writing, there is evidence that Eldritch is now engaged with the Sisters of Mercy project in ways unheard of since the twentieth century. Despite an accumulation of cigarette ash and cat hair, Eldritch's home studio has had more new Sisters material pass through it in these last two years than in the previous twenty. Perhaps this is a herald of a late-period flurry, the likes of which have not been seen since Leonard Cohen came down from the mountain.

Laurence Elliot continued in the March Violets until the band's end in 1987. He did not participate in any of the live performances or recordings when the March Violets reformed.

Reg Forbes (Riot Reggie/Reggie Riot) died in early 2019.

Jenny Foster fronted a band called Princess Pang for several years and then studied Eurythmy. She is currently living and teaching in New Jersey.

Lucas Fox has been based in Paris for more than three decades. He currently broadcasts on Radio Perfecto, regularly attends Motörheadbangers (the official Motörhead fan club) events and is currently writing his erotically explicit autobiography. His most recent records are the Pink Fairies' *Resident Reptiles* (2018) and the remastered *On Parole* (2020), featuring his 1975 recordings with Motörhead.

Keith Fuller has worked for Leeds City Council's Forestry team since the early 1980s. He enjoys photography as a hobby and contributed to the official Merciful Release fanzine *Underneath the Rock* in the 1990s. He has been married since 1985 and has two children.

Rosie Garland is now a writer and performer. Her latest poetry collection is *What Girls Do in the Dark* and her latest novel is *The Night Brother*. She also performs 'twisted cabaret' as Rosie Lugosi the Vampire Queen. She sang co-lead vocals in the reformed March Violets between 2007 and 2015.

Ken Giles: Although he built 'the recording studio of my dreams' in Wakefield in the early eighties, he instead went on to have a forty-year career in sales, distribution, export and manufacturing of leading-edge, high-end professional audio products, especially those of Drawmer and Soundfield. He lives in West Yorkshire and Languedoc-Roussillon and regularly visits his in-laws in Finland.

Daniela Giombini wrote for several years for *Rockerilla,* an Italian music magazine. She then founded a booking agency, Subway Productions, and organised Italian tours for bands like Nirvana, Hole, Lemonheads and Mudhoney. After having worked as a painter and sculptress, she now writes for the online Italian newspaper *Kulturjam.*

Stuart Green moved to 'that London' in 1983. After 'stumbling through his degree' he found himself in music management working for Björk, Arcade Fire, These New Puritans and Fat White Family among others. He remains friends with many of the contributors to this book.

Stan Greenwood lives in Bingley, West Yorkshire. He plays in Skeletal Family and in his local band the 1960 Four.

Paul Gregory (Grape) has worked at Leeds Grand Theatre 'on and off for twenty-odd years.' He still sings with the Expelaires, who reformed in 2014, releasing the *Sick of Lies* EP the same year and their debut album, *Feedom,* in 2016, thirty-eight years after the band formed. He is also in Black Chapel, an offshoot of the Danse Society.

Ben Gunn (Ben Matthews) has not spoken on the record about the Sisters of Mercy for thirty-seven years.

Graeme Haddlesey died suddenly at the age of forty-two. Graeme's ashes were scattered on the pitch at Anfield, home of his beloved Liverpool FC. Gary Marx performed father of the bride duties at both his daughters' weddings.

Dave Hall spent many years as a hugely successful flyposter, as manager of Red Lorry Yellow Lorry and Rose of Avalanche, and as a concert promoter and band merchandiser. 'Poacher turned gamekeeper', he now develops legal poster sites across the UK. He regularly attends Pilates and Yoga classes.

Reg Halsall: After a large VAT dispute ended Troubadour in the mid-1980s, he continued doing freelance tour management, including for Megadeth, Anthrax and Boney M. He then worked for Virgin Media for twenty years and is now a sales leader at Avon Cosmetics based out of Swindon.

John Hanti still also owns SST. He oversees the day-to-day operations of the business as well as the real estate that houses all of its various music and media operations, including five recording studios and 'one of New York's favourite audio/visual production stages' used by, among others, Alicia Keys, the Rolling Stones and Lenny Kravitz. He lives in Las Vegas.

Carl Harper ('Tich') and **David Harper** ('Tubby') both live in West Yorkshire: Leeds and Ilkley, respectively.

Tony Harris is still a recording engineer. He has also worked for the last twelve years at the National Sound Archive based at the British Library 'digitising all kinds of recordings on all kinds of formats.' He is 'still dragging Dave Allen out for the occasional breakfast and gossip.'

Mick Harvey: After the Birthday Party ended, he was a Bad Seed for more than twenty-five years, until 2009. Other than his work with Nick Cave, he is best known for his recordings with PJ Harvey, which span nearly twenty years. As a solo artist, he has written soundtracks for television and film and made a series of albums dominated by an array of cover versions, most significantly of songs by Serge Gainsbourg.

Werner Herzog (Werner Stipetić) remains one of the great artists of world cinema, as both a documentary and fiction film-maker. He has also acted, and has directed numerous operas and plays. He has yet to produce a rock music album.

Max Hole became Executive Vice-President of Universal Music in 2004, overseeing the promotion of Bon Jovi, Amy Winehouse and Justin Bieber, among others, with special responsibility for the company's Asia/Pacific business. In January 2013, he became Chairman & CEO of Universal Music Group International (UMGI). He retired due to illness in 2015. He lives in west London.

Danny Horigan (Daniel Mass) lives and works in Leeds and still sings in Salvation. After leaving Merciful Release, the band released several singles and EPs (including one produced by Wayne Hussey) and two albums before splitting in 1990. They reformed in 2007 and continued to gig and record.

Steve Hulme (Stevie Vayne/Stevie Dead Vayne): The death of Johnny Thunders in 1991 prompted Hulme to quit rock 'n' roll. He became a player in the international dance music scene in Leeds, London, New York City and Ibiza, where he has been living 'in vibey bliss' since 2005, with his Cuban wife and Spanish stepson.

Dave Humphrey moved to Bristol and fronted God Bless You between 1983 and 1989. They released one 12-inch single with 'Sugar' as the A-side and 'Magic and Mystery' as the B-side.

Wayne Hussey still tours and records as a member of the Mission. He also regularly performs as a solo artist. His autobiography, *Salad Daze,* was published in 2019. He is working on a second volume continuing his story after he left the Sisters of Mercy in 1985. He lives in São Paulo and in rural Brazil with his wife Cinthya.

Paul Ireson: After his time at Priestley's and Red Rhino, he worked for Rough Trade. After leaving the music business, he taught Design Technology and Electronics. He still lives in York and has started a band late in life, singing and playing guitar.

Tony James created Sigue Sigue Sputnik in 1982. After that band split up, he joined the Sisters of Mercy for the *Vision Thing* album and the ensuing 1990 and 1991 tours. His final appearance in the band was on *Top of the Pops* performing 'Temple of Love' in 1992.

Mark Johnson worked in music retail with Virgin Megastores and HMV for twenty-eight years. He has lived in Ireland since 1994. *Whippings & Apologies* was resurrected in 2018 in the form of a 'best of' compendium, including a new twelfth issue.

Nick Jones continued to release independent records on KARBON, simultaneously managing the Folk Devils, the Scientists and Ghost Dance, until leaving Notting Hill altogether to care for his parents. He resurfaced after their passing to promote free music festivals and gigs in Bognor Regis, West Sussex, where he still lives, peacefully retired and happily married, next to a graveyard.

John Keenan has lived in Leeds for fifty-three years and has promoted events there for forty-four of them. He continues to 'make things happen, for my own enjoyment as much as for everyone else's.'

Dave Kentish died in the mid-1990s.

Andy Kershaw remains best known as a radio broadcaster, especially as a champion of African music. In 2005, he was awarded an honorary degree by the University of Leeds. His autobiography, *No Off Switch*, was published in 2011. There is no mention of the Sisters of Mercy in it.

Duncan Kilburn returned to work for Reuters in 1985 and was posted to Hong Kong in 1988, where he would live for the next ten years. Sailing his boat, the aptly named 'Scots Wha Hae', halfway round the world he finally settled in South Australia and, 'missing the crazy world of the early-eighties music industry, now teaches Film to ten-year-olds, which he finds remarkably similar.'

Tony Kostrzewa: The Red Rhino record label was closed down when Red Rhino Distribution financially collapsed in 1988. When the Red Rhino record shop closed in 1992, Kostrzewa and his family moved to Leeds. He died in 2008.

Bob Krasnow continued as Chairman of Elektra until his sudden resignation in 1994. He then set up his own company Krasnow Entertainment. He died in 2016, aged eighty-two.

Martin Lambert is a chef by trade and still lives in the Wakefield area. He is married to Molly and still meets up with many of the God Squad. He is still an avid gig-goer with his 'gig buddy of more than thirty years, Mr Gary Marx.'

Jon Langford is a painter and musician. He moved to Chicago in the early 1990s and since then he has played in numerous bands: the Waco Brothers, Pine Valley Cosmonauts, Men of Gwent and Bad Luck Jonathan, among them. He has remained a Mekon for forty-four years.

John Lee played in two bands, Satori and Chant, in the early 1980s. He was resident DJ at the Dry Dock in Leeds 1993–98 and more recently started the *Soulful!* club night in Harrogate. He is now retired, lives in Knaresborough and is learning to draw. He intends to republish the *Damaged Goods* fanzine.

Lisa Levine: After working for record labels and producing music videos, 'she and her husband moved to Seattle and raised a couple of stellar humans who are now older than she was when she first started going to see the Sisters.' She had a midlife reinvention and is now a writer and a life and health coach.

Yaron Levy provides tour management and sound engineering services, including to Ocean Colour Scene for fifteen years and for Feeder since 2001. He also does splitter bus tours, which he 'really enjoys for their intimacy and camaraderie, which often takes me back to where – and when – I started out in this industry: getting my break with the Sisters.'

Kevin Lycett: The original Mekons reformed in 2017, toured and released an album of new material. Lycett also continues to create music with various collaborators and is a member of Soviet Leeds, a performance outfit that stages pieces about radical history. He is a busy visual artist, producing paintings and prints, which can be seen at www.kevinlycett.co.uk.

Tony Mallett spent most of his working life as a journalist and editor, much of it in Brussels. He died in Turkey, aged fifty-eight, in July 2020.

Mike Mansfield: After the Sisters of Mercy's 1985 Albert Hall concert, he continued to film live music performances, most notably for Jean-Michel Jarre. He also directed some episodes of *The James Whale Radio Show* and the pilot episode for (the unmade series) *Tiger Bastable: The Case of the Nazi Mindbender*.

Gary Marx (Mark Pearman) is 'mostly retired'. He and Kathryn Wood were married in 2001. They share their home in Wakefield with two badly damaged guitars, an ill-fitting Sex Pistols T-shirt and Stéphane Audran: 'I think it's her I see in the bedroom from time to time.' If you averaged out the time he's spent in the company of Andrew Eldritch since leaving the Sisters of Mercy 'it would equate to roughly twenty minutes a year.' Marx is open to the idea of reducing that still further and believes Eldritch is as well.

Merb (Ian Hill) joined the police in late 1980s, became a traffic sergeant and served the full thirty years. He recently retired and is currently living on the coast of Portugal, near Lisbon with his wife, son and 'a crazy labradoodle'.

Les Mills continued to manage the Psychedelic Furs until the end of their *World Outside* tour. With the band in terminal commercial decline, he fired staff from his Southwark office and resigned as the Psychedelic Furs manager on 25 April 1992.

James Mitchell: After Flesh for Lulu, he 'worked in the film business, wrote a book and had kids.' He currently has a property/building company and a fledging start-up 'for unique body confidence products'. He lives in London.

Patricia Morrison (Patricia Rainone): After the Sisters of Mercy, Morrison released a solo album in 1994 and then played in the Damned for eight years. She lives in England with her husband Dave Vanian and their daughter Emily.

Roger Nowell (Trotwood) is currently Paul Weller's guitar tech and is guitar tech/stage manager with Culture Club. He still plays bass in Skeletal Family. His girlfriend is Sarah Adams, sister of Craig.

Rodney Orpheus (Rodney Campbell) still tours and records with the Cassandra Complex, while also pursuing a career as an executive in cutting-edge media technology companies. He has also written extensively on the magick of Aleister Crowley. He lives in London.

David Owen is a freelance graphic designer. He lives in a farmhouse 'in the middle of nowhere' on the North Yorkshire Moors. 'The Hollow Men back catalogue is hopefully going to see the light of day' in 2021.

Romano Pasquini is a bass player and tour manager. He has played in the A-10, Yage, Jahmila, Sonic Assassin and Punkafarai with his brother, Pippo. He now lives in the South of France and plays in the Sonic Preachers.

George Peckham operated his company, the Master Room, until the late 1990s when he retired. His autobiography, *Porky's Prime Cuts* was published in 2018 and recounts his time in bands in Liverpool in the 1960s and mastering records for three decades. He describes 'a life full of sex (a lot), drugs (a little) and rock 'n' roll (more than enough).'

John Peel (John Ravenscroft) continued broadcasting, including his BBC Radio One show featuring Peel Sessions, until his death in 2004. After his early support for the Sisters of Mercy, his enthusiasm rapidly cooled; he played one song by them on air after 1985.

Johnny Plumb died in September 2013.

Ruth Polsky was hit and killed by an out of control taxicab outside the Limelight club in Manhattan on 7 September 1986. Her seven years as a promoter and booker transformed the New York City music scene, and the fortunes of a host of bands, particularly those from the UK.

James Ray (Eric Mansfield) writes, records and releases music with the Black Hearted Riders. He lives in Northumberland and Spain. He is currently writing and filming a documentary about Spanish gypsies.

Mick Robson: After Naked Voices and the Sisters of Mercy, several other artists from Yorkshire recorded at Ric Rac Studios in Wortley: Skeletal Family, Bill Nelson, Shed Seven, the Pale Saints, the Bridewell Taxis and the Grumbleweeds.

Henry Rollins (Henry Garfield) was the singer in Black Flag until 1986 and in the Rollins Band until 2006. He now hosts a weekly radio show on KCRW and the *Henry & Heidi $1.99 Show* podcast.

Andrea Ross (Angel Corpus Christi) is still a San Francisco-based singer, songwriter and accordionist. She is 'working on her next musical offering consisting of songs one-minute in length, and practising hula-hooping while playing accordion.'

Herman Schueremans has promoted concerts in Belgium for forty-five years, with huge success. Between 2004 and 2012, he was also a member of the Flemish Parliament. He currently promotes for Live Nation and is the main organiser of Rock Werchter, TW Classic and Werchter Boutique festivals.

Claire Shearsby worked as a DJ and sound engineer for many years, including for American thrash metal band Overkill on tours in Japan and the US and at European festivals. She DJ'd at the Sisters twenty-fifth anniversary gig in Leeds in 2006. She still lives in Leeds and now works as a Medical Guide Communicator, taking Deafblind people to hospital appointments. She lives with Mick Brown and with a cat called Billy and a dog called Chicken.

John Spence is in his fortieth year as a recording engineer and is 'still very busy with clients old and new.' He has worked in many different studios but is still mainly based at Fairview in Hull. He has no plans to retire.

Boyd Steemson resigned from Eldritch Boulevard (the previous name of The Sisters of Mercy Limited) in 1994. He then managed XC-NN and Tin Star, two bands featuring Tim Bricheno who played in the Sisters of Mercy 1990–92. Steemson is currently CEO of TotalRock Radio based in London.

Jim Steinman: As well as 'This Corrosion', Steinman co-produced 'Dominion'/'Mother Russia' on the Sisters of Mercy's 1987 album *Floodland*. He also co-wrote and co-produced 'More' on *Vision Thing*. As a songwriter and producer, his records have sold more than 190 million copies over five decades. He died in 2021.

Tim Strafford-Taylor left Leeds at the end of the 1980s to work in IT. His approach to this is the same as to music – 'make it up as you go along'. He is 'slapping the same old bass', with the Outriders, his band in Nottingham, where he now lives, with his wife of thirty years and two children.

Adam Sweeting: After leaving the *Melody Maker* in 1986, Sweeting has written on rock, classical music and television for the *Guardian*, *Telegraph*, *Uncut*, Classic FM and *Gramophone*, and on motor racing for *Motorsport*. He co-founded The Virtual Television Company and the arts website www.theartsdesk.com. He has written books on Simple Minds and Bruce Springsteen.

Howard Thompson quit the record business in 1999 but 'missed all the free records/CDs that came with it', so he started an inter-net radio station. After a few years, he moved to WPKN, a terres-trial, independent, community radio station broadcasting out of Bridgeport, Connecticut, where he's been Music Director for more than ten years. On his show, *PURE (*first and third Fridays of the month, 1 p.m. Eastern), the Sisters of Mercy are among Howard's most played artists. @howardwpkn

Nick Toczek: After he stopped publishing *Wool City Rocker* and promoting gigs, he continued as a rock journalist and became established as an authority on the activities of racist groups in the UK and the USA. He also toured as a performance poet, lectured at Bretton Hall College in Wakefield, became a best-selling children's poet and has been a visiting writer in schools in more than forty countries. He lives in Bradford.

Pete Turner continued in tour production management and as a sound engineer. He has toured with Boyzone, Ant and Dec, 5ive, All Saints and – 'as a reward from the gods' – with Roxy Music and Bryan Ferry solo. His last work with the Sisters of Mercy was at summer festivals in 1996. He is in his late sixties and still enjoys 'a bit of sound work and driving the big lorries.' He lives in Bridlington.

Alan Vega (Boruch Alan Bermowitz) died at the age of seventy-eight in 2016. After contributing to *Gift*, he continued to perform and record in Suicide, released several solo records, participated in numerous musical collaborations and had a long career as a visual artist.

Steve Watson (Stevie Sex Pistol/Winker) became Assistant Tour Manager for the Mission and played in 3,000 Revs with Adam Pearson and Paul Gregory. He also worked for Dave Hall's company, DNA Productions. He lived in Leeds and died in August 2019.

Jez Webb 'held on to Craig and Wayne's coat-tails and toured the world with the Mission.' He returned to the Sisters of Mercy for the *Vision Thing* tour. He has been working for bands ever since, including Depeche Mode, the Cure and Robbie Williams. 'The Sisters truly did change my life,' he says.

Mike Wiand owned the Warehouse in Leeds until 1988. He then opened clubs in Miami, Dallas and Baltimore and was hired to open the first three House of Blues clubs in Boston, New Orleans and Los Angeles. Throughout his time in Leeds, he was a member of the National Security Agency. When he died in 2014, he was given a military funeral at Arlington National Cemetery.

Phil Wiffin: His last outing as the Sisters of Mercy's lighting designer was on the 1991 US *Vision Thing* tour. For twelve years after that, he worked with a range of artists from Suede to David Sylvian. He now works mostly in events, although in 2017 he did the lighting for the Mission on their UK dates supporting Alice Cooper.

Mark Wilson (Vince Berkeley) is semi-retired from his career as a software engineering consultant. He is a governor at a Leeds university and 'is writing a book, *Priests I Have Known*, with his brother Richard.' Since the 1980s heyday of Pink Peg Slax, he has continued writing, singing lead vocals and playing lead guitar.

David Wolfenden played in Red Lorry Yellow Lorry until 1990. The band briefly reformed and recorded a new album in 2013, *A Strange Kind of Paradise*, which remains unreleased. Wolfenden still plays in the Expelaires. He also records with Caroline Blind as Voidant. He lives in Bramley, a western suburb of Leeds.

Robert Worby played in the Mekons until the late 1980s. In the 1990s he worked with Michael Nyman, primarily composing film scores. He then began presenting contemporary music and documentaries at BBC Radio 3 and continues this work today. He has composed experimental electronic music since the 1970s and is currently a member of the Langham Research Centre, performing and making records. His solo LP *Factitious Airs* was released in 2019.

Notes on Sources

All quotations are taken from interviews carried out for this book between May 2016 and March 2021 apart from:

Chapter 1: The Swamp

p. 9 'and what a fine, fetid swamp': Andrew Eldritch, as quoted by the author, *The Quietus,* November 2016, at https://thequietus.com/articles/21215-sisters-of-mercy-leeds-andrew-eldritch-interview.

p. 18 'a housing estate of utter grimness': ibid.

p. 19 'it was a documentary': ibid.

p. 19 'I must have gathered from that': ibid.

p. 19 'oversized toilet': Andrew Eldritch, as quoted by Tina Jackson, *Underneath the Rock* Issue 5, October 1992.

p. 19 'glamorous DJ': ibid.

p. 20 'I just can't think of that happening anywhere else': ibid.

p. 20 'I practically lived in the F Club': ibid.

p. 21 'The Expelaires were like the house band': ibid.

Chapter 2: Cat People

p. 30 'She was there at the birth of it': Eldritch, *The Quietus*, November 2016.

p. 31 'Everybody thought fondly of the Fenton': ibid.

p. 33 'the representative of camp': ibid.

p. 33 'expressing what's basically serious to you' Christopher Isherwood, *The World in the Evening* [Kindle edn], Vintage Classics, London, 2012.

p. 34 'You could always tell when I'd taken over': ibid.

p. 34 'groovy': Eldritch, *Underneath the Rock* Issue 5.

Chapter 3: Under the Jungle Sky

p. 37 'perfectly reasonable way to live': Andrew Eldritch, unpublished part of interview with author for *The Quietus*, conducted August 2016.

p. 38 'We were taking a lot of medication': ibid.

p. 43 'the last two kids to be picked': Eldritch, *The Quietus*, November 2016.

p. 47 'played a variety of cheap and/or borrowed guitars': Gary Marx, letter of provenance written for his Shergold Masquerader guitar, sent to Barry Briggs (aka Quiff Boy), June 2013.

p. 48 'wrote the song during a blizzard in Edmonton': Sylvie Simmons, *I'm Your Man: The Life of Leonard Cohen*, Vintage, London, 2013, p. 185.

p. 48   'The name's nice and ironic': Andrew Eldritch, as quoted by Adam Sweeting, *Melody Maker*, January 1983.

Chapter 4: Slow, Slow, Quick, Quick, Slow

p. 52   'So it came to pass that our intrepid sonic explorers': Anonymous (presumed to be Andrew Eldritch), 'THE MAKiNG OF . . . the first single', the official website of the Sisters of Mercy, at http://www.the-sisters-of-mercy. com/mek/mekddone.htm.

p. 57   'Andrew went off to York with the master tape': ibid.

p. 58   'the nation seems to be packed to bursting point': John Peel, *John Peel Show*, 4 November 1980.

p. 60   'Hell is probably run by cockroaches': Andrew Eldritch, *Underneath the Rock* Issue 3, February 1992.

p. 61   'tingle, tingle, tingle': Andrew Eldritch, Canadian radio interview, 18 June 1984.

p. 63   'Geoff Travis gave it one listen': Andrew Eldritch, as quoted by Adam Sweeting, *Melody Maker*, February 1982.

p. 63   'Nobody likes being compared to Bauhaus': Andrew Eldritch, as quoted by Richard Newsom (Mr Spencer), *Sounds*, December 1982.

p. 64   'I am indeed pretty fucking good at alienating everybody': Andrew Eldritch, *Underneath the Rock* Issue 10, May 1994.

Chapter 5: White Witch Ceremonies

p. 65   'Marx has connected his guitar to a record-player pre-amp': Anonymous (presumed to be Andrew Eldritch), 'SISTERS

BIOGRAPHY', the official website of the Sisters of Mercy, at http://www.the-sisters-of-mercy.com/gen/biog.htm.

p. 66 'That was a real balls-up because of the bad sound': Andrew Eldritch, as quoted by Mark Johnson, *Whippings & Apologies*, September 1981.

p. 67 'We don't see the need to play in every toilet every week': ibid.

p. 68 'He fucking hated us': Eldritch, *The Quietus*, November 2016.

p. 69 'When we'd sound-checked the main band': John Spence, 'The Sisters of Mercy 1980–85' Facebook group, August 2017.

p. 70 'while lurking at a Furs sound-check': posted by thinman (widely assumed to be Eldritch) on Burned Down Days, the Psychedelic Furs' now-defunct 'officially unofficial' online forum, August 2004.

p. 70 'first gig in Leeds at the F Club': Andrew Eldritch, as quoted by the author in *The Quietus*, September 2019, at https://thequietus.com/articles/27065-psychedelic-furs-sisters-of-mercy-interview.

p. 70 'density': ibid.

p. 71 'I have to credit Duncan Kilburn': ibid.

p. 73 'general demeanour onstage at the time': Andrew Eldritch, unpublished *Quietus* interview, August 2016.

Chapter 6: Electric Warriors

p. 89 'I was in the middle of my A Levels': Ben Gunn, as quoted by Mark Carritt and Steve Trattles, *Whippings & Apologies*, August 1983.

p. 92   'Attached to the mic like it was a failing life-support system': Sweeting, *Melody Maker*, February 1982.

p. 92   'These are the finest legs in rock 'n' roll': ibid.

Chapter 7: Metallic K.O.

p. 99   'It's always a good idea to have someone who': Andrew Eldritch as quoted by Bill Astbury, *Box of Rain* Issue 4, late 1981.

p. 100   'Motörhead compared to SOM are Mickey Mouse': Dave McCulloch, *Sounds,* May 1982.

p. 103   'completely thrown . . . [and] completely jealous': Tony James, *The Sputnik Story*, 2012 at http://www.sputnikworld.com.

p. 103   'big idea band': ibid.

p. 103   'We watched the band': Tony James, 'A Tale of Two Singers' in TJ's Blog Archive, 2009, at http://www.carbonsilicon.com/articles/a-tale-of-two-singers.

p. 103   'if he would leave this unheard-of group': James, *The Sputnik Story*.

p. 103   'couldn't entice him away from the Sisters': James, 'A Tale of Two Singers'.

p. 106   'country-folk': Eldritch, *The Quietus,* November 2016.

p. 108   'did have a habit of turning up wearing Mickey Mouse sweatshirts': Marx, Heartland forum, 2003.

Chapter 8: The Hyacinth Girl

p. 112   'mentally wayward': Andrew Eldritch, as quoted by Tina Jackson, *Underneath the Rock* Issue 8, August/September 1993.

p. 112 'There were a million videos': John Ashton, 'Sex WAX n Rock n Roll' YouTube Channel, 2015.

p. 118 'incredibly funny postcard mailing list': James, 'A Tale of Two Singers'.

p. 119 'The crossover between machine and guitars': ibid.

p. 122 'I thought: this band's going to go the distance': Andrew Eldritch interview with Kenny Garden, *Underneath the Rock*, Issue 6, February 1993.

p. 122 'didn't foresee a career as musician': Andrew Eldritch, as quoted by the author in *The Quietus*, August 2017, at https://thequietus.com/articles/23082-sisters-of-mercy-interview-wayne-hussey-craig-adams-gary-marx.

Chapter 9: Heartland

p. 126 'That is mischievous but not exactly untrue': Andrew Eldritch, unpublished *Quietus* interview, August 2016.

p. 127 'For a time Andrew got obsessed with a long distance phone number in New York': David Owen, 'The Sisters of Mercy 1980–85 Facebook group', September 2020.

p. 128 'Even in the dark room Andrew never took off his leather jacket or his dark glasses': anonymous, attributed to 'Jeremy', *I Was a Teenage Sisters of Mercy Fan*, Nikolas Vitus Lagartija, May 2017, at https://sistersfan.blogspot.com/2017/05/the-first-encore-leeds-october-1982.html.

p. 133 'didn't have any trouble understanding Aswad': Andrew Eldritch, taped interview for *Sounds*, Richard Newsom (Mr Spencer), November 1982.

p. 139 'the Violets turned rancid': Andrew Eldritch, interview on WNYU *Music View,* 9 September 1983.

Chapter 10: Choose Your Masks

p. 146 'I wore them because I used to bite my nails': Eldritch, *The Quietus,* November 2016.

p. 146 'ties together with every kid of my generation's Alice Cooper fetish': ibid.

p. 147 'It was a very tolerant and inclusive place': ibid.

p. 147 'the audience's attitude changed to me': Andrew Eldritch, taped interview for *Sounds*, Richard Newsom (Mr Spencer), 25 September 1984.

p. 149 'ludicrously democratic': Andrew Eldritch, as quoted by Sweeting, *Melody Maker*, January 1983.

p. 149 'to work a desk': Andrew Eldritch, *The Quietus*, August 2017.

p. 154 'We chose not to get in bed with': Eldritch, *The Quietus,* November 2016.

p. 154 'the hunky Goth singers': Simon Reynolds, *Rip It Up and Start Again: Postpunk 1978–1984*, Faber & Faber, London, 2006, p. 421.

Chapter 11: Upon Thy Belly Shalt Thou Go

p. 157 'ferocious electrical dancing': Roger Hill, *Rockaround* on BBC Radio Merseyside, May 1984.

p. 158 'The Sisters' macabre fusion of hideous raw power': Adam Sweeting, *Melody Maker*, March 1983.

p. 158 'He unleashes a torrent of prowling malevolence': Elissa Van Poznak, *NME*, March 1983.

p. 160 'The original was about how love is just a kiss away': Andrew Eldritch, Canadian radio interview.

p. 160 'we are the Children of Altamont': Andrew Eldritch, as quoted by Dave Dickinson, *Extra Kerrang!*, July/August 1985.

p. 160 'the trip turned sour': Andrew Eldritch, Canadian radio interview.

p. 160 'as part of the rock 'n' roll tradition . . . the new spiritualist, ludicrous, positive punk bands': Eldritch, WNYU, September 1983.

p. 161 'We don't know who the fuck Alien Sex Fiend are': Andrew Eldritch, quoted by Dickinson, *Extra Kerrang!*.

p. 162 'This record is completely unarguable': Andrew Eldritch, handwritten on a copy of the test pressing of *The Reptile House* EP given to Steve Sutherland, 1983.

p. 163 'There are no windows in the Reptile House': ibid.

p. 163 'Recording the vocal was challenging': John Spence, 'The Sisters of Mercy 1980–85 Facebook group', August 2017.

p. 164 'The mixing process was not difficult': ibid.

p. 165 'The last track especially promises something to hold on to': ibid.

p. 165 'They weren't into recording that much': Andrew Eldritch, as quoted by Marcel Anders (translated from German), *Visions*, July 1992.

Chapter 12: Seven Samurai

p. 171 'everything seemed to click': Andrew Eldritch as quoted by Mr Spencer and Martyn Strickland, *Sounds*, February 1986.

p. 176 'It was my first experiences in a band': Andrew Eldritch, *Underneath the Rock* Issue 10.

p. 176 'I loathed my childhood and everything to do with it': Andrew Eldritch, as quoted by David Sinclair, *The Times*, November 1987.

p. 180 'They had an admirable attitude towards their audience': Johnny Marr, *Set the Boy Free*, Century, London, 2016, p. 170.

Chapter 13: The Western Allies

p. 188 'HermanShermanHe'sNotGerman': Andrew Eldritch, private correspondence with the author, August 2016.

p. 190 'doom glam': Danceteria flyer/press release #54 for the 13 April concert, 1984.

p. 190 'a boring old twat . . .': Andrew Eldritch interview with Declan Allen at Kingston Polytechnic prior to gig on 30 June 1983.

p. 195 'the gesture of total atomic oblivion': Andrew Eldritch, as quoted by Richard Newsom (Mr Spencer), *Sounds*, October 1984.

p. 195 '*Spannung macht Stimmung*': Andrew Eldritch quoted in *SPEX*, November 1983.

p. 196 'a really good guy': Bobby Startup, as quoted by Trevor Ristow, *Waiting for Another War: A History of the Sisters of Mercy Volume 1: 1980–85*, GKW Filmworks, 2019, p. 94.

p. 196 'adorable' : Lisa Levine, as quoted in ibid, p. 97.

p. 197 'painfully close to the heavy metal end of things when they dirge out', David Sprague, *Sense of Purpose*, December 1983.

p. 197 'slight, dark figure', Khaaryn, *Truly Needy*, early 1984.

p. 199 'personal differences': Ben Gunn, as quoted by Jayne Houghton, *ZigZag*, August 1984.

Chapter 14: New Skin for the Old Ceremony

p. 206 'Have I got a guitar player for you': Andrew Eldritch, WNYU *Music View*, April 1984.

p. 208 'Elvis meets Kierkegaard': Andrew Eldritch, as quoted by Chris Roberts, *Melody Maker*, October 1990.

p. 211 'going into a shop in Bedford': Max Hole, 'Max Hole explains the record company and the video', *UKRockHistory* YouTube channel, 2014.

p. 211 'There are some pretty groovy guys working in London': Andrew Eldritch, quoted by Nancy Rapchak and Philip Puckett, *Rockpool*, June 1985.

p. 214 'When I'm rich and famous': Andrew Eldritch, quoted by Don Watson, *NME*, May 1984.

p. 217 'a vision of heaven with everyone on speed': Andrew Eldritch, *Underneath the Rock* Issue 2, February 1992.

p. 217 'rescued, revived and mastered': Salvation, *Clash of Dreams* CD sleeve notes, 2014.

p. 219 'intense young man': Andrew Eldritch, *Underneath the Rock* Issue 8.

Chapter 15: Detroit's Finest

p. 228 'American blowjob': Wayne Hussey, *Salad Daze*, Omnibus, London, 2019, p. 234.

p. 231 'He was the most rock solid bass player ever': Andrew Eldritch, unpublished *Quietus* interview, August 2016.

p. 232 'went to the bottom floor of Danceteria': Bob Beiner, 'The Sisters of Mercy 1980–85 Facebook group', April 2017.

Chapter 16: The Pilgrims' Progress

p. 239 'you in that sort of bozo gut-wrenching heavy metal way': Andrew Eldritch, Canadian radio interview.

p. 240 'I owe a lot to him': Andrew Eldritch, *The Quietus*, November 2016.

p. 245 'decided to give me a friendly kick and I fell off the stage': Wayne Hussey, *Jackie* Issue 1,115, 18 May 1985.

p. 245 'Of course there was a post-mortem after the show': Hussey, *Salad Days*, p. 236.

p. 245 'detoured through Leeds': Gary Marx, letter of provenance.

Chapter 17: (After the Gramme)

p. 269 'Of all the bands in the world': Henry Rollins, *Get in the Van*, 2. 13. 61, Los Angeles, 1994, p. 107.

p. 270 'The best part was seeing the poor Sisters': ibid.

p. 270 'Another night of music and bottles': Gary Marx, *The Eternal Flame* No. 1, late 1984.

p. 273 'I'd never really talked to the guy': Eldritch, *Underneath the Rock* Issue 5.

Chapter 18: Too Dark to See

p. 279 'The doctor said, "How do you relax?" and I said I don't':

Andrew Eldritch as quoted by Jane Simon, *Sounds*, March 1985.

p. 279 'No thank you. This has gone far enough': Andrew Eldritch, as quoted by Steve Sutherland, *Melody Maker*, March 1985.

p. 282 'shiny black van with heavily tinted windows': Mark Burgess, *View from a Hill* [Kindle edn], Mittens on Publishing, Leeds, 2014.

p. 284 'Cliff Richard haircut': Eldritch, *Underneath the Rock* Issue 8.

p. 284 'The person in those videos is my stupid twin brother': Andrew Eldritch, *Underneath the Rock* Issue 14, Winter 1995.

p. 284 'people he engaged in conversation began to change colour': Adam Sweeting, *Melody Maker*, October 1984.

p. 286 'we sold out and the crowd': Wayne Hussey, *NITV*, October 1984.

p. 286 'an all round superhuman good guy': Andrew Eldritch, *Underneath the Rock* Issue 3.

p. 291 'because basically they're bombed out of their boxes': Eldritch, *Sounds*, October 1984.

p. 294 'If you want it to, being involved with music': ibid.

p. 294 'I've walked around for an awful number of years now': ibid.

p. 295 'the chapeau shop': Eldritch, *Underneath the Rock* Issue 8.

Chapter 19: All the Clouds That Lour'd Upon Our House

p. 298 'had an infatuation with a thing called Zoids': Tony Harris as quoted by Robert Cowlin, 'All I Know for Sure: The Making of First and Last and Always', 2017, at https://

heavyleatherblog.wordpress.com/2017/03/11/all-i-know-for-sure-the-making-of-first-and-last-and-always/.

p. 298 'arrogant bastard who writes sensitive lyrics': Eldritch, *Sounds*, March 1985.

p. 299 'I had to teach myself at an early age': Andrew Eldritch, taped *Sounds* interview, 25 September 1984.

p. 299 'the brink': ibid.

p. 300 'wanted a really clean hi-fi sort of sound': Tony Harris as quoted by Cowlin, 'All I Know for Sure'.

p. 300 'Dave and I kept out of it': ibid.

p. 301 'at the request of Craig': Gary Marx, as quoted by Cowlin, 'All I Know For Sure'.

p. 302 'after the world tour that will follow the release of the album I'll leave the group': Andrew Eldritch in Daniela Gombini and Romano Pasquini's *Tribal Cabaret* of March 1985, as quoted in 'The 1985 Split – the real truth is never spoken??', Nikolas Vitus Lagartija, *I Was a Teenage Sisters of Mercy Fan*, July 2016, at https://sistersfan.blogspot.com/2016/07/the-1985-split-real-truth-is-never.html.

p. 303 'there isn't a detail of life or anybody else's life': Eldritch, *Sounds*, March 1985.

p. 303 'So I've calmed down a bit': Eldritch, *Melody Maker*, March 1985.

p. 304 'Even I've not decided how far I'm prepared to push it': Eldritch, *Extra Kerrang!*.

p. 304 'I'm very aware of how fast the blood's going around': Eldritch, *Melody Maker*, March 1985.

p. 304 'None of the songs on the album are about being a victim': ibid.

p. 304 'twelve fresh lemons I have to have every night': ibid.

p. 304 'I've spent so long doing this that I can't distance the two': ibid.

p. 304 'Greatly overindulged in': Eldritch, *Sounds*, March 1985.

p. 305 'We've sacrificed a great deal of our lives for this': Eldritch, *Extra Kerrang!*.

p. 305 'get into big school': Eldritch, *Underneath the Rock* Issue 5.

p. 305 'It's difficult to comprehend sometimes. Dying': Hussey, *Sounds*, March 1985.

p. 306 'My brain works quicker than my mouth, and that's an advantage': Eldritch, *Sounds*, March 1985.

p. 306 'into us, them, and people I don't talk to': Eldritch, *Sounds*, October 1984.

p. 306 'to demolish Liverpool just by thought-power': ibid.

p. 306 'The French half of Belgium can go fuck itself!': Eldritch, *Extra Kerrang!*.

p. 306 'Motown, the MC5 at its urban wasteland': Andrew Eldritch, as quoted by Paul Du Noyer, *NME*, March 1985.

p. 306 'how beautiful napalm is': Andrew Eldritch, *Sounds*, October 1984.

p. 307 'an enraged ex-boyfriend': Andrew Eldritch, as quoted by John Robb, *Louder Than War*, November 2016, at https://louderthanwar.com/interview-andrew-eldritch-depth-trump-brexit-new-album/.

Chapter 20: Waiting for the Summer Rain

p. 310 'over-produced and over-dramatic outing': Dave Henderson, *Sounds*, March 1985.

p. 310 'mockdespair, rock theft and semi-glam appropriation of Joy Division': David Quantick, *NME*, March 1985.

p. 310 'a cross between Bauhaus and Siouxsie and the Banshees': Chris Heath, *Smash Hits*, March 1985.

p. 310 'sung through a tunnel darkly': Jim Reid, *Record Mirror*, April 1985.

p. 310 'have successfully accumulated a startling array of timeless jewels': Ted Mico, *Melody Maker*, March 1985.

p. 311 'To find a band so acutely in tune': Dickinson, *Extra Kerrang!*.

p. 312 'No generations will breed from this diamond': Henderson, *Sounds*.

p. 313 'God forbid, but these songs': Mico, *Melody Maker*.

p. 313 'the mental strain was the real problem': Gary Marx interview on the Heartland forum, 2003.

p. 313 'I was killing myself on the road': Andrew Eldritch interview with Paul Du Noyer, *Q* Issue 16, January 1988.

p. 316 'it shook him up so much': Gary Marx interview for *Artificial Life*, March 1985.

p. 317 'It's about time someone got up': Eldritch, *Extra Kerrang!*.

p. 320 'hadn't had the balls to leave when I did': Marx, Heartland forum, 2003.

p. 324 'A hairy scary moment': Wayne Hussey, post on the Mission's Facebook account, September 2015.

p. 324 'I was in such an altered state': Andrew Eldritch, *Underneath the Rock* Issue 11, October 1994.

Chapter 21: Non-Alignment Pact

p. 326 'a Duran Duran-type reception': Wayne Hussey, as quoted by Nick Robinson, *Wot!*, July 1985.

p. 327 'It was the loudest concert I've ever heard in my life': Tom G. Warrior as quoted by Jimmy Martin, 'Walk On In Darkness: Tom G Warrior's 13 Favourite LPs', *The Quietus*, September 2017, at https://thequietus.com/articles/23198-tom-g-warrior-of-celtic-frost-s-baker-s-dozen.

p. 329 'Oslo got rained off pretty much': Andrew Eldritch interview, Stockholm, 17 May 1985, as quoted in 'Rain from Heaven – Oslo 16 May 1985', Nikolas Vitus Lagartija, *I Was a Teenage Sisters of Mercy Fan*, June 2017, at https://sistersfan.blogspot.com/2017/06/rain-from-haven-oslo-16th-may-1985.html.

p. 329 'We thought that Oslo was a capital city': Eldritch interview, Stockholm, 17 May 1985.

p. 330 'You get into the routine of working certain hours': Andrew Eldritch interview with Danny Fields, *Underneath the Rock* Issue 1, June 1991.

p. 330 'I like the idea of concerts': Andrew Eldritch interview with Ted Mico, *Melody Maker*, November 1987.

p. 331 'in an all-boys together': Eldritch, *Underneath the Rock* Issue 6.

p. 331 'feel like a person: Eldritch, *Underneath the Rock* Issue 1.

p. 332 'I think what will happen is we'll keep the basic nucleus': Wayne Hussey interview on DRS 3 radio, Basel, 25 April 1985.

p. 332 'Wayne is covering both guitar parts': Andrew Eldritch interviewed with Pascal Stevens (translated from the French), 'Elle Ta Soeur? Elle Va Bien, Mercy', *Télémoustique*, 1985.

p. 332 'I'm tired, I'm not feeling well': Andrew Eldritch, as quoted by Federico Guglielmi, *Il Mucchio Selvaggio* No. 89 (translated from Italian), June 1985.

p. 332 'two gorgeous handcrafted books': Federico Guglielmi, *L'ultima Thule* blog, October 2013, at https://lultimathule. wordpress.com/2013/10/22/sisters-of-mercy.

p. 333 'In the last two years I have been very busy': ibid.

Chapter 22: Twilight of the Idols

p. 337 'Two of my favourite people work A&R for Elektra': Eldritch, *Rockpool*.

p. 337 'It is no good resigning yourself to an independent state': ibid.

p. 338 'So, it was agreed after some discussion': Robert Webb, 'Sisters of Mercy, Rock Video Shoot, "Black Planet" – 1985', at https://www.robertwebb.com/som.htm.

p. 344 'his clipped sarcasm and reluctant monotone': *East Village Eye*, October 1985.

p. 344 'We've got one final date in Britain': Eldritch, *Rockpool*.

Chapter 23: Life Out of Balance

p. 348 'almost completely used up as cannon fodder': Eldritch, *Underneath the Rock* Issue 10.

p. 348 'sad beyond words when I think about the First World War': Eldritch, *Underneath the Rock* Issue 3.

p. 352 'ruined in some sort of film laboratory accident': Robert Webb, 'Rock Video Shoot'.

p. 353 'all pumped up': ibid.

p. 353 'bleary-eyed and walking funny': Hussey, *Salad Daze*, p. 331.

p. 353 'I went to Mexico for the day': Andrew Eldritch, as quoted by Steve Sutherland, *Melody Maker*, September 1987.

p. 354 'looking almost as dishevelled as when I'd met him just a few weeks before': Hussey, *Salad Daze*, p. 335.

Chapter 24: Eldritch, Wrath of God

p. 364 'The stuff Andy's doing now is softer and slower': Wayne Hussey as quoted by Kaz, *Mass Murder*, early November 1985.

p. 365 'no one would use the name': Eldritch, *Melody Maker*, September 1987.

p. 365 'Andrew wanted to start making songs as himself': Wayne Hussey as quoted by Neil Perry and Greg Freeman, *Sounds*, February 1986.

p. 365 'putting together cassettes of demos': Wayne Hussey, 'Chapter 19: Foreign Tongue in Familiar Places', unpublished manuscript of *Salad Daze*.

p. 367 'With the Cult tour fast approaching': ibid.

p. 368 'He couldn't sue us': ibid.

p. 370 'Andrew and I': postcard from Werner Herzog and Andrew Eldritch to the A&R department of Warner Music UK, January 1986.

Chapter 25: Poison

p. 374 'featuring the same line-up': Neil Perry and Greg Freeman, *Sounds*, February 1986.

p. 377 'Ian Astbury and Billy Duffy joined us onstage': Wayne Hussey, 'Chapter 19: Foreign Tongue in Familiar Places', unpublished manuscript of *Salad Daze*.

p. 378 'but the show was cancelled': ibid.

p. 384 'like a disco party run by the Borgias': Andrew Eldritch, as quoted by Paul Elliott, *Classic Rock*, November 2016, at https://www.loudersound.com/features/sisters-of-mercy-i-wanted-to-sound-like-a-disco-run-by-the-borgias.

Epilogue: Ozymandias/Songs of the Free

p. 386 'Our version of the Fall': Eldritch, *The Quietus,* November 2016.

p. 386 'There's got to be a good way of doing it': Eldritch, *NME*, March 1985.

p. 388 'I don't make music for you': Eldritch, *Classic Rock*, November 2016.

p. 388 'There's a difference between being a musician and being a pop star': ibid.

p. 389 'simply preening': ibid.

p. 389 'The most unlikely people end up being stars': Eldritch, *NME*, March 1985.

Acknowledgements

In 2016, I offered John Doran of *The Quietus* a long article on the early years of the Sisters of Mercy and the Leeds music scene that birthed them. He agreed to publish it and I agreed not to be paid. I am in his debt. In that article – and its two sequels in *The Quietus* – this book originated.

Paint My Name in Black and Gold also grew out of the work of a host of Sisters researchers, collectors, enthusiasts and writers. Nikolas Vitus Lagartija's *I Was a Teenage Sisters of Mercy Fan* blog was key. Nik's forensic research into the early history of the Sisters revivified my feelings for the band and initiated my desire to write about them. Nik also read the early manuscript of the book and caught several errors. Nik, I thank you and I salute you. As I do Phil Verne, not just for the extraordinary The Sisters of Mercy 1980–85 group that he curates on Facebook, but also for providing me with copies of bootlegs recordings and other artefacts, many of them extremely rare. Thanks also to Quiff Boy (aka Barry

Briggs) who oversees the Heartland forum, a treasure trove of opinion and primary material. To paraphrase Al Pacino, I thought I was out but they pulled me back in. Thanks also to 'Being 645', Robert Cowlin, Bruno Bossier and of course Trevor Ristow, author of *Waiting for Another War*, which provided *Paint My Name in Black and Gold* with several choice US anecdotes.

Paint My Name in Black and Gold is primarily structured around original interviews. That approach became clear to me right at the outset. The fascinating time I spent in Leeds with John Keenan, and with Ben Farvak and Daniel Mass from Salvation (in the Faversham and the Fox and Newt respectively) set the pattern. They were the first interviewees; there have been seventy-six others. Whether or not they have been quoted, I thank them all. This includes Andrew Eldritch, who agreed to talk about Leeds and the Sisters for that first *Quietus* article. If not for that decision, this book would not exist.

Some interviewees gave especially long interviews and/or were repeatedly pressed on the minutiae of decades-old trivia and on matters more serious over the following weeks and months. Therefore I am very grateful to Kevin Lycett, Jon Langford, Les Mills, Boyd Steemson, Howard Thompson, Lucas Fox, Ken Giles, Dave Beer, Grape, Jez Webb, Merb, Dave Wolfenden, Stuart Green, Duncan Kilburn, Nick Jones, John Ashton and Dave Allen.

Special thanks go to those who did particularly heavy lifting, giving me hours and hours of their time and thousands and thousands of words (and even some remarkable photos): Claire Shearsby, Wayne Hussey, Craig Adams and Mark Pearman. Conversing with each of them – by whatever method – has been a great pleasure and central to writing this book. Mark's contribution to *Paint My Name in Black and Gold* has been immeasurable. I'm deeply grateful for the clarity of his analysis and his humour, not only when discussing His Favourite Year, but also less joyful episodes.

Thank you to Rob Manuel for playing matchmaker between me and Mathew Clayton, the Head of Publishing at Unbound; to Alex Eccles, my editor; to Richard Collins and Edward Wall, who were intimately involved in revising and improving the manuscript; and to my friends Clark Sargent and Jon West who read draft passages of the book.

To all those who pledged: without you there would be nothing. Also supportive of the fundraising process (along with the Heartland forum and the Sisters of Mercy 1980–85 group) were John Robb and *Louder Than War*, and the following Facebook groups: Leeds Music Past & Present; The Sisters of Mercy Facebook Group; Ribbons; Merciful Release; The Leeds Warehouse 80–88; Le Phonographique; and The F Club Leeds.

Thanks and love to my parents Richard and Ann, who bought me my first Sisters records from Discovery Records in Leamington Spa. My mum also drove Clark and me to my first ever concert: the Sisters of Mercy supported by the Scientists at Lanchester Polytechnic in Coventry on 14 March 1985. She can still recall the car being buffeted by the vibrations created by the good Doktor as she waited to pick us up outside the venue.

During the researching and writing of this book my youngest child was born – and my older children began hearing what they referred to as 'Alice in Her Party Dress' and 'Hey Now Now' among their bedtime songs. To Louis, Adèle and Joséphine, I say this: I love you, and this book is why Daddy was on his computer a lot. My wife is a remarkable person: she's been pregnant, short of sleep for long periods of time, worked her job, been a mother to three children during a pandemic and still supported me in my endeavours to write a book about a band in which she has no interest whatsoever. *Je t'aime*, Elisabeth.

And finally, a thank you to whichever teenage boy put 'Floorshow' on the record player of the sixth form common room sometime in the autumn of 1984. At the time, I had no clue what it was or who the band were, but I knew it was *exactly* what I was looking for.

Unbound is the world's first crowdfunding publisher, established in 2011.

We believe that wonderful things can happen when you clear a path for people who share a passion. That's why we've built a platform that brings together readers and authors to crowdfund books they believe in – and give fresh ideas that don't fit the traditional mould the chance they deserve.

This book is in your hands because readers made it possible. Everyone who pledged their support is listed below. Join them by visiting unbound.com and supporting a book today.

Philip Aberer
Gareth Absalom
L&O Adams
Greg Adomaitis
Knoe AgentOrange
Suleiman Al-Sabah
Alex Mish Dani
Richard Allison
Johan Åman
David Anderson
Phil Anderson
Kevin Athow
Corinne Aviad
Martin Aylward

Emma L. Baird
Stephen Baishya
Richard Baker
Laurens Bakker
Chris Baldwin
Vince Baldwin
Jason Ballinger
Douglas Baptie
Iain M Barker
Paul Barnsley
Bruce Barrow
Jackie Bates
David Batey
A.G. Baxter

Chrissie Beardmore
Lee Beggie
    (EastMidsWhizzKid)
Being645
Pete Bell
Greagoir Belle
Julian Bentley
Marc Oliver Berger
Roman Berndt
Simon Bessant
Beau Betts
Alessandro
    Bianco (Negro
    dell'Audiofracasso)

Nikki Biddiss

Peter Bingham

Anthony Robert Bird

Johan Birgander

Bruce Bishop

Amanda Blackburn

Rich Blackett

Simon Blackmore

Looke Blackstaffe

Konstantinos Blounas

Mark Blunden

Robert Blurton

Tod Bod

Becki Bodey

Fredrik Bökman

Jan Bollansee

Jon Bond

Étienne Bonmariage

Gaylord Bonnafous

Sara Bonnell

Crispin Boon

Alastair Boone

Andrew Boulton

Kate Bowgett

Innes Bowman

Clive Brace

Chris Bradley

Les Bradley

Steve Bradley

Abigail Brady

Stuart Braithwaite

Pete Bratach

John Bravin

Shelleyan Brecht

Dan Brida

Barry Briggs

Lorraine Broertjes

Gavin Bromley

Jonathan Brook

Dave Brown

Stephen Brown

Nick Browne

Brian Budd

Bryan Burford

David Burgess

John Burke

Ian Burns

James Burt

Richie Butler

Laurence Byrne

Davina Caborn

Mike Cambridge

Andy Camm

Eduardo Canas

Stefano Caneparo
(Skeggia
dell'Audiofracasso)

Victoria Carroll

Pierre Carron

Jack Catchpoole

Nika Cejnek

CellThree

Martin Chalk

Anthony Chefles

John Chesshire

Brydon Cheyney

Joe Chillingworth

Graham Chisnall

John Cholmondeley

Graham Christensen

Juan Christian

Rene B Christiansen

Christin

Barbara Ciszewska

Citizen of Wakefield

Mi Cl

Matt Claridge

Simon Clark

Dan Clayton

Mathew Clayton

Simon Clifford

Simon Cobb

Andrew Cocker

Jeremy Coffey

Martin Coldrick

Steve Collier

Sharron Connor

Ollie Conraculix

AJ Constance

Dom Conway

Porl Cooper

Ian Cornwall

Angel Corpus Christi

Supporters

Benjamin Corrigan

Neil Corry

Paul Coughlin

Steven Cowan

Robert Cowlin

Robert Cox

Steve Craig

Kath Craigs

Jeremy Cravos

Greg Crichton

Toby Crispin

Roi Croasdale

Andrew Croft

Charles Croft

Chris Cropper

Jo Cumming

Stephen Cuthbertson

Stu Czuba

Jez D'Netto

John Daly

Mattias Danielson

Danny & Marion

Erik Dardel

Nicholas James Davey

Micky Dazzler

Jan De Boeck

Patrick De Cnodder

Rosana De Oliveira
    Sorva

Serge De Pauw

Chris Dearle

An Deirfiur

Iggi Demello

F.J. DeSanto

Anton Desmazeau

Stephen Dillon

Marèn Din Armagh

Jason Dodman

Alastair Doggett

Vanessa Doidge

Paul Donlon

Sam Donohoe

David Downie

Eric Drass

Tony Drozd

Simon Duckels

Shane Duggan

Diederik Duivenvoorden

Oliver Duke-Williams

Kevin Dunbar

Bill Duncan

Darren Duncan

Geraldine Dunne

Stephen Dunne

Simon Dunnigan

Chris DuPilka

John Durnian

Eva Duse

Felix Dziubas

L. Edel

Sarah Edkins

Piers Edminson

Gary Edwards

Sandra Egan

Frank Ehrmann

Sebastiaan Eldritch-
    Böersen

Elenchus

David English

Diego Entonado

Eric Esser

Borja Estévez

Geraint Evans

Will Evans

Jon Ewing

Robert Fakes

Benoît Farvak

Matthew Faulkner

Julien Favre

Patrick Federli

Gordon Finlay

Paul Fletcher

Fabrizio Floris

Michael Foggin

Alison Forbes

Bill Forbes

Nikos Foskolos

Michael Foster

Colin Fox

Jenny Foxe

Pierre Frankignoul

Robert Frederickson

Josiah Frosting

Trevor Fry

David Galbraith

Heidi Gallagher

Paul Gallagher

Majda Gama

David Gammack

Kenny Garden

John Garner

Russell Garrett

Graham Geldard

Sean Ghostparty

Will Gibb

Martin Gilder

Kieron Gillen

Chris Gilliland

Nigel Girvan

Dion Giunta

Jürgen Gizzi

Martin and Helen
    Glassborow

Marc Goebert

Leo Goldsmith

Monika Gombert

Paulo Gonçalves

Paul Goodman

John Goodwin

Dom Gourlay

David Grainger

Peter Granström

Peter Grant (gift)

Grape

Robert Gray

Chantal Gregoire

Anthony Gregory

Judith Griffith

Mick Griffiths

Matthew Grimes

Richard Grosvenor

Gal Gur-Arie

Peter Haas

Paul 'Bruce' Haden

Craig Haggar

Les Hale

Tim Hall

Paul Hammond

David Hancock

James Hanson

Jase Hardcastle

Michael Harding

Jason Hardy

Deborah Contessa
    Hargreaves

Kim Harjo

Sean Harkin

Steven Harrington

Buff Harris

Mirjam Hartstra

David Harvey

Richard Hawkins

Rob Haworth

Bobi Hayderer

Daniel Haydock

Jane Hector-Jones

Alexander Heinrich

Frank Hemsley

Kieran Heneghan

Nicole Hess-Waldron

John Hindmarch

Michael Hiney

M Hinrich

Roger Hirst

Robert Hobbs

Brian Hodges

Steven Hodgson

Marc Hoffman

Stephen Holden

Richard Holland

Henrik Hollbox

Paul Hollins

Lene Holm Jensen

Craig Holmes

Cristian Holmes

Simon Holmes

Robert Holmqvist

Richard Holtom

Filip Hoop

Dennis Hope

Carsten Hopf

Danny Horigan

Carl Horrocks

Ethan Huber

Keith Hudson

Martin Hudson

Supporters

Hugh

Darren Hughes

Gary Hughes

Tally Hugo

Richard Hunter

Nik Hurrell

Mike Iampietro

Graeme Jackson

Christopher Jacobs

Oscar Jacobsson

Saskia Jagemann

Tamas Jakab

Darren James

Franc James – Francs

David Jefferies

Toby Jeffries

Keith Jenner

Mary Jirsa

Ian Johnsen

Mark Johnson

Jason Jolliffe

Dominic Jones

Laura Jones

Morten Jordal

Michael Jordan

Robin Jordan

Craig Joyce

Billy Jubb

Rowan Jubb

Aleph Kali

Åke Källback

Jonas Karlsson

Anthony Keaveny

Grahame Keeping

Ian Kelly

Nayab Khalid

Dan Kieran

Andy Kilbride

Jason King

Richard King

Ned Kirby

Oliver Kirk

Lucien Kloeckner

Matt Knadler

Susanne Kohlert-Schildt

Jakub Skinny B Konecny

Martin König

Marko Koski-Vähälä

Richard Kovitch

Alex Koziol

Andreas Krinke

Daniel Kunert

Seth Lachner

Axel Lademann

Peter Lankester

Patrice Laurendeau

Daphne Lawless

Mel Laycock

Yan Le Gat (Sentenza)

David Lees

Lisa Levine

James Lile

Nikki Livingstone-
   Rothwell

Paul Lockett

Jon Love

Ryan Love

Tobias Low

Andy Lowe

Nikolaus Löwe

Lauri Löytökoski

Peter Lundahl

Alex Lungley

Paul Lunt

Dave Lupton

Joe Luscombe

Mark Lyth

Glenn Macdonald

Emile MacDonald-
   Williams

Phil Mahoney

Richard Maides

Paul Maidment

Catherine Makin

Thomas Mang

Cheryl-Lynne Mansell

Rob "Subscribe to the
   B3ta newsletter"
   Manuel

Boris Maringer

Chris Marsh

JF Marsh

Andrew Marshall

Darren Marsland

Chris Martin

Craig Martin

Nicolas Martin

Billy Mason

Dubravka Matovinović

Ade Matthews

Dave Maud

Indigo Maughn

Andrew McAinsh

Steve McBurney

Gregory McCartney

Alex McCauley

Paulo McClean

Mary McCoy

Gary Mccrindle

Andrew Mcdonald

Rich McGann

David McGillveray

Paul McGlone

Killian McGowan

James McIe

Keith McIvor

Kathleen McKee

Padraig McKenna

Liz McLaughlin

Tim McMillan

Bryan McPhail

Anthony McQuillin

Keith Medgett

Alex Meehan

Menno Meerbach

Edwin Megens

Thorsten Melchers

Daniel Melia

George Mensink

Adam Mercado

Heather Merryweather

Indrek Mesikepp

Scott Millar

Steve Milner

Mark Milward

Chris Mitchell

David Mitchell

Dominic Mitchell

John Mitchinson

Jean-Paul Monseu

Ander Monson

Anna Montag

Beth Moore

Stuart Moore

Richard Morgan

Matthew Morley

Steve Morrison

Ian Morse

Alice Moss

Richard Mosses

Ian Mowat

MRFS

Anne Murphy

Tania Murphy

Jane Alice Murray

Alan Mustafa

Tony Muzi

Tony and Chris Muzi

Rob Myers

Hugh N

Craig Naples

Al Napp

Carlo Navato

Gary Naylor

Fraser Neilson

Craig Newton

Jo Nightingale

Maria Nightingale

Al No

Matthew North

Andy Nunwick

Tim O'Gorman

Brian O'Rourke

Björn Odendahl

Björn Odendal

Johnson Okpaluba

Gramps Oldman

Eirik Olsen

Jonas Olsén

Alexander Ord

Richie Orwat

Neil Pace

Steve Pace

Dave Page

Per Ottar Pahr

Juanjo Paneque

E. Pardee

Gary Parker

Jonathan Parker

Chris Partington

James Parton

Rupe Patel

John Paterson

Matt Patterson

Jason Paul

Wim Pauwels

Dan Pawley

Spencer Pawson

Aly Peacock

Tony-Sue Peacock

James Peake

Neil Perry

Erick Pessoa

Derren Phillips

Jan Piatkowski

Maria Pickering

Neil Piper

Marcin Piwcewicz

Ralph Plowman

George Poles

Chrissa Poliou

Justin Pollard

Philip Porter

John Potter

Steve Potz-Rayner

Tereza Považanová

Alex Pradervand

Tobias James Pritchard

Clair Quentin

Dan Quine

Tennie R. Rabbit

Geoffrey Rabe

Dallas Rasmussen

Christopher Rawley

Michael Read

Jonathan Reber

Marc Reckert

Nicholas Redding

Charlie Redfern

Matt Redman

Derek Redpath

Mike Reichel

Chris Reid

Raul Remujo Aragón

Bruce Rennie

Anders Rensberg

Karen Reyniers

Kester Richards

Trevor Ristow

Paul Rizos

Ben Robards

Alun Roberts

David Roberts

Victoria Roberts

Don Robertson

Tracy Robertson

Andrew Robinson

Derek Robinson

Ed Robinson

Paul Robson

Steven Jacques Roby

Matthew Rochford

Gonzalo Rodríguez

Tom Rodwell

Carsten Roekens

Kenn Roessler

Simon Rogerson

Nikolai Romanov

Neil Ronketti

Nuno Rosa

Christopher Rose

Karl Rossin

Adrian Rostill

Emily Rounds

Andy Rouse

Rob Rowell

Jonathan Rowles

Ruffers

Anthea Rutherford

Richard Ryan

Robert Sadler

Michael Sadowski

Christin Sager

Tim Sapsford

Clark Sargent

Jen Saxena

Adam Say

Draillia Scarabae

David Scarborough

FKA Hlavacek von Schüttenhofen
Eric Schubert
Mark Anton Schulz
Kristian Schuster
Mario Schweikert
Bill Scott-Kerr
Paul Scrutton
Ian Senior
Mark Seton
Mike Shallcross
Jez Shanahan
Tim Shannon
Tony Shannon
Andy & Sharon Swift
David Sharp
Stephen Sharp
Jon Sheard
Ivan Shiel
Jeanette Shin
Seyed Shirsavar
Alessia Signorelli
Mel Silver-Ford
Eskil Simonsson
Alan Sims
Alistair Singer
Judge Singh
Paul Slater
Craig Smith
Dave, Heather & Mark Smith

Lily Smith
Mike Smith
Simon Smith (Big Si)
C Snedden
Anzu Solas
Hartmut Spiekermann
Karl Spracklen
Iain Stables
John Stancik
Dr Michael Starr
Christian Stenerud
Alan Stephen
Paul Stephenson
Neil Stevens
Alan Stewart
Cobham Still
Dan Stockwell
Martin Stokes
Rob Stout
Vitaliy Stranger
William Streek
Tony Stuart
Rob Stubbs
Andrew Sunaitis
Anders Svensson
Adam Sykes
Łukasz Szymczyk
Peter Tags
Alex Tasker
Clive Taylor
Andy Telemacque

Andy Theyers
Stephan Thiemann
Jon Thompson
David Thomson
Troy Thorstad
Martin Thrane
Thomas Thyssen
Zacharias Tienhaara
Gareth Tilley
Karl Tomlinson
Mark Topping
Ross Tregaskis
Michael Trempelmann
Steffen Trempelmann
Matt Triggs
Michael Trinder
Terry Truman
Ralf Tuchscherer
Gavin Tucker
Andrew Turner
Melanie Turner
Peter Turner
Marek Urbanik
Adrian Utteridge
Romy Vager
Veronika Valigurska
Teus Van de Pol
Fabian van Langevelde
Paul van Leipzig
Koen Van Tichelen
Ferencz van Weert

Supporters

Kurt Vandaele
Jaimie Vandenbergh
Joost Vandoorne
Zsolt Varga
Tom Vaughan
Nico Verdijsseldonk
Greg Viar
Craig Vincze
Marge von
 Munchingindahausen
VonConway
Ian Waddington
Tim Waddington
Simon Wadsworth
Nigel Waghorne
Matthew Wainwright
John Walker
Steve Walker
Zelda Wall
Nigel Wallbank
Simon Waller
David Walton
Pete Walton
Andrew Ward
Katie Ward
Roger Ward

Robin Wardell
Al Warr
Roger Warwick
Matt Washington
Simon Waterman
Paul Watson
Dave Wealleans
Jez Webb
Richard Weeden
Jack Weeland
Gary Weight
Wolfgang Weiss
Tony Welland
Fraser Welsh
Paul Weston
Matthias "vicus" Weyh
Jamie White
Thomas Wigley
Fraser Wilkes
pygmydanny' Willems
Alexis Williams
Alyn Williams
Helen Williams
Owen Williams
Robert Williams
Bryan Willis

Svante Natanael Winblad
Daniel Winnwa
Adela Wittgenstein
 Safarova
Christian Wojtysiak
Mark Wolstenholme
Darren Wood
Alex Woodcock
Rob Woodcock
Ben Woodhams
Benjamin Woods
Zoe Woods
Nick Wright
Kai Wüst
David Wynne
Mike York
David Young
Jan Zaehle
George Zahora
Dawid Zarach
Phoebe Zeitler
Pavel Zherebtsov
Oliver Zissing